# The User's Manual For The Brain

## The Complete Manual For Neuro-Linguistic Programming Practitioner Certification

*Bob G. Bodenhamer, D.Min.*

and

*L. Michael Hall, Ph.D.*

Crown House Publishing Limited
www.crownhouse.co.uk

First published by

Crown House Publishing Ltd
Crown Buildings, Bancyfelin, Carmarthen, Wales, SA33 5ND, UK
**www.crownhouse.co.uk**

and

Crown House Publishing Company LLC
6 Trowbridge Drive, Suite 5, Bethel, CT 06801, USA
**www.chpus.com**

First published 1999.
Reprinted 2000, 2002 (twice), 2005, 2007

**British Library of Cataloguing-in-Publication Data**
A catalogue entry for this book is available
from the British Library.

**13-digit ISBN 978-1899836321**
**10-digit ISBN 1899836322**

LCCN 2003106531

Printed and bound in the USA

# Acknowledgments

The book you have in your hand is the product primarily of my teaching Neuro-Linguistic Programming at Gaston College in Dallas, NC. It has developed over a period of six years in a classroom setting. Obviously, when anyone writes a book, they draw from numerous sources and many individuals. Though I would desire to give credit to all that have contributed to this volume, I cannot possibly recognize the many teachers and others who have influenced my life. I would, however, like to acknowledge the following people who have contributed specifically to this volume:

- To my deceased mother, Mae Bodenhamer, who constantly encouraged me to study.
- To my father, Glenn Bodenhamer, who encouraged me to work hard.
- To the co-founders of NLP, Richard Bandler and John Grinder.
- To my NLP instructors, Gene Rooney, Tad James and Wyatt Woodsmall.
- To my students at Gaston College whose inspiration, especially in those earlier years, inspired me to continue the development of a comprehensive NLP training manual that has resulted in this volume.
- To Dr. John Merritt, Associate Dean of Community Education at Gaston College, for his giving me the privilege and opportunity to teach in his department and who has provided constant encouragement.
- To his able secretary, Sandy Hamilton, who works diligently in assisting those of us who instruct in the department.
- To L. Michael Hall, Ph.D. for his invaluable contribution to this book and for the privilege of working with him on many projects.
- To Peter Young who has tirelessly labored in assisting me towards a more excellent copy.
- To Martin Roberts, Ph.D. and the people at Crown House Publishing who have done so much for the advancement of NLP through publishing the labors of so many authors.
- To my niece, Mandy Collette, who has brought "life" and "youth" to our home.
- Last of all and most importantly, to my wife, Linda, whose constant support and encouragement through 34 years of marriage has allowed me to follow my dream.

To all these people and to many more, I say thank you.

*Bob G. Bodenhamer*
*August, 1999*

# Table Of Contents

## Part Four: Advanced Neuro-Linguistic Programming Modeling

# Table Of Figures

# *How To Use This Manual*

To get the most out of your studies of **Neuro-Linguistic Programming** and this book, we suggest the following:

1) Obtain and devote a notebook to your reflections, insights, practices, and exercises. The neuro-muscular action of actually **writing** will reinforce your learnings in kinesthetic ways and "drive in" the knowledge in ways that transcend conscious understanding. Further in the future, you will probably find it helpful and insightful to return to your notes, insights, ideas, and practice drills.

2) When you come to exercises, "thought" experiments, and laboratories – don't cheat yourself. Stop. Do the exercise. Involve others in your study. Several of the exercises involve up to five people, although you can go through most exercises with just two people.

3) Build your own indexing system between parts of **the Manual.** This will reinforce your learning of NLP, the components in the domain, and give you practice in moving around inside the Manual.

4) We have included **Key Sentences** and **Concepts** in text boxes. Upon request, you may purchase **Overhead Mats** for you to create training overheads that parallel the text boxes. These will enable the NLP Trainer to align their training with the student's Manual.

# Introduction

## The Story Of "Magic" In Human Neuro-Linguistics

*"NLP is an attitude and a methodology that leaves behind a trail of techniques."*
Richard Bandler

*Neuro-Linguistic Programming* (NLP) represents a relatively new discipline dating back only to the mid-70s. Behind NLP stands a respectable body of knowledge. NLP originated from several different intellectual disciplines as organized by two co-founders—Richard Bandler and John Grinder.

It happened once upon a time when Dr. Grinder served as a professor of linguistics at the University of California in Santa Cruz. Bandler came there as a student to study mathematics and computers. Dr. Grinder, in fact, had already published several books in the field of linguistics known as Transformational Grammar.

Bandler discovered that he had a "natural" gift for modeling and hearing patterns. He discovered he could detect and replicate **patterns** in Gestalt Therapy from minimum exposure. He became an editor for several of Fritz Perls' books in Gestalt Therapy. Being familiar with Perls' work, Bandler began to study Perls' techniques. As he discovered that he could *model* Perls' therapeutic procedures, he began experimenting with clients using the techniques.

After enjoying immediate and powerful results from that modeling, Richard discovered that he could model others. With the encouragement of Grinder, Bandler got the opportunity to model the world's foremost family therapist, Virginia Satir. Richard quickly identified the "seven patterns" that Virginia used. As he and John began to apply those patterns, they discovered they could replicate her therapies and obtain similar results.

As a computer programmer, Richard knew that to program the simplest "mind" in the world (a computer with off-and-on switches) you break down the behavior into component pieces and provide clear and unambiguous signals to the system. To this basic metaphor, John added his extensive knowledge of transformational grammar. From transformational grammar we borrow the concepts of deep and surface structure statements that transform meaning/knowledge in the human brain. From this they began to put together their model of how humans get "programmed," so to speak.

Thereafter, world-renowned anthropologist Gregory Bateson introduced Bandler and Grinder to Milton Erickson, MD. Erickson developed the model of communication that we know as "Ericksonian hypnosis". Since 1958, the American Medical Association has recognized hypnosis as a useful healing tool during surgery. As Bandler and Grinder modeled Erickson, they discovered they could obtain similar results. Today many of the NLP techniques result from modeling Ericksonian processes.

From these experiences and their research into the unifying factors and principles, Bandler and Grinder devised their first model. It essentially functioned as *a model of communication* that provided a theoretic understanding of how we get "programmed" by languages (sensory-based and linguistic-based) so that we develop regular and systematic behaviors, responses, psychosomatic effects, etc. This model went further. It also specified ways for using the components of subjectivity for creating psychological (mental-emotional) improvement and change.

From that point, NLP expanded. The model expanded by incorporating materials from other disciplines: cybernetics (communication within complex systems both mechanical and living), philosophy, cognitive psychology, studies of the "unconscious" mind, and neurology. Today, NLP has institutes worldwide and numerous authors have applied NLP to medicine and health, therapy and psychological well-being, business, education, athletics, law, Christian ministry, etc.

## The Study Of Excellence

NLP primarily focuses on studying *excellence*. In the 1983 book, *Neuro-Linguistic Programming, Volume I*, the authors subtitled NLP, *"The Study of the Structure of Subjectivity."* The subjectivity that most NLP theorists, developers, and presenters have focused on involves **those highest and most excellent facets** of human experience—high level experiences of creativity, excellence, genius, etc. Co-developer Robert Dilts has especially focused on this area, writing a series of books and numerous journal articles on *"The Strategies of Genius."*

> *NLP offers a model for learning how to recognize excellence and how to emulate it.*

Teachers who want to improve model the best teachers. NLP offers a model for learning *how to recognize excellence and to emulate it.* NLP focuses on recognizing excellence and how to specifically chunk it down into the component elements and the syntax (or order) for installing it in others.

In this step-by-step fashion, the NLP model instructs us how to achieve excellence. Do you wish to improve your ability to communicate? NLP provides a model for communication excellence. Would you like to know how to build and maintain rapport? NLP chunks these skills into teachable formats. Does your child have difficulty spelling? NLP has identified the structure of excellent spellers and the process for training them to become champion spellers. Would you like to conduct successful negotiations in committee meetings? NLP offers a high quality performance model for negotiating with others around difficult issues.

Counselors usually experience a great thrill when they help to bring about positive change in people. NLP offers not only a state-of-the-art theoretical foundation for such, but also the techniques for bringing about personal change.

## The Experiential Nature Of NLP

As you read and use this NLP Training Manual, you will discover *the experiential nature of NLP.* What does that mean? It refers to the emphasis in NLP on *modeling, experimenting,* and *testing* in contradiction to theorizing and hypothesizing. When people ask in our trainings, "Does NLP 'work'?", we get them to put it to the test, right then and there to see if a particular pattern "works" for them. Expect this hands-on immediate testing of the model.

This suggests that the best way to understand NLP involves **experiencing** it. Let us do this as we begin. The following *mental exercise* (a "mind" experiment) will introduce you to NLP. As you read the instructions, take time to follow the directions. This will enable you to become more attuned to what a unique creation you have in your mind-and-body and nervous system. We will work with the natural processes of your mind. By doing this, you will discover many of *the mechanisms* by which you can learn to take control of these processes. In the following paragraphs, the three dots ... mean "pause, experience, notice, feel, think," etc.

> *NLP provides the methods and technology for the "how to" of the managing of our thoughts.*

To the extent that these processes and mechanisms lie outside our awareness—to that extent they control us. As you develop familiarity with these unconscious processes, you learn to manage them. In doing so, you will find these processes worth learning. NLP provides **the methods and technology** for the "how to" of the managing of our thoughts.

### Experiment #1

*Recall some pleasant experience* from your past. Various things will pop into your mind. Whatever pops up in your mind, allow yourself to go with that memory for now. If you don't seem to find such a memory, then allow yourself to simply imagine a pleasant experience. For some people, closing the eyes helps in this process. Once you have this pleasant experience, permit it to remain in your awareness.

Now that you have this pleasant thought in mind—just notice its visual aspects. As you recall the experience, what specifically do you see? Notice the picture of the memory. If you do not visualize well, then imagine what the pleasant experience *feels* like. Or, allow yourself to just *listen* to some pleasant sounds—words or music—enjoy that kind of an internal pleasant experience.

Now that you have the picture of the memory, make the picture larger. Let it double in size... and then let that picture double... Notice what happens. When you make the picture bigger, what happens? Do the feelings intensify?

Now shrink the picture. Make it smaller and smaller. Allow it to become so small you can hardly see it... Stay with that a moment... Does the intensity of the feelings decrease? Experiment now with making the picture bigger and then smaller. When you make it smaller, do your feelings decrease? And when you make it larger, do your feelings increase? If so, then running the pictures (sounds, feelings) in your awareness in this way functions as it does for most people. However, you may have a different experience. Did you? No big deal. We all code our experiences in our minds uniquely and individually. Now, put your picture of that pleasant experience back in a format where you find it most comfortable and acceptable.

Maintaining the same picture now, move the picture closer to you. Just imagine that the picture begins to move closer and closer to you, and notice that it will. What happens to your feelings as it does? ... Move the picture farther away. What happens when you move the picture farther away? Do your feelings intensify when you move the picture closer? Do your feelings decrease when you move the picture farther away? Most people find this true for the way their consciousness/neurology works. When you moved the picture farther away, the feeling probably decreased. Notice that as you change the mental representation in your mind of the experience, your feelings change. This, by the way, describes how we can "distance" ourselves from experiences, does it not?

Suppose you experiment with the color of the picture? As you look at your pictures, do you see them in color or black-and-white? If your pictures have color, make them black-and-white, and vice versa if you have them coded as black-and-white… When you change the color, do your feelings change?

Consider the focus of your images: in focus or out of focus? Do you see an image of yourself in the picture or do you experience the scene as if looking out of your own eyes? What about the quality of your image: in three dimensional (3D) form or flat (2D)? Does it have a frame around it or do you experience it as panoramic? Experiment by changing *how* you represent the experience. Change the location of the picture. If you have it coded as on your right, then move it to your left.

## Debriefing The Experience

> *NLP works primarily with mental processes rather than content.*

Did it ever occur to you that you could change your feelings by changing **how** you **internally represent** an experience? The strength of NLP lies in these very kinds of *processes of the mind*. NLP works primarily with mental *processes* rather than with *content*. Here you have changed how you feel about an experience by changing the quality and structure of your images, not their content. Thus, you made the changes at the mental *process* level while leaving the content the same.

Question: What would happen to a person if they made all their *unpleasant pictures* big, bright and up close? What would happen if they made all their *pleasant experiences* small, dim, and far away? … The person would become an expert at feeling depressed, miserable and unresourceful, would he not?

On the other hand, consider what would happen if a person coded their *pleasant experiences* as big, bright, and up close... will it not create a more positive outlook on life? And, what if they made their *unpleasant experiences* small, dim and far away? The negative would have less influence on their life.

NLP has taught us to appreciate with a new freshness the depth and meaning of the old proverb, *"For as he thinketh in his heart, so is he…"*[i] Consequently, much of what we do in NLP occurs as a result of these natural processes that describe how we humans *process information* in our minds. NLP directs us how to change the process by changing the mental codings. What you just experienced, we call *submodality codings and shifting* in NLP.

Your mind performs six primary representational functions (excluding maintaining internal physical functions such as breathing) in order to "make sense" of the world—*it creates representations* of pictures, sounds, words, generates feelings, smells and tastes. Through the five senses you gather or input information and store it in like manner. Your mind then retrieves this information in the same code or format that you stored the experience. If you store information visually, you will retrieve it as a picture. If you hear and store a noise, you will retrieve the information as a sound.

> *By changing the coding (submodalities) of an experience, you can change your feelings and your internal state.*

We call this coding or storing of information *an internal representation* (see Figure 1:1). In experimenting with a pleasant experience, you retrieved the visual part of the internal representation of a pleasant experience. Quite possibly your pleasant experience also had sounds. By changing the coding of an experience, you can change your feelings and your internal state. When the internal state changes, behavior changes.

The brain uses this *encoding method* to control the messages to our nervous system which then determines/creates our neurological experiences. This *brain "software"* enables us to make decisions and to respond quickly. Doing this consciously would overwhelm us. As we understand these coding procedures, a practitioner of NLP can then bring about change by simply *changing the coding.* Depression, trauma, grief, guilt, anxiety, phobias, beliefs, values, all emotions and human states operate according to their own individual structured codings.

As a Master Practitioner and Trainer of NLP, I (BB) use the techniques of NLP on a regular basis to bring about structural change in my clients.

## Formal Definition Of NLP

Having experienced NLP, let us now give you a formal definition of Neuro-Linguistic Programming.

*Neuro* refers to our *nervous system/mind* and how it processes information and codes it as memory inside our very body/neurology. By *neuro* we refer to experience as inputted, processed, and ordered by our neurological mechanisms and processes.

*Linguistic* indicates that the neural processes of the mind come coded, ordered, and given meaning through language, communication systems, and various symbolic systems (grammar, mathematics, music, icons). In NLP we talk about two primary language systems. First, the "mind" processes information in terms of pictures, sounds, feelings, tastes and smells (sensory-based information) via the "representational systems." Second, the "mind" processes information via the secondary-language system of symbols, words, metaphors, etc.

*Programming* refers to our ability to *organize* these parts (sights, sounds, sensations, smells, tastes, and symbols or words) within our mind-body organism

> *Taking control of one's own mind describes the heart of NLP.*

which then enables us to achieve our desired outcomes. These parts comprise the programs we run inside our brain. Taking control of one's own mind describes the heart of NLP.

NLP has become famous for the techniques it offers to bring about effective and lasting change. For example, NLP has a technique called *The Fast Phobia Cure* developed by Richard Bandler. Using this technique, we can now cure a phobia in ten to fifteen minutes. We have used the procedure to cure phobias of water, bees, elevators, heights, public speaking, small places, airplanes, etc. Best of all, we have done it in just minutes—with the effect lasting (in some cases) years! *The Fast Phobia Cure* represents just one of many techniques for such change.

We have used *Time-Line Processes* to remove traumatic pictures from the minds of traumatized people. Additionally, we have even learned to use the NLP patterns of *Reframing, Swishing, Collapsing Anchors*, etc, conversationally, which means that we do not have to use these patterns in an overtly "therapeutic" way. We can speak in a way that facilitates a person *to think* in new ways thereby leaving them feeling more whole and empowered—with "renewed minds." Language (and languaging) works that powerfully!

> *"NLP is an attitude and a methodology that leaves behind a trail of techniques."*
>
> Richard Bandler

However, NLP involves so much more than just a toolbox of techniques. Richard Bandler says, **"NLP is an attitude and a methodology that leaves behind a trail of techniques."** The attitude of NLP involves one of *intense and excited curiosity*. It involves the desire to know what goes on behind the scenes. With this kind of attitude of curiosity, we want to know what makes the human mind work.

Second, NLP involves an attitude of *experimentation*. With such an experimental attitude, we "try things," and then try something else, and then something else… always trying, getting results, using the feedback, and experimenting with something else. If something doesn't work, we try something else, and we keep doing so until we find something that does work. Bandler and Grinder possessed such an attitude of curiosity and experimentation in their original discoveries that brought about NLP.

The methodology of NLP involves *modeling*. As Bandler and Grinder modeled excellence in Perls, Satir, and Erickson, they produced the original format of NLP. Modeling thus describes the methodology that produced the trail of techniques.

In the book *Turtles All The Way Down: Prerequisites To Personal Genius*, John Grinder makes a noteworthy comment concerning NLP:

> Neuro-Linguistic Programming is an epistemology; it is not allowed to make substantive decisions, to offer the comfort of the "correct path." It offers the opportunity to explore, it offers a set of pathfinding tools. It is for you to select and explore these paths, whether you find comfort or challenge or hopefully, I would say, the comfort of challenge… (pausing) …. The finest compliment that I ever got from Bateson, was the statement to me that NLP was a set of Learning III tools. Now, if that's true then it becomes incumbent upon me, Judith, Ann, Richard, Robert…, the co-creators of this technology, to make some statement about context. As you say without that movement to some ethical considerations, we have not done what is considered a socially responsible job … In a fragmented, technical society which doesn't have that kind of matching between the "emanations from the outside and the emanations from the inside," it becomes incumbent on the individual to develop their own personal culture in the sense of the ethical frame within which they employ the tool.[ii]

## Thought Questions To Assist Your Learning:

1. How would you explain NLP to a 10-year-old child?
2. What would you use to illustrate NLP?
3. How would you explain NLP to a business associate?
4. What about the NLP model makes it so experiential?

[i]Proverbs 23:7 (KJV).

[ii]Judith DeLozier and John Grinder, *Turtles All The Way Down: Prerequisites To Personal Genius* (Bonny Doon: Grinder, DeLozier and Associates, 1987), p. 221.

# Part One

*The NLP Model And Techniques*

# Chapter 1

## The Content Of The Model:
## The Representational System

**What you will learn in this chapter:**

- The representational systems that make up conceptual processes
- The modalities that run conceptual processes
- Your own favorite modality
- Your driver (primary) submodalities
- Our new discovery concerning the limitations of submodality shifts
- The secret of what "controls" submodalities
- How to read eye-accessing cues
- Characteristics of the representational system (rep system)
- How certain predicates inform you about the representational system (rep system)
- How to listen for representational system (rep system) in everyday language

> *All of our experiences result as a product of what we see, hear, feel, touch and smell. In NLP we refer to these senses as the representational system.*

We rely on our senses to gather information about the external world. Within our bodies we have numerous sense receptors. We have no other way to take in information from the world than through these neurological mechanisms. All of our experiences, in fact, result as a product of what we see, hear, feel, touch, and smell (more than just these five senses exist, but these describe the five most central senses). In NLP we refer to these senses as *the rep system*. When we analyze individual skills we find that they function via the development and sequencing of these basic rep systems.

In the NLP model, the five senses do far more than just funnel in information. Each system receives information and then activates memories to produce behavior. This activity takes place within the realm of the neural connectors of the mind. As we receive information from our senses, our brain codes

> *In the NLP model, the five senses do far more than just funnel in information. Each system receives information and then activates memories to produce behavior.*

them in the same manner. For instance, when we receive information visually, our brain codes this information as *a picture*. The brain codes information received auditorily as *sounds and words*. We refer to the internal words we form from sounds as *auditory digital*. "Digital" means that something is either on or off. A digital distinction has nothing in between like an analogue distinction. Most words represent an existing referent or not. Only a few words allow us to represent a continuum or range of distinctions. And, information taken in through our feelings, the brain codes as *a feeling or emotion*. When you recall information, the brain accesses and expresses the memory in the same manner it stored the information.

An illustration: we have written this text using Microsoft Word™. So to store it we use a Microsoft Word™ file. Then later, to retrieve it we must likewise begin by retrieving it from that same format. If we store a memory visually, we will recall and describe that memory using visual language. Thus, we preserve the format of visual. If we hear something and store it as a memory of sounds, we will recall and express that experience using auditory language. *Speak, hear, sound* and *loud* serve as examples of auditory words.

Our mind codes our learnings in the way we learned them. When we recall these memories, we recall them in the same rep system (see Figure 1:1). Suppose you bought a car. Suppose that you had already seen a picture of a car that you particularly liked. At the car dealership you would look at his inventory. In choosing a car to purchase, you would compare the car the dealer had with the stored memory of the car you wished to buy. Thus you used the visual rep system both to store and code the memory of the car you desired to purchase. You used the visual rep system to see the car you wanted to consider buying. And you used the visual rep system to recall the memory of the car you desired to purchase and to compare it with the car you wanted.

Of course, we store and code most memories using more than one of our five senses. In NLP we emphasize primarily the three senses of visual, auditory and kinesthetic (VAK). Should smell and taste comprise part of the memory, your mind will use them. However these two senses play a lesser role. The term *representational system* arises from the fact that we *re-present* information primarily visually, auditorily and kinesthetically. As we grow from infancy to adulthood, most people begin to favor one rep system over the others.

I (BB) primarily represent information using the auditory and verbal systems; I use words like, *hear, explain, loud, harmonize, listen,* etc. Now, listen! Whereas I (MH) once primarily used the kinesthetic system, and now use the visual and auditory-digital systems. I use words like *see, imagine, say to yourself,* etc.

| Incoming information | Internal information | Subjective experience |
|---|---|---|
| From outside world (Enters our heads through our senses) | Enters our nervous system and is interpreted as: | Information constructed or recalled as: |
| Visual (Eyes) ———————▶ | Pictures ———————▶ | V – Visuals, Pictures |
| Auditory (Ears) ———————▶ | Sounds ———————▶ | A – Sounds, Noise |
| Kinesthetic (skin/body) ———————▶ | Feelings ———————▶ | K – Sensations, Feelings |

**Figure 1:1** *Making Sense of the World*

With this we have now provided you with a secret key for matching and gaining rapport with us! Feed back these key words that express the way of thinking for you and match the way we "think" with the way our brains work best!

In American society, roughly 20% of people process primarily kinesthetically, 60% do so visually, and 20% auditorily. These statistics only represent the general tendency. In actual experience, people change rep systems from moment to moment. Depending upon the subject at hand, they will process primarily visually one moment and then auditorily the next.

For those who present information publicly (ministers, teachers, public speakers), do you *use all three of the major rep systems in your presentations*? If you code most things primarily visually, then you probably (unconsciously) use visual terminology, which means that it will only fit or match between forty to sixty percent of your audience. To do that leaves out those people who process auditorily and kinesthetically. This could very well provide part of the answer why churches do tend to take on the personality of the pastor.

> *The way people represent information using the rep system will come out in their words.*

NLP asserts that the descriptions people use to describe an event do not only occur metaphorically, but that they also provide a literal description of what a person does inside their head in coding and representing information. This means that the way people represent information using the rep system will come out in their words. If someone says to you, "I see your point," then they may want to inquire about some visual images! To establish rapport and communicate with that person, we must paint them a picture of our meaning!

If somebody says, "I just don't *feel* right about this," they want some kinesthetic representations. If you ask, "Can't you get the picture?" and then proceed to paint them a picture, you would probably not gain rapport. You thereby *mis*match their kinesthetic way of "thinking" with your visual "thinking." But respond in feeling terms and you will establish rapport and they will understand your communication.

Suppose you want to try to convince a kinesthetic person to visit your club. You could say, "I just know that you would *feel comfortable* in our club. We have a *warm* group of people. In fact, at our meetings people *get lots of hugs*. I *feel* that you would become highly *impressed*." We have here italicized the kinesthetic words by which we "predicate" a statement of some sort. Using a specific sensory predicate enables us to match and pace. A kinesthetic person can *get a feel* for this kind of talk.

By giving people back their words (using their languaging), we "speak their language" and they think of us as one of them. And people tend to like people who think and act like them.

Knowing the primary representation system of others thus becomes an extremely important piece of information for effectively communicating with them. If your spouse asked, "Honey, can you *see* us going to the club tomorrow? I really liked what I *saw* at the club. The people *appeared* so friendly. And I'd describe the speaker as *a picture of perfection*, wouldn't you? I believe we should go to this club more often." You wouldn't reply, "Yes, I agree. I also had a good *feeling* about that club. I *felt* the director's *delivery* really *spoke* to me and I felt moved. And the people *made me feel* right at home." No! That would completely *mis*match her visual rep system. A congruent reply would go, "Yes, I agree with you. I can *see* us at that club tomorrow. The people not only *appeared* friendly, but *showed* themselves as truly friendly. I also found the speaker's talk *attractive* because of all *the word pictures* he drew."

> *Pacing plays an essential role in rapport building.*
> *Pacing involves having enough flexibility to enter the other person's model of the world.*

*Pacing plays an essential role in rapport building.* Pacing involves having enough flexibility to enter the other person's model of the world. We do this by using their language patterns and vocabulary in communicating with them. When pacing an individual, determine their primary rep system and feed it back to them as you talk. In the above illustrations, the first speaker primarily used a visual rep system. The reply of the second person *mis*matched as he used kinesthetic predicates. This can result in a loss of rapport. The second example demonstrates pacing the first person via matching the visual rep system by using visual predicates. Here is a transcript of an auditory mismatch between a visual and an auditory. This is followed by a piece of pacing communication.

**Auditory:** I think we need to *talk* about this car some more. I have *listened* to all you have *said* about this vehicle. However, I discern some differences in what you *say* and what I *hear* you *saying*.

*Mismatch:* Yes, I can *see* that you have not *perceived* all that I have tried to *reveal* to you about this car.

*Pace:* Yes, I agree that it *sounds* like we have not *communicated* on the same *wave length*. However, I know that as I *describe* the car further to you, you will *hear* what I *say* in a way that will sound more understandable to you.

## The Representational System Preference Test[1]

For each of the following statements, please place a number next to every phrase. Use the following system to indicate your preferences:

    **4 = Closest to describing you**
    **3 = Next best description**
    **2 = Third best**
    **1 = Least descriptive of you**

1. **I make important decisions based on:**

    _4_ gut level feelings.
    _1_ which way sounds best.
    _2_ what looks best to me.
    _3_ precise review and study of the issues.

2. **During an argument, I am most likely to be influenced by:**

    _1_ the other person's tone of voice.
    _3_ whether or not I can see the other person's argument.
    _2_ the logic of the other person's argument.
    _4_ whether or not I feel in touch with the other person's true feelings.

3. **I most easily communicate what is going on with me by:**

    _3_ the way I dress and look.
    _4_ the feelings I share.
    _2_ the words I choose.
    _1_ the tone of my voice.

**4.** **It is easiest for me to:**

__1__ find the ideal volume and tuning on a stereo system.
__2__ select the most intellectually relevant point concerning an interesting subject.
__4__ select the most comfortable furniture.
__3__ select rich, attractive color combinations.

**5.**

__2__ I function as very attuned to the sounds of my surroundings.
__1__ I function as very adept at making sense of new facts and data.
__4__ I function as very sensitive to the way articles of clothing fit on my body.
__3__ I have a strong response to colors and to the way a room looks.

## SCORING THE REPRESENTATIONAL PREFERENCE TEST

### STEP ONE:

Copy your answers from the test to the lines below. Transfer the answers in the exact order they are listed.

| 1. | | 2. | | 3. | | 4. | | 5. | |
|---|---|---|---|---|---|---|---|---|---|
| 4 | K | 1 | A | 3 | V | 1 | A | 2 | A |
| 1 | A | 3 | V | 4 | K | 2 | D | 1 | D |
| 2 | V | 2 | D | 2 | D | 4 | K | 4 | K |
| 3 | D | 4 | K | 1 | A | 3 | V | 3 | V |

### STEP TWO:

Add the numbers associated with each letter.
Make five entries for each letter.

| | V | K | A | D |
|---|---|---|---|---|
| 1. | 2 | 4 | 1 | 3 |
| 2. | 3 | 4 | 1 | 2 |
| 3. | 3 | 4 | 1 | 2 |
| 4. | 3 | 4 | 1 | 2 |
| 5. | 3 | 4 | 2 | 1 |
| Totals: | V 14 | K 20 | A 6 | D 10 |

## STEP THREE:

The comparison of the totaled scores give the relative preference for each of the four major rep systems.

### Representational System Practice[2] (Homework)

Genie Laborde includes in her book, *Influencing With Integrity*, a handy instrument for assisting you in determining your preferred rep system. You can determine which system you prefer most, which one you prefer second and which one your conscious mind does not use much. The system that gives you the most difficulty to translate and match probably reflects your least used system. I have used several instruments but I have found this instrument the most helpful to me. I have reproduced her instrument in its entirety.

Example 1. My future looks hazy.

> Match:
>> Visual: When I look to the future, it doesn't seem clear.

> Translate:
>> Auditory: I can't tune in to my future.
>> Kinesthetic: I can't get a feel for what seems to be going to happen.

Example 2. Sarah doesn't listen to me.

> Match:
> Auditory: Sarah goes deaf when I talk.

> Translate:
>> Visual: Sarah never sees me, even when I'm present.
>> Kinesthetic: I get the feeling Sarah doesn't know I'm alive.

Example 3. Mary gets churned up on Mondays when the boss expects the report.

> Match:
>> Kinesthetic: Mary gets agitated and nervous on Mondays.

> Translate:
>> Visual: Mary can't focus on Mondays when the report comes due.

> Auditory: Mary hears lots of static on Mondays when the report comes due.

Complete the following for increased awareness of rep systems. This model offers good practice for future use. This exercise will wire your mind to match predicates when you next hear one of these. **Note:** I have added a third translate for Auditory Digital.

1. My boss walks over me like I'm a door mat.
   Match:
   Translate:
   Translate:
   Translate:

2. I get the feeling I'm unappreciated.
   Match:
   Translate:
   Translate:
   Translate:

3. I have trouble looking back to that problem.
   Match:
   Translate:
   Translate:
   Translate:

4. I guide this project by the seat of my pants.
   Match:
   Translate:
   Translate:
   Translate:

5. She seems like such a sweet girl.
   Match:
   Translate:
   Translate:
   Translate:

6. I ask myself, "How did I ever get into this?"
   Match:
   Translate:
   Translate:
   Translate:

7. I can imagine what she's like.
   Match:
   Translate:
   Translate:
   Translate:

8. Something tells me I'm making a mistake.
   Match:
   Translate:
   Translate:
   Translate:

9. I've tried to get a handle on what my boss means.
   Match:
   Translate:
   Translate:
   Translate:

10. I keep stubbing my toe on unexpected obstacles.
    Match:
    Translate:
    Translate:
    Translate:

11. Joe paints a clear picture of disaster ahead.
    Match:
    Translate:
    Translate:
    Translate:

12. Smells like a dead fish to me.
    Match:
    Translate:
    Translate:
    Translate:

## Predicates & Process Words

In communication—*we cannot not communicate*. I (BB) first learned this truth while studying communication skills. The instructor put it this way, "You cannot *not* tell your story." Thus, every time we open our mouths we verbally represent our model of the world. This applies to the rep system as well. People who primarily sort and code their thoughts auditorily will primarily produce auditory predicates. Visual processors will do this visually and kinesthetic processors will do it in that system. It only makes sense. If we think in terms of sights, sounds, and sensations, it shows up in our external language maps—words.

Accordingly, if we but *listen to the specific predicates or process words* (primarily verbs, adjectives and adverbs) that a person uses, we can discover that person's primary rep system. These predicates thus become *language cues* (linguistic markers) of the person's internal processing (rep systems).

What value or importance does this awareness of predicate use in another person's languaging have? A person's use of predicates provides a major indicator of how that individual "makes sense" of the world and constructs their "internal reality." Predicates thus provide us a major clue as to the person's subjective reality—a "royal pathway" to their thinking-feeling and responding.

Predicates also greatly assist us in establishing rapport with people. If rapport refers to getting into a state of harmony, accord, and affinity with someone, then predicate awareness and use empowers us to quickly learn to "speak the other's language." It enables us to quickly hear and utilize the same language patterns that the other person uses. This, in turn, endows our words with a greater likelihood that the person will understand them. I (BB) like to think of rapport as "jumping inside another's nervous system and suddenly making sense of how they understand reality." When we get into rapport with someone else, *we join that person* (mentally and emotionally) in their model of the world. No wonder matching a person's predicates provides great value for communication excellence.

We know of no easier way to gain solid rapport with another than by matching predicates. Doing so, you verbally mirror the individual's *way of thinking* when you reflect back their primary rep system predicates.

> *By matching predicates, we exquisitely pace in a graceful and elegant process.*

By matching predicates, we exquisitely pace in a graceful and elegant process. After consciously practicing this for a while, you will find yourself unconsciously matching predicates. When you do this mirroring in matching and pacing repeatedly it becomes an unconscious pattern in your responding and languaging. Matching predicates provides a simple yet profound way to accomplish deep rapport. Further, when we give a person back their favorite kind of process words, these words make so much sense in their reality that they just "slide in." In other words, the person will not have to translate your words into their words nor notice the inherent meaningfulness of your languaging.

## Predicates

For your convenience, I am including a thorough list of predicates. For months I kept such a list on my word processor during sermon preparation. My purpose was twofold. First, I desired to broaden my vocabulary. And second, I desired to make sure I was including all three rep systems in my message. If you desire to include everyone in your conversation, you need a vocabulary that includes all three.

## VISUAL

| | | |
|---|---|---|
| admire | foggy | reveal |
| appear | foresee | scan |
| attractive | form | see |
| blurred | gaze | shiny |
| bright | glance | show |
| clear | glare | sight |
| cloudy | gleam | sightsee |
| colorful | glow | sparkle |
| conceal | graphic | spy |
| dark | hazy | staring |
| dawn | illuminate | strobe |
| disappear | imagine | surface |
| display | obscure | twinkle |
| envision | observe | vanish |
| exhibit | look | veil |
| expose | peer | view |
| eyed | perspective | visualize |
| faced | picture | vivid |
| flash | preview | watch |
| focus | reflect | |

## AUDITORY

| | | |
|---|---|---|
| announce | harmonize | request |
| answer | harsh | resonance |
| argue | hear | sang |
| asked | hum | shout |
| attune | inquire | shriek |
| call | insult | shrill |
| chatter | lecture | sighs |
| cheer | listen | silences |
| complain | loud | silent |
| crescendo | melodious | sound(s) |
| cry | mention | stammer |
| deaf | mumble | talk |
| discuss | noisy | tell |
| echo | outspoken | translate |
| explain | overtones | unhearing |
| expression | question | utter |
| growl | quiet | vocal |
| grumble | recite | yell |
| gurgling | reply | |

## KINESTHETIC

| | | |
|---|---|---|
| angle | grapple | slip |
| beat | grasps | smooth |
| bends | grinds | soft |
| bounce | hard | solid |
| break | hold | spike |
| brush | hug | stuffed |
| burdened | hurt | suffer |
| carry | irritate | sweep |
| clumsy | mushy | thick |
| comfortable | movement | touch |
| concrete | pinch | trample |
| crouching | plush | tremble |
| crumble | pressure | twist |
| exciting | pull | unbudging |
| feel | rub | unfeeling |
| firm | run | warm |
| fits | scramble | wash |
| flop | scrape | weigh |
| force | shaky | work |
| grab | skip | |

## OLFACTORY/GUSTATORY

| | | |
|---|---|---|
| bitter | salty | spicy |
| fragrant | savor | stale |
| fresh | smell | sweet |
| odor | smoky | taste |
| pungent | sour | |

## UNSPECIFIED PREDICATES

| | | |
|---|---|---|
| be conscious | decide | nice |
| be cognizant | experience | notice (v or a) |
| become aware | feel that | perceive |
| believe | insensitive | process |
| change | know | question |
| clear (v or a) | learn | sense |
| conceive | light (v, a or k) | think |
| consider | motivate | understand |

### Predicate Phrases[3]

## VISUAL

| | |
|---|---|
| an eyeful | mental picture |
| appears to me | mind's eye |
| beyond a shadow of a doubt | naked eye |
| bird's eye view | paint a picture |
| catch a glimpse of | photographic crystal |
| clear cut | plainly seen |
| clear view | pretty as a picture |
| dim view | see to it |
| eye to eye | shortsighted |
| flashed on | showing off |
| get a perspective | sight for sore eyes |
| get a scope on | snap shot |
| hazy idea | staring off in space |
| horse of a different color image | take a peek |
| in light of | tunnel vision |
| in person | under your nose |
| in view of | well defined |
| make a scene | |

## AUDITORY

be all ears
be heard
blabber mouth
clear as a bell
clearly expressed
call on
describe in detail
an earful
express yourself
give an account of
give me your ear
grant me an audience
heard voices
hidden messages
hold your tongue
idle talk
inquire into
key-note speaker
loud and clear

make music
manner of speaking
outspoken
pay attention to
power of speech
purrs like a kitten
rap session
rings a bell
state your purpose
tattle-tale
to tell the truth
tongue-tied
tune in/tune out
utterly
unheard of
voice an opinion
well formed
word for word

## KINESTHETIC

all washed up
be felt
boils down to
catch on
chip off the old block
come to grips with
connect with
control yourself
cool/calm/collected
firm foundations
floating on thin air
get a hold of
get a handle on
get a load of this
get in touch with
get the drift of
hand in hand
hands on
hang in there
heated argument

hold it, hold on
hot-head
keep your shirt on
know-how
lay the cards on the table
light headed
make contact
moment of panic
pain-in-the-neck
pull some strings
sharp as a tack
slip through
slipped my mind
smooth operator
start from scratch
stiff upper lip
throw out
tap into
topsy-turvy
turn around

## DIGITAL

doesn't compute

factor in

get an account of

hash it out

the bottom line

## Matching Predicate Exercise

This exercise requires three people. Decide person "A," "B," and "C." "A" serves as the operator, "B" role plays as the subject or client and "C" role plays as the advisor or meta-person.

1. "B" leaves the room and plans a two to three minute monologue about a present issue in their life. Make this first monologue positive.

2. When "B" returns, he tells the monologue to "A." "A" responds to "B" using the same type predicates (visual, auditory, kinesthetic) that "B" used.

3. At the conclusion of the exercise, "B" tells "A" how well he did in matching her predicates. Give the positive remarks first by sharing where he matched your predicates. Afterwards, share where he mismatched or missed your predicates. "C" serves as the meta-person by sharing their agreement or disagreement with "B."

4. Round robin—"A" becomes "B". "B" becomes "A". Repeat the exercise as above.

## Eye Accessing Cues

NLP's model for understanding and changing behavior utilizes the rep system as *the basic building blocks* of subjectivity. These systems describe the process by which we understand, represent, and operate on the world. All human experience results from external and internal perceptions of sensory data. To use this understanding, we must develop the ability to recognize rep systems as a particular person uses them. Amazingly, *we can do just that!* Doing this provides cues about their ongoing representational functioning. Then we can simply match their predicates to gain rapport.

Beyond predicate awareness, we can utilize other indicators about a person's ongoing representing. We can notice their other *accessing cues*. Such cues tell us what system people access and when they access a particular modality. In the early days of NLP, Bandler and Grinder made this discovery. They noticed that when they asked certain questions in class, people would look in the same direction before they answered. From those preliminary observations, John and Richard formulated NLP.

> *Internal and external processes that people experience correlate with both eye movements and predicates.*

They discovered, as Woodsmall (1990) later wrote, that the "...internal and external processes that people experienced were correlated with both eye movements and predicates." In *The Structure of Magic, Volumes I and II* (1975/1976), Bandler and Grinder described the rep system theory, which now serves as **the foundation** of NLP. However, the first description of eye accessing patterns occurred in their classic work (1979), *Frogs Into Princes*, a publication that launched NLP into its present popularity. As these eye movements provide us such information, we can then use it to establish rapport.

Think about some time when you have noticed that people move their eyes while they talk and listen. These eye movements do not occur randomly. Each movement of the eyes functions to indicate certain neurological processing. The patterns go as follows: when most right-handed people move their eyes *up* and to the left, they recall pictures previously seen (visual process of remembered material). When they move their eyes up and to the right, they construct an image putting together pieces which they may not have ever seen.

> *John and Richard discovered that we can observe a person's lateral eye movements and positions and thereby recognize when a person represents information visually, auditorily or kinesthetically.*

Eyes moving *level* in the head to the left indicate recalling of remembered words. Eyes moving level to the right indicate the constructing of sentences. If the eyes go *down* and to the left, the person engages in an internal dialogue—usually about highly valued values and principles. Here a person has a synesthesia (combination, merging) of two senses— they *speak feeling words to themselves* as they consider something of importance. When eyes move down and to the right, they access kinesthetic awareness (feelings, sensations) and emotions. Eyes centered and defocused often indicates the person is making pictures; however, many also process internal dialogue this way.

The eye movements and positions do not create the internal experience, but *reflect and indicate* internal neurological information processing. Yet because the brain and nervous system work interactively as a holistic system, when we consciously manage our lateral eye movements, this can help to stimulate the corresponding portion of our representational brain. Thus, when I look up and to the left, I stimulate that part of my brain that stores pictures from my past. Ask a family member to recall their first bicycle and notice where the eyes go.

Woodsmall (1990) wrote about the scientific basis for eye accessing cues:

> "Scientists have discovered a basic and ancient mechanism in the depths of the brain that physiologically relates eye movements to sensory memory recall. Called the "reticular formation," this dense bundle of nerves serves as a sensory filter for the brain, deciding which messages are significant enough to be sent to the conscious mind for attention.
>
> The nerves that control eye movements, a set of three nerves (the oculomotor, the trochlear and the abducens) which we'll refer to simply as the oculomotor nerves, originate and derive from the reticular formation area. It is thought that whenever the eye is moved to a particular position, either instinctively or intentionally, the reticular formation is activated to send a beam or impulse to the brain to stimulate a particular sensory motor recall." (p. 12).

> *The chart does not apply to everyone.*
> *Left-handed people and cerebrally reversed people may have a reversed pattern.*

The following chart (Figure 1:2) identifies the eye movements and positions of most right-handed people. As you view the chart, it portrays a person as you look at them, hence, from your point of view. The arrows indicate what you see as you look directly at them. Figure 1:3 provides the same information giving the linguistic cues present with each eye position.

Does this chart hold true for everyone? No. A left-handed person, and anyone cerebrally reversed, will have their remembered and constructed sides reversed. Several people differ from this chart in just that way as a left-handed person. Their visual remembered and auditory remembered occur on the right side. The visual construct and auditory construct occur on the left side. However, some may still access auditory digital and kinesthetic in conformity with the chart, though these may reverse as well.

Further, some people's eye accessing patterns do not occur in a way that shows as much distinction as indicated by the chart. They make much more subtle movements. For them, one has to observe much more closely to detect the different positions. As you watch the eyes, listen closely to the person's predicates. Their predicates will provide redundant information about their processing/representing. Once you map someone's eye patterns, you will find that they will tend to use the same pattern regularly and consistently.

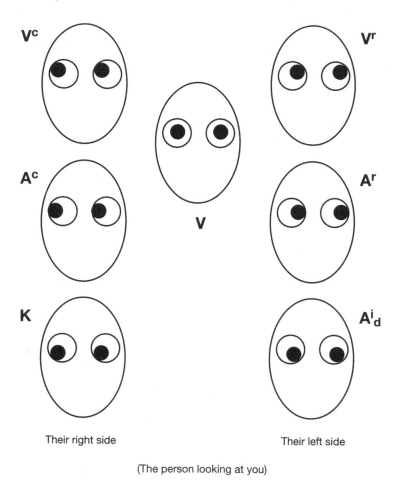

Their right side                Their left side

(The person looking at you)

(Young, 1999)

*Figure 1:2 Eye Position Chart*

What does this have to do with rapport? Everything. When someone moves their eyes up, you can pretty well guess about them internally seeing pictures. So if you speak to them using visual words, you get on their wavelength. As you watch, notice how many people will move their eyes into position before they speak. As they do, you have a better than probable chance of knowing, before they even speak, the rep system they will use!

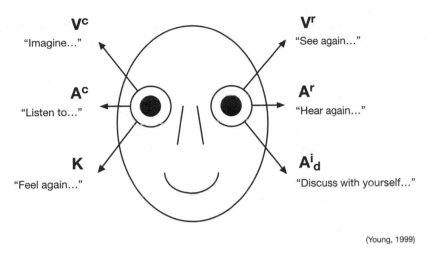

(Young, 1999)

*Figure 1:3 Language Accessing Cues*

Recently, I (BB) sought to establish rapport with a client. Her eyes and head went down and to her left. So I asked, "As you think about the things we've talked about, what conclusions do you now reach?" This state so fit her internal world that it gave me continued rapport and assisted her in becoming aware of her internal dialogue.

Do take care to use this discreetly. Avoid staring. Most people will not appreciate it if you begin to stare at them. Use television talk shows to develop your skill at this. Since "the eyes are the window of the soul" we now can use that idea in a creative way to develop our communicative skills.

Knowing these eye accessing patterns can further help us in building and maintaining rapport if we use them as cues as to when to talk and when not to talk. As predicates inform us about *what* system a person uses and usually has consciousness about, so we refer to this as the "lead system."

## Lead System

> *Accessing cues inform us about the rep system that people use to retrieve information. Our lead system frequently will differ from our primary rep system.*

Our lead system frequently will differ from our primary rep system. Suppose I ask, "What is your name?" and your eyes go down and to the left. That suggests that you used the auditory digital system to lead. I also know that while you have moved your eyes down and to the left, you will not both listen and process internal information. For that millisecond, or minute, I need to stop, quiet myself, and give you the time to get the information. Once we share information, people have to process it. They have to "go inside" so to speak, and access their own internal understandings of the information. They may look up and visualize, they may move their eyes down into auditory digital, or they may access kinesthetic sensations. To maintain rapport, pause and give them time to process the information.

If you don't, if you continue talking while a person accesses information, you may very well lose rapport. In that time period where they "go inside," they don't/can't hear you. What will continually interrupting another's "thinking" thought processes do? It will prevent you from ever gaining rapport as it prevents the person from completing their thoughts. So, watch eye movements. When a person's eyes move to access information through their lead system, give them processing time.

*Possible Anomalies* (Young, 1999)

- Eyes go to the opposite side from the diagram: possible lateral reversal. The person may have a left-handed preference?
- Eyes consistently go to one location first and then off to others: lead system being accessed to enable the person to do what you ask.
- Eyes consistently do not go to one particular location at all: the person may have blocked V, A or K and so avoid that place.
- Eyes go to atypical locations, for example, they look up and say, "I feel…" This may be a synesthesia pattern.
- Eyes are motionless: they do not seem to move at all. If they really do not move at all there is immediate access. No search is necessary, as when someone is asked their name.
- They may not have heard or understood what you have said: they have gone blank. They may have tranced out—they are busy thinking other thoughts.
- Eyes move back and forth, for instance the eyes move repeatedly left and right: they may be searching, or scanning, or they may be comparing two images.
- Eyes consistently go to wrong locations: the person may just have sorted things differently and habituated to a different style of functioning. They are probably under-performing neurologically.
- Eyes seem to go all over the place: this may indicate confusion or agitated internal state. They may also need to learn where to put different classes of information in terms of VAK.

## Exercise: Mapping Eye Patterns

*Elicitation Questions For Eye Accessing Patterns*

Use the following questions to assist you in mapping someone's eye patterns. In doing this, make sure you look at the person you want to map when you ask them the question. If you look down at the question when you ask the question, their eyes will dart before you can look back at them! This process works best if you ask the questions conversationally. Then the person doesn't become self-conscious and try to "see" themselves responding! If you use this as an exercise and you play the recipient, just allow yourself to have permission to respond freely and spontaneously, not caring if you notice the movements of your eyes. Self-awareness (self-reflexive consciousness) in this process messes things up because the person's second thoughts go to, "How did my eyes just move, let me visually remember that now!" So just allow yourself to relax so that you can respond naturally and gracefully.

Peter Young (1999) points out:

> The language you use affects another person's internal processing, it influences first what mental operations the person engages in. If you want them to use a particular representational system then your language should signal this clearly.

Conversely, if you want to find out how they will process left to their own devices, use non-sensory language. If you say "Remember a time when . . ." you leave it to the subject to choose the way in which they will do this. So it might be by seeing again a particular scene, or hearing again a person's voice, or feeling that old familiar feeling that goes with such an event, or tasting or smelling the particular tastes and smells that are forever associated with such times.

**Warning:** Sometimes when you ask for memories of past experiences, you may immediately get kinesthetic responses as the old memories may have painful feelings attached. Suppose you ask the question, "What color graced your bedroom walls as a child?" and the person had experienced severe trauma as a child in the bedroom? Don't expect a visual recall eye pattern in that moment. You will immediately get a kinesthetic response with other sensory feedback like a reddening of the face and a tearing of the eyes. When this happens, sometimes I (BB) say to the client, "You have some emotion attached to that memory, don't you?" This will maintain and deepen rapport.

$V^r$: *Visual Remembered*. Recalling an image or picture.
See the color you most favored as a child.
See the color that graced your bedroom walls at that time.
See yourself yesterday. What did you wear?

$V^c$: *Visual Constructed*. Making up pictures you have never seen.
Imagine your car as green with yellow dots on it.
Imagine yourself with red hair.
Picture a traffic light with the green light at the top and the red light at the bottom.

$A^r$: *Auditory Remembered*. Remembering sounds or voices previously heard.
Listen to your favorite song. What does it sound like?
Listen again to the very last statement I made.
Listen to the sound of ocean waves lapping on the shore.

$A^c$: *Auditory Constructed*. Creating and inventing new sounds.
Name the seventh word in "T'was the Night Before Christmas."
Hear me sounding like I had Donald Duck's voice.
Hear the sound of a large rock hitting water.

**Note**: As you map from these questions, observe the person closely because he or she may go to auditory recall to remember what the sounds sound like before they construct what you will sound like as Donald Duck.

K: *Kinesthetic*. Feelings, sensations, emotions.
Feel yourself rubbing your hand over a very fine fur coat.
Feel your love for the one person you love the most.
Imagine diving into a very cold stream or pool.

$A_d$: *Auditory Digital*. Internal talk, dialogue, self-conversation.
Go inside and repeat to yourself the choices you had concerning the last major decision you made.
Recite the words of your favorite verse to yourself.
Talk to yourself about what you really want out of life.

## Group Eye Accessing Exercise

I.   *Eye Accessing Patterns Exercise Number 1*

A.   Get into groups of three. Choose "A," "B," and "C." "A" begins by asking "B" questions from the elicitation question list. Follow the questioning order as they appear on the sheet. "A" observes "B" closely as to where their eyes go in response to each question. "C" positions themselves beside "A" to corroborate "A's" findings. Use the additional questions should you need them.

B.  Once "A" satisfies themselves that they have mapped "B" accurately, do a round robin.

C.  Warnings:

1.  "B" concentrates on answering the questions and not on the placement of their eyes. For "B" to concentrate on the placement of their eyes will contaminate the exercise. Concentrating on the eyes will result in the accessing being in relationship to this rather than in answering the questions.

2.  You may use other questions should the ones provided not elicit adequate eye movements. However, take care with that. For instance, suppose you desire a kinesthetic response. You ask the question, "Can you imagine yourself feeling warm?" The problem may arise that this question will elicit a visual remembered response first and then a kinesthetic response. The word "imagine" presupposes images or pictures. Therefore, phrase your questions to get the response you want. Remember, "communication" involves the response you get.

## II. Eye Accessing Patterns Exercise Number 2

A.  In this exercise use the same group, with each person serving exactly as they did in the first exercise. You verify the findings of your first exercise with this one. If you mapped your partner correctly in the first exercise, their eye patterns from this exercise will confirm the patterns of the first exercise.

B.  "B" role plays as a spouse, child, client, customer, etc, and talks for five minutes about something they would like to do or purchase. As "B" talks, make a conscious effort to include all three rep systems, that is, include what you see, hear and feel about the product you wish to purchase or what you would like to do. "A" can ask any questions necessary to clarify what "B" does on the "inside" while talking.

C.  "C" positions themselves beside "A" to permit their observing clearly "B's" accessing patterns. "A" and "C" determine, through observation, "B's" accessing patterns.

D.  Round robin

## Characteristics Of The Primary Representational Systems

Your **Primary** rep system contributes to defining your "personality type" (how you develop and express your overall "powers" or "functions" as a person). Studies indicate a direct correlation between an individual's primary rep system and certain physiological and psychological character-istics. The following generalizations about these characteristics offer some patterns to look and test for. We have found that the more we used these patterns in our personal and professional lives, the more ways we have found to utilize and appreciate this information, and we believe you will too.

> *Your primary representational system contributes to defining your "personality" type.*

### Visual

People who specialize in the visual system often stand or sit with their heads and/or bodies erect, with their eyes looking upward. Their breathing is often shallow and high in the chest. When a visual person accesses a picture, they may even stop breathing for a moment. As the picture begins to form, their breathing resumes. Their lip size will often look thin and tight. Their voice tones will come out in high tones and loud volume with rapid and quick bursts of expression. Organization and neatness charac-terize the visual. Noise can distract a visual. They learn and memorize by seeing pictures. So they generally become bored by lectures and remember very little. Visuals like, want, and require visual aids for learning. They take more interest in how a product looks than how it sounds or feels. Visuals make up approximately sixty percent of the population.

Since visuals organize their world visually, they can more easily let go of emotions. By creating new pictures rapidly, visuals can install new pictures with the accompanying emotions to replace old ones. For a visual person, "As he or she sees, so he or she becomes." Visual people tend to easily create new pictures and change their internal states.

In terms of body types, a great many visuals have thin, lanky bodies with long waists. They hold their posture in a straight and erect way. Give a visual space; don't stand too close. They must have plenty of room in their field of vision so they can see things.

*Auditory*

People who operate primarily from the auditory rep system will tend to move their eyes from side to side. Their respiration will operate in a rather regular and rhythmic way from the middle of the chest. When you ask them to describe an experience, they will concentrate first on the sounds of that experience. This will result in their breathing adjusting to express those internal sounds they hear. Often they will give forth a sigh.

Having processed information in terms of sounds, auditory individuals will happily respond using their own sounds, and with musical language. They often have a "gift of gab." Often they will go to lengths to explain a concept or event. Auditory people even take pride in enunciating thoughts clearly and with good sound quality. They can even tend to dominate a conversation because of their abundance of words. When they so alienate people through too much talking, they become the "loners of our culture." They talk to themselves a lot. They frequently have an intense sound sensitivity and can become easily distracted. Because of this heightened sense of sound, unpleasant or harsh sounds will distract them.

People with auditory focus learn by listening. Inasmuch as the auditory channels address information in a sequential way, they too will "think" and memorize by procedures, by steps and by sequences. Auditory people like for others to tell them about the ongoing progress of things. Since they give supreme importance to sounds, match their tonality and predicates in your conversation with them. Treat their ears very well. When you match their predicates and tonality, it sounds good to them because it fits their inner reality. People with this rep system make up approximately twenty percent of the population.

In body form and shape, auditory people tend to have a moderate form in between the skinny visual and the heavy kinesthetic. Often their hand gestures will point to their ears. An externally oriented auditory person will lean forward while talking. When sounds occur internally, they will lean backwards. They will keep their voice rhythmic and even. Speak clearly with an auditory person.

*Kinesthetic*

Those who use the kinesthetic system **primarily** express themselves with their eyes down and to the right. They use action predicates indicating sensation, movement, action: *touch, feel, grasp, warm,* etc. They breathe low in the stomach. It makes sense for someone who feels deeply to breathe deeply. Their breathing will change with their feeling states. Their lips usually look full and soft. Voice tone for a kinesthetic will often sound low, deep, breathy and/or soft. They typically speak slowly and use long pauses as they access their deeply stored information. If they take an internal orientation, their bodies will look and feel full, round and soft. If, however, they take an external orientation, their bodies will look and feel hard and muscular.

Many kinesthetic people will move verrrry slooowly. To motivate a kinesthetic, give them a physical reward or pat them on the back. Kinesthetic types love touching. You can also get up close to a kinesthetic person, they love closeness. Kinesthetic people do tend to have difficulty in getting out of negative emotions. If they feel sad, the sadness may lead them into depression. Then that heavy sensation will lead them to become even sadder and so it continues into an ever descending loop. A plus for most kinesthetic people lies in their ability to feel deeply and love deeply. To motivate a kinesthetic, get hold of their feelings. Kinesthetics represent approximately twenty percent of the population.

*Auditory Digital*

A person who primarily uses the auditory digital rep system essentially operates at a meta-level of awareness *above* the sensory level of visual, auditory and kinesthetic. As a consequence, this individual comes across as if in "computer" mode. I (MH) like to say that if a person has too much college, they will more likely move into the world of auditory-digital! I (BB) have noted that these people become the researchers and the accountants in our society. Woodsmall (Hall, 1989/1996) noted that such individuals love lists, criteria, rules, meta-communication, etc.

The eye movement and position for this meta-representational system will operate on a lateral movement pattern, like auditory processing, except when accessing information and then they will tend to move their eyes down to the left. They will breathe in a restricted and uneven way. Their lips will often look thin and tight. The posture for the auditory digitals usually involves an erect head with shoulders back and arms crossed. The voice will come across in a monotone and robotic manner, like a computer talking. They will often have a soft and full body type. And yet, because the auditory digital mode will often exhibit characteristics of the other rep systems, they may very well vary widely from the above description.

## Submodalities—The Qualities of the Modalities

A key element of the rep system, and hence of NLP, concerns that of the **elements or qualities** of the rep system. These rep system elements offer a major contribution of NLP to the domain of personal change and the technologies that make such transformation possible. Our internal processes function with a profound *literalness*. Consider the following statements:

"I feel pretty dull today."
"I hear you loud and clear."
"Something smells fishy about his proposal."
"I have a bright future."

These seemingly metaphorical sayings can actually enable us to track back to the individual's internal map-making in terms of their rep system "modes" (modalities). Until the discoveries of NLP, most people treated such language as "just metaphors." Today, however, we know better.

With the insights of NLP, we know that such metaphors typically cue us about the person's internal representing of the world and so we hear such as literal descriptions of the speaker's internal world. Brains often use the metaphorical language that we speak to run some literal internal program.

> **Submodalities** *represent one of the most basic components of the way the brain functions.*

*Submodalities* represent one of the most basic components of the way the brain functions. Given that we use three primary modes (modalities) for "thinking," these modalities (VAK) mean that we represent the world in our minds by sights, sounds, and sensations. We also use smell and taste, but typically they play a minor role.

The modality of language exists at a higher logical level than these sense modalities inasmuch as words function as *symbols about* these sights, sounds, and sensations. For now, we want to focus on the primary level sensory-based representations—our VAK representations—and describe how we can make further distinctions in these internal representations, namely, their qualities.

> *The modality of language exists at a higher logical level than these sense modalities inasmuch as words function as* **symbols about** *these sights, sounds, and sensations.*

In this NLP Practitioner Training Manual, we have included the latest discoveries about the role meta-states play in what works and what doesn't work in NLP. For you to understand this, you need to understand some terminology. These terms consist of "logical levels," "primary levels,"

"Meta-levels" and "Meta-states." As the manual progresses you will find further explanation. In the meta-state model as developed by Michael, the "primary level" refers to our thinking about, responding to, and the meaning we give to, the **world outside our internal experience**. Hence, "primary states" describe those states that result from our experience of the outside world. States such as fear, anger, sadness, joy, happiness, etc., describe those everyday states that we access from our primary level experience of the outside world.

Meta-states do not refer to those states of mind we have from our external experiences. Meta-states refer to those **internal states** we have about our internal experiences. Our brains have the unique quality for abstracting. In NLP you read and hear a lot about "logical levels." Logical levels refer to higher level abstractions. Consider the following:

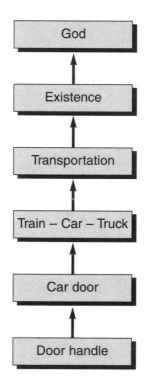

*Figure 1:4* Levels of Abstraction

In Figure 1:4 note how with each word going up, you move to a higher level of abstraction. Start with the word "transportation." We know that "transportation" functions at a higher logical level

> *Higher levels modulate lower levels.*

than does the word "car," for transportation includes "cars", but it includes more. The word "car" includes the term "car door" but it includes more than just a car door, etc. Hence, each word functions as a higher order abstraction in that it contains what lies below it and **more**. Important to the meta-state model concerns the discovery by Gregory Bateson that **higher levels modulate lower levels** (1972). The term "Meta-levels" refer to higher logical levels.

In the meta-state model, we utilize the power of higher levels in the modulation of lower levels. The brain has the unique ability to **internally** apply one thought to another thought. The brain abstracts to another state level and reflects that state to another state. Suppose you experience a primary state of fear from some external event. Internally you may choose to apply the thought of "appreciation" to your fear and take appropriate action to any external threat. Or, you may choose to apply another state of consciousness called fear to the fear you had from the primary state of fear. Thus, you fear your fear. Guess what you will get? Paranoia. You fear your fear and the higher level fear modulates and increases your primary state of fear and suddenly you experience paranoia. But, notice the difference in outcome states when you apply the meta-level state of appreciation to fear. What do you get? You sure don't get paranoia, do you?

- *Primary levels* refer to our experience of the outside world primarily through our senses.
- *Primary states* describe those states of consciousness from our primary level experiences of the outside world.
- *Meta-levels* refer to those abstract levels of consciousness we experience internally. As the meta-levels connect with the body (kinesthetic) we have a "state" containing emotions.
- *Meta-states* describe those internal states of consciousness we have "about" or "above" lower level states.

Michael formally defines meta-states:

To *model the structure of subjective experience*, we begin with **states**—*states* of mind, body, & emotion, hence *mind-body or neuro-linguistic states*. What mechanisms drive these states? *"Thoughts"* (mental representations, ideas, meanings, etc.) as *processed & embodied* in our nervous system. When our consciousness *goes out* to some reference outside of us (a person, event, or thing), we experience a **Primary state**. But when our thoughts-and-feelings come back to reference our thoughts-and feelings, we have a **Meta-state**.

In **a Meta-state,** conscious awareness *reflects back* onto itself. We call this *self-reflexive consciousness*. Thinking-about-thinking generates thoughts-feelings at higher logical levels so that we experience states-*about*-states. Rather than referring to something "out there" in the world, Meta-states refer to something *about* (@) some previous thought, emotion, concept, understanding, Kantian category, etc. Korzybski talked about Meta-States as "abstractions about abstractions" or a second-order abstraction.

As a **Meta-class of life,** we live our lives *at Meta-levels.* There we experience beliefs, values, domains of understandings, conceptual and semantic states, "core" or transcendental states, etc. To model human excellence (or pathology) we have to "go meta" (Bateson) and recognize the Meta-levels as they play in the *systemic nature of consciousness* (i.e. it operates reflexively and recursively).

By **Meta-stating** we *bring a* mind-body *state to bear upon* another state. In this way we *set a frame-of-reference* that, in turn, governs all of the lower levels. It operates as an *attractor* in a self-organizing system. Bateson noted that the higher levels organize, drive, and modulate lower levels. In this way we create our *Model of the World* or map which we then use as we navigate through life.

Our layered Meta-states becomes our reference system for "making sense" of things. It *frames* our meanings (semantics). When we change our internal universe, we *reframe* our understandings, beliefs, values, and meanings. Since we give meaning according to *context,* our Meta-states describe the structure of our mental contexts.

In **Outframing** we make the ultimate meta-move of going above all frames to *set* an entirely new frame-of-reference. We can engage in *Meta-magic* by this maneuver to re-set our whole reality strategy (1999).[4]

So to summarize, primary levels refer to our experience of the outside world primarily through our senses. Primary states describe those states of consciousness from our primary level experiences of the outside world. Meta-levels refer to those abstract levels of consciousness we experience internally. Meta-states describe those internal states of consciousness we have "about" or "above" lower level states. Meta-states describe the mind's ability for self-reflexive thought—thoughts about thoughts about thoughts, etc. Meta-states come directly from the human experience of self-reflective consciousness as we reflect or apply one state to another state. The point: when we have a thought about another thought, the second thought will modulate to some degree the primary thought. A meta-state transcends the primary state, and as it transcends, that makes it a higher logical level from the primary thought.

> *The words we apply to our internal representation function at a higher logical level. Hence, our language modulates our internal representations.*

Later we will cover more about meta-states and how they inform submodalities. For now, note that the words we apply to our internal representation function at a higher logical level. Hence, our language modulates our internal representations. Or to put it another way, words "control" our internal representations.

### Experiment # 1

So... recall a pleasant experience again. Do you see that experience that you found so pleasurable? Now look closer at *the qualities* **of that picture**: color or black-and-white; three-dimensional or flat like a photograph; do you see yourself in the picture (dissociated) or do you look through your own eyes as if you have stepped into the picture (associated); does the picture have a frame around it or do you have it coded as panoramic? Does it move like a movie or does it look more like a still picture? Do you see the picture far off or close; bright or dark, or in between; in focus or out of focus? Where do you have this picture located—up to your left, in front of you? These *qualities* of your representations identify a number of what we call *submodalities*.

Now let's do the same with the **auditory system**: dDo you have sounds in your representations of pleasantness? Would you describe those sounds as loud or soft? What about the tone—soft or harsh? Full or thin (timbre)? What direction does the sound come to you from? Fast or slow? How clearly do you hear this sound? Do you hear in stereo or mono?

What about the **kinesthetics** that go along with this internal experience? How intensely do you feel the sensations? Do you feel any texture, weight, heaviness or lightness, shape or form, temperature? Where do you feel these sensations in your body? Any smells or tastes?

Identifying and making these distinctions in our internal representations provides specific details for this domain of *submodalities*. In a way, they function as the "building blocks" of the representation system—the very qualities of our awareness that make up their properties. These distinctions, in turn, provide the brain and nervous system the messages, or commands, for how to feel and respond. In a way, they fulfil the category of distinctions that Gregory Bateson called "the difference that makes the difference." Yet they do not do so at what we might call "the submodality level." They do so at a level meta to the rep systems themselves. Now you won't read about this in NLP literature itself. We have just recently (1998) come to this understanding. But more about **how** submodalities **actually work** later.

> **Submodalities** essentially function as the
> building blocks of the rep system.

Regarding submodalities, Woodsmall (1989) wrote:

> "If the mind/body is capable of making any distinction, then it must have some way of making that distinction; and the way it in fact does so is by differences in the submodalities by which the alternatives of the distinction are internally represented." (p. 4).

This means that the human brain determines the parameters of our experiences by using these submodality distinctions. The brain represents all experiences, emotions and even beliefs using modalities (rep system) and especially **the qualities or properties** of these modalities (that is, the submodalities). Submodalities provide us another understanding of the proverb about "as a man thinketh, so he is." This truth shows up as the heart of the Cognitive-Behavioral model. If our cognitions (thoughts) control our inner subjective reality and move us to begin to literally "realize" such externally in behavior, then it lies within submodalities that these cognitions control the human system. This has given rise, in NLP, to the saying, "Submodalities determine behavior."

How do you know the difference between *what you believe* and *what you do not believe*? Traditionally in NLP we have assumed the following:

> You have different words, different voices, different tones, you hear these voices perhaps in different locations, or, if you code primarily visually, you will have very different *quality* of pictures for those you believe versus those you do not. You tell the difference by representing the beliefs differently. The distinctions between these two beliefs lie at the submodality level.

Bandler and MacDonald (1988) have written that if you change the submodalities of a belief, you can change the belief (pp. 67-75). Similarly, with Time-Lining we use the metaphor of a "line" designating "time." This seems to work because of the physiological fact that submodalities *in-form* our autonomic nervous system about how to respond. Thus, all of the changes made through Time-Line processes, as well as any process, occur ultimately at the submodality level.

Yet this does not accurately explain submodalities. Actually, to even note or detect these **qualities** of our representations—we have to go meta or above the internal representation. The word "meta" comes from a Greek word meaning "above" or "beyond." Try it for yourself. Think about a pleasant experience until you step into it so much that you fully experience it again. Now think **about** that experience. How did you code your pictures in terms of distance, clarity, color, etc? And your sounds—how did you code the volume, tonality, tempo, distance, etc? As you *think about* **the qualities** of your internal representations—the submodalities—do you not have to *step back* or *go meta*? Do you not have to get *out of content* by moving to a higher level and then notice their *structure?* Of course.

But so what?

This shows and suggests that when we alter **the quality** or **properties** of our internal representations, we do **not** do so "at the submodality level." But we rather do so at a meta-level of awareness.

---

> *When we alter the quality or properties of our internal representations, we do not do so "at the submodality level." But we rather do so at a meta-level of awareness.*
>
> *The qualities (submodalities) of our pictures do not exist at a level lower than the picture. They occur **inside** and exist as **part of** the representation.*
>
> *And so what does this mean? It means that we cannot change some experiences with only submodality shifts.*

---

The problem with the old view about submodalities lies in part with the term itself. By labeling **the quality and properties** of the representations "sub," the language created—by presupposition—the idea that we have moved to a lower logical level. But we have not.

The **qualities** of our pictures do not exist at a level lower than the picture. Try to picture any visual image that does *not* have color or black-and-white, closeness or farness, clarity or fuzziness. These do *not* represent "members" of the class—but **qualities of** the picture. They occur *inside* and exist as *part of* the representation.

When I (BB) try to process submodalities at a lower logical level, my mind goes blank because submodalities do not exist at a lower logical level. Submodalities exists as a part of the representation system and not apart from it. For instance, a car door can exist apart from the car as a separate entity and therefore the car door exists at a lower logical level from the car. Also, transportation exists at a lower logical level from existence and as such transportation can exist as a separate conceptual reality—but not so with submodalities. But a submodality like color cannot exist separately from the visual modality. A loud sound cannot exist as a separate entity from sound, for without sound you could not have loud or soft, high pitch or low pitch, etc. Therefore submodalities exist as part and parcel of the representation system.

> *We cannot change some experiences with only submodality shifts. This powerfully applies to belief change.*

And so what does this mean? It means that we cannot change some experiences with only submodality shifts. This powerfully applies to belief change. Think about something that you do **not** believe. Can you *represent* what you do not believe? Can you even turn up all of the submodality properties of the representation making it closer, brighter, more life-like, etc.? When you do, do you suddenly "believe" it? I don't. For example, get an image that represents the awfulness of Adolf Hitler. Note the submodalities. Now get an image that represents a great person like Mother Theresa. Note the submodalities of Mother Theresa. Now put the submodalities of the image of Adolf Hitler into the submodalities of Mother Theresa. This may prove difficult but go ahead and do it. Do you believe that Adolf Hitler represents a person like Mother Theresa? Of course not—when you see Adolf Hitler your words which operate meta to the image will modulate the meaning of the image.

In understanding this model, let's review the difference between two basic levels of thought. The first level we call the level of the Primary State. The Primary States of consciousness define those everyday states of consciousness wherein we experience thought-and-feelings "about" something in the world "beyond" or "outside" our nervous system. In these states our thoughts relate to things "out there" and our bodies experience the primary emotions like fear-anger, relaxation-tension, glad-mad, attraction-aversion, etc.

The second level of thought refers to those abstract states of thought that Michael calls meta-states. Meta-states of consciousness define those thoughts about thoughts, feelings about feelings and states about states. Here our thoughts-and-emotions relate to and "about" the world "inside" ourselves. We can hate our hatred and minimize and/or eliminate our hatred. Thus, as Gregory Bateson has said, higher level thoughts modulate lower level thoughts (1972). By the process of Meta-stating ourselves, that is, bringing one thought to bear on another thought, we can increase a state as fearing our fear, minimize a state or even eliminate a state. When we really get tired of hating someone or something and then start hating our hatred, we may hate our old hatred right out of existence. What happens when you bring forgiveness to bear on your bitterness? What happens when you bring forgiveness to bear on your guilt? What happens when you bring appreciation to bear on frustration? Anger? Guilt? Sadness? Try it, you might like it.

Now, concerning beliefs: **beliefs** do not exist at the primary level — but at a level meta to representations. To believe in something, anything, we have to *"say 'Yes' to the representation."* We have to confirm it. To **disbelieve**, we say "No" to the representation. To **doubt,** we say, "Maybe it is, and maybe it isn't." These phenomena occur at a meta-level and therefore need a meta-representational system to carry them, and that primarily means *words*. With beliefs we have moved from thinking about something outside us in the world to thinking about some internal representation of what we have already experienced in the world.

So what?

This means that to turn a thought into a belief or a belief back into a *mere* thought, we have to move to a meta-level and confirm or disconfirm the thought. Mere submodality shifting will often not work in shifting these beliefs. Submodality shifting that effects the saying "Yes" or "No" to a thought will alter the belief. In Part III we will give you models for shifting submodalities that work and work well.

### Digital and Analogue Submodalites

| |
|---|
| *A digital submodality functions either on or off. An analogue submodality varies over a continuum.* |

In looking at the submodalities, you will note a distinction even within the submodalities. Consider the visual submodalities. What difference exists between a picture that we code in color or black-and-white and a picture we see as far off or close? We will represent a picture as *either* black-and-white *or* in color. We have no choices for anything in-between. However, we can represent a picture as far off or close *or anywhere in-between*. Some submodalities then function like a light switch. We can code it one way or the other, but nowhere in-between. We can code a picture as a movie or a still shot, but not both. We refer to this as *a digital submodality*. A submodality that we can vary over a continuum we refer to as *an analogue submodality*. Location operates as an analogue submodality.

Most people learn to appreciate the submodality structure of experience by experiencing these distinctions via changing them. When an event happens, the event occurs as a fact of history. We cannot change what occurred "out there" beyond our skin. But once we take cognizance of that fact and *represent* it inside our heads/nervous systems—then thereafter we respond, *not* to a fact of history, but to our memory *of* that event (we respond to our "map" rather than the "territory"). So, while we cannot change external history, we *can change our memory* **of** that event (our internal map). When we do, the change takes place at the submodality level. How we feel about a certain event usually depends upon a few critical submodalities.

### Experiment # 2—*Discovering Confusion & Clarity*

What causes you confusion? Consider something that you find confusing… As you recall that experience, notice how you represent it—pictures, sounds, sensations, words, etc. And just let that confusion come, and experience it fully… for a little bit.

You probably have a picture of it. So notice that picture and check for its submodality distinctions:

- Color: in color or black-and-white?
- Dimensions: 3D or flat?
- Inside/Spectating: associated or dissociated?
- Edges: panoramic or framed?
- Motion: a movie or a still picture?
- Distance: how far away?
- Brightness: bright or dark?
- Focus: focused or out of focus?
- Location: where located?

You can also allow yourself to take time to identify the *qualities* of the auditory and kinesthetic systems. After you do, take a break … Think of hot fresh bread baking in the oven. Good.

Now, think about something you truly know. What do you know without question? What do you feel certain about? Allow yourself to think of something about which you *feel certain*. Do you feel certain that the sun will rise tomorrow? Do you feel certain the politicians will play partisan politics in Washington? Do you think you will eat tomorrow?

As you think of anything that you feel certain about, run the same kind of analysis with the pictures, sounds and sensations you have of that certainty. Fully elicit the submodalities of this picture of certainty as you did with confusion. As you do, you will discover some differences. List those differences.

Ooopps. We did it to you again! We quoted verbatim the traditional NLP approach using the "Confusion to Understanding Pattern." But if you picked up on the new distinctions about multiple levels of awareness and that submodalities work at a meta-level, then you might have had an uneasy sense about this pattern. In exploring this, we have found that nobody that we know uses this process for moving from confusion to understanding.

Why not? Because **understanding** (like belief) operates at a meta-level. To *understand* we have to have a pattern, structure, or model that orders and organizes things. Merely making pictures brighter, sounds closer, kinesthetic sensations more compelling will not create "understanding."

Now that you know *the meta-level governs and creates the difference that makes a difference*, you have some really powerful transformational energy at your fingertips—or "mind"-tips! When you go meta and bring a new **quality** to bear on the representation—a **quality** that makes a difference— then you can change that experience.

In a belief, we bring the **quality** of *confirmation* to bear on the thought. In dis-belief, we bring the **property** of *dis-confirmation* to bear on the thought. In understanding, we bring the **quality** of order to bear on the confusing thoughts. The submodality quality may make the difference—but it does so from a meta-level. After all, as Bateson so repeatedly argued, the higher meta-levels always modulate the lower levels.

So take the image of confusion and put it in the same submodalities that you use to code certainty all you want, and you won't turn it into "understanding." If your picture of confusion occurred in black-and-white and of certainty in color, then make your picture of confusion colorful. Now you have colorful confusion, do you not? Merely changing the submodalities of confusion into the submodalities of certainty will not change how you feel about that particular state of confusion. Nor will your state of confusion give you a feeling of more certainty. After all, close and colorful have **not** given you any way to order the confusion.

But move above the confusing images, sounds, and sensations and bring an organizing structure to bear upon it. You could use a metaphor or story, a diagram, or piece of explanation, but whatever you use that **organizes** the pieces and gives it structure, that allows you to now "understand" the relationships between the parts — suddenly and completely brings order out of chaos. In this move, we did not change anything except the relational structure of the internal representations.

> *When you change a submodality and it changes other submodalities you have discovered a driver submodality.*

In changing one's internal representations through changing **the quality** of the modalities, you will discover that some submodalities play a more critical role than others to make such changes. We refer to such submodality distinctions as *driver submodalities*. And these "drive" because they create a new frame of reference for the thought.

For instance, in turning the sights, sounds, and sensations of confusion into the coding of certainty, if changing the location of the representations simultaneously changed other submodalities and brought order or structure, then this **property** set a new frame.

Changing the submodalities of one image into the submodalities of another image we call *submodality mapping across*. In mapping across, usually two or three submodalities will typically change other submodalities. When this happens, you have a *critical submodality* or *driver* submodality. A submodality that drives other distinctions and brings about significant changes when mapped across into another image provides a key change mechanism in human personality. In changing one experience using submodality mapping across, using the driver submodalities describes a crucial piece of understanding in helping people.

Even though we cannot change historical facts, as making those external events to have never happened, **we can change** our current internal representations of those events. And, as we change the internal representations, we signal different cues to our brain and body about how to feel about it. By changing how we feel, we change our response. This describes the heart of how NLP and its patterns for renewing the mind work. Rep systems, eye accessing cues, submodalities, meta-states, etc, describe some of the key elements in how we structure our subjective experiences. Later in this work you will discover several models for working directly on submodality shifts.

Another building block of subjective experience lies in *how we sequence* these elements. We refer to the sequencing of our rep systems in the production of thought and behavior as *strategies*.

## Conclusion

With *this model of human subjectivity* and how we "work" through our nervous system (neurology) to generate our unique model of the world that then initiates us into a particular neuro-linguistic *state of consciousness*, we have a model for understanding and working with the particularities of human subjectivity. Most of all, it gives us specific things that we can do to *connect* with people, create a relationship of rapport, and understand their reality from their point of view.

## Thought Questions To Assist Your Learning:

1.  Using what you now know about rep systems and eye accessing cues, identify the favorite rep systems of five close associates or family members.
2.  What did you learn in this first session about *how* you process information?
3.  How will you use this to improve your own learning strategies?
4.  Find some old letters, journals or reports that you have written and underline or highlight all of these process/predicate words.
5.  With the eye accessing chart before you and some blank paper, watch talk TV interview shows to track both the eye movements and people's use of language. What did you notice about the "lead" rep system in contrast to the system used to represent information?
6.  Explain in your own words how higher logical linguistic levels modulate lower submodality levels.

# Chapter 2

## The Basics

## Connecting With People:
## Building And Maintaining Rapport

**What you can expect to learn in this chapter:**

* Sensory Acuity—What "Up time" means
* How to use the representational system to gain immediate rapport
* How to "pace" (match) people for rapport
* How to use predicates in pacing
* How to pace non-verbal aspects of experience

---

*Sensory acuity refers to the ability to notice,
to monitor, and to make sense of the
external cues from other people.*

---

### Sensory Acuity

In NLP we use the concept of sensory acuity in training our ability to see
and listen more effectively and consciously when comprehending non-
verbal communications. Sensory acuity refers to the ability to notice, to
monitor, and to make sense of the external cues from other people. The
other person constantly and inevitably sends out unconscious external
signals of some of their internal processing and state. As we develop our
own *sensory acuity skills*, this allows us to "read" those cues. If so much of
the communication messages come to us non-verbally, then developing
our sensory acuity skills becomes essential to becoming truly an accomplished communicator. Developing our sensory acuity skills enables us to
recognize the quality of another's signals in terms of their congruency
and incongruency.

By developing and using our sensory acuity we make available to ourselves
a great deal of the non-verbal aspects of communication. These non-verbal
areas of communication comprise the fuller picture of communication.
Knowing and using these levels enables us to build and maintain rapport at
these levels—levels that usually operate unconsciously for the sender.
Furthermore, sensory acuity of these non-verbals provides us with a set of
indicators with which we can gauge the level, depth, and quality of rapport.

### For Daily Practice

Developing sensory acuity skills requires time and practice. As you allow yourself to believe that *you will develop these skills* as you continue to practice them on a daily basis, you will find yourself surprised at times at seeing, hearing, and sensing parts/details of the communication process that previously went unnoticed. To do this, "chunk down" the pieces into small enough chunks to work with without feeling overwhelmed. Shortly, we will introduce you to some new things to watch for in people. We will offer them to you in chunked-down, bite-sized bits. Then, on a daily basis, begin to observe these in those people with whom you come into contact. Once you master one area, go on to the next one. Genie Laborde (1984) wrote:

> "You can train your sensory acuity in fifteen minutes a day for a week or two by allowing yourself to look closely and listen carefully."

She pointed out that our culture (generally) does not give us permission to stare. How do we become proficient at rapport building, looking intensely at people, but without staring? We can do this non-intrusively at home, work, restaurants, TV talk shows, etc., without offending or drawing people's attention to our interest! As you become a better observer of people, you will develop your sensory acuity so that you can learn how people respond to various communications. Once you have learned their response to certain stimuli, you can then adapt your communications to them to get the response you want. After all,

> "The response you get specifies the meaning of your communication to the other person in spite of your intent."

Below we have listed five crucial areas wherein you can begin your daily practice.

---

*Things to look for:*

1. *Breathing*
2. *Color changes*
3. *Minute muscle changes*
4. *Lower lip changes*
5. *Voice sounds/tones*

---

1.   **Breathing**. A person's breathing patterns tells a great deal about them. A change in breathing usually indicates a change in internal state. As you begin to observe the variety in people's breathing, notice *where* they

breathe. Do they breathe in their chest or from their stomach? You can also detect differences in *the tempo* of breathing. Notice the *pattern* of breathing while in conversation. If, while conversing, the other person's breathing changes, seek to identify what thought-feeling shifted within them. You can count on breathing shifts to almost always function as a signal of an internal state shift. As you learn to calibrate to these shifts, you will have an answer to your questions before they verbally give them to you. *Calibrating* a person means that you can recognize certain states in an individual by their non-verbal signals.

Sometimes it becomes difficult to see their breathing because of heavy clothing or shallow breathing. Also, starring at the chest of some people may get you in trouble(!). So watch the tops of their shoulders. Usually, you can pick up their breathing patterns by watching their shoulders move. This also works well for it allows you to observe their face as well. To further strengthen your observational skills of breathing, turn the sound down on your TV set and observe the breathing of the actors. As you develop this skill, begin to watch the pulse rate of people. You do this by observing their heart beat on the carotid artery in the neck or observing the pulse rate on the temple.

2. **Color Changes.** At first this may seem impossible. However, if you begin to recognize the extent to which you already have expertise in this, then you can become aware of how your unconscious mind already picks up on these color changes. You can then bring this skill into conscious awareness as you practice awareness of a few things. First, think in terms of contrast. This will help you notice color changes. Notice that a person's face does not have just one color. Faces have areas of pink, cream, brown, grey, green, blue, lavender and yellow. These colors constantly change as a person talks. Facial colors also tend to reflect the internal state of the person. For instance, detect the differences between the color under the eye with the color of the upper cheek. Secondly, notice how these colors change as the person changes subjects. Often I will change the subject matter in order to have the person reflect an opposite emotion. This will allow me to calibrate the person's response to different feeling states.

3. **Minute Muscle Changes.** As the color of the face changes to reflect internal states, so do the muscles of the face change. The facial muscles change as to tension and relaxation to reflect internal states. Watch specifically the small muscles around the mouth, at the jaw line and at the outer corners of the eyes. Often when people feel tense, the forehead will tense and the muscles around the eyes will crease. The phrase "tension headache" speaks literally about the process. Anticipate these changes to function in an idiosyncratic way. Each person will respond in his own way

to his own internal state. By listening to what the person says and observing his unconscious body signals, you can *calibrate* what each muscle tone means in that person's system. As your skills develop, you will become proficient at observing muscular tension and relaxation in other parts of the body.

4. **Lower Lip Changes.** We doubt that anyone consciously controls the shape of their lower lip. Indeed, we would probably find it impossible to control the lower lip consciously anyway! Given this, our communication partner will give us some direct unconscious signals if we observe their lower lip. As you begin to observe someone's lower lip, take care that you don't get into trouble! Just notice the changes in size, color, shape, edges, texture, movement, stretching and tumescence (swelling or filling). Do not attempt to interpret. Only as you have begun to notice distinct changes, then begin to calibrate as to the internal state the changes indicate. Calibration becomes possible as we make mental photographs of what each state indicates for a given person. Then we take that picture and compare it with what we see in the other person and whether or not we see the same or different state we are calibrating to.

5. **Voice Sounds/Tones.** Obviously, voice tone plays a significant role in communication. Learning to hear the sound quality of a person's voice represents a skill essential in becoming an excellent communicator. Again, changes in a person's voice signify internal state changes. Begin by listening for changes in volume, pitch, rhythm, tempo, clarity, and resonance. A good way to do this, again, involves listening to the radio or TV. In this way you do not have to worry about the content. Begin to detect the shifts in tonality, pitch, etc. Each of these changes reflects a different internal state on the part of the individual. Once you develop adeptness at this, you will notice just how much more attuned you have become to truly listening, understanding, and entering into another's world.

As your acuity develops, start connecting voice shifts with breathing patterns, muscle movements, lower lip configuration and color changes. Remember, to chunk this down into learnable bites. As your skills develop in one area, move on to the next. With time it will unconsciously come together. The secret to this involves: practice, practice, practice.

## Directions for Group Work

You will need three people (triads) to do most of the exercises. Each person in the group will choose a letter: "A," "B," or "C."

"A" - begins as the operator (therapist, teacher, salesperson, etc).
"B" - role plays as the subject (client, student, customer, etc).
"C" - is the meta-person (observer, adviser, helper, etc).

## *The Observer/Meta-Person's Role*

1. Monitor the time allotted for each exercise.
2. Make sure the exercise follows the guidelines as written.
3. Give high quality feedback to "A" when requested. "C" does not intervene unless the exercise progresses poorly or incorrectly.
4. Assist "A" in maintaining a good "Resource State." Should "A" become discouraged, confused or apprehensive, "C" assists "A" respectfully back into their Resource State.
5. Observe "B's" reaction to "A." Should "B's" reaction to "A" become incongruent, make note of this and inform "A" during the debriefing period. Do not break in during the exercise.
6. During the debriefing period following the exercise, give high quality feedback to "A." Make complimentary statements first followed by a tactful summation of needed improvements.
7. Follow the same procedure in number 6 above with "B."
8. "C" requires of the triad a high quality exercise. Much learning can take place during the exercises. "C" insures that each benefits from the exercise.

Should "C" observe that "A" operates below their potential with the specific exercise, then "C" "stretches" "A" by requesting that the next exercise be more challenging.

## Calibration: Sensory Acuity Exercises

1. Form groups of four. Each person takes five minutes each and tells four learning experiences. Three of the experiences will relate a true and positive story. Share a fourth false story but one you wish had truth for you. The false story can come in any sequence of your presenting your four stories. After each person tells their learning experiences, the other three pick which one they believe to be false. Use your sensory acuity skills in determining which one you believe to be false. Give sensory-based descriptions as to why you believe the story contains false information.

2. Form groups of three. "A" begins by holding a dollar bill at waist level. "B" encircles the dollar bill with their hand about mid-way up. "B" stands ready to catch the dollar bill when "A" drops it. "B" calibrates each time "A" drops the dollar bill until "B" figures out "A's"

unconscious movements, etc., prior to "A's" dropping the dollar bill. "A" will give off unconscious signals before dropping the dollar bill.

When "B" catches the dollar bill three times in a row, then you know you have determined "A's" pattern. "B" notices what they calibrate to catch the dollar bill. "B" gives back to "A" sensory-based descriptions of their unconscious movements. "C" serves as the meta-person.

3.  Do a round robin.

## How to Gain Rapport: Matching and Mirroring

*How do you gain rapport at the unconscious level?*
*You become LIKE the other person through a process called* **Matching** *and* **Mirroring***.*

*How* do you gain rapport? How does one establish communication at the unconscious level? Actually, gaining rapport at the unconscious level occurs simply: you *become like* the other person. When people look, sound, act, and move like each other, they tend to *like* each other. Same-sized pendulums, when placed together on a wall and suspended with a taut wire, will gradually synchronize their swings. Nature thus seems to love for the physical world to move into a state of harmony. We too can gain rapport with people by **acting like them** through a process called *matching and mirroring*.

The next time you go into a restaurant, notice the tables alive with conversation. If you look carefully, the conversants will sit, talk, and gesture in very similar manner. They will seem to operate as if *in sync*. Do we match and mirror in large group meetings? The next time you attend a large group meeting, look down the row of chairs. Notice how many people sit in similar positions. Do these people do this consciously? No. They have entered into a rapport with each other at an unconscious level.

### An Example of Rapport

As a Christian professional, Karen felt her life caving in around her. It went back to a time in her life when at seven years of age, a fifteen-year-old neighborhood boy sexually abused her. The abuse continued for some time. Now at thirty-six, feelings from those horrible experiences began to resurface. She sought help from a minister friend of mine who had some training in NLP. Because of his limited training, he referred her to me (BB).

The referring minister said that Karen desperately wanted help. Such clients usually come most receptive for therapy, and Karen fitted that description. When we met

> *When people become like each other, they like each other.*

at the minister's office, I arrived first and waited with him for Karen's arrival. I knew of Karen, but had not met her. Upon arriving, Karen said, "Hello Bob!" and sat down in the chair in front of me.

Now the first task of the therapist always involves *establishing rapport*. I did not have to do that with Karen. She did it. When she sat down in front of me, she took a position in her chair that reflected my posture. Her posture mirrored mine. She crossed her legs in the same way. She even placed her head in her hand in a way that matched mine. She also matched my voice. Did Karen do this consciously? No. All of this mirroring and matching occurred unconsciously. Without my training in NLP I might not have noticed her mirroring and matching me.

What elements can we match and mirror? We can match and mirror another's physiology, voice, posture, gesturing, facial expression, blinking, words, tilt of the head, etc. When a person with whom you desire rapport tilts their head, do the same. If they tilt their head to the left, tilt your head to the right. In this way you mirror them exactly as you sit across from them. Their left corresponds to your right. Notice the curvature of their spine and align yourself with their posture. When they talk, take note of their gestures. As you respond, use the corresponding gestures. Give them back their gestures as you respond. But do not match their gestures while they talk otherwise your matching might not occur outside of their conscious awareness!

You may wonder, "Won't the person notice my mirroring? How should I respond if they accuse me of mimicking them?" Not surprisingly, this rarely happens. We have mirrored and matched people for years and almost never get caught!

Just once did I (BB) get caught. During a therapy session, the client said, "You are sitting like I am sitting." I responded, "Well, yes, now that you mention it, I am. How is it that you noticed?" By the way, that client worked as a practicing psychotherapist. She said, "My boyfriend has become a student of NLP and he told me about mirroring and matching." So she came cued to notice!

> Crossover mirroring refers to mirroring a portion of a person's physiology with a different portion of your physiology.

So *match and mirror people discretely*. You can delay your matching and mirroring by a few seconds. If they shift, wait a few seconds and then match their shift. You may also use crossover mirroring. *Crossover mirroring* refers to mirroring a portion of a person's physiology with a different portion of your physiology. If they move their leg, you can move your arm. You may match a person's breathing by moving your finger up and down at the same rate as their breathing. Such discretion will keep their conscious minds from becoming aware of your mirroring them.

You can also match facial expressions and blinking. You can match the tension in facial muscles. Note their lower lip and shape your lower lip to mirror their lower lip. Take note of the rate of their eyes blinking and match with your eyes.

An excellent way to gain deep rapport involves matching someone's breathing. When someone talks, they breathe out. Match them by breathing out while they speak. When they take a breath, take a breath as well. When you speak to them, talk while they breathe out and inhale with them. If you have a difficult time observing someone's breathing patterns, notice the tops of their shoulders. The rise and fall of their shoulders will reveal their breathing pattern.

A great portion of communication occurs through the auditory tonal channel. As you match someone's voice tone you have another marvelous avenue for gaining rapport. Match the tone, speed, quality, and volume of their voice. If someone has a soft voice, then match their softness. Should they speak rapidly, then you match their voice with the same speed. If they speak loudly, you speak loudly. Matching someone's voice provides an excellent tool in gaining instant rapport.

## Mirroring Exercise

### Body Molding

1. "A" faces "B" with "C" sitting (or standing) behind "B's" line of peripheral vision.
2. "C" places themself in an unusual posture with unusual facial expressions. Don't overdo it because "C" must hold this position for a few minutes.
3. "A" directs "B" to take on the same posture and facial expressions as "C." Thus, "A" gives good sensory directions to "B."

4.  You can "stretch" this exercise further by asking "A" not to use words but gestures and grunts to mold "B."

### Behavioral Mirroring

Do this exercise with 5 people. Person number 5 serves as the meta-person.

1.  "A" and "B" role play a short interaction. Keep very short...not over 2 minutes.
2.  "C" and "D" observe and listen carefully to "A" and "B's" role play. "C" observes "A" and "D" observes "B." "C" and "D" reproduce "A" and "B's" skit; and importantly, they mirror "A" and "B's" physiology (posture, gestures, facial expressions and breathing), and match their voice tonality, pitch, speed, quality and volume. "C" and "D" may have "A" and "B" repeat their skit once or twice.
3.  "E" serves as the meta person and coaches where necessary. "E" only interrupts should the exercise become badly out of order. Should "C" and "D" forget the exact words, just *ad lib*, concentrating on mirroring physiology and matching voice tonality, etc.
4.  Should "C" and "D" become overwhelmed, chunk down and reproduce only those areas recalled.
5.  Do a round robin. "E" becomes "A," "A" becomes "B," "B" becomes "C," "D" becomes "E", and repeat.

## Difference Between Matching & Mirroring

In building rapport, we match and mirror physiology, tonality and words. What differs between these two verbs of matching and mirroring? The difference lies in degrees. When you *mirror* someone, you take on and "become" their mirror image. If they have crossed their right leg over their left leg, you cross your left leg over your right leg. Since you stand opposite them when you face them, you mirror them by crossing opposite legs. In *mirroring* their words, you give back to them their exact words.

If you *match* someone's words, you do not give back to them their precise words. You rather seek to match their general rep system. If they say, "I don't see what you are saying," you match by responding, "Sure, let me show you what I mean." A mirroring response would go, "I know you don't see what I am saying." In *matching* physiology with someone who has crossed right leg over left leg, you would match them if you crossed your right leg over your left leg. This works similarly to cross-over mirroring. In mirroring we do precisely as the person does; in matching, we match more generally.

## Matching & Mirroring An Angry Person

After attending an introductory conference on rapport building skills, a lady inquired, "How do you match and mirror an angry person?" Her father would often get angry and shout at her. Shouting became a pattern of behavior for him. In matching and mirroring someone in an angry state, simply match and mirror their physiology and tonality. However, as you do, do *not* match the angry *content*. In other words, do not use threatening language.

Suppose someone angrily said, "Why aren't you doing a better job?" In your reply, match their voice tonality. Tonality includes the pitch, speed, quality, and loudness of their voice. While you so respond, give them back the gestures they used while questioning you and do all of this in *a non-threatening way*. You could respond, "How do you evaluate my work as not good?"

---

*Rapport Summarized:*

*How do we gain rapport with people? We gain rapport by matching and mirroring the other person's expressions.*

| *Physiology* | *Tonality* | *Words* |
|---|---|---|
| *Posture* | *Pitch* | *Predicates* |
| *Gestures* | *Speed* | |
| *Facial expressions* | *Quality* | |
| *Breathing* | *Loudness* | |

---

Practicing these skills empowers us to gain rapport with anyone. You will find such rapport skills applicable to many areas of your life. Today you may have special needs to establish rapport with your spouse or child. Tomorrow your place of employment may require you to get into rapport with a supervisor, co-worker or subordinate. Even in leading a committee or a group, rapport skills greatly facilitate understanding and help to eliminate misunderstandings and unnecessary conflict. Because groups have leaders, identify the leader and establish rapport with him or her. In this way you can pace and lead the entire group. Life will present you with many opportunities to use your rapport skills.

## Knowing When You Have Rapport

How do you know when you have rapport? James (1990) offered five indicators of rapport.

1. Check your matching of the person's physiology, tonality, and words.

2. Notice if you experience an internal feeling like a feeling in the stomach. It may, at first, feel somewhat uncomfortable. Thereafter you may feel it as warmth of unity with the other person.

3. Within about a minute after you detect this feeling, you may notice changes in the other person's color. You may feel this blushing feeling in yourself as well.

4. You may hear statements indicating that the other person feels connected, "I feel like I have known you before." "I find it so easy to talk with you." This commonly expresses the interpersonal state of two people in rapport. Each feels "at home" with the other.

5. You can lead and the other will follow. This indicates a certainty of rapport. Test for rapport by doing something different—leading out in a new response physiologically or verbally. If you scratch your ear, then so will the other person. If you shift your position, a sign of rapport lies in the fact that they shortly do too. If you lead verbally in visual predicates and notice that the other shifts to the same, then they have followed your lead. We can do the same with the subject. Does the other follow? Yes? Then you have rapport.

## Homework

1. Establish rapport with as many people as you can this coming week. Practice, practice, practice.

2. Match and mirror someone near you in a restaurant. Notice your skills in doing so that establish rapport.

3. When you go up to a counter to purchase something, practice establishing instant rapport with the person at the counter.

4. Train your consciousness to closely observe different facets of non-verbal communication. On Monday watch for color changes in faces. Tuesday, watch for lower lip size. Wednesday, observe people's breathing patterns. Thursday, notice the variety of body builds and their relationship to the rep systems. Friday, listen for voice tonality and quality. Saturday and Sunday, look for eye accessing patterns.

5. Use your television time to develop your sensory acuity. Tune into a talk show with your eye accessing chart before you.

## Thought Questions To Assist Your Learning:

1. What do we mean by the phrase "sensory acuity"?
2. How can a person develop and increase their "sensory acuity"? Describe.
3. Why does matching or pacing another person's rep system or physi-ology create "rapport"?
4. List the non-verbal facets that you have a natural skill for noticing or pacing. Then list all of the items that you seldom, if ever, notice.
5. What does "calibration" in NLP mean?

# Chapter 3

## Perceptual Positions

| | |
|---|---|
| **1st Position:** | *Self, from one's own eyes—total self-reference.* |
| **2nd Position:** | *Other, from eyes of another person—total other-reference.* |
| **3rd Position:** | *External Viewer, from any other position—totally dissociated.* |
| **4th Position:** | *From the perspective of the system—associated in the perspective of the whole system.* |
| **5th Position:** | *From the perspective of the universe—taking on multiple perceptual positions with ability to change rapidly among them.* |

The realization that we humans operate from three basics ways of looking at experience offers tremendous potential in state control and in the enhancing of our communication. In NLP we refer to these ways as being the first, second and third perceptual positions. When you associate into your own body, you live in **first position**. This permits you to look at the world from your own viewpoint. In the first position, you do not take into account anyone else's position. You simply think, "How does this conversation or communication affect me?"

**Second position** means you walk in the other person's shoes. You take into consideration how a communication or event would look, feel and sound from another person's point of view. In the second position, you imagine yourself entering the other person's body. In this position you imagine looking at yourself through their eyes. What do you look like, sound like, and what feelings do you get from the other person's viewpoint of you? In the second position you develop ability in experiencing empathy. This position gives much flexibility when involved in conflict with someone. From the second position you can appreciate how they feel about your conversation and behavior. Build rapport before going second position. And, by going second position, notice how the rapport deepens. Second position offers an extremely valuable model in deepening rapport.

**Third position** offers a way of dissociating from the entire event or conversation. In the third position you become an independent observer. Third position allows us to operate from the position of objectivity. Ask yourself, "How would this conversation or event look to someone totally uninvolved?" Imagine yourself being out of your body and off to the side of the conversation between you and the other person. You can see both yourself and the other person.

Recent NLP literature offers two additional Perceptual Positions to the first three. We give them here:

## The Fourth Perceptual Position

Dilts (1997) specified the Fourth Perceptual Position in his *Visionary Leadership Skills* manual. He defined the Fourth Position as "We"—from the perspective of the system. In this position, we have "associated in the perspective of the whole system." To take fourth position, step aside and adopt the perspective of the whole system so that you can there consider what would contribute to the best interest of the system. A linguistic format for this position goes: "If we consider our common goals…"

## The Fifth Perceptual Position

Atkinson (1997) in an unpublished manuscript entitled *Five Central Ideas* suggests another perceptual position—"a universal perceptual position." This results from applying the universal quantifiers (all, always) to our perspective. Doing so "springboards us to the valuable idea of a universal perceptual position." (p. 24). This provides the widest and largest-level perspective of all.

By taking this meta-position to everything, we can then learn to take on multiple perceptual positions and even change rapidly between them. Doing so increases our flexibility of consciousness so that we don't get stuck in any one position.

This may involve "over-viewing through time"—seeing things as they progress through and over time. *None of these positions offers a superior position to the other*. Each position has equal importance. The wise communicator knows how to move at will from one position to the other.

Just think what would happen if you got stuck in either position. A person stuck in first position would find himself or herself an egotist. Do you know anyone who lives in first position? A person stuck in second position would live constantly over-influenced by other people's views. In my NLP classes, after I (BB) explain the second position, and how those who live in second position tend to let the state of others *determine* their state, I say, "Second position functions as the position of co-dependency." Just about every time I do this, I will hear several sighs come from students as they realize what and how they have caused themselves to allow others to control their states.

| A person stuck in: | Becomes |
|---|---|
| First position | = Egotistical |
| Second position | = Caretaker, rescuer |
| Third position | = Cold and unfeeling |

A person stuck in third position would become detached and unfeeling. Others perceive these people as "cold hearted." Indeed, I have found that those who live in third position find themselves as the loners of the world. Many, but not all, also will have the characteristics of the Auditory Digital person. These people provide society its thinkers and philosophers. Living life detached permits a person to analyze objectively.

Everyone moves from one position to the other. For most, *moving* from one position to another flows with everyday life. The ability to move from one to the other, either consciously or unconsciously, permits one to act with wisdom and respond appropriately. By moving among the perceptual positions, you will add richness and choice to your conversations.

## Exercise: Perceptual Positions

Try this experiment. Recall the last major argument you had with someone. Associate into your body (first position) by seeing what you saw, hearing what you heard, and feeling what you felt. Do you still feel the same negative emotions you felt then? Now, imagine yourself floating out of your body and floating into the body of the person you argued with (second position). Look through their eyes at yourself. Notice how you looked during the heat of the argument. What tone of voice did you use? How do you feel as you look at yourself and hear your tone of voice? Now, imagine yourself dissociated from the total event (third position). Move yourself off to the side where you can see both yourself and the person arguing with each other. How do you view the argument from this dissociated position? Notice your reaction and feelings and how they differ in each position. Has your perception of the argument changed now that you have been in all three positions? Would you have given a different response to the person had you done this during the argument?

## The Aligning Perceptual Positions Pattern

Sometimes our ability to perceive things from out of our own eyes (first-person perception) and from out of the eyes of another person (second-person perception, the "empathy" perspective), and from an observer position (third-person perception) gets out-of-alignment. Structurally, each of these perceptual resources can operate as separate "parts."

These *three perceptual positions* refer to the three ways that we can "look" at the world. As we have seen, conceptually, we can become stuck in one position or another. Those *stuck in first-person position* can become totally self-referencing in their view of things so that they think-and-feel in highly "narcissistic" ways. They will process things only in terms of themselves. Those *stuck in second-person position* tend to become totally other-referencing in their perspective and can get stuck in the role of rescuers and caretakers to the exclusion of taking care of themselves. People *stuck in third- position* may take a historical view, a cultural view, etc., so that they become so dissociated from their body and emotions that they seem more like robots than people (Satir's "Computer" stance—see Chapter Twelve).

Not only can we get *stuck* in one position, but we can experience an out-of-alignment between these perceptual positions. Problems may also arise from having parts of ourselves react from different perceptual positions. When that happens we end up working against ourselves. *Aligning perceptual positions* in all rep systems, results in inner congruence and personal power. This pattern also enables us to resolve inner conflict and attain internal alignment.

Use this **triple description pattern** whenever you or another lack a full awareness or perspective on a given problem. Take all three positions to broaden your thinking-feeling. This can truly enrich perspectives in such situations as conflict resolution, mediation, influencing others, personal flexibility, etc. The technology enables us to gain an expanded perspective and information on problem situations.

*The Pattern*

1. **Identify target information**. Specify a limitation, a problem or a situation in which you (or another) feel stuck. "Please describe the situation in which you would like to have a more congruent response."

2. **Identify the visual, auditory and kinesthetic factors within each perceptual position.**

   a. **Visual**: What and how do you see the situation? From what perceptual position? If you have two or more "conceptual parts" or entities that reference this same subject, check what perceptual position each part uses. Do some parts see the situation as an observer or from the eyes of another person? Locate the position of each part. Point out (internally or externally) where you find them. Do some of the parts seem closer to the situation than others? How does each part see the situation? What does each part actually see? What differences occur between them?

b. **Auditory**: What sounds and words do you hear about the situation? From what perceptual position do you hear these things? If you have two or more parts in reference to it, what does each part say? Listen for the pronouns that each part uses. A part in *the observer mode* will have a neutral voice and will refer to "he" or "she." An "other" voice will typically refer to "you" with a more judgmental tone. The "self" voice will use "I" and "me." Where exactly in your body do you hear each part? (Side positions often indicate other or observer; self usually comes from vocal chord area.)

c. **Kinesthetic**: What do you sense about the situation? From what perceptual position? For multiple parts, where do you sense each part in your body? What emotions do you experience with each part? Do you have any neutral parts as if you only observe and don't experience life?

3. **Realign perceptual positions in all rep systems.** For the Observer alignment (3rd position), go through the VAK checks.

   a. **Visual**: Ask the observer part, "Would you communicate any information you have gathered to the self part?" Continue the dialogue until self and other similarly view the situation.

   b. **Auditory alignment**: Ask the observer part, "Would you shift pronouns to support the self using 'I', 'he,' or 'she?'" Also, please use "self" tone of voice.

   c. **Kinesthetically**: Ask the observer part, "Would you be willing to shift feelings to those compatible with self feelings." Also move feelings to the place where "self" holds feelings.

4. **Align your self in terms of the VAK perceptual positions.** "Make sure you see from your own point of view and out of your own eyes. Make sure your voice location arises from your own vocal chords and that you use 'I' pronouns. Make sure that all feelings come from inside the 'self' and reflect resourceful states."

5. **Do another alignment (2nd position) in the same way.** "Please adjust your perceptions to make them compatible with the view held by self." Move the location of "other" to the place occupied by self. Please move

the voice you hear to the vocal chord area and have it represent 'self', bringing any enriching information to the 'self' position. Align feelings from 'other' to those of 'self.' Integrate feelings in such a way as to make the 'self' more flexible and resourceful.

6.   **Run an ecology check.** Do all the parts feel aligned and in harmony?

7.   **Future pace.** Allow yourself now to become aware of new behavioral possibilities. "Describe any new abilities and behaviors that now become available to you. And you can notice yourself performing in the future as the 'self' part increases in richness and flexibility." If the "other" part objects to integration, you can request that this part return to the person to whom the thoughts and feelings belong.

## Thought Questions To Assist Your Learning:

1.   Without referring to your notes, list and describe the five Perceptual Positions.
2.   Which position do you favor so much that you tend to use it as your default Perceptual Position?
3.   Which Perceptual Position feels like the biggest stretch for you?
4.   Do you have any Perceptual Positions in which you can become "stuck?"
5.   What procedures will facilitate you (or someone else) developing more flexibility of consciousness about Perceptual Positions?

# Chapter 4

## NLP Presuppositions
## For Building Resourcefulness

*Thinking Theoretically About Theory*

**What you can expect to learn in this chapter:**

- The theoretic foundations of the NLP Model
- The central presuppositions that create empowerment
- The critical difference between "map" and "territory"
- The NLP attitude in communicating
- The systemic nature of NLP
- The importance of flexibility
- The attitude that helps us to take a positive attitude

### Keeping The Context In Mind

To discern the proper meaning of a thing, we have to *keep it in context*. The original context arose from therapy, family systems, gestalt perceptual psychology, foreground/background, computer science, etc. It has everything to do with **communication** and with **the structure of excellence** in various human behaviors. To forget that context or to judge it by another context or criterion, inevitably leads to misunderstanding, unnecessary and inaccurate judgments, and the missing of some resources we can use to improve our lives.

The context of NLP concerns accessing the mindset, state, and skills necessary for understanding and bringing about successful communication and personal change. As such it concerns **how processes work**, not the source or origin of those resources. It stays away from theory, morality (right and wrong judgments) and explanations, as it focuses on *what* does work and *how* we can model it.

In its therapeutic concern, NLP aims to discover state-of-the-art methods for getting people out of their small, limited, inaccurate, and painful perspectives that keep them locked into dysfunctional habits. Thus it addresses the issue of *changing the meanings* that people attribute to things which keep them limited and in pain. Without prescribing meaning, NLP suggests effective methods for changing meanings, how to alter perception, how to take on new and different frames of reference, etc.

Accepting the epistemology of General Semantics, NLP corresponds to the Cognitive-Behavioral proposition that with regard to things *inside* human psychology, *thinking itself* plays a central and crucial role. Thus how we map our internal reality about the territory makes all the difference in the world.

NLP also operates within the context of *resources*. It assumes that in order for a person to make positive change and model excellence, one needs lots of feelings of confidence and certainty that such changes can occur. This involves finding enough resources to bring to bear upon a person. In NLP we commonly access curiosity, flexibility, a sense of possibilities, a desire for change, etc. NLP itself makes no assumptions whatever about where these resources come from.

NLP recognizes that "mind" involves more than the surface information at any given moment within the conscious mind. Based upon numerous scientific experiments and models about human neurology and "mind," NLP seeks only to access these not-conscious facets of mind that run the autonomic nervous system.

Having first modeled Satir and Perls, NLP asserts the value of viewing a person as "response-able" ("at cause") for their own life. This stands in contradistinction to some psychologies which view a person as a victim of early childhood training, genetics, birth order, trauma, etc.

## NLP's Theoretical Assumptive Presuppositions

We now want to shift from **applied neuro-linguistics** to a more philosophical perspective about the NLP model. To do that we want to step back and consider the model in terms of its theoretical underpinnings. We have structured this chapter around a list of the *Key Presuppositions of NLP* as formulated by Bodenhamer (1995)[5]. All of the primary therapeutic techniques of NLP go back to these presuppositions.

We have noted before that the NLP developers and community do *not* think of NLP as a theory, but as a model. How does a theory differ from a model? A theory goes into explanations of *why* a system works. NLP does not do this. A model simply describes, in a step-by-step fashion, *how* to use the model.

Does that mean that NLP has no theoretical underpinnings? Of course not! Every system and every model operates by some assumed theoretical understandings about the world, people, God, etc. Some systems spend a lot of time and energy on developing their theories, defending their theories, arguing against the theories of other systems, and using the scientific method to run experiments on the validity of the theories. NLP does not do this.

What does NLP do? It simply assumes a certain ideology—and announces these *presuppositions* up front. In other words, it lays its epistemological premises on the table admitting, "We can't prove these ideas." "We cannot demonstrate that they stand as 'true,' or 'right,' or that they comprise any 'ultimate reality,' but we do accept them. We do so because we find them useful in the task of making changes and accomplishing things."

Korzybski (1933, 1994) described epistemology (the branch of philosophy that studies the nature of knowledge, its presuppositions and foundations, and its extent and validity) in very similar terms. He argued that once we realize that we don't deal with "reality" directly, but only indirectly via our nervous system and sense receptors, and we understand the fundamental difference between "map" and "territory"—then we also realize that we can never "say" everything about anything—we cannot so simplify the territory of reality. Nor can we, via our human powers, ever "state" the foundational principles of the universe—we have to operate linguistically, and therefore mentally, from "undefined terms" and assumptions. So, for the sake of *science and sanity*, Korzybski argued that we take the approach of announcing our "undefined terms" up front.

NLP does precisely this—*announcing its "undefined terms" and undefined beliefs in the list of "the NLP Presuppositions."* Where did these come from? From the theoretical underpinnings that were found in the systems that were modeled: gestalt psychology, family systems therapy, Ericksonian hypnotic-medical communication, general-semantics, cybernetics, information systems, transformational grammar, cognitive-behavioral psychology, and Batesonian anthropology.

Consider now these presuppositions and test them for yourself. We believe you will find that they do not contradict the beliefs/values of most people. NLP offers unsurpassed tools for working with subjectivity.

## The NLP Presuppositional Beliefs

The importance of our presuppositions lies in how they operate as *unspoken beliefs*. We inevitably and inescapably have operating presuppositions that control our "undefined terms" and understandings. A belief, as a concept, theory, paradigm, etc., describes **a basic structure** in our model of the world that we hold as true. Often we hold varying degrees of beliefs. We believe some things strongly, other things not as strongly. Beliefs that we hold very dear and that drive our thoughts and actions we call *core beliefs*. We use them as our presuppositions.

> *Beliefs act as **major neurological filters** that determine how we perceive external reality.*
> *Our beliefs about what we value as important or not important powerfully shape our perceptions.*

Beliefs act as *major neurological filters* that determine how we perceive external reality. Our beliefs about what we value as important or not important powerfully shape our perceptions, as do other unconscious neurological filters (the Meta-programs of introversion/extroversion, motivated by wants or avoidances, gestalt versus detail thinking, etc. See Hall & Bodenhamer, 1997c).

If you use a computer, whether you know it or not, your computer has some kind of *operating system* by which it runs. We have written this text on IBM compatible computers that utilize the Windows operating system. In a similar way, NLP also has an *Operating System* by which it *runs*—these "NLP Presuppositions." They enable the system of processes, technologies, insights and skills to function.

---

*Mental Processing Presuppositions:*
1. "The 'map' is not the 'territory'" ("the menu is not the meal").
2. People respond according to their internal maps.
3. Meaning operates context-dependently.
4. Mind-and-body inevitably and inescapably affect each other.
5. Individual skills function by developing and sequencing of rep systems.
6. We respect each person's model of the world.

---

*Presuppositions about Human Behavior/Responses:*
7. Person and behavior describe different phenomena. We "are" more than our behavior.
8. Every behavior has utility and usefulness—in some context.
9. We evaluate behavior & change in terms of context and ecology.

---

*Communicative Presuppositions:*
10. We cannot *not* communicate.
11. The *way* we communicate affects perception & reception.
12. The meaning of communication lies in the response you get.
13. The one who sets the frame for the communication controls the action.
14. "There is no failure, only feedback."
15. The person with the most flexibility exercises the most influence in the system.
16. Resistance indicates the lack of rapport.

**Learning—Choice—Change Presuppositions:**
17. People have the internal resources they need to succeed.
18. Humans have the ability to experience one-trial learning.
19. All communication should increase choice.
20. People make the best choices open to them when they act.
21. As response-able persons, we can run our own brain and control our results.

| Incoming Information from outside world enters our heads through our senses: | | Internal Information enters our nervous system (brain) and is interpreted as: | Subjective Experience Information is constructed or remembered as: |
|---|---|---|---|
| Visual | eyes | (V)—Pictures | (V)—Visuals, Pictures |
| Auditory | ears | (A)—Sounds | (A)—Sounds, Noise |
| Kinesthetic | skin/body | (K)—Feelings | (K)—Sensations, Feelings |

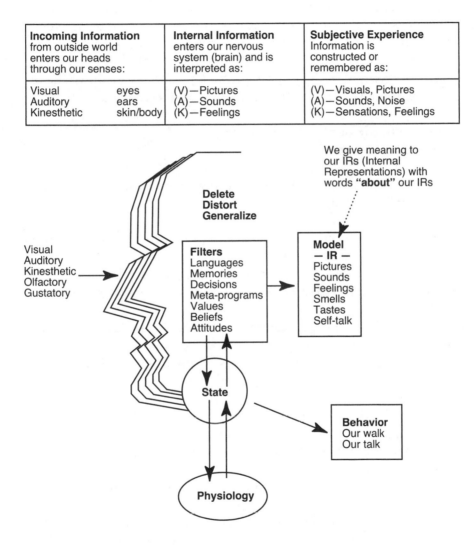

*Figure 4:1 The NLP Communication Model*

## The Operating System Of Presuppositions

### Mental Processing Presuppositions

#### 1. *"The 'map' is not the 'territory'" or "The menu is not the meal"*

Just as *a "map"* does not actually consist of *the "territory"* it represents, the words we use do not comprise the event or item they represent. *Territory* exists as the reality—out there, beyond our skins, made up of billions of stimuli per second—an ever-changing world of dancing electrons, ultimately energy. "Map" describes what exists in our bodies (neurological reception of those energy manifestations) and what exists in our heads ("mental," conceptual understandings *about* the territory). So we have two levels of phenomena here—external reality and internal, subjective reality.

What goes on inside our head concerning an event does not comprise the event, it only comprises our *perception of* that event. This understanding critically impacts everything about us! Why? Because when we experience an external event, we try to *make sense* of it. In

> *What goes on inside our head concerning an event does not comprise the event, it only comprises our **perception of** that event.*

our attempt to make sense of that event, we construct internal representations (IR) in our minds *of* it. These internal representations include information received through all of our senses. In other words, our IR have the VAKOG components as their constituent makeup, plus language.

Based upon this General Semantic foundational fact, NLP makes wonderful use of the fact that internal representations do *not* exist at the same logical level as the event itself. This distinction explains why we can only relate to the world out there via our *neuro-linguistic processing*. God gave us numerous portals (senses, sense receptors) to the world—and yet we exist "apart" from it while still within it.

The next conclusion this leads to involves the neurological impossibility— we can never *represent* an external event *exactly* as it exists out there. Consider: I see an apple. I make an internal picture of it. The rods and cones of my eyes give me the internal sense of "color." My other senses enrich this picture. But regardless of how rich, varied, or complete, my picture of it functions only as a "map" of it. If you look at the same apple, you will *not* entertain *exactly* the *same* picture—because your nervous system, neural pathways, etc., do not work *exactly and precisely the same way* as mine. Two individuals see an accident from a very similar position (never the "same") but when they report it, *differences* between their reports arise. Why?

Because of the differences in their perception arising from differences in their individual neuro-linguistic processing and internal representations.

The basis of the difference? Each represented the accident using slightly different nervous systems and minds! "The 'map' is not the 'territory'." Or, in other words, "The menu is not the meal." We do not operate directly on the world, but on our individual perceptions *of* the world. Regardless of the external event, as subjects, we each construct our own internal subjective reality *of* it and that internal construct determines us—our thoughts, emotions, response.

> We can never **represent** an external event **exactly** as it "exists out there."
>
> Therefore,
>
> "The menu is not the meal."

## 2. People respond according to their "maps"

*We do not operate directly **on** the world, but on our individual perceptions **of** the world.*

With the map/territory distinction, our "map", as our perception of the territory, determines or controls both our perceptions and our responses. We respond to the world, not *as* the world exists—but *according to our "map" of it*. This underscores the ultimate importance of addressing our human "maps" of the world.

These neuro-linguistic "maps" consist of our beliefs, values, attitudes, language, memories, and other psychological filters. Within our consciousness, we experience these internal "maps" as simply our "thoughts" through our rep system (see Figure 4:1). Yet "as we so think—so we are." In this way our internal representational "maps" interact with our physiology to produce our states. Then our state drives our behavior. This means that our perception operates as our projection. It determines our actions.

David Seamands (1988) in *Healing for Damaged Emotions* told about the work of the famous plastic surgeon, Maxwell Maltz. Dr. Maltz began to notice that many patients experienced the same personality problems after surgery as before. Even though his surgery dramatically improved their appearance, they still saw themselves as ugly (p. 58-59).

How could someone have obvious physiological changes made to their face through plastic surgery and yet act as if blind to the change? Everyone else noted the improvements in their appearance. But the individual insisted that they could see no changes. You know the answer. Though externally their faces had changed, their internal "maps" had not.

*We respond according to our internal "map" of the world.* So does everybody else. Everybody uses their model to guide their perceptions, thoughts, emotions, and actions. This includes your spouse, children, friends, parents, authority figures, etc. Before we can expect someone to change their thinking, emoting, responding, etc., their internal "map" must change. To assist someone in changing that, we must develop enough flexibility in communicating that we can assist them in shifting their internal "map."

> *Before we can expect someone to change their thinking, emoting, responding, etc., their internal "map" must change.*

### 3. *Meaning operates context-dependently*

> *All words require some context for meaning.*

This presupposition relates to the first one. It states that *all words require some context for meaning*. In themselves, words contain no meaning. A statement or an act in one context may mean something entirely different in another context. When I tell my father, "I love you!" that meaning differs from telling my wife, "I love you." The context of the statement determines or frames the meaning of the statement.

O'Connor and Seymour (1990), write,

> "Events happen, but until we give them meaning, relate them to the rest of life, and evaluate the possible consequences, they are not important. We learn what things mean from our culture and individual upbringing." (p. 131)

To paraphrase the Jewish proverb, "As a person appraises (constructs meaning, calculates, reckons) in his soul, so he is."

> *"There is no content in content worth knowing."*
>
> Tad James

Since meaning operates in a context-dependent way, **context (frame)** primarily controls meaning—the context we accept as given or the frame that we attribute. Tad James stated, "There is no content in content worth knowing." This emphasizes this fundamental NLP principle—namely, internal experience, and change of that experience, occurs through how we have used our mental processes to *code* or *recode* the content. So, change the structure of internal images, etc., and you change the experience.

This contextual process, or structural point of view, identifies the heart of NLP. When we remain "in content" we live in the "map." Only when we move from content to process do we rise *above* a map and understand its structure *of* the territory.

When a client says, "I am depressed," we don't ask, "What causes your depression?" His answers to that will not heal anything! Finding external cause doesn't heal the internal pain—it only provides **reasons** that support that pain! Not wise. An internal problem exists as it does because of its structure. So ask, *"How* do you do that?"

This *how* question enables us to move from the content level of the depression to the process level. Expect confusion. The client will usually respond, "What do you mean? *'How'* do I do that?" Help the person shift, "Sure. You experience this tremendous skill called 'depression,' don't you?" "Well, yes." "So *how* do you get yourself into such a state? If I took your place for a day, what would I have to do to think and feel as you do?" "What do you do inside your mind-body to create the depression?" In this way, we search for the process (the neuro-linguistic process) within the client that enables them to code and then experience depression. Once we discover the structure, we lead the client to change the structure. And that changes the experience.

> The **how** question enables us to move from the content level of the problem to the process level.

## 4. Mind-and-body inevitably & inescapably affect each other

Though we talk about "mind" and "body" *as if they operate independently of each other*—they do not. They can **not** operate so. In General Semantics we describe this kind of separating of inseparable phenomenon as a "false-to-fact" "elementalism." Korzybski (1941/1994) argued strenuously that *elementalism* arises from primitive minds and language forms and works to our detriment. When we put hyphens between terms we can create a more holistic and systemic understanding.

Today, many in the medical community have also come to understand just how much mind-body function as one. After all, the "mind" occurs within the body (the nervous system) and when we inject psycho-dynamic drugs into it the "mind" becomes greatly affected! Likewise, when we inject thoughts, either pleasant or unpleasant, into the "mind", the body becomes affected. The mind-body functions as a cybernetic whole.

> *The mind-body functions as a cybernetic whole.*
> *The mind-body interaction further explains what we call the "placebo effect."*

The mind-body interaction further explains what we call the "placebo effect." For years doctors have experimented with inert "sugar pills" (placebos) up against active medicine to see if the effect of a drug occurs because of the chemical effect within the drug or because the person *believes* that they have received "medicine." Since we test almost all drugs up against placebos, we have an immense literature of comparison. And to the chagrin of some doctors, many experiments have shown not only a significant reduction in symptoms by placebos, but many have shown as good results, and sometimes placebos will out-perform the active drug! Studies have indicated repeatedly that one's belief about a particular medication tremendously affects the effectiveness of the medication.

More recently, Frank (1973) and Kirsch (1990) along with other studies have looked at "the placebo effect" in therapy. Here "the placebo" does not consist of inert pills, but in universals such as (listening, sympathy, giving of hope, encouragement, faith in a client, belief in the therapist or in the intervention, etc.).

Where do you feel your emotional pain in your body? In what body organ do you now feel your emotions? That place could very well become your next locus of illness. Today we trace many physical illnesses to emotional stress: ulcers, ulcerated colitis, migraine headaches, arthritis, asthma, allergies and even cancer. In therapy we see people who come in with stomach problems, high blood pressure, headaches and skin lesions and leave without such physiological problems once they experience healing in their mind-emotions.

Modern medical research today about the mind-body connection relates that we have roughly one hundred billion individual nerve cells within our bodies. Most of these nerve cells occur in the brain. Each of our one hundred billion neurons connect to at least one thousand others. Yet these connections between nerve cells do not occur in a direct and mechanical way like we attach electrical wires.

Neurophysicist Paul A. Goodwin (1988) explains:

> "...they connect neurochemically, through a device known as a synapse—actually just a very small gap between adjacent neurons, the gap being architecturally supported by other cells, known as glial cells. Within these synaptic connections, different neurochemicals are used to communicate, transmit an electrical nerve impulse from one neuron to another. So far, about sixty different neurochemical transmitters have been identified that serve the purpose of communication between neurons." (p. 24)

The nerve cell synapse has receptor molecules that either permit or do not permit the neurotransmitters to enter the nerve cell and communicate information. Goodwin used the analogy of a lock and a key. The receptor molecules function like keyholes that permit or do not permit the neurotransmitter entrance. The pain-killing drug acetaminophen (Tylenol) and other similar drugs work due to this process. Acetaminophen serves to plug up certain receptor molecules (keyholes). This "plugging" prohibits the entrance of the neurotransmitter into the nerve cell. Thus, the nerve cell will fire less than it normally would. As a result of a decrease in the firing of the nerve cell, one feels less pain.

Neurotransmitters occur primarily in the brain, though we find them throughout the body. Goodwin (1988) made a profound deduction that applies to the mind-body connection:

> *"Can it be that the body can be cured of an illness through the medium of the brain just by one's **belief** that it can be done? The answer to this question seems to be a qualified 'Yes' ..."*
>
> Paul Goodwin

"Exploring the implications of this point further, we find that transmitter molecules normally associated with the brain are also produced by various parts of the body. For example, the adrenal gland produces dopamine-like hormones that can be utilized by the brain. This finding recently led to a potentially effective treatment for Parkinson's disease. Other normally brain-related transmitter-receptor molecular complexes have been found to make up the walls of certain cells in the immune system. These findings all tend to establish a strong chemical communication relationship between the body, the brain and, indeed the *mind*. Since the immune system is involved, can it be that the body can be cured of an illness through the medium of the brain just by one's *belief* that it can be done? The answer to this question seems to be a qualified "Yes," as is indicated by many documented instances of spiritual healing as well as by clinical evidence regarding the placebo effect." (p. 33)

## 5.   *Individual skills function by developing & sequencing rep systems*

| |
|---|
| *The rep system has two key components in the NLP model: submodalities and strategies.* |

How we use our rep systems (VAK) in thinking-emoting and behaving generates our **skills.** Our mind not only takes in information through the senses, but also processes and stores information. It then uses these pieces of sights, sounds, sensations, smells, etc., to build up skills. In NLP we call *strategies* the sequencing of these pieces of sights, sounds, sensations, etc., which make it possible for us to take action. Knowing how we receive, store, process and elicit information plays a crucial role for rapport building and assisting someone to renew their mind. The rep system has two key components in the NLP model: submodalities and strategies. We have already looked at an introduction to submodalities. Now let's look at an introduction to the NLP strategy model:

## Strategies

| |
|---|
| *The key phrase about human **syntax** or structure lies in this phrase—"the sequencing of rep systems."* |

NLP takes the view that **skills** arise and function through "the development and sequencing of our rep systems." The key phrase about human *syntax* or structure lies in this phrase—"the sequencing of rep systems."

Consider the fact that every day you get out of bed in the morning. *How* do you accomplish this task? *What enables* you to produce this behavior of physically getting out of bed? What do you do inside your head that enables you to put your body in motion and to get yourself out of bed?

Do you first hear the alarm clock ($A^e$—auditory external)? What happens next? You may have said some words, "Oh no, it is time to get up" ($A^{id}$—Auditory digital, internal). What did you do next? Maybe you had the feeling of *not* feeling like getting up ($K^i$—kinesthetic internal or "emotion") and the kinesthetic sensation that you gave that judgment to consisted of feeling stiff in your back ($K^i$—kinesthetic negative). But then you knew that if you didn't get up you would get to work late and lose your job ($A^{id}$—more words about the job, your future). So, you had an internal dialogue with yourself about the necessity of getting up to go to work ($A^{id}$—Auditory digital words). When this knowledge reached a certain threshold it informed your body to move out of bed ($K^e$—kinesthetic external).

Taking all of these sequential pieces as a step-by-step formula for your *motivation strategy* for getting up in the morning, we have:

$$A^e \rightarrow A^{id} \rightarrow K^i \rightarrow K^i \rightarrow A^{id} \rightarrow A^{id} \rightarrow K^e$$

A strategy describes the sequencing of rep systems, which provides a design whereby we can produce a certain outcome. Robert Dilts (1980) wrote, "All of our overt behavior is controlled by internal processing strategies" (p. 26). Your brain has a strategy for generating all such experiences such as learning, teaching, motivation, preaching, spelling, loving, hating, paying attention, and for all observable behaviors.

> A **strategy** *refers to any internal and external set (order, syntax) of experiences which consistently produce a specific outcome.*

Formally, *a strategy* refers to any internal and external set (order, syntax) of experiences which consistently produces a specific outcome. Most of our strategies for living, relating, thinking, interacting, etc., develop at a young age. Unconsciously we learned that a specific sequence of the rep systems would produce a certain result. From then we generalized that strategy to all occasions calling for that result.

Consider the power of a good strategy versus a poor strategy regarding the task/behavior of spelling. A useful and productive spelling strategy goes along the following lines. First, you hear a word ($A^e$—auditory external), then you make a picture of the word ($V^c$—visual construct) and looking at it you feel good/right about its correct spelling ($K^{i+}$). Then, to rehearse the spelling, you retrieve your picture of that word ($V^r$—visual recall). Good spellers usually look up or straight ahead as they internally see the word and have a good feeling of rightness about it. Seeing the word, you can now spell out the word verbally ($A^{id}$—auditory digital, internal). Then with the feeling of familiarity for spelling it correctly ($K^{i+}$—kinesthetic internal), you spell it externally ($A^{de}$—auditory digital external). The spelling strategy for champions goes: $A^e \rightarrow V^c \rightarrow K^{i+} \rightarrow A^{de}$.

O'Connor and Seymour (1990) identify that dyslexics have demonstrated the usefulness of the spelling strategy. Teaching this strategy to dyslexic children often cures

> *Champion spellers visualize the word before they spell it.*

many of their dyslexia. Most dyslexics do not visually see or visually recall the words they wish to spell. They attempt to spell the word auditorily or kinesthetically. Spelling a word auditorily (phonetically) means you sound out the word to yourself. This strategy greatly limits how much material you can hold in memory.

> *Teaching the spelling strategy to dyslexic children often cures many of their dyslexia.*

Conversely, attempts to spell out a word kinesthetically makes the task difficult. An example of spelling kinesthetically would consist of memorizing the letters of the word by a certain touch. Spelling phonetically (auditory) does not work much better. Spelling champions never spell auditorily. "Wun wunders why foenick spelling methuds arr stil tort in skools." (pp. 182-184)

Each internal representation of a strategy also includes submodalities. Thus, the picture of the visual recall of the spelling strategy will have its own submodalities. The kinesthetic internal will have its own kinesthetic submodalities. We will devote an entire chapter to strategies—see Chapter Fifteen.

*Spelling strategy: exercise for students*

1. **V$^r$** Determine the position of visual recall of the student and have the student select their favorite color.

2. **V$^e$** Spell the word in large letters and in the favorite color of the student. Hold the word in the position of the student's visual recall. The student visualizes, that is, makes a picture of the total word or part of the word. (It may work easier for the beginning student to chunk down and visualize the spelling of only three letters of a word at a time. For example, "believe." Repeat steps 2 through 4 until the person learns the entire word.)

3. **V$^r$** Remove the word then lead the student to shift their eyes into their Vr position and ask the student to see or recall the word or that part of the word they seek to learn.

4. **A$^e$** Have the student spell the word out loud.

5. **K$^e$** The student copies down the word.

6. **V$^r$** Hold the word in the student's visual recall position and ask them to again see the word and make an internal picture of the word. Then, remove the word and ask them to go to visual recall and see the word.

7. **K$^e$** Ask them to write the word down backwards. Repeat steps 6 and 7 until they can write the words down backwards. This will insure that they "lock" the word in their visual memory.

8. **V$^e$** The student examines a list of words.
   Examples:        a) bilieve
                    b) believe
                    c) beleive
                    d) bealeave
                    e) beleev
                    f) beleave

9. **V$^r$** The student shifts their eyes in their visual recall position and recognizes the correct spelling of the word from the list.

10. **K$^e$** The student writes down the correct word.

11. **V$^e$** The student examines a sentence containing the spelling word. Example: "How do you spell believe?"

12. **V$^r$** The student shifts his eyes to his visual recall position and recalls the color-coded word.

13. **K$^e$** The student corrects the spelling word if they see it incorrectly spelled, or they write "C" next to the sentence if spelled correctly.

The ability to recall words improves by practicing the above strategy rather than by just rereading the spelling words. As the student's recall ability improves, they will become more able to more accurately recall under the stress of an exam.

## 6.   We respect each person's model of the world

If "the 'map' is not the 'territory'," and if everybody operates from their own "map", then everybody processes information in their own unique way. One will code experiences associated (in your body), another dissociated (outside your body seeing yourself). One will create their "map" comprised mainly of pictures, another with sounds. Recognizing the map/territory difference, we also recognize that people will map reality out in different ways. This enables us to respect their right and responsibility for dealing with the world. When we respect their model of the world, we respect them as persons and that enables them to trust whatever assistance we can offer.

An *occupational hazard* for any professional communicator arises at this very point. If we don't *respect their* "map" even with all the errors and distortions we believe it contains, we create unnecessary conflict and prevent ourselves from getting heard at all! If we disrespect another and their model of the world, we won't spend the necessary time in listening, supporting, and validating. We will jump right into the fray "preaching" at them, at the errors in their "maps", and evoke in them strong defensiveness.

During my first twenty years as a pastor, I (BB) found myself unable to help some people. I really desired to help them, but after the first session, they did not want to see me again! What evoked that response? I did not respect their model of the world—or at least they felt that I didn't. Why not? Because I immediately started "preaching" to them. They would share some problem they had that involved some sinful behavior and I would immediately apply scriptures to show them the error of their ways! I took a most confrontational approach in counseling.

I now have completely changed my style. Today I begin by listening sympathetically to needs and problems. I do not necessarily agree with what I hear, but I do begin from a position of respect for them and their "map." Only after I discover their positive intent behind behavior do I resort to scripture. Incredibly, the first intent behind the behavior hardly ever violates scriptures. By accepting their model of the world, I establish rapport and get their permission to help.

## Presuppositions About Human Behavior/Responses

### 7.   *Person & behavior describe different phenomena*

*We "are" more than our behavior.*

If "the meaning of our communication lies in the response we get", then some of the most important information we can pay attention to involves a person's behavior. To say this, implies that one's behavior does *not* define them. It may express them—their values, style, etc. But it does not *identify* them.

By realizing that when a person performs a particular behavior and that this differs from their ultimate identity, then we can expect and hope that in another situation or another time that person may behave differently. That makes behavior contextual. Provide another context, and the person may behave in a drastically different way. We make a major mistake in our relationships whenever we equate a person's worth or identity with a particular behavior. That "people *behave...*" identifies people at a higher level than behavior. The opposite does not hold true: "behaviors people..." does not make sense because people are far more than any particular behaviour in any particular context. Although, if you *identify* a person with a behavior, you essentially have used the second formula!

## 8.   *Every behavior has utility and usefulness—in some context*

*All behavior functions from positive intentions.*

This statement does *not* mean that we can conclude that any given behavior comprises "the correct behavior." Of course not. Rather, this statement asserts that within the context of a person performing a behavior, the behavior fulfills some need for them. Furthermore, that behavior—in other contexts (time, space, person)—has value and use.

> *The NLP model starts from the assumption that all behavior has a positive intent driving it.*

The NLP model starts from the assumption that *all behavior has a positive intent driving it.* Thus, every behavior has a useful value in some context. Again, this does *not* approve of immoral, unethical or damaging behavior. It rather **separates person from behavior** and recognizes that, as "behavior", there probably exists some context in which a behavior has value. When we engage in inappropriate behavior, we seek to accomplish something, something of value, something important—and so we do the best we can with the resources we have. Our intent, at the time, involves a positive intent, but gets filtered through limited understandings and erroneous ideas—precisely the reason for "renewing the mind" in order to become transformed.

Even when we find a person doing something in order to "do evil" (that is, hurt someone, take revenge, etc.) if we asked again and again, "In doing this, what positive value does it serve in you?" we will always find some Meta-level outcome of value.

In working with people, we seek first to discover *the positive intent* behind the behavior. We assume it exists and go pursuing it. And here shows the wonder of this approach—even *if* it did not exist previously, by asking about it, pursuing it in the life of a person—they have to create that internal representation to make sense of our words and thereby *internally create* it within themselves! Having worked with the Department of Corrections for several years in the State of Colorado, I (MH) have found that even (worst case scenario!) in those who have suffered from "a criminal mind", that this approach offered hope. For many, this approach gave them the chance to believe in themselves, to believe that they have a God-given "image and likeness" at their core—and that they do not exist as genetically flawed persons somehow created without dignity and values.

## 9. *We evaluate behavior & change in terms of context & ecology*

As we act, behave, and respond to people and events, this presupposition challenges us to develop awareness of the impact of our actions and to check the *ecology* of our responses. In other words, our behaviors do not occur in a vacuum, but in a system of other actions, ideas, feelings, etc. Accordingly we should take into account the total system (individual, family, co-workers, etc.) and evaluate our behavior in terms of that context and its usefulness therein. Seeking to make changes in ourselves and others will have systemic implications. Let us evaluate the desired change in such a manner so as to make the change congruent within the person and the system.

When we work with many of the parts within human "personality," each part must also take into account the ecological question about the whole person. "Will this have any negative consequences that I need to consider?"

We can also extend *ecology* to the person's larger relational systems: "Would this change in a congruent way with the other people in this person's life?" Considering the larger frames of reference helps us to make sure that our communication, behavior and change works for us rather than against us. Rooney (1986) wrote:

> "The concept of ecology refers to the concern that any changes made at one point in a human system must be compatible with and adaptable to the other parts of the system."

> *"The concept of ecology refers to the concern that any changes made at one point in a human system must be compatible with and adaptable to the other parts of the system."*
>
> Gene Rooney

NLP tools for rapid change work enable us to easily bring about changes in one partner that, ecologically, will have various effects upon others. To prevent doing more harm, *the ecology check* enables us to take care in anticipating the effect of change upon the other persons in the system.

## Communicative Presuppositions

### 10. *We cannot not communicate*

Since communication involves the sending of signals to another—even when we attempt not to send a message to another—that comprises "a message" and the indicators or signals of that message will leak out. Even when we don't put our thoughts, feelings, ideas, beliefs, understandings, decisions into words and express them to another—such internal phenomena get communicated non-verbally in a multitude of ways.

## 11. The way we communicate affects perception & reception

> How you say what you say often has more importance to the communication than what you say.

A great portion of communication occurs via non-verbal channels. This means that we always and inevitably not only communicate by *what* we say (verbally) but also by *how* we say things (the non-verbal facets: tone, volume, facial expressions, breathing, posture, etc.). These messages exist as *para*-messages. Sometimes, however, one of our messages may refer to (reference) another message.

Saying, "I love you!" carries one meaning. Saying it sarcastically another. Saying it with fingers crossed another. Saying it in tears—yet another. *The way* that we use our para-message signals can tremendously affect the way people hear, perceive, and receive us. Many people give more weight to tonality or physiology or eye contact or some other non-verbal facet than to the linguistic content. Others reverse that. This suggests the importance (and power) of congruency—aligning all of our communication channels so that they communicate the same message and don't conflict or contradict each other. Congruence makes our communicating believable.

## 12. The meaning of your communication lies in the response you get

Communication refers to the exchange of information. It operates as dialogue in a system of feedback responses from sender and receiver, not a monologue. The response of the person with whom we communicate reflects the effectiveness or ineffectiveness of our communication. If they respond to our communication in the manner we desire, we have succeeded. If their response differs from our desired outcome, we can simply send other signals. This model leads to a non-blaming style.

> When you measure the effectiveness of your communication with the response you get, you take 100% responsibility for the communication.

Regardless of your intent in communication, the response you get indicates what you communicated to the other person—in spite of what you intended. Take it as feedback and use it. I (BB) view this as "taking one-hundred percent responsibility for my communication." *Responsible communication* means that I always have the option to make changes in my communicating until I get my outcome. If I only take partial responsibility for my communication, I will more likely give up trying.

What do you want from another when you communicate? Identify your desired outcome for conversing. Taking full responsibility for your communication helps you to order your communication signals until you get the response you desire. Sales people sometimes say that they make eighty percent of their sales after the fifth call. That sounds as if such persistent salespersons have taken full responsibility for the communication exchange.

### 13. *The one who sets the frame for the communication controls the communicating*

We all live within a frame of reference. Even a simple act of looking at a picture presupposes various frames of references. What do we focus on— its overall configuration or some detail? Do we do one and then the other? Do we see it in terms of its beauty, in terms of what it took to create it, in terms of its value financially, in terms of its usefulness, etc.? We learn a great many of our frames from within the culture of our maturation. Afterwards, we live within those frames as unconsciously as a fish lives in water.

> *The frame governs perception, meaning, emotion, behavior and values.*

Yet the frame governs perception, meaning, emotion, behavior and values. To live within a frame means to use some paradigm that gives meaning to things. To get out of that frame, or to set a new frame, thereby reframes and invites a whole new world of meaning.

Therefore, in relating and communicating—he who sets the frame truly governs the interpersonal field that results. The power of setting a frame lies, in part, in that whoever sets the frame essentially does so apart from consciousness. Consequently, people lack awareness of it and therefore cannot bring their conscious values to bear upon it. In communication, people frequently set Win/Lose frames or Win/Win frames; Dignity Preserving frames/Dignity Denying frames, etc.

### 14. *"There is no failure, only feedback"*

What would not happen if you receive 'failures' as feedback? What would happen if you did not receive such as feedback? What would not happen if you did not receive such as feedback? It seems to us that if everyone received everything that happened to them as feedback, they would all become ferocious learning machines.

> *It seems to us that if you, and ourselves, received*
> *everything that happened to us as feedback, we*
> *would all become ferocious learning machines.*

If you communicate with someone and fail to get the response you want, what do you do? *You alter your communication*—the stimuli that you present —until you get the response you want. In this way, you turn failure into feedback. Feedback, not Wheaties, comprises the breakfast of champions.

Living life by this presupposition changes all areas of life, but especially those areas that demand persistence and the wisdom of learning from "what doesn't work." People tend to give up too easily. Many marriages would not end in divorce if the couples considered communication as feedback rather than failure. Thomas Edison's 10,000 experiments (some say 1,000 experiments) in search for a filament to work in his light bulb illustrates this principle. When asked, "It must be hard to have failed 10,000 times!" Edison replied, "I didn't have 10,000 failures. I just found 10,000 ways *not* to make a light bulb." No failure—only feedback!

How many relationships end because people "fail" to get what they want immediately? How much business ceases because people take "failures" as a reason to quit or back off?

### 15. The person with the most flexibility exercises the most influence in the system

In any system, the one with the most flexibility over their own behavior (not that of others) will exercise more choices and therefore will exercise more influence in the system. Accordingly, the more choices you have in your communication toolbox, the less chance you will get stuck. For instance, should you become angry, you lose flexibility and you also lose control of the processes of communication. We recommend learning to use the NLP toolbox so that you radically increase your choices. Known as the *Law of Requisite Variety*, this belief as it applies to NLP encourages us to dissociate from our emotions so as to maintain choice in our communicating.

### 16. Resistance indicates the lack of rapport

We often read "insult" or "resistance" as trouble, failure, difficulty—and throw up our hands. We just give up on the person. We speak with people one time, get resistance, and never return; and so, we lose the joy and rewards of the relationship we could have had with them.

> I (BB) hold this belief:
> "I don't have resistant
> clients. I just lose rapport
> and I will re-establish it."

Why? In addition to using that as a trigger for "feeling bad," we simply lack the skills necessary for working with and overcoming the resistance. Consider the power of this presupposition about resistance. It shifts responsibility to us—in *how we handle it.* Believing this empowers us to re-establish rapport even with the grouchy— the grumpy, the out-of-sorts, the hurting. This belief also enables one to continue communicating even in the face of anger and sarcasm without taking it personally. It keeps us matching their internal reality by "saying words that agree with their internal model of the world."

The NLP model teaches us how we *can* overcome resistance. We can overcome resistance even with irate people. Obviously, establishing and maintaining such rapport plays an essential role in communication and therapy.

Rapport moves us into a more harmonious state with another. When two people adopt the "same mind" about something—they enter into rapport. Detecting resistance from someone signals to us that we have lost rapport.

## Learning—Choice—Change Presuppositions

### 17. *People have the internal resources they need to succeed*

NLP looks upon people as having an inherent ability for coping, and for creating the resourcefulness that they need to attain their definition of success. In saying people have the resources within, NLP takes an educational approach. *Educare* literally refers to "calling or leading out" (e-ducare, "to bring out" as something latent). Bandler has said repeatedly, "People work perfectly well, they just run very poor programs (depression, procrastination, defensiveness, etc.) very well!"

As communicators and therapists we seek to assist people in accessing their own resources—in "equipping" them to develop more skill. People only need some help in discovering and accessing their resources. In saying this, bear in mind that we do not say you have "everything" in place, we say you have all the resources you need to get "everything" in place. As an example, you may need to further your education or to obtain specific training in order for you to have success. In NLP we say you have the resources necessary in order for you to obtain the education and/or training you need to have your success. You have the "wiring" in your neurology to produce that success.

## 18. Humans have the ability to experience one-trial learning

The human body exists as quite a system. Each of us lives as an amazing bio-electro-chemical information processing unit—one that gives us the ability to learn *very rapidly!*

If a child gets thrown into a pool of water, that child may grow up *never forgetting that* and always remembering to experience fear (intense and inappropriate fear) at every sight and thought of going into water. Such learnings usually take place when we simultaneously experience an intense or high emotional level. This ability of the human brain to learn quickly provides opportunity for the NLP communicator/therapist to assist clients in rapid change.

## 19. All communication should increase choice

> *The more choices an individual has, the more wholeness that individual experiences.*
> *In NLP we seek to increase choice.*

This NLP trainer, as do many other NLP trainers, believes that the more choice an individual has, the more wholeness that individual experiences. Indeed, a great way to break rapport with an individual results when you remove choice. If you box them in, they often get really agitated. Give them choice and they experience happiness.

Speaking therapeutically, most problems we confront in working with people consist of their "stuckness" in some perceived problem. They live at what we call the "effect" of some perceived "cause." The outcome of the therapy moves in the direction of taking the client from "effect" to "cause" where they experience choice as to how they want to live their lives. The more choice you give a client the more satisfaction they experience from you as their therapist.

> *NLP outcome therapy moves in the direction of taking the client from "effect" to "cause" where they experience choice as to how they want to live their lives.*

## 20. People make the best choices open to them when they act

How frequently do we experience high levels of frustration with people because we do not understand the choices they make? How many times do we scratch our heads and say, "Don't they know better? What's wrong with them?" Thinking-feeling and saying such indicates our frame of reference: "Others should operate from my model of the world" frame!

This presupposition shifts that. Here we start from the working assumption that people come from their own model of the world and that they make the best choices available to them in that model. This thus answers our question, "No, they do not know better."

Starting from the assumption that people make the best choices available to them at the time enables us to approach them with compassion, to forgive them. This fosters gentleness, kindness, optimism, and hope.

Does that not hold true for you? Consider some time when you behaved (mis-behaved!) in a manner below your expectations... Didn't you attempt to do the best you knew? If you had had a better choice for coping, wouldn't you have opted for that?

Who knowingly makes a choice that will work good-and-well to their own detriment? People make stupid, ugly, sinful, and destructive choices while thinking that somehow it will make things better for them. Realizing this about others and ourselves enables us to treat everyone with more kindness and gentleness about our human fallibility and stupidity.

This realization supports the value and importance of forgiveness. Imagine for a moment what would follow if you held this belief toward the members of your family? What would result if you practiced this presupposition with the people at work? At church? Among your friends? With clients? Doing so will obviously affect the way you communicate with your significant others. They will sense that you believe in them and their abilities! And they will love you for it.

### 21. *As response-able persons, we can run our brains & control our results*

Mind (Greek: *nous*) refers to "mind, disposition, practical reason, understanding, thought, judgment." The majority of people seem to believe and act as if they have no control of their minds. Bandler (1985) wrote:

> "Most people don't actively and deliberately use their own brains. Your brain is like a machine without an "off" switch. If you don't give it something to do, it just runs on and on until it gets bored. If you put someone in a sensory deprivation tank where there's no external experience, he'll start generating internal experience. If your brain is sitting around without anything to do, it's

going to start doing something, and it doesn't seem to care what it is. *You* may care, but *it* doesn't...

I want you to find out how you can learn to change your own experience, and get some control over what happens in your brain. Most people are prisoners of their own brains. It's as if they are chained to the last seat of the bus and someone else is driving. *I want you to learn how to drive your own bus* (my italics). If you don't give your brain a little direction, either it will just run randomly on its own, or other people will find ways to run it for you—and they may not always have your best interests in mind. Even if they do, they may get it wrong!" (pp. 7-8)

NLP offers *neuro-linguistic processes for taking control of our thought processes.*

> *NLP offers neuro-linguistic processes for taking control of our thought processes.*

## Conclusion

Now you know the operational system of beliefs and values that drives the NLP model—a reality frame of presuppositions about how the human mind-body system works. In NLP, we simply start from these assumptions rather than spend lots of time studying, "proving," deleting, validating, etc., them. This does not mean that such conceptual studies prove useless or worthless; much to the contrary, it only means that in the hands-on, experiential and transformational model of NLP—we make experience and pragmatics change our focus.

> *In the hands-on, experiential and transformational model of NLP—we make experience and pragmatics change our focus.*

## Training Exercises

1.  Write down the 21 Presuppositions of NLP in your own handwriting and keep it with you throughout the week for constant review. (One student of mine [BB] typed out the presuppositions each morning for months when he first entered his office in the mornings.)

2.  Share the NLP Presuppositions with 3 people every day.

3.  Write an explanation about which Presupposition will have the most *profound* impact on you.

4.   Write an explanation about which Presupposition will have the most *pervasive* influence on you.

5.   Which Presupposition(s) do you already use in living?

## Thought Questions To Assist Your Learning:

1.   Which Presupposition(s) do you already use in living?
2.   What do we mean in NLP by "The NLP Presuppositions?"
3.   What does "epistemology" mean and how does it relate to NLP?
4.   What epistemology does NLP use and rely on?
5.   If you could adopt and integrate one or two of the Presuppositions that would really transform you life—which two would you choose? Why?
6.   What do we mean by "systems" in NLP?
7.   Define "strategy."
8.   Many of these Presuppositions imply ethical concerns and issues. Which ones, for you, speak about ethics?
9.   Which one of the Communication Presuppositions do you find the most compelling or insightful?

# Chapter 5

## NLP As As Communication Model:
## Excellence In Communicating

*Modeling Exceptional Communicators*

**What you can expect to learn in this Chapter:**

- The basic factors in the NLP communication model
- The NLP "guideline" in communicating
- "The Three Qualities of Exceptional Communicators"
- How to create a well-formed outcome
- The factors that complicate communication

*Life thrives on communication.* Growing up in the rural mountains of North Carolina, I (BB) saw little value in becoming proficient in English. What good would conjugating verbs and diagramming sentences do me?! What did split infinitives have to do with real life—on a farm? Simple life didn't need that! Then I left the farm.

As I entered the larger world, my perceptions began to change. After I became a minister, I took a refresher course in English and literature prior to tackling college-level work. What an act of wisdom—for a change! As I spent the next ten years in college and seminary, I served as a pastor the last eight years I was in school. Out of those experiences, I discovered just how much *language and communication* drive Christian ministry. To an incredible degree we minister by communicating.

To me, a Christian minister, like a salesperson, essentially "sells" the message of the gospel. At that time I read extensively in order to improve my communication skills. I studied Zig Ziglar's *See You At The Top* (1984) and *Closing The Sale*(1984a). I read everything I could put my hands on to aid me in improving my speaking and listening skills. Such became my passion. In witnessing and ministering to people, I desired to enhance my ability to communicate effectively. Though such books assisted me in improving my effectiveness as a communicator, not until I came across *the NLP model of communication* did I discover **the best model of all** about how language and non-language messages work. I then discovered the power and grace of the NLP model for equipping a person to become a truly professional communicator!

I (MH) also believe that *communication lies at the heart of all human experiences.* Our very bodies operate by innate "communication systems" of immense complexity so that our central and autonomic nervous systems interact with each other and the world "outside" our skin in a way that keeps us alive, healthy, and vigorous. Even our cells "communicate" with each other! But how a signal races down a neuro-pathway via bio-chemical-electrical processes and transfers and transforms "information" (messages, differences) in that cortical context—well, even the neuro-physiological scientists hardly have a clue.

My discovery of NLP occurred in the context of teaching basic communicative skills (skills for asserting, negotiating, listening, disclosing, conflicting respectfully, etc.) in the context of Christian churches. I found an article in *Leadership Journal* about NLP. Thereafter I devoured the NLP literature and incorporated much of it into a book on communication skills, *Speak Up, Speak Clear, Speak Kind* (1987).

Almost immediately I discovered the NLP "Ten-minute Phobia Cure" (the "Visual-Kinesthetic Dissociation Pattern"). When I ran it with several clients and saw *the immediate and dramatic response* (in contrast to three to six months of de-sensitization of phobic responses using relaxation and cognitive-behavioral processes), I became truly excited—and curious. Ultimately, all I did with the person comprised "saying words." All this person did to experience this tremendous personal transformation involved "listening to those words," and "thinking about them inside his head." I *communicated* to him; he *communicated* to himself. What literally, actually, and exclusively **transformed** this person from a reactive phobic person who automatically accessed a state of intense fear to a calm and cool person? *Verbal communication* alone transformed this person.

**How does this phenomenon that we call "communication" work?** How can the "saying" and "listening to" words have that much creative and re-creative power? How do words (as mere symbols) *work* anyway? How do written and spoken symbols alter actual internal physio-psychological processes? Can we say that some words function in a "healing" way and other words actually generate "hurt," "trauma," "distress," etc.? What mechanisms govern this?

So, of course, ultimately I took my doctorate in Cognitive-Behavioral psychology, with an emphasis in psycholinguistics, and wrote my dissertation on *Languaging: The Linguistics of Psychotherapy. How Language Works Psycho-Therapeutically.* Our ability to use words as symbols describes our uniqueness as humans. We humans have this tremendous power (and a dangerous one at that) of *speaking our "reality"* (subjective, internal reality) *into existence.*

Now, given this crucial role of "communication," symbols, symbolism, language, words, higher level processing of information, etc., in human experience, *the more we know about how "communication"* (sending and receiving of messages) *works, and the more skilled we can become in "communicating" effectively and with power*—the more effective we will become in getting the outcome we desire from our communication. This brings us to the...

## Three Qualities Of Exceptional Communicators

When the founders of NLP observed professional communicators in many fields, they discovered that successful communicators possessed three qualities. Thus anyone can become an exquisite communicator by developing these three skills. An NLP presupposition states, "The person with the most flexibility of behavior controls the system." Successful communicators will change their communication and behavior to attain their outcomes.

In this chapter we address the first of these qualities. We have already studied number two (Chapter Two) as we considered reading non-verbal feedback through our sensory acuity. In the same chapter we studied rapport building skills, which applies to number three as you begin to learn flexibility in communication. This entire work concerns itself about giving you more flexibility of behavior as we assist you in filling up your communication toolbox with a vast array of tools. These tools will enhance your proficiency in communication through many choices which provide for more flexibility in communication.

---

*The Three Qualities Of Exceptional Communicators*

1. **Identify explicit and achievable outcomes.** *Successful communicators know from the outset the direction and purpose of their communication.*
2. **Use sensory awareness to notice responses.** *These skills enable them to live in the now, in sensory-awareness, and provide them with necessary feedback about their progress toward their outcomes.*
3. **Flexibly alter behavior to achieve outcomes.** *Successful communicators develop the flexibility of behavior to continually change and adjust their communications to achieve their outcomes.*

---

## Well-Formed Outcome Model: Keys To An Achievable Outcome

Consider "goal setting." In recent decades, many have written about the process of effectively setting goals. Many years ago I (BB) memorized the acrostic for S.M.A.R.T. goals:

S – Specific
M – Measurable
A – Attainable/Assignable
R – Realistic/Rewarding
T – Timeable/Tangible

Goal setting functions as a prerequisite to success in most areas of life. Yet sadly, 95% of Americans still do not set goals. Who do these 95% work for? The 5% who do!

> *An outcome represents a goal developed with specificity that endows us with a very clear understanding of what to **do**.*

The NLP model enables us to go beyond mere "goal setting" into *desired outcome development*. Here we do not talk just about setting goals but about setting outcomes. How do they differ? Goals are described in general terms, outcomes in specifics. An outcome represents a goal developed with specificity that endows us with a very clear understanding of what to *do*.

Suppose you set a goal to "increase participation in a work team" or to "enhance the dynamics of the group." Both represent worthwhile objectives. Yet neither describes anything specific enough for *a behavioral outcome*. Those two phrases lack specificity. What plans do you plan to use to achieve them? In what areas do you expect to accomplish these desires? How will you know when you have reached them? A good outcome statement answers such questions. Once you have taken a goal through **the well-formed outcome model**, you greatly increase the probability of achieving your outcome.

The specificity of the well-formed outcome model facilitates concentration on what you internally see, hear, and feel. Your attention will direct itself toward external and internal resources necessary in achieving the outcome. Notice what happens internally when you think about the following:

sound … internal sound … pleasant internal sound
… low-pitched internal sound

As you became aware of each of these words and phrases, *your attention becomes more focused*. As you become aware of how you represent them in your mind, you notice the increasing specificity in the language—and that *specificity focuses consciousness*. Your internal processes make the necessary adjustments in order for you to experience the meaning of these word and phrases. Specifying an outcome immediately changes what you see, hear and feel.

None of us has the ability to experience "conscious awareness of every-thing." Roughly two million bits of information per second impinge on the human nervous system. Yet our consciousness can only entertain seven plus or minus two pieces of information at a time (Miller, 1956).

| |
|---|
| *The **well-formed outcome** **model** enables us to direct our attention toward our desired outcomes.* |

Few of us hold more than two or three items in our mind, consciously, at a time. Our minds must select. A well-formed outcome enables us to create specific pictures, sounds, feelings and words. Then that image activates our abilities and resources for achieving that outcome. This empowers us to take advantage of what we find presently available in our environment to attain our outcome.

The well-formed outcome model aids us in specifying *who* we will become. The model will enable us in the development of an image that we find both achievable and appropriate. Often people ask, "Isn't this just positive thinking?" We explain, "Not exactly. For while positive thinking obviously helps, NLP goes beyond mere positive thinking to providing *a way to think productively* so that we can get ourselves to take the kind of effective actions that will move us to the fulfilment of our objectives."

Now, given the value of this *well-formed outcome process,* a well-formed outcome should have the following characteristics:

| |
|---|
| 1. *Stated positively in terms of what we want.* |
| 2. *Described in sensory-based language.* |
| 3. *Self-initiated and self-controlled.* |
| 4. *Appropriately contextualized.* |
| 5. *Maintains appropriate secondary gain.* |
| 6. *Builds in/includes the needed resources.* |
| 7. *Ecological for the whole system.* |

## 1. Stated Positively

> In fact, the human mind does not directly process a negative.

A representation stated in the positive motivates the mind more than a negative representation. Actually, the human mind does not directly process a negative. Suppose someone says to you, *"Don't* think of poverty!" To process that statement, you will have to think by mentally representing "poverty." You may then try to negate it by crossing it out, letting it fade away, etc., but first you have to *represent* it. If you tell a child to *not* go into the street, then first of all, the child will probably see themselves "going into the street!" And children, unfortunately, often forget to negate the representation after creating it! ("Don't eat those delicious cookies!") This realization about mental processing informs us about how and why we often end up doing exactly the opposite of what we ask of others or ourselves. We need to ask ourselves, "What kind of image does my question or statement create in the person's mind?"

By definition, an outcome describes what we positively want to accomplish. It describes something you want, not what you don't want. We feel far more motivated to accomplish a positive outcome than a negative outcome. So we should not state outcomes using negations: "I am going to stop smoking." That describes what we aim to *not* do (a negation). Every time you think of your outcome of *stopping* smoking, you internally imagine doing that very thing you want to stop doing. You have to think of what you don't want to be doing—smoking. And, as we think, so we will become.

We should phrase it as a positive outcome: "I will take care of my health." To think of this outcome, we imagine looking and feeling healthy. And if we think (represent) health, we will more likely experience health since we continue to send positive messages not only to our "mind," but also to our neurology.

We also recommend that in your visual construct of your outcome you make the image of yourself having your outcome dissociated. So, once you have created an image of yourself having your outcome, make sure you see yourself in the picture. Why? Well, think of it this way: if you formulate your outcome associated (you do not see yourself in the picture), then your brain will tell your body that you already have your outcome. The reason—the brain does not know the difference between imagination and reality. Imagine yourself going over to your refrigerator and opening the door. Next open the vegetable drawer and pull out a lemon. After closing the vegetable drawer and the refrigerator, imagine yourself going over to your counter and taking out a knife and cutting board. Next, slice the lemon in half, then in quarters. Afterwards, pick up a one-quarter slice of lemon and imagine squeezing the lemon juice into your mouth. Now, is your mouth watering? For most people, this simple exercise will cause your mouth to water. How come? After all, you don't have a lemon in your mouth. It happens because through the processes of imagination your brain activated your salivary glands and your mouth watered. Likewise, if you recall your outcome images associated, your brain will instruct your body that you already have the outcome—and you will not have as much motivation to obtain your outcome as you will if you recall it dissociated. Your brain will tell your body from a dissociated position, "I want that. I don't now have it but I can have it. Let's go get it!"

To begin designing some well-formed outcomes, use the following questions to formulate your outcome (or a client's outcome). These questions assist in establishing a well-formed outcome:

*What specifically do you want?*
*What will having that do for you?*
*Have you stated your outcome positively?*
*Do you see yourself having your outcome?*

## 2. Described In Sensory-Based Language

*We will reach our outcome through the mental processes of creating an internal map of our outcome in terms of sights, sounds, and sensations—what we will see, hear, and feel.*

Having stated our outcome in positive language, we can now ask, "What will I see, hear and feel when I have my outcome?" This step will let us know *when* we have our outcome—our *evidence procedure*. In NLP, we base outcomes on sensory experience (seeing, hearing, feeling). Why? Because the mind processes information in these terms. Our individual skills arise from how we develop and sequence our rep systems. In other words, we will reach our outcome through the mental processes of creating an internal map of our outcome in terms of sights, sounds, and sensations—what we will see, hear, and feel. These processes, in turn, determine our internal state. And our internal state coupled with our physiology ultimately drives our behavior. And by means of our behavior, we create our outcome.

Further, code the desired outcome in a dissociated image so that you see, hear, and feel it as "out there." This will set up a neurological direction so that you will have a feeling of wanting to move toward it.

> *How will you know when you achieve your outcome?*
> *What will you see when you have your outcome?*
> *What will you hear when you have your outcome?*
> *What will you feel when you have your outcome?*

### 3.  Self-Initiated And Self-Controlled

While we can control *our own* thinking-and-emoting responses to life, we cannot control other people—especially their thoughts-and-emotions. Often we hear someone ask, "How can I change my spouse's behavior?" Easy. "Change your behavior and responses in some way that leaves your spouse without the need for their old program. Now what do *you* need to do that?" Changing others **directly** lies outside our control. Changing them **indirectly** by *changing ourselves*—we can do that! The well-formed outcome works with changes that *we* can initiate, maintain, and manage. To put our outcome at the disposal of others only disempowers us and invites failure.

> *Changing others directly lies outside our*
> *control—changing them indirectly by*
> ***changing ourselves**—we can do that!*

> *Do you and you alone control your outcome?*
> *Does your outcome involve anyone else?*
> *Can you both initiate & maintain the responses needed to reach your outcome?*

### 4.  Appropriately Contextualized

We need to design our well-formed outcome to fit into all the appropriate contexts of our lives. When we fail to do such, we build an over-generalized outcome that can cause problems in other areas. So we ask, "Where and when do you want this particular outcome? Under what conditions? What other constraints of time, energy, context, etc., do you need to consider as you build the outcome representations?"

> *In what situations would having your outcome become inappropriate or useless?*
> *Where, when, how & with whom do you want this outcome?*
> *Do you want your outcome all the time, in all places and without any limitations?*

## 5. Maintain Appropriate Secondary Gain

> *In changing behavior, if we do not preserve the secondary gains from the old behaviors, and provide alternative ways of attaining them, the desired behavior changes will probably not last.*

All of our present behavior provides us with positive values and outcomes. If it didn't, we would not perpetuate and maintain it. In psychology, clinicians refer to this feedback as *"secondary gain."* We talk about this in NLP as **the ecology of the entire system** (a personal, human system of thoughts-emotions, relationships, etc.). A person who smokes *gains something* from smoking. If they did not, they would not smoke. An individual who eats too much gains something from over-eating. If they did not, they would not over-eat. Therefore in changing behavior, if we do not preserve these secondary gains, and provide alternative ways of attaining them, the desired behavior changes will probably not last. This undoubtedly explains why so much change doesn't last. Use the following questions to discover the secondary gains you may have hidden inside your current behaviors:

*What would you lose if you accomplished your outcome?*
*When, where & with whom would not having your outcome feel OK?*
*Would you have to give up anything that you deem important to have this outcome?*

## 6. Build In The Needed Resources

To reach our desired outcomes—we need *resources*! A well-formed outcome will therefore have the needed resources included within it so that we imagine and represent such as part of the outcome achievement. Many people set goals which they simultaneously "can't imagine" themselves really experiencing! This indicates that they have not built in the needed resources.

*What do you have now, and what do you need, to get your outcome?*
*Have you ever done this before?*
*Do you know anyone who has done this before?*

## 7.  *Ecological For The Whole System*

> Changes made at one point in a human system must fit together with, and adapt to, the other parts of the system in a healthy way.

A major strength of NLP concerns *ecology*. Ecology, as the science of the relationship between an organism and its environment, in NLP speaks about our concern that changes made at one point in a human system must fit together with, and adapt to, the other parts of the system in a healthy way. In defining a well-formed outcome, we therefore give consideration both to the individual and to other people in the system. Human systems include family, work relationships, school, friends and community. If we gain from one area at the expense of another area, this benefit will not last. NLP says that "We need to evaluate behavior and change in terms of context and ecology."

The following four questions derive from Cartesian logic. These four questions offer some useful and powerful linguistic patterns. The theory of Cartesian logic asserts that if an outcome (or any theory) will hold true in all four questions, then you can view your outcome as attainable. As you process your outcome through these questions, notice if you get a negative internal feeling ($K^{i-}$) or an objecting thought. If so, you probably will need to alter your outcome until you have positive thought-feelings about outcome. These questions provide a powerful means of discovering if your outcome truly fits your needs. You may want to memorize these questions and see just how helpful they become in your communications and change-work:

> *What will happen if you get it?*
> *What won't happen if you get it?*
> *What will happen if you don't get it?*
> *What won't happen if you don't get it?*

## Cartesian Coordinates

**Note:** In the chart on the next page the ~ symbolizes "not." So this illustration reads: Theorem = AB, Inverse = A not B, Converse = not AB, Non-Mirror Image Reverse = not A not B. Or, I (BB) like to think of it in terms of (–) and (+). In this manner it would read: Theorem = (+) (+), Inverse = (+) (–), Converse = (–) (+) and The Non-Mirror Image Reverse = (–) (–).

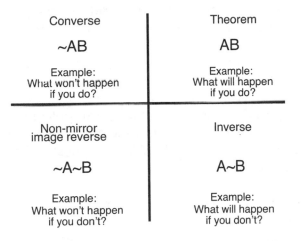

| Converse | Theorem |
|---|---|
| ~AB | AB |
| Example:<br>What won't happen<br>if you do? | Example:<br>What will happen<br>if you do? |
| Non-mirror<br>image reverse | Inverse |
| ~A~B | A~B |
| Example:<br>What won't happen<br>if you don't? | Example:<br>What will happen<br>if you don't? |

*Figure 5:1 Cartesian Coordinates*

Overdurf and Silverthorn (1996) in *Beyond Words* provide a couple of excellent metaphors in explaining Cartesian Logic. They utilize the analogy of a glove and suggest that **the inverse** of the glove would consist of *the glove turned inside out*. The *converse* of the glove would comprise the other glove or its opposite.

*The non-mirror image reverse* of the glove would include everything else in existence other than the glove. Another way of viewing the non-mirror image reverse in the context of the theorem of a problem would involve saying that the non-mirror image reverse of the problem includes everything the problem does not consist of. The power of this? Once we impose the non-mirror image reverse on the problem, *the problem cannot hold up*. This results because "the everything else" of the non-mirror image reverse engulfs the problem. That which defined the problem disappears.

Julie Silverthorn gives another example to provide a visual metaphor. She talks about preparing Jell-O. Consider having a Jell-O mold inside a larger and deeper pan or dish. If you poured Jell-O into the mold you would have a Jell-O form. But if upon pouring the Jell-O inside the mold, you then discover that the mold has a leak, then all of the Jell-O would first go into the mold. Then it would flow out and into the inside of the larger dish. Eventually, the mold and the dish would both fill up, and in doing so, the Jell-O inside the larger dish would engulf the Jell-O mold. The Jell-O mold would then, in effect, disappear and essentially serve no purpose.

In *the non-mirror image reverse* pattern, the "everything else" engulfs the theorem and if the theorem holds no purpose for the individual, it will disappear as a problem.

In addition to the above questions, these additional questions can also assist in formulating a well-formed desired outcome:

> *Can I test the outcome?*
> *Can I chunk down the outcome into achievable pieces?*

We should give special care to avoid making our outcomes too global. In a well-formed outcome, we need to break the outcome down into a step-by-step procedure. Such will then allow us to achieve the outcome via a systematic, patterned and teachable way.

> *Do I know the first step to take?*
> *Do I feel I can achieve the first step?*
> *If I reached the outcome would it fit with my values?*
> *Can I find more than one way to achieve the outcome?*
> *What appropriate personal anchors exist in the context in which I desire the outcome?*
> *Do I have sufficient information about the internal state necessary for reaching the outcome?*
> *Do I have the image of the outcome firmly in my mind?*
> *Do I have the sounds, pictures, words and feelings of the desired outcome in mind?*
> *Does my internal state drive my behavior in the direction of obtaining the outcome?*

Peter Young provides the following Well-Formed Outcome visual:

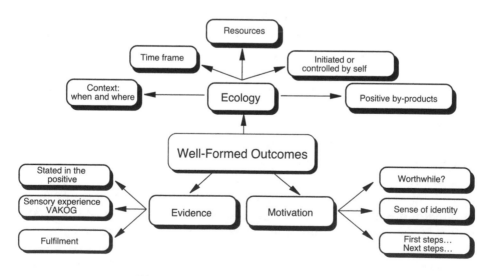

*Figure 5:2 Well-Formed Outcomes*

## Well-Formed Outcome Exercises

### Exercise 1

You will do this exercise by yourself. Begin to look around the room. Look at the physical structure of the room, furniture and other people. Notice four or five different colors and name them to yourself. After noticing colors, notice the different geometric shapes within the room. Do you see squares? Rectangles? Circles? Pyramids? Triangles? Name these shapes to yourself. Listen to the different sounds both within the room and outside. Do you hear people talking? Do you hear any appliances humming? Can you hear automobiles outside? Name the sounds you hear. How many did you hear? How do you feel today? How does your head feel? Stomach? Lower back? What tastes do you experience? Do you notice any odors in the room? How would you gauge your overall emotional state today?

### Exercise 2

Form a group of three and choose "A," "B" and "C." "C" will serve as the meta-person or observer. "A" chooses an outcome relating to the study of NLP. "B" will serve as the operator. "B" takes "A's" outcome through each step of the well-formed outcome outline. "B" asks "A" each question under each step. You make no other intervention. Keep your exercise to asking the questions from the Well-Formed Outcome model. Notice the changes in "A" as "A" processes each question. Did "A's" outcome change any during the questioning? When "B" finishes with "A," do a round robin. "A" becomes "B." "B" becomes "C." And "C" becomes "A," etc. After completing a round robin with an outcome relating to your study of NLP, choose an outcome of your choice and repeat.

## Overview of the NLP Communication Model

If we break down the term "communication," we discover that it involves a **"communing"** (*"co"*-with; *"union"*-coming together) **of meanings**. This noun-like word (communication) then actually refers to *a process*, namely, the ongoing feedback process of clarifying messages sent and messages received between two or more persons attempting to relate and understand each other. In this process, it takes two persons who keep relating (sending) back and forth their meanings by means of their words and gestures until they begin to share meanings with each other (whether they agree with them or not). Ultimately, they co-create a phenomenon that we call "a state of understanding." The communication process thus involves a relational and interactive phenomenon.

*"Talking"* thus radically differs from *"communicating."* While it takes only one to "talk"(!), it takes at least two people to "communicate." Most people can easily "talk." All they need do involves opening their mouth and letting a flow of words gush forth! After we have "said words" to or at another person, we can know *what* we said and even *how* we said it by simply having some recording device to pick up the signals we sent out. That holds true for "talking." It does **not** hold true for "communication." In "communication" **we never know what we have communicated**! Why? Because we never know *what the other person heard*!

This indefiniteness of knowing what messages get sent and heard in "communication," leads to the frequent (usual?) experience of *the mismatching of meanings* between people. Meaning-sent and meaning-received fail to match. Accordingly, to become more professional and elegant in our "communicating", we must address this mis-matching of messages. This identifies one of the central problems in the interactive process of "communicating."

## Facets of Communication

### Complexities That Affect Communicating

Basic communication theory operates from the information processing functions that we label: (1) *processing*—thinking, evaluating, reasoning, interpreting, etc.; (2) *outputting*—in language (verbal) and behavior (non-verbal); and (3) *inputting*—receiving data, listening, hearing, etc. This operates **representationally.** This means that *words do not mean, people mean*. Words function merely and solely as vehicles of meaning, symbols of referents other than themselves. We use words as symbols of our ideas, thoughts, beliefs, understandings, etc. We use them to *transfer* our ideas into the head of another human being. **Language** occurs in various modalities of awareness: visual, auditory, kinesthetic (sensations), smells, tastes, and words.

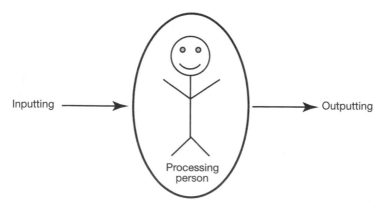

*Figure 5:3  Linear Model of Communication*

What problem do you see with this model? Primarily it portrays the communication process as if it operates in a linear way. What problem does this pose? It makes "communication" reductionistic and too simplistic to describe the complexity that typically occurs when we seek to "communicate." For one thing, when someone talks, my mind doesn't wait before I start processing! I process and output (primarily non-verbally) *as* the speaker continues—*and* if the speaker has their eyes and ears open, they will simultaneously process my response, and communicate to themselves internally about that, etc.

**# 1.** Complexity # 1 that enters into this process involves how "communication" functions as **a cycle of interactive events** involving the speaker-listener. This means that when we *co*-mmunicate we inevitably generate *a co-created phenomenon* (or experience) *of speaker-auditor* in interaction, exchanging, testing, misunderstanding, giving feedback, receiving feedback, etc.

**# 2.** Nor does the complexity end there. Complexity # 2 adds one of the most basic NLP presuppositions: **The meaning of your communication resides in the response you get!** Or to restate it, the response you get indicates *the meaning of your "communication" to the other person regardless of your intent!*

In NLP, we use this as our major *communication guideline* for developing our skills in becoming more professional and elegant as communicators. This guideline reveals that *we never know what we communicate*—until we get a response. Then that response assists us in figuring out what we must have communicated to the other person! "Tell me, what did you 'hear' me say? Oh, no, I didn't mean that, let me back up and see if I can provide a different set of signals and words so that I can more accurately communicate my meanings."

Obviously, this approach empowers us to realize that *there is no "failure" in communication, only results, responses and feedback!* I don't need to blame or accuse others of "not getting it," "not listening," "distorting my messages," etc. That almost always provokes others to respond defensively. Not good. By accepting **this non-blaming frame of reference**, I start with the realization that others live in their own worlds (and boy, some people *really* live in their own worlds!). And as I adjust myself to that "reality" (even though I may not like it at all), I don't need to go around moralizing about it!

**# 3.** This brings us to adding complexity # 3 of the model: *Expect yourself and others to always, inevitably, and inescapably* **contaminate** *the "communication" process!* Part of what you and the other "hear" in the communication interchange involves what each brings to the communication encounter in addition to what each inputs from the other.

NLP adds to the communication this piece—*we all operate "internal filters."* Our brains and nervous systems do *not* see, hear, or record the information that comes to us in a "pure" form as does an audio or video recorder. We do *not* photographically hear "meaning" or "see" events. We see and hear in the context of our internal world—a world of meaning, values, beliefs, understandings, and experiences. In NLP we refer to this as our internal "references," that is, those conceptual filters that determine our reality. Metaphorically, we all have our own "library of references." To therefore "make sense" of things, we go within and use our own personal and subjective references. Linguists refer to this internal trip as a "Trans-derivational Search (TDS) to our referential index." The referential index defines the person, place or thing doing or receiving the action of the verb. Did you do your own trans-derivational search to your referential index when you read those words?

In the late 50s and early 60s, Noam Chomsky and his associates created the field of *Transformational Grammar.* This domain of knowledge sought to specify how language works in the human nervous system in terms of translating, transferring, and transforming surface sentences into the deep structures inside our neurology. Using some of the formulations of General Semantics about levels of knowledge (abstraction), the transformational grammarians created a model of deep, pre-linguistic "knowledge" inside our nervous systems and how that "knowledge" gets transformed into language and then into the surface statements that we utter as we attempt to communicate what we "sense" deep inside. Bandler and Grinder built NLP using some facets of the Transformational Grammar model.

What does this have to do with an average communication event like a presentation, a conversation, therapy, telling jokes, reading a book, etc.? Everything! Because it means that neither you nor I receive any information (signals, messages) in its pure form. *We contaminate everything with "our stuff."* I hear you through my belief filters, my value filters, my mental processing filters, my cognitive distortions, deletions, and generalizations.

And because I do—you never know how I filtered your words, gestures, non-verbal movements, etc. No wonder we have to work so hard to communicate effectively! Somehow we have to take into account the "meaning systems" that others use in processing our information. Sometimes we have to stop talking about our subject, mentally step back, and talk about our process of communicating—we "meta-communicate"— talk about our talk.

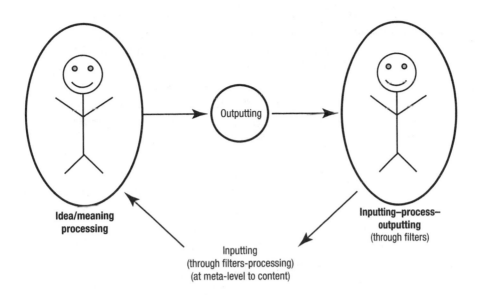

**Figure 5:4** *The Complexity of Communication*

**Complexity # 4.** We haven't finished identifying the layers of complexity yet because *all "communications" occur from within some "state" of consciousness.* By "state" we refer to some mind-body or neuro-linguistic state of being. More commonly we speak about "state" as one's "attitude, mood, feeling, place, space," etc.

As we learn to take our state, and the other person's state, into consideration as we communicate, we essentially become aware that neither we nor the other exist as dead machines, but as energized beings. I suppose we could talk about the "state" of an audio recorder, the "state" of a video recorder. But the "status" of such would only comprise its mechanical condition.

Not so with humans. What comprises a *state of consciousness* in a human being? Because it refers to our mood, attitude, emotion, physiology, mind-set, etc., it refers to all of the things going on "mentally" in our heads *and* all of the things going on "physically" in our bodies. And we all "never leave home without" our heads-and-bodies! We drag them everywhere we go—and so they generate our ongoing and ever-changing states.

The importance of this? Our states create "state-dependent" or "state-determined" communication, perception, learning, memory, behavior, and emotion. **State-dependency** means that *how* (and sometimes what) you communicate, perceive, learn, remember, emote and behave *depends* on your current mind-body state of consciousness. When we feel depressed we can remember, think, perceive, communicate and behave out of depressing awarenesses so easily! When we feel angry, we can see and remember other angry events with such ease. When we laugh and joke and feel pleasant, we see the world through eyes of humor and playfulness. Our states seem to open up that "library of references" inside us so that we have special access. And, when we get into one state, it often precludes us from having access to the resources of another state. When fearful or angry, we find it much more difficult to get to the resource of calmness.

In NLP we use the communication guideline that *"We never know what we have communicated."* The meaning of our communication lies in the response we get. When we do not get the response we want, we need to develop the ability to change our behavior and to continue eliciting responses until we get the one we want! NLP offers the skills necessary for flexibility of behavior in communication.

If indeed we all live in our own unique world driven by our own meanings and history, then how can we ever really **connect** with another human being? What skills and tools will facilitate truly and deeply **connecting**? In this work we have introduced you to a major gift in NLP for just this—the NLP strategy for *building and maintaining rapport*, the model of *Sensory Acuity* and the *Well-Formed Outcome* model. What do we mean by rapport? **Rapport** refers to "a relationship of mutual trust and harmony, a feeling of connectedness, a sense of communicating on the same wavelength."

In NLP we analyze rapport by examining precisely how we have *matched* (or paced) some aspect of another person—their breathing, language, values, posture, etc. We say that we have entered into rapport with another when we speak (literally) the same language as that person. In doing so, we "enter into their model of the world." We enter the other person's model of the world when we use the same mental processes as the other. If they think visually, we similarly think visually. Should they process their thoughts auditorily (in sounds), we match them by thinking auditorily. If they use a lot of feeling or kinesthetic thought processes, we do the same. *This enables us to enter their model of the world.*

By rapport we metaphorically enter into the other's way of making sense of reality. It gives us access to their way of thinking and meaning-attribution. We speak of such rapport as "walking in the other person's shoes" to thereby come to appreciate their point of view. Walking in the other's shoes may involve modeling their tonality or physiology. As we do, their speech becomes our speech; their physiology becomes our physiology.

To establish rapport requires that we identify and then match the other's internal processes. As a Christian minister, I (BB) sometimes find this difficult. I had a client once who desired to leave her husband and marry a younger man. She thought she loved this younger person. I could find no justification for her leaving her husband. So how could I enter her "model of the world" when I did not accept her *outcome*? I could, however, accept and identify with her *pain*. She did experience a lot of hurt, confusion, and distress. Her pain came from her childhood. So I accepted *that* model of the world. We can establish rapport with a person's emotions and thought processes without accepting their behavior. Matching or pacing a person's model of the world does not mean conceptually validating that reality model—only understanding it.

The key lies not in preaching or becoming judgmental in cases of our perception of people's inappropriate behavior. The key to rapport with them, and then success in leading them to a more holistic, healthy outcome, lies in first discovering the purpose behind their inappropriate behavior and matching their positive intent. The intent of the behavior will often surprise us. Once we get deep enough to the root cause of their behavior, we will find a positive intent.

The NLP model of building rapport enables us to *empathize* with others. We do this by entering into their style of processing information. In that sense, we become their servant.

## Dimensions of Communication

> *Ray Birdwhistell said that only 7% of communication arises from the words used, while a full 93% of what we communicate arises from voice tonality and body signals.*

In an article entitled, "Kinetics and Context: Essays on Body Motion Communication", Ray Birdwhistell said that only 7% of communication arises from the words used, while a full 93% of what we communicate arises from voice tonality and body signals. He further said that 38% of effective communication arises from voice tonality (tonality includes tone, speed, quality, volume, etc), while the other 55% of communication involves physiological factors.[7] This refers to communication that comes through posture, gestures, facial expression and breathing.

Have you ever given someone a gift and their verbal response indicated that they loved the gift (they said so), but on another level, their non-verbal communications (their voice tonality and physiology) "told" you that they didn't really *love* the gift? Which communication did you believe? More than likely, you sided with their non-verbal signals. When a person says "yes" with their mouth while their head shakes side-to-side, we experience incongruity. So what do we believe? What do we decide? A great many people go with the unconscious signal of the head-shaking "no."

These findings inform us as to why most people believe the non-verbal communication over the verbal. Non-verbal communication, more often than not, functions unconsciously—outside of our conscious awareness. The person talking lacks awareness of their unconscious signals. Yet our unconscious mind often picks up on these unconscious communication signals.

I (MH) have a little different take on this. C.E. "Buzz" Johnson (1994) explored this research about the parts of meaning that come from the different communication media (words, tonality, body gestures) which he called "The 7%, 38%, 55% Myth." Tracing back the source to Albert Mehrabian's (1971) works, *"Silent Messages"* and *"Nonverbal Communications,"* he quoted Mehrabian as saying, these numbers "have to do only with what he calls the resolution of inconsistent messages... incongruencies." Mehrabian further added, "there are very few things that can be communicated non-verbally."

He explained that the original research sought to identify the *"attitude"* (the person's emotion behind their words) carried in the tonal component and tested this using *single words,* Johnson argued that we must handle with great care the implications of that research. Johnson (1994) further noted,

> "If you've ever played charades, you know that words and language are by far the most effective way of expressing complex and abstract ideas."

Now he certainly did not argue against the existence and power of the non-verbal channels of communication. Of course not. Yet,

> "Words and language are probably the primary motivation factors for human beings and they can be enhanced by proper congruent totality and body language" (p.36).

Bandler and Grinder (1975) argued that given these different facets of communication, neither operate as more or less important than the other *per se*, but can in a given context. Accordingly, we should take them all as

**para-messages**—on an equal footing—and search out what each signal or message means, especially if they differ.

Similarly, much of my (BB) training in communication has focused on the area of verbal communication. The NLP model slightly shifts this emphasis onto *the total communication process* which includes the non-verbal communication messages as well. What does this mean practically? It means that to communicate effectively, my unconscious communication must congruently reflect my verbal communication. We call this incredibly powerful factor *"congruency."* If I want people to believe my communications, then what I say verbally must congruently match my tone of voice, physiology, posture, breathing, etc.

> *Gestures and voice tonality speak volumes while words speak pages.*

The 7%, 38%, 55% findings suggests why many people (if not most) always believe the *how* of a person's communications up against *what* they actually say. How often have you noticed someone's eyes, voice, facial expressions and gestures communicate congruently that they really did like a gift? Didn't that communicate most powerfully to you? Such represents the importance of recognizing and working with all of the communication dimensions!

So, as you undoubtedly have guessed, *congruency* plays an extremely important role in the area of building rapport and trust in your communication. In the area of communication and relationship building, we must send out our messages congruently. This means that *what* we say (auditory) and *what we express* via feelings (kinesthetic) must match what others see (visual) in us as we communicate to them. Gestures and voice tonality speak volumes while words speak pages.

[Let us note one disclaimer at this point. The *behavioral equivalent* for one person for "trust," "honesty," "sincerity," "conviction," etc., will often differ from what another person attributes as the behavioral equivalent. Thus, to some people, when a speaker "raises their voice" that *means* (equates to) excitement, enthusiasm, conviction. To others, it *means* "being obnoxious, insecure, unsure, etc." Similarly, when a person folds their arms across the chest some people will *read* that as meaning "defensive, closed, rigid," while others will *read* it as meaning "getting calm, attempting to listen, relaxed." This means that we also need to know and take into account *the behavioral meaning equivalent* of non-verbals for any given audience. The stories of cross-cultural mis-readings can provide both amusing entertainment and tragic misunderstandings.]

## Thought Questions To Assist Your Learning:

1. How would the NLP "Communication Guideline" alter or affect your communication style?
2. Recall and list (without looking if possible) the three Qualities of Exceptional Communicators.
3. Which criteria of Well-Formed Outcomes do you already do very well? How did you learn to do this?
4. Which criteria of Well-Formed Outcomes do you need to learn and develop?
5. What impressed you about all the "complexities" that contribute to the Complexity of Communication?

# Chapter 6

## Framing For Resourcefulness

**What you can expect to learn in this chapter:**

- How meaning completely depends upon Frames
- A number of empowering frames in NLP
- How to shift frames (reframe) to transform meaning
- How to use the Pretend Frame
- How to use the Dissociative Frame

The dissociative frame of reference provides many resources for the person who knows when and how to use it. First we will study some of the primary frames of reference as presented in NLP. Then we will apply it to the process of learning to effectively handle feedback (commonly called "criticism") and finally we will apply it to phobias and traumas. As a way of viewing things—stepping out of a picture, remembered experience, or even an ongoing current experience—and take a second position (Chapter Three) empowers us to cope with things without going into state. Choosing when to do this, to what degree and when to stop doing this provides us with a flexibility of consciousness of much value.

> *In NLP the process of framing refers to putting things in different contexts (frames of reference), thus giving them different meanings.*

## Part I—Using Different Frames Of Reference

In NLP the process of framing refers to the putting of things in different contexts (frames of reference) in order to give them different meanings. Some of these frames appear implicitly in other sections of this training manual.

*Frames Found In The Well-Formed Outcome Model*

- You first read of the **Outcome Frame** in the early part of our training dealing with the Well-Formed Outcome model (Chapter Five).
- That model also contained the **Ecology Frame**. You will remember that ecology deals with the way your actions fit into the wider systems of family, friends and co-workers.

- The **Evidence Frame** also appeared in the Well-Formed Outcome model. This frame concerns itself with clear and specific details. In the Evidence Frame you ask, "What will I see, hear and feel when I obtain my outcome?" The **Evidence Frame's** usefulness reveals itself not only in the Well-Formed Outcome Model but also in most areas the NLP Practitioner works in.

In this chapter we shall explore numerous frames and provide patterns for using these frames. To shift to a different frame typically will reframe one's perspective and therefore one's meaning. And when we do this, our very world changes. This transformation of meaning alters our neuro-linguistic and neuro-semantic "reality" so that we see things differently, feel different emotions, act and speak in different ways, etc.

### Backtrack Frame

> In the Backtrack Frame you mirror their words.

The Backtrack Frame offers a simple but most effective model. The frame utilizes the skills you have learned from building rapport through matching, mirroring, pacing and leading. Using this frame you recapitulate the information you have up to that point by using the other person's key words and tonalities in the backtrack. Most summary statements distort the other person's words. However, in the Backtrack Frame you mirror their words. Therefore, using the Backtrack Frame really helps in maintaining rapport. This frame demonstrates its helpfulness in meetings, especially when you need to update new people and in the checking of agreement and understanding of all the participants. The frame gives you time to think about what you're going to do or say next.

### Backtracking Exercise

1. Let "B" think of something they would like to accomplish. As "B" tells "A" about the outcome, "A" asks of "B" questions that will elicit from "B" high quality sensory-based information.

2. As "B" answers "A's" questions, "A" silently identifies the process words or predicates that "B" uses. "A" may wish to take notes of the statements and/or predicates.

3. Then "A" backtracks by saying, "Now let me make sure I *heard* you correctly, you said ..." For the first several responses, "A" accurately matches the process words "B" used. Then let "A" begin to deliberately mismatch some of the responses.

4. "C" stands behind "A" with hands on "A's" shoulders (thumbs on "A's" back). When "A" matches "B's" responses according to "C's" memory, "C" squeezes their right thumb into "A's" back. When "A" mismatches "B", "C" squeezes their left thumb into "A's" back. "A" and "C" should pay close attention to "B's" responses to the mismatches. There will probably occur some incongruence in "B's" response. See if a mismatch effectively causes incongruence. A mismatch usually works about the same as a slap in the face!

5. Continue for a total of 7 – 8 minutes each round, stopping only for only *very* brief conferences when "A" and "C" disagree about a match or mismatch.

6. **Stretch:** Try to match "B's" predicate *sequencing*, e.g., "I've been *telling* myself for some time that I could *look* at things differently." Reply, "So you've been *saying* to yourself that a different *outlook* may be necessary." (10 minutes each)

### *"As If" Frame*

> *The "As If" frame assists in problem solving by pretending that something has already happened which enables the exploration of possibilities.*

The "As If" frame assists in problem solving by pretending that something has already happened which enables the exploration of possibilities. Some NLP trainers refer to the "As If" frame as the "Pretend Frame." Pretend that you have moved six months or a year into a successful future. Then, look back and ask yourself, "What steps did I take that led me to this successful outcome?" From this future perspective you may discover new and important information that previously you did not have available to you in the immediate present. We often live too close to the problem and that sometimes hinders our seeing the total picture. This frame assists us in seeing the problem from a future perspective.

The "As If" frame works with groups or committees. Suppose a key person has not shown up for the meeting. Using this frame just ask, "If they had come, what would they do?" If you have a person present who knows the absentee well, this person may very well provide some valuable information.

Interestingly, the "As If" frame works not only with *time switch* as given in the example above, but also with *person, information* and *function switches.* The following examples demonstrate lead-in statements for each switch:

*Types of "As If" Frames*

1.  **Time Switch**: Pretend that you have moved six months or a year into a successful future. Then, look back and ask yourself, "What steps did I take that led me to this successful outcome?"

2.  **Person Switch**: "If you could become anyone you wanted to become, who or what would you become and how would they handle this problem?"

3.  **Information Switch**: "Let's just suppose that you had all the information you needed, then what do you suppose...?"

4.  **Function Switch:** "Just pretend that you could change any part of the situation..."

The "As If" frame provides a valuable communication tool when dealing with people who resist change. Pretending as a rule does not create as threatening an environment as when we face real change. Since the frame tends to remove the threatening aspects of change, people's minds become open to new choices.

*"As If" Frame Exercise*

1.  "B" selects something they find themselves stuck in and desire to move forward.

2.  "B" imagines moving into the future and looking back on how they easily handled the stuck state. "A" assists "B" by using lead-in statements such as: Let's suppose that..."; "Let's pretend that..."; "If you began to imagine that..."; "When you act as if..." Or, "A" may say something like this, "Now notice yourself handling the problem that used to bother you, and see and hear yourself effectively coping with the problem using new behaviors."

3.  "A" directs "B" in running a movie of themselves performing as they desire with the new resources they have discovered.

4.  "A" asks "B" if the movie appears satisfactory to them. Re-associate them into the problem and have them run a movie of it. "A" then asks "B", "Are you satisfied in dealing with this situation by using these new behaviors?" This "ecology check" determines if the person as a whole has total agreement with the change.

5. If "B" answers "no", "A" recycles them to number 1 and continues. If "B" answer "yes", proceed with the following steps.

6. Do a Break State.

7. Test. "A" asks "B", "Think of the stuck state one more time." Typically, as "B" begins to think of the stuck state, they will automatically move to the dissociated state of seeing themselves successfully solving the problem as in step number 2.

8. The goal of this exercise provides "B" with some new choices rather than getting stuck in limited choices or no choices.

## The "Agreement" Frame Pattern

> *To achieve an agreement frame, both must move to a higher logical level that encompasses all of the concerns, perceptions, and frames of reference.*

When two people in conflict lack agreement about something, they will continually butt heads. Often disagreements will arise because they are looking at a situation from different points of view, and do so in categorical ways. To achieve an agreement frame, both must move to a higher logical level that encompasses all of the concerns, perceptions, and frames of reference. This pattern enables us to facilitate the process whereby people or groups in conflict can reach quality agreements with each other. Remember, you never solve a problem at the level of the problem. You must chunk higher to agreement.

### The Agreement Frame Pattern

1. **Identify the current frames**. Ask each person for a specific description of their outcome. "What do you want specifically?" "What values, beliefs, and criteria drive this goal?" "What do you evaluate about this as really important?" (These questions not only gather important information, but also pace each person so that each feels heard and understood. It also begins to construct meta- or higher level outcomes for an agreement frame.)

2. **Identify common elements**. Find a common element at a higher level that brings the two parties into agreement. Chunk up to a higher positive intent that both can agree on. "Jack wants a blue chair and, Jill, you want a red one. It seems that, at least, you both agree on purchasing a chair, right?" By pacing the higher-level want, it moves the parties there.

3.  **Identify a higher level category**. If you get a no, then move the parties up to the next category. In the example, you might use "furniture." "Do you both agree that you want to purchase some piece of furniture?" Continue until you find some level (category) of agreement. "So you could both agree on an expenditure for the house, right?"

4.  **Utilize the parties' meta-outcomes to formulate the larger level agreement frame.** "By purchasing X, what will that do for you, Jack?" "And if you purchase Y, what will that do for you, Jill?" "When you get that outcome, what does that do for you?" Continue this until the parties agree to the other person's higher level intent. "So you both want a comfortable and attractive home?"

5.  **Frame the negotiation using the higher level agreements**. Move back down from the general frame of agreement to specific exchanges. "Would purchasing this blue chair meet the criteria of comfortable and attractive?" "Would letting Jack decide this one and Jill the next purchase meet your joint criteria of having equal input into decisions?"

6.  **Confirm agreements**. During the process, continually identify and solidify all levels of agreement reached and their importance to each party.

## Part II—Dissociative Frame For Handling Criticism

In the area of communication, one of the most difficult tasks we face involves the handling of criticism. How can we accept criticism as feedback and not get sucked into heavy emotion and do something foolish? Indeed, the problems we often have in handling criticism constructively lie in dealing with our feelings about being criticized. If we could handle those immediate negative emotions, we could respond constructively to the criticism.

In your study of NLP you are learning the value of dissociation in the removal of emotion from an experience. Drawing upon this neurological phenomenon, Steve and Connirae Andreas developed a procedure for handling criticism. They learned this procedure by modeling people who operated successfully in turning criticism into feedback.[8]

You need to maintain a resourceful state throughout the procedure. Recall a time when you were on top of the world. Choose a specific time when you felt like you could conquer hell with a water pistol. Associate into that time. See what you saw. Hear what you heard and feel what you felt. You may wish to create a self-anchor of this experience. If at any time during this procedure you begin to become aware of losing your resourceful state, fire your resource anchor.

1. *This procedure requires a dissociative state. See yourself at some distance* (see Figure 6:1). If you have difficulty getting this picture of yourself, imagine seeing yourself in a photograph. To assist yourself in maintaining the dissociation, imagine a piece of plexiglass between you and the dissociated picture of yourself about to receive some criticism. Thus, since you see yourself "out there," any negative feelings you had during that time will seem "out there," and you can feel curious about those feelings.

2. *Dissociate from the criticism by seeing that you over there receiving the criticism.* You will see that other you "out there" ready to deal with what is going to happen. Now see "out there" someone who criticizes you and that you have had difficulty dealing with. Watch yourself just prior to the other person's criticizing you. As soon as the criticism starts, see that you out there immediately dissociate. See another version of you step out of the first you, so that that they have dissociated from it. Now you see yourself twice in the picture. You are watching yourself receiving criticism. Thus you experience a double dissociation. I (BB) have trouble doubly dissociating myself by seeing myself twice. It trances me out too much to even function consciously. Other students have reported the same difficulty. Fortunately, the procedure offers another option. So, double dissociate yourself by dissociating once (that is, seeing yourself once in the picture) and then see the words of the critic printed out in the air or on an imaginary blackboard.

3. *Make a dissociated movie of the content of the criticism.* Notice if you can make a complete movie of the criticism. Watch the dissociated you in the picture ask the other person questions until you can gather enough information to make a clear movie of what the person means. Oftentimes criticisms come to us so vaguely that we cannot make a clear representation. Such statements like, "You are rude" or "You are insensitive." Acknowledge the other person by saying, "I too feel concerned about that. Could you more specifically describe to me how I act in a rude way?"

4. *Evaluate the criticism.* Now that you have gathered sufficient information to run a clear representation of the criticism, decide what part of the criticism you agree with and what part you disagree with. Running a movie of the events as you understood them and comparing it with a movie of the events as the critic understands the situation works quite well in evaluating the criticism. Check for areas where the movies

match and mismatch. Should your memory of the event appear signif-
icantly different from their criticism, gather more information by
asking questions.

**1. "Watching yourself watch yourself receiving criticism:"**

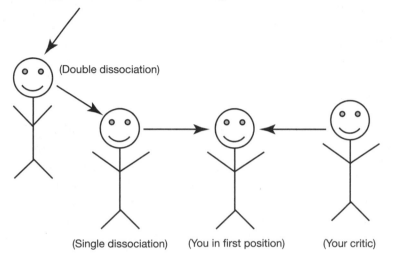

**2. "Watching yourself receiving criticism and seeing the words of the critic out on a banner (whiteboard, movie screen, out in the air, etc.):"**

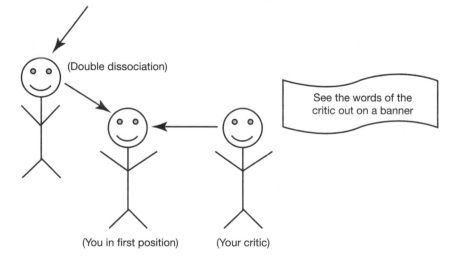

*Figure 6:1  Dissociative Frame for Handling Criticism*

5. *Decide on your response.* You now have all the information you need to
respond. Your response will include what you agree with in the criticism and what you disagree with. Steve and Connirae write:

"Exactly what response the you in front of you selects depends upon your goals as a person, your values, your relationship to the other person, etc."[9]

In responding to the critic, respond first to those areas in the criticism that you agree with. Then share those areas you disagree with, and explain why you disagree. This will help to maintain rapport with the person. If you need to apologize, do so.

6.  *Change your behavior as a result of receiving new learnings from the criticism.* If you have learned something about yourself from the criticism that needs changing, then begin now to re-adjust your behavior in the future. Future pace by actually imagining yourself in a similar situation in the future and notice how you will respond. Practice this procedure two or three times to install it in your unconscious mind.

7.  *Incorporate the part of you that learned this process.* You have just observed yourself "out there" learning new ways to respond to criticism. Do you not wish for that learning to become a part of you? Sure, you do. If you have placed up a piece of Plexiglas, please remove it. Then reach out with your hands and pull that new you inside and give yourself time to integrate totally into your unconscious mind.

## Part III—Dissociative Frame for Phobias and Trauma

Since, to a great extent, we develop our personality as a product of our memories, reframing negative memories with the Fast Phobia Cure will help us develop a more positive and resourceful identity. Richard Bandler describes the Fast Phobia Cure in *Using Your Brain For A Change*.[10] Associating into our memories causes us to re-experience the emotions. On the other hand, dissociating from the memory usually removes us from the emotions of that memory. Utilizing the power of dissociation, the Fast Phobia model permits us to erase the negative emotional impact of unwanted memories. As a result of this erasure, we recode both the visual and kinesthetic aspects of the memory. Would we not find this a useful technique?

You can perform this procedure on yourself. However, you will probably get better results having someone take you through the steps. The following procedure will work with most people. Those people who have difficulty visualizing may encounter difficulty. The Fast Phobia Cure has contributed to making NLP famous. The procedure offers not only a useful model in erasing the effects of a phobia, but also in recoding any unwanted memory. I have used it extensively in the removal of the visual component of my client's images from sexual, physical, and emotional abuse.

Removing this visual component often drastically reduces the negative emotions from the memories of the abuse.

1. **Establish a resource anchor**. In dealing with painful memories, the possibility always exists of the client associating into a very painful memory. To prevent this from happening, we begin by establishing a resource anchor, which we could use to pull the person out of a bad experience. Have the client associate into a time when they felt safe and secure. Anchor that state kinesthetically. Then test your anchor. Follow the steps to setting an anchor.

   Earlier in my NLP work, I established a resource anchor. Presently, I rarely do it. When a client associates into a bad memory, I get them to change their state by having them stand up and walk around. While walking, I encourage them to breathe from their abdomen. Also, you can shout or do anything that *breaks the strategy* of their emotional experience. However, go ahead and establish a resource anchor both for your practice and their comfort. Later, you may wish to stop the practice. (We will cover anchoring in Chapter Thirteen.)

2. **Acknowledge the mind's ability for one-trial learning**. A phobia represents an amazing achievement! Imagine it: people never forget to have the phobic reaction. Hurt from strong emotional experiences operates in similar fashion. When the correct trigger fires, the person immediately goes into hurt. Say to the client,

   "How amazing that you *always* remember to feel afraid or hurt when you think of the bad memory! I can't even remember to take out the garbage. You remember to feel phobic (or afraid, or hurt) every time you recall the memory. How amazing. If you can learn to feel phobic or hurt from a one-time experience, you can unlearn to feel phobic or hurt from another one-time experience, right?"

3. **Imagine a blank movie screen** (see Figure 6:2). Walk the client into an imaginary movie theater and have them sit down seeing the blank movie screen in front of them. Once the person has the imaginary movie screen, have them place a black-and-white photograph of themselves on the screen. Direct the person to make a photograph of them just before the onset of the bad memory, when they still experienced safety.

4. **Next, dissociate the client once more from their body and move into an imaginary projection booth.** Invite the person to look out of the projection booth at themselves sitting in the theater seat observing a black-and-white picture of them on the movie screen. They will see the back of their

current self observing the even younger self up there on the screen. Take a few moments to solidify this experience of a double dissociation.

5.  **Now, the client runs a black-and-white movie of the bad memory or phobia all the way through to the end of the event to a scene of comfort/security.** The client experiences a double dissociation from the memory. They now watch themselves watching the movie. This will begin to remove the emotion from the event and to recode it from a different perceptual position. Should the client still experience deep emotion from the movie, have them send the screen farther away.

    On one occasion I had a client cut off the bottom half of their body before running the movie. The client's father raped her at the age of ten years old. So, I led the client in removing the abused part of her body from the image. After running the phobia model on just the upper part of the body, she put the bottom half on and ran the movie. This worked beautifully. Tad James tells of having to take one lady out into the ticket booth before she could run the movie. Do whatever it takes.

6.  **Once the client runs the movie to the scene of comfort/security, ask them to freeze frame and either white out or black out the picture.** The client will probably see just a blank screen.

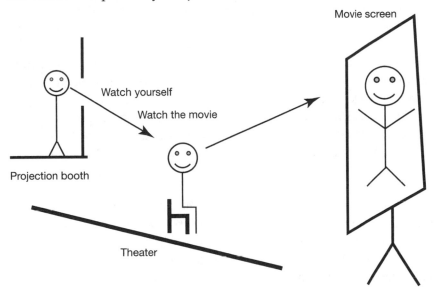

*Figure 6:2 Visual–Kinesthetic Dissociation Pattern (Fast Phobia Cure)*

7.  **Lead the client to associate into the movie at the end where they blanked out the movie.** The client will leave the projection booth and enter their body in the theater seat. Then lead them to associate into the

image of themselves that appeared on the screen at the end of the movie, the place of comfort/security. Guide them carefully and graciously. Use your language carefully so they follow your directions exactly. Check with them regularly to make sure they do what you want them to do. "Have you now re-associated fully into the you at the end of the movie? You are looking through your own eyes and you are seeing what you saw then, aren't you? You are hearing the same sounds you heard then?" Give your directions clearly and precisely.

8.  **Run the movie backwards, in color, and associated**. "You have seen movies run backwards, haven't you?" Once you get a yes, make sure they associate into the movie, and they see everything in color. "Now run that same movie backwards, and do so really fast. Do it in one or two seconds." You can anchor them to a sound as you say, "Whiiisssshhh." By watching their eyes, you will know when they run the movie backwards and how fast they did it.

9.  **Repeat the Process. Ask the person to repeat steps 7 through 8 three to five times making sure that they break state, clear the screen and start at the end. Do so until the kinesthetic disappears. If you desire, they can repeat the process until the image disappears as well.** Removing the image completely will remove *all* of the kinesthetics. The person may still recall the event; however, they will barely get any image or words. In running the movie backwards, lead the client to re-associate at the end of the movie. Make sure the client does not go to the end of the movie associated as that will re-install the phobia or trauma. When they run it backwards say, "Now, clear your screen. Put yourself back at the end of the movie. Go straight to the end of the movie. Just imagine yourself at the end when you experienced comfort/security. See what you saw and hear what you heard. Now, run the same movie backwards in color. Repeat until it disappears."

10. **Test & Future Pace to see if the client can access the phobic state.** See if their non-verbal response matches their earlier state of the phobia or trauma. You may say, "Imagine living in that situation right now." Or, if you know the content, elicit the stimulus more explicitly. For a phobia of water say, "Imagine walking out into a swimming pool into deeper and deeper water." If you get any of the phobic response, check out how accurately they followed the procedure and re-run the phobia cure making sure they follow the exact procedures.

[Note: When the phobia cure does not produce the effect I would like, I use the Swish Pattern to reinforce the change.]

## The Fast-Phobia Cure (Simplified)

1. **Establish a resource anchor**. You may set a resource anchor in order to bring the client out of trauma should they associate into the traumatic event. I do not use this any more for I have learned that when a client associates into a traumatic event, just have them stand up really fast, and breathe deeply from the abdomen. This will dissociate the client from their traumatic state.

2. **Acknowledge to the client the mind's ability of one-trial learning.** "How amazing how you always remember to feel afraid or hurt when you think of the bad memory. I can't even remember to take out the garbage. You remember to feel phobic (or afraid or hurt) every time you recall the memory. How amazing!"

3. **Imagine a blank movie screen.** Walk the client into an imaginary movie theater and have them sit down seeing the blank movie screen up there in front of them. Once the client has the imaginary movie screen, have them place a black-and-white photograph of themselves on the screen. This photograph represents their younger self just before the onset of the bad memory when they felt safe and secure.

4. **Next, the client dissociates once more from their body and moves into an imaginary projection booth.** The client should now look out of the projection booth at themselves sitting in the theater seat observing a black-and-white picture of themselves on the movie screen.

5. **Now, the client runs a black-and-white movie of the bad memory or phobia all the way through to the end of the event.** The client watches themselves watching the movie, experiencing a double dissociation from the memory. They watch themselves watch the movie.

6. **Once the client runs the movie to the end to a scene of comfort/security, ask them to freeze frame and white- or black out the picture**. They will just see a blank screen.

7. **Now, lead the client to associate into the screen where they blanked out the movie.** They leave the projection booth and enter their body in the theater seat. Then have them enter the movie and associate into the image that appears on the screen. Have them associate into the image of themselves at the end of the movie after they survived the trauma. Guide them carefully and graciously. Use your language carefully.

8. **Direct them in running the same movie backwards, in color and associated**. "You have seen movies run backwards, haven't you?" Once you get a yes, make sure they associate into the movie, and invite them to see everything in color. "Now run that same movie backwards and real fast. Do it in one or two seconds." You can anchor them to a sound as you say, "Whiiisssshhh." By watching their eyes, you will know when they run the movie backwards and how fast they did it.

9. **Repeat the Process. The client now repeats steps seven through eight until the kinesthetic disappears. If you desire, they can repeat the process until the image disappears as well.** Make sure they do *not* go to the end of the movie associated—that will re-install the phobia or trauma. After they have run it backwards say, "Now, clear your screen. Put yourself back at the end of the movie. Go straight to the end of the movie. Just imagine yourself at the end when you were OK. See what you saw and hear what you heard. Now, run the same movie backwards in color. Repeat until it disappears."

10. **Test & Future Pace by seeing if the client can access the phobic state.** See if their non-verbal response matches their earlier state of the phobia or trauma. You may say, "Imagine walking into that situation right now." Or, if you know the content, express it more explicitly. For a phobia of water, say, "Imagine walking out into a swimming pool into deeper and deeper water." If any phobic response reveals itself, check out how accurately they have followed the procedures and re-run the phobia cure making sure they follow the exact procedures.

## Other Editing Tools

From the double dissociation position of the projection booth you can not only rewind, you can do numerous other things to change your submodalities. You can make other choices as well. From there you can program your brain to process the film in ways to give you a great range of perspectives and reframes on the memory.

1. **Associate a resourceful memory.** Recall the memory of a time when you felt creative, confident, powerful, etc., from the past. See what you saw at that time. Now turn up the brightness on that memory. When you are fully associated into this resourceful state—bring into that scene the negative stimulus (dog, spider) that you fear, or the traumatic memory, and merge the two memories until they integrate and you see yourself handling the situation with your resources.

2. **Alter your sound track**. Re-process the way you hear yourself and others talk. How would you want to make your voice different? Or the voice of someone else? What qualities would make the memory less intense? What voice would you like to have heard? Install an internal voice to help you through this situation.

3. **Add tonal qualities to the sound track that make it better.** Take an unpleasant memory and put some nice loud circus music behind it. Watch the movie of it again; how do you feel? Put circus music to other memories of anger and annoyance.

4. **Apply your spiritual faith**. If in your spiritual belief system you can bring in your heavenly Father, a loving heavenly Father, etc., then split your screen and see through the eye of your faith your Guardian Angel hovering over the earthly scene of your memory. See and hear your Angel caring and loving you. Perhaps you hear, "I am with you." "I will help you." See Jesus touch you with his healing hand.

5. **Symbolically code the memory**. For instance, you might want to make the people in your memory transparent. Color them according to how you think/feel about them. Draw a line around the three-dimensional people in your memory, make them two-dimensional and color them according to your evaluation of them.

6. **Humorize your memory**. Since laughter gives us a great distancing skill, use your humor so that you can laugh this emotional pain off. How far in the future do you need to transport yourself before you can look back on a memory and laugh at it? What difference lies between a memory you can laugh at and one that you can't? Do you see yourself in one, but not in the other? Do you have one coded as a snap-shot and the other as a movie? What difference lies in color, size, brightness? Imagine the hurtful person talking like Donald Duck. Turn your opponent into a caricature cartoon character with exaggerated lips, eyes, head, hands, etc.

## Thought Questions To Assist Your Learning:

1. What other words can you think of that describe what we call "Frames" and "Framing" in NLP?
2. List all the Frames that you recall in this chapter or know about in NLP.
3. When or where would you use the Backtrack Frame?
4. Describe a time when you used the "As If" Frame in a creative and productive way.

5.  How skilled would you gauge yourself at this time in using the
    Dissociative Frame in handling criticism, phobias, negative emotions
    and traumatic experiences?

---

**We recommend John Grinder and Michael McMaster's
(1983)** *Precision: A New Approach To Communication;* **and
Bob Bodenhamer and Michael Hall's (1997)** *Mindlines:
Lines For Changing Minds* **for further reading on frames.**

---

# Chapter 7

## The Art Of State Management

**What you can expect to learn in this chapter:**

- The meaning and importance of resourcefulness
- The NLP State Management model
- How to interrupt disempowering states
- How to access, elicit, and amplify states
- How to anchor states

When you add your internal representations (the stuff in the mind) and your physiology (the stuff within the nervous system and body) you then have the component pieces of "a state of consciousness." Such states come and go throughout a day. Some enhance our lives and therefore empower us; some limit our lives and therefore disempower us. Can you tell the difference? Can you identify the triggers that induce the various states that you find yourself experiencing? Can you then alter your state?

> *The ability to manage state describes the difference between those who achieve their outcomes and those who fail to achieve their outcomes.*

In NLP, we call the effective management of states "state control." And success at reaching desired outcomes (goals) comes to those who know how to manage state control, does it not? And does not this, in fact, describe the difference between those who achieve their outcomes and those who fail to achieve their outcomes? The difference lies in the ability to put yourself into supportive and enhancing states so that you can then produce the behaviors that move you to reach your goals.

Developing the ability to direct and manage your states highlights the key to your main source of "power." By power, we refer to your ability to think, emote, speak, behave, respond, etc., in the ways that you so desire. This offers another facet of the art of learning to effectively "run your own brain" and neurology. To do this necessitates understanding your states, and your subjective factors that drive your states.

The problem with regard to state management does not lie in the fact that people do not have the personal resources to do such. The problem lies in knowing how to access the resources, how to amplify resourceful states, and how to do so when we most need such resources! The problem lies in that when we get into an unresourceful state, our resources seem less available.

In this NLP manual, we offer the following information about state management in order that you can get the most out of all of the material that follows. With these skills, you will tap into your powers to access learning states, relaxation states, states for clarity, creativity, curiosity, respect, passion, etc.

---

*State Management*

1. *State Understanding*
2. *State Awareness*
3. *State Alteration*
4. *State Utilization*

---

## 1. State Understanding

A first key lies in understanding the dynamics of states and the factors that comprise our states.

What creates any given state that you find yourself in?
If you saw a "state of consciousness" what would it entail?

> *The two main components of states involve: internal representations and physiology; the condition and use of your physiology.*

The two main components of states involve: internal representations and physiology; the condition and use of your physiology.

Internal representations, to a great extent describe your habitual patterns of representing things to yourself which you learned from your earliest models—your parents. This makes up the source of a great many of our beliefs, attitudes, values, and understandings which, in turn, form and pattern the kinds of representations you utilize. Internal representations include what (content) and how (form/process) you picture and talk in your mind.

Ultimately, what matters in your experience lies in how you represent things to yourself. As you learn to represent things in a way that empowers you rather than creates limitations for you, you learn the value of enhancing representations. You can represent things in a way that puts you in a positive state.

Keep in mind that you always have a choice about how to represent things to yourself. We like to describe this as representational power. Also, the kind of behavior that you produce when in a state also depends on your model of the world. These mapping functions that you have engaged in, also made up of internal representations, have become your stable "sense" of the world—your internal map for navigating reality.

So as you learn to take control of your own communications with yourself, you can learn how to produce the VAK signals to send regularly to your brain for what you want (your desired outcome). This will run a new program in your neurology and eventually produce positive results. It will keep you in a much more resourceful state.

Your physiology includes a multitude of things: muscle tension, what you eat, your breath, posture, overall level of biochemical function, etc. These things also greatly affect your state. Physiology includes posture, biochemistry, nervous energy, breathing, muscle tension and/or relaxation.

Internal representations and physiology work together to form a cybernetic loop or "system" that make up your unique "personality."

Another important awareness: we all perceive the world from within the context of our states. Such "state perception" explains why we experience certain perceptions at certain times. And since we always operate out of some state of consciousness that state always creates and filters the way we process things.

When we feel physically vibrant and alive, don't we perceive the world differently from when we feel tired or sick? The condition of our physiology changes the way we represent and experience the world. In this way our internal world always affects our external world. Thus, our internal representation that describes how we experience an event does not precisely describe what happened, but merely a personalized re-presentation of it.

## 2. State Awareness

The next step involves developing the ability to pay attention and identify our current and ongoing states. Making this discernment enables you to make finer discriminations: what internal representational factors determine this state? What physiological factors contribute?

But a problem arises that prevents much state awareness. When we experience states repeatedly, over time, etc., they become habitual so that we lose consciousness of them. They then become like the air we breathe and we cease to notice them. So we have to learn to take a moment and gauge our states, and then make an overall ecological evaluation.

Is this neuro-physiological state enabling and full of confidence, love, inner strength, joy, ecstasy, belief, etc., and tapping your wellsprings of personal power? Or do you find it dis-abling (even paralyzing)? What characterizes it? Confusion, depression, fear, anxiety, sadness, frustration, etc.?

Some states give us power to do things, to think clearly, emote accurately, feel good, take effective action, etc. Such states empower us. Other states operate as "impotent states." Getting into an unresourceful state doesn't mean you have become a "bad" person or even that you have something wrong with yourself. It only means that you have gotten into a "bad" state. And as goes the state, so goes the behavior. Yet we exist as far more than our behaviors. The behaviors simply express how and what we think and feel at the moment.

## 3. State Alteration

Now the process whereby you learn to take charge of yourself and your states (state control) means developing the ability to effect the states you access, elicit, induce, and amplify in yourself (and others).

The good news: everyone's state is altering all the time, and thus we experience a wide range of states of awareness. But how do you alter your consciousness? Answer: examine your IR and your physiology, note their component parts, and then alter those components of your experience.

> *But how do you do such altering of your consciousness? Answer: examine your IR and your physiology, note their component parts, and then alter those facets of your experience.*

If you do a contrastive analysis between two opposing states, you will gain important information about how your neurology and brain operate. For example, what do you find when you compare the modality and submodality differences between self-esteem and self-contempt? What differences do you discover between how you language self-esteem and how you language self-contempt?

By exploring the language and the submodality qualities of the images, sounds, and sensations in these states, you will learn which ones operate most impactfully on you (your driver or kicker submodalities as well as your driver Meta-states). Or, if you really get playful and curious, you might begin to discover what happens to your experiences when you turn the submodalities of relaxation into how you normally code stress.

Or, what happens when you turn the submodalities of resourcefulness, adult strength, and choice into those painful regressive states that characterize an old trauma. Pay close attention to the meta-states that govern the submodalities.

As you contemplate altering your state, identify what resource you need that would make a positive difference in the pattern that you currently find unsatisfactory. If the pattern that does not work for you involves "losing your head" and yelling angry words when stressed, then what resource would you need at that point? The ability to delay your reaction? Calmness of soul? A sense of confidence and self-esteem? An awareness of what you want to accomplish?

All resources do not work equally with everybody. What do you need? What would make a difference in your neurology? Do you know?

Try on several and experiment until you find something that makes a difference. The person who knows how to tap into their resourceful parts, to access those states, to alter their current states, etc., will become the one who achieves personal excellence in their chosen area.

## 4. State Utilization

Utilization means using your power to alter and access states. It describes your power to apply a resource when you need it. In other words, becoming resourceful alone will not be enough. The objective is to become resourceful when you need a particular resource.

State utilization refers to developing the abilities to call on the kind of internal representations and physiology shifts that you need when you need them. Then you could experience life much more as a matter of choice. For example, you could find yourself "snapping your fingers" (or firing off some other anchor) when you chose and suddenly finding yourself going into the most dynamic, resourceful state at will. How valuable would you find that? What if you could access and then amplify any given desired state? What if you could get into a state where you feel excited, confident, where your body crackles with energy and your mind feels alive with new and creative ideas? This describes what we mean by "utilization."

## The Pattern

Take a moment to think of a time when you have felt powerful. Now represent things in a way that puts you in such a resourceful state where you feel empowered. Represent how things will work, not how they can't or won't. Forming internal representations of things working begins to access the internal resources that will tend to produce that state. It works like magic!

Knowing the dynamic of how internal representations and physiology work together to create states (out of which behaviors spring) enables you to work backwards. This will let you know what specific things to do to elicit the state you want. Make the kind of generalizations about yourself that will effectively govern and direct your states.

We all can change our states in a matter of moments. We can "fly into a rage" or "fly into a calm." The ability to effect our own state in moments simply reflects a mechanism within our personality. Once we learn to access and elicit a state then we can anchor it. Associate or link it with certain behaviors, words, gestures, symbols, etc., so that you can quickly and easily get back into that state. This will cultivate in you a powerfully resourceful state of representations and physiology. Later in this work we will give a complete explanation of anchors and how to set a self-anchor.

> *People who excel tend to become masters at tapping into their own most resourceful parts.*

Such utilization will set you apart from most people who take little conscious action to direct their states since they attempt to direct so little of their own thinking, emoting, speaking and behaving. They just let them happen. People who excel tend to become masters at tapping into their own most resourceful parts. They don't wait for the state to "naturally" appear, they access, elicit, amplify and anchor their resourceful states. This makes them less and less dependent on, and determined by, the winds of fate that blow their way. They aren't so much at the mercy of whatever comes their way.

*Exercise*

Practice identifying an enhancing state of excellence in groups of 3. Person "B" states a resource they do not yet have, but would like to have (e.g. confidence, poise, self-worth, enthusiasm, love, energy, etc.).

Persons "A" & "C" elicit, access, and amplify this enhancing state in terms of internal representations. As "B" fully accesses the state that expresses this belief, have them adopt its physiology. "Sit or stand or hold yourself in such a way that it expresses a physiology of excellence in a way that seems congruent, believable and attractive for you."

## The Skill Of Elicitation

*How to Elicit and Work With Subjective States*

One of the most crucial NLP skills consists of the ability to do effective elicitation. This skill enables you to discover the structure of subjective experiences wherever you find them in yourself and others. The skill of eliciting also enables you to learn how to effectively transform experiences. It plays a crucial role for effective communicating, persuading, motivating, etc.

1. **Move to an up time state.** Get all of your sense receptors open to inputting sights, sounds, sensations, etc.

2. **Assist the person in accessing the state.** This becomes important in order to elicit good clean information about a person's experience. The person needs to get into the state. "Think about a time when you were honestly and completely confident (honest, forthright, in love, etc.)." Eliciting the structure of almost any experience without that person being in state reduces your ability to explore effectively the state they are experiencing. That removes it one level from the thing itself and will give you more of the person's theory about it rather than the experience itself.

3. **Elicit as pure a state, or experience, as possible.** If you ask for a "strong belief," pick something that the person doesn't have laden with emotionally significant issues, like, "I'm a worthwhile person." Pick, "I believe the sun will rise tomorrow." "I believe in the importance of breathing." The mental processes involve the same kind of thing, but the less emotionally laden content will give you "cleaner" information.

4. **Express yourself congruently and evocatively.** In eliciting, remember that your tools consist of your words, your tones and your tempo, your physiology and other non-verbals. So be evocative, and sound like what you speak about.

5. **Allow people time to process things.** If they aren't accessing, then have them pretend (use the Pretend or "As if" frame): "What would it be like if you could?"

6. **Begin with unspecific words and unspecified predicates (e.g. think, know, understand, remember, experience, etc.).** This allows the person to search for the experience in their own way.

7. **Follow up with specific predicates.** As you notice the accessing of a certain rep system, help them by then using sensory-specific words. "And what do you see...?"

8. **Use good downtime questions to assist the person in locating and identifying the experience.** To do that you will need enough content so as to ask good questions. Downtime questions involve those questions the answers to which are not on the edge of consciousness. The person has to go inside to their unconscious mind to find the information. "How many green lights did you go through to get here today?" In the upcoming anchoring section (Chapter Thirteen), you will receive complete instructions in how to set a downtime self-anchor.

9. **Once the person begins accessing, focus on the form and structure of the experience by getting the person's submodality coding.** If the person gets stuck in trying to think of something, ask, "Do you know anyone who can?" "What would it be like if you stepped into their shoes for a few minutes and did it?"

Eliciting helps the person you're talking with to become conscious of factors normally outside their range of conscious awareness. This means your own patience, positive expectation, and acceptance will make it easier (and safer) for the other person to access the information.

## Conclusion

The desired outcome of NLP as a whole involves making accessible more resourcefulness in people. To do that we need to have a general pattern for understanding how we get into "states" of mind-and-body, and how we can evaluate those states for resourcefulness. In this chapter you learned about these state management skills.

## Thought Questions To Assist Your Learning:

1. What two factors primarily govern your states?
2. What ways have you developed to interrupt your unresourceful states?
3. Practice "scaling" your states (from 1 to 10) for a few days. What did you learn by doing that?
4. What submodalities really drive and amplify your states?
5. What do we mean by "state management" in NLP?

# Part Two

*The NLP Language Model*

# Chapter 8

## The Meta-model of Language:
## Structure and Meaning

*The Heart Of The "Magic"*

**What you can expect to learn in this chapter:**

- The heart and structure of "magic"
- The NLP Meta-model of language
- Distinctions that indicate ill-formedness
- How to challenge impoverished "maps"

As we have explored the NLP communication model about how we create, process, and exchange messages with each other, this raises the question of *how does "the structure of magic" work?* How do we "make meaning" with symbols, words, and sentences anyway?

We have already noted that to "think" we use the rep system of the senses. This enables us to *present* to ourselves *again* ("re-presentation") information that we originally saw, heard, felt, smelled, or tasted. As we use our senses we also *code those understandings in words*. Thus we can represent a pleasant summer day at the beach by using the specific sights, sounds, sensations, and smells of that experience or we can use an even more short-cut system, we can say "relaxing day at the beach."

The words function within us as **a symbol** of the sensory representations, and those sensory representations function as a symbol of the actual experience. Thus if we begin with the experience (the territory), our VAK representations operate as a neurological "map" *of* the experience. Then our sensory-based words ("pleasant day at the beach") provide us a basic linguistic "map" *of* the neurological "map." And given the way our minds work, we can then use even more abstract and conceptual words ("pleasure", "comfort") as a higher level linguistic "map" *of* the other linguistic "map," etc.

> *Given the fact that words function in our consciousness as a "map" of reality (and not even the first level "map"), then words work to provide us a scheme, model, or paradigm about that reality.*

Given the fact that words function in our consciousness as a *"map" of reality* (and not even the first level "map"), then words work to provide us a scheme, model, or paradigm *about* that reality. To the extent that the words correspond in an isomorphic way ("form", "similar") to the territory they represent—they give us an accurate "map." To the extent that they do not, they give us a distorted map with significant parts left out (deleted), or with parts over-generalized or messed-up.

NLP began here. Linguist John Grinder had studied, and contributed to, the field of Transformational Grammar for years—a field that sought to understand how the coding, meaning, and significance at the Deep Structures of experience (at the neurological levels) become transformed into language (at the linguistic levels). Thereafter (1975), he and Bandler put together *the Meta-model of language for therapy.*

| The Territory | Neurological | Neurological (Conscious Exp.) | Sensory-Based (Linguistic Sorting) | Evaluative-Based (Meta-linguistics) |
|---|---|---|---|---|
| Territory of sensory-based reality out there. | Processing sense-receptors bringing information into our nervous system (NS) | Awareness of experience. What we pay attention to and what we delete. VAK representations of the experience | Naming and describing words (signifiers); names of objects, entities, categories (nouns); of actions (verbs); qualities (adjectives, 'submodalities') and relationships (prepositions), etc. First Linguistic "map" of the experience. | Language that describes the meaning, the language, and our feelings, etc, about the experience.<br><br>Second Linguistic "map" (Meta-words) of the experience. |

They developed this model of language elegance by modeling Fritz Perls and Virginia Satir. Bandler and Grinder noticed their use of certain powerful questions in gathering information and another set of powerful questions that essentially enabled the person to reorganize their internal world. From a linguistic analysis of their language, Bandler and Grinder developed this Meta-model. (*"Meta"* comes from Greek and means "beyond, over, about, on a different level.") The Meta-model specifies how we can use language to clarify language. It does so by re-connecting a speaker's language with the experience out of which it came.

> *The Meta-model specifies how we can use language to clarify language. It does so by re-connecting a speaker's language with the experience out of which it came.*

Obviously, the business of communication involves *language use*—it involves "sharing the word," and it involves living the word. The more we know about the neuro-linguistic processes at the root of language processing and languaging ourselves and others—the more effective our ability to handle this most incredible tool.

## Deep Structure/Surface Structure

The Meta-model provides us with a tool to get to the experience behind a person's words. When we speak, none of us gives a complete description of the thoughts behind our words. If we attempted to completely describe our thoughts, we would never finish speaking. Why? Because none of our verbal descriptions can fully or completely (exhaustively) say everything about an experience. As a speaker, we will always have a more complete internal representation of what we wish to communicate than what we can put into words. We inevitably shorten the description.

Now we call the complete internal representation (experience) of what we seek to communicate the "Deep Structure." Most of this Deep Structure lies in unconscious parts of mind and neurology—some of it at levels *prior* to words, some *beyond* where words can describe. As we seek to present, articulate and clarify our experiences, we do so in what we call "Surface Structures"—the words and sentences that represent *transforms* of the deeper levels.

While Transformational Grammar has not proven adequate to fully explain language acquisition, syntactic structure, etc., the Meta-model does not depend upon the validity or adequacy of Transformational Grammar. The Meta-model only presupposes that below (or above, depending upon the operational metaphor), there exists another level or layer of abstraction—prior to the Surface Structure out of which the Surface Structure arose. Because the human nervous system and "mind" constantly "leaves characteristics out" (Korzybski) or "deletes" (Bandler and Grinder) or functions as a "reducing valve" (Huxley), Surface Structures as cognitive "maps" suffer impoverishment. The Meta-model with its challenges involves a process whereby a person expands and extends the cognitive map, making it richer and fuller.[11]

> We call the complete internal representation (experience) of what
> we seek to communicate—*the Deep Structure*.
> The words and sentences that we speak we call **Surface Structure**.

Bandler and Grinder noted that in the process of moving from the Deep
Structure in our neurology (our neurological "map") to the Surface
Structures that come out of our conscious minds and mouths, we do three
things, which they termed "modeling processes." For the most part, we do
this naturally and apart from consciousness. First, we *delete* much if not
most of the material in the Deep Structure. Every second, approximately
two million pieces of information feed into the brain. Obviously, the brain
must screen out much information or else we would go crazy. Read the
following:

> *Paris in the*
> *the spring.*
>
> > *A snake in the*
> > *the grass.*
> >
> > > *A kick in the*
> > > *the rear.*

Lewis and Pucelik (1982) presented this in their treatment of the Meta-
model (p. 7). Did you notice as you read that you deleted one of the "the's"
in each of those sentences? Unless you put yourself into a detailed state of
mind (a proof-reader's state of mind) you made sense of the sentence by
quickly and unconsciously deleting the second "the."

Second, we *distort* the meaning and structure of information as we simplify
our description of the experience. We alter our perceptions using our
brains. A story in Eastern philosophy relates how a man walked along the
road and saw a snake. Immediately he yelled, "Snake!" But then, as he
approached it, he saw it more clearly as a rope, and not a snake.

"Beauty" lies in the eye of the beholder. The ability to distort enables us to
enjoy works of art, music and literature. Thus we can look at a cloud and
turn its vague shapes into animals, people and all kinds of things—we do
it by using our brain's power of distortion. Our ability to distort makes it
possible for us to have dreams and visions about our desired future.

Third, we *generalize* information. When new learnings come into our brain, our brain *compares* the new information with similar information previously learned. Our minds compare and generalize old similar material with new data. This process allows us to learn quickly. We do not have to relearn old concepts. Our brain utilizes them in new learnings. Although many kinds of cars exist, we relate to such through the category or class that we call "cars." Mapping out experiences, events, people, learnings, ideas, etc., through categories enables us to compare, contrast, group, subgroup, etc. This helps us handle increasingly large amounts of information, process information through logical levels, and move into more and more conceptual levels of reality.

While other mapping functions exist, the Meta-model uses these three. They describe the key processes whereby we move from the Deep Structure within our mind-neurology to our Surface Structures that show up in our language and languaging. In summary, we delete, distort and generalize information as we create our model of the world.

> *Meta-model questions*
> ***reverse*** *the process of going*
> *from Deep Structure to*
> *Surface Structure.*

What does this Meta-model consist of precisely? It consists of thirteen (in this model) language distinctions and thirteen sets of questions. These challenging questions inquire about the ill-formedness that shows up in the Surface Structures and this enables the speaker to restore the material deleted, distorted, and generalized. Meta-model questions *reverse* the process of going from Deep Structure to Surface Structure. The model reverses the abstracting process—we "de-abstract" via the Meta-model, we take a person *back to experience*. The Meta-model thus uncovers missing information in the client's communication and model of the world—often crucial information without which they live in the world with an impoverished "map." Some ask, "When do you stop asking Meta-model questions?" Good question. You stop when you have your outcome.

We have abbreviated the following description to provide an overview of this neuro-linguistic model. We would recommend that you obtain a complete description of the Meta-model and do a more in-depth study (Bandler & Grinder, 1975, Hall, 1996b).

> **The questions of the Meta-model restore:**
>
> 1. *Distortions*
> 2. *Generalizations*
> 3. *Deletions*

## Distortions

### 1. *Nominalization*

By nominalization we refer to those kinds of nouns that originated from process. They function meta to experience and symbolize whole chunks of experience. Young (1999) states, "They are iconic, like the symbols on a computer screen. When you metaphorically 'double-click' on the icon, it opens up to reveal something of the experience(s) it stands for." Nominalizations take processes and freeze them so that the process movie becomes a still picture. A nominalization can be a word that represents a process, movement, action (verb) or ideas, understandings, and concepts such as memories, rules, principles, values and beliefs.

> *Linguistically, nominalization refers to changing a Deep Structure **process** (movement, action, etc.) into a Surface Structure **static event**.*

Linguistically, nominalization refers to changing a Deep Structure *process* (movement, action, etc.) into a Surface Structure *static event*. The classic NLP description that tests for a nominalization versus a true noun asks: "Can you put it in a wheelbarrow?" If so, you have a noun! If not, then behold—a nominalization!

Another way to determine a nominalization involves seeing if the suspected word will fit in the blank of the following phrase: "An ongoing_____." A *process word* like a nominalization will make sense in that syntactic environment whereas a concrete noun will not.

Nominalizations delete large amounts of information. Consider the statement, "Our poor *relationship* really bothers me." "Relationship" functions as a nominalization, even though we generally treat it as a concrete noun. But we cannot see, hear, smell, or taste a relationship. We can't put a relationship in a wheelbarrow. Changing the verb "relating" into the pseudo-noun "relationship," nominalizes the verb. Other examples of nominalizations: *education, illness, respect, discipline, friendship, decision, love, fear, strategy* and *sensation*.

We often describe medical diseases using nominalizations. When a friend recently told me (BB) that he had ulcers, I asked, "How are you ulcerating yourself?" He immediately replied, "I have been working too many hours."

Lewis and Pucelik (1982) state:

> "In an article entitled 'Language, Emotion and Disease,' Dr. Wallace Ellerbroek makes some astute, if unorthodox, observations. Staff psychiatrist at the Metropolitan State Hospital in Norwalk, California, Dr. Ellerbroek's article addresses the effects of language on our perceptions and behaviors. He contends that '...each word you use as a label for something makes you see it in an entirely different way.' He cites the case of 'essential' hypertension, a medical condition for which the cause is unknown. His description includes the process of denominalizing the medical term, a rare action in the field of medicine in which nominalizations abound. Contrary to the generally accepted medical model, he states, 'Remember, I called all diseases 'behaviors,' in other words, things that people do... When I found a patient with elevated blood pressure (140/90 mm/Hg or more), I said to myself not 'He has hypertension' but 'He is hypertensioning.'"
>
> This transformation of the nominalization 'hypertension,' the name given to a specific set of medical conditions, back into a verb or process of 'hypertensioning' not only altered Dr. Ellerbroek's perception of his patients but also his behaviors toward them. This, says Dr. Ellerbroek, changed his patients' responses to treatment in a dramatically positive way. The implication is that as we begin to alter our language, as in the above example, we change our perceptions of the *processes* of health and disease. Ultimately, this gives us more choices about our physical and emotional conditions." (pp. 87-88):

To challenge nominalizations, we reverse the process. As a person has changed a process into a thing, we now direct him or her to *change the thing back into a process*. We do that by using the format: "In what way do you do the process of (<u>nominalization</u>)?" This question then assists the person to reconnect with the experience in a way that recognizes their role in the process.

**Examples:**

> I have a poor relationship.
> You have no respect for me.
> Our system of education stinks.
> Communication is a problem in their marriage.
> Management made poor decisions.
> His desires got him into trouble.
> Her behavior is unacceptable.

This exercise will provide you with new insights, and new understandings.

## 2. Mind Reading

We engage in mind reading when we think and assert that we know the thoughts, motives, intentions, etc., in another's mind. We do this when we say, "I know exactly how you feel." In spite of communicating sympathy, typically such statements trigger pain, resentment, misunderstanding, etc. Mind-reading Surface Structure reveals much more about *the speaker's internal experience* than the others. Accordingly, when we utter mind-reading statements, we *project* our own perceptions, values, issues, history, etc. Thus they usually have little to do with the person to whom we speak.

To challenge mind reading, ask, "How specifically do you know how I feel (think, intend, etc.)?" In response to this question, the speaker will then offer more of their internal world-model (Deep Structure). The question will allow the speaker to question assumptions and recover the source of the information.

**Examples:**

> I know he doesn't care.
> She knows better.
> I'm sure you're aware...
> I can tell you don't like me.
> He isn't interested.
> You think...
> You're upset.
> I know that you are wondering.

## 3. Cause-Effect

The over-used accusation, "You *make* me mad!" illustrates a cause-effect statement. This sentence implies that you directly make or cause me to feel mad as if I have no choice in the process. However you create this effect— when you do, I must feel this way. It seems to imply that you have a kind of psychic power over me. Words that indicate the presence of cause-effect statements include: *make, if then, as you... , then, because,* and almost any present tense verb. One of my students, John Burton, says "the word 'because' is the most influential mind changer than any other word." "Because... ?"

To challenge such statements, ask, "How specifically do I cause you to feel bad?" "By what process do I 'make' you have these feelings, thoughts, or responses?" "Do you have no choice whatever in how you respond to this stimulus?" Such responses invite the speaker to expand and enhance their map about cause-and-effect in human relationships. It empowers the speaker to take responsibility for their own feelings, thoughts, and responses. It facilitates the speaker to adopt a more pro-active response by exploring their choices.

One of the larger-level purposes of therapy involves empowering a client to recognize their response-able powers and to own their responses as their own. Clients generally feel that they suffer the effects of the causes of others. Effective counseling leads them to realize how they also stand 'at cause.' So we lead them to take control of their own lives and responses as they claim their own powers: the power to think, feel, speak, and behave.

**Examples:**

> I'm late because of you.
> When you believe in me, I can do it.
> You make me feel _____.
> I would do it, but I'm mad.
> I feel badly that I hurt him.
> Just asking that question **you begin to understand**.
> You will begin to relax as you learn the Meta-model.
> Since you're reading this sentence, you can think of several more examples.
> Because _____.

As you progress in your knowledge of NLP, you will learn the importance of getting a statement into the form of a Cause-Effect for reframing. In order to do this, you simply ask a person this question, "How is that a problem for you?" This will direct the person you are communicating with to describe the problem in Cause-Effect terms. We cover this completely in our book *Mind-Lines: Lines for Changing Minds.* Such questioning "gets on the other person's 'map'" quickly. It prepares the person for processing the reframes you will direct towards them. And, it also serves as an excellent information-gathering tool. For instance, a client seems quite agitated. Obviously the client has allowed some external event to agitate them. I ask, "How is that a problem to you?" The client will give me more information as to the specifics of their problem. One client spoke about her husband's irritating mannerisms. I inquired, "How are his mannerisms a **problem for you**?" She said, "He pisses me off." Now I had her set up for a reframe. I immediately replied, "What would happen if you pissed on your belief that he can piss you off without your permission?" Well, you can read about that in *Mind-Lines*. It just seems that when you reverse Cause-Effect you find the solution. The point—no one can make you have any thought-feelings that you choose not to have.

When we live at "Cause-Effect" we box ourselves in:

**Figure 8:1**  *Living at Cause-Effect*

When we challenge our Cause-Effect(s) (and others) we dissociate ourselves (and others) from our box(es) and give ourselves permission to ask, "Does this type thinking serve me (you)?"

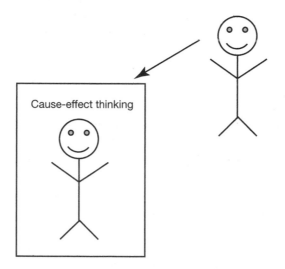

**Figure 8:2**  *Dissociating from Cause-Effect*

Before moving from Cause-Effect, we would like to make one more important point. That point is how the question "Why?" often involves Cause-Effect ill-formedness. Dennis and Jennifer Chong in their thought- provoking book, *Don't Ask Why: A Book About The Structure Of Blame, Bad Communication And Miscommunication,* point out that often when we ask the question "Why?" we are in fact looking for reasons and explanations. They conclude that, "Once you have the *reason* or *explanation,* you have the *cause.* You know what *made* you do it. The questions 'Why?' therefore seeks the elucidation of the relationship between two classes of variables or things: the class of variables that are the cause and the class of variables that are the effects" (p. 81). Thus, asking "Why?", rather than looking for solutions to the problem, will often deepen the problem by eliciting reasons and justification.

Imagine someone in your life whose behavior does not match your expectations. This works well with children. Now, note when you asked them, "Why did you do that?" if they don't have a justifiable reason their unconscious mind will create one. So, have you assisted them out of their box or have you in fact anchored them deeper into their box? Asking the *why of justification* tends to deepen the problem rather than solving the problem as the person looks for and finds reasons and justifications for their behavior. Instead of asking "Why?" try asking, "What is your purpose in doing this behavior?" This question tends to dissociate them from the problem—gets them out of their box. (We will cover this type of questioning when we get to Milton Model hypnotic language patterns in Chapter Ten.) Once the person gives you their purpose in performing their behavior, you can say something like, "Well, the behavior you are doing will not get the response you want from me. But, doing (X) is more likely to get it. You have the choice to behave as you so choose. But, I will choose my response to your behavior."

The Chongs illustrate this "out-of-the-box" thinking with the following example of the nine dot square:

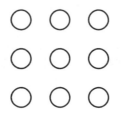

*Figure 8:3 Outside-of-the-Box Thinking*

Now, as you look at the nine dots, connect all nine dots using only four straight lines. Also, do not lift your pen off the paper nor re-trace over a line you have already drawn.

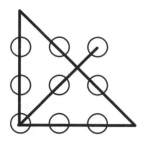

*Figure 8:4 The Solution*

To solve the problem, one must step outside the boundaries and limits of the square. Cause-Effect thinking locks us inside the box. Challenging our Cause-Effect thinking requires that we step outside our limiting belief boxes and ask, "Does this type thinking serve me?" If not, change it. After all, your thinking consists primarily of thoughts.

We contend (contrary to some in NLP) that asking some forms of "Why?" can serve us. I (MH) address this in Chapter Three of my book *Neuro-Linguistic Programming – Going Meta: Advanced Modeling Using Meta-levels.* You may also find this chapter on our (http://www.neurosemantics.com) website. Here I list the various forms of "Why?"

**The Why of Causation/Source**
"Why do you act (feel, think) that way?"

**The Why of Explanation**
"Why do you judge yourself so harshly?"

**The Why of Teleology/Outcome** (final effects, desired outcomes)
"Why do you do that?" (That is, "What do you seek to accomplish in doing that? For what purpose?")

**The Why of Value/Importance** (values, frames of references, beliefs)
"Why do you do that?" (That is, "What value does this hold for you?")
"Why do you find this important and significant?"

In that chapter I (MH) conclude:

The inhibition of the *why?* question has also created a general aversion to exploration of past "causes." With some NLPers that I have known, this has seemed to create a state of intolerance about listening or pacing a person's Problem State. They have taken the *why?* inhibition so literally and seriously (not exactly "the spirit of NLP"!), that they become distraught when they even begin to work with someone's story that involves very much historical content. They want to rush forward to giving out solutions with interventions of cure before they even begin to pace the person's model of the world.

By way of contrast we do see a more balanced approach in some of the Time-Lines processes and especially the Re-Imprinting Process of Robert Dilts. These NLP patterns certainly take a more balanced and thoughtful approach to "past" sources of difficulties and pains (that is, past beliefs, decisions, experiences, etc.). It even uses the TDS process for tracking down earlier occurrences of mapping problems around "self," worth, dignity, purpose, destiny, etc.

In this section on Cause-Effect, we just wish to warn you about the dangers of asking the *why of reason/justification*.

## 4. Complex Equivalence

We generate a complex equivalence whenever we use a part of an experience (an aspect of the external behavior) to become equivalent to the whole of its meaning (our internal state). Thus when we become aware of the external cue, we then assume the meaning of the whole experience. "You did not tell me that you love me this morning; you just don't love me anymore." Here a person has equated certain **external behaviors** (saying words that express love to someone) and an **internal state** (feeling loved). The construction of complex equivalences utilize words of equation: *is, that means, equals*, etc. A person makes one external phenomenon identical with another internal phenomenon.

We therefore take experiences that occur on different logical levels and confuse those levels so that we conceptually make some External Behavior (EB) equal to some Internal State (IS).

We challenge a complex equivalence by asking about the equation, "How specifically does my not telling you that I love you (EB) mean that I don't love you anymore (IS)?" "Have I ever failed to tell you that I loved you and yet you knew that I truly did love you?" Such questioning enables the speaker to identify the complex equivalent belief and recover additional material deleted and distorted. "When I saw Joe's face turn red (EB), I knew he was angry (IS)." This Complex Equivalence (CEq.) leads to Mind-Reading (M-R). "When you raised your voice (EB), it means you are angry" leads to a Cause-Effect (C-E).

In a Complex Equivalence we have mentally created a relationship between a word or words and some experience which those words name. Lewis and Pucelik (1982) explain:

> "For every word learned, everyone has a somewhat different internal experience. These specific experiences associated with words are called complex equivalents. Usually, the subtleties between people's understanding of words are irrelevant. However, there are words that sometime lead to misunderstanding between people. Words like *love, relationship, partnership, fear, power, trust, respect,* and any expressions linked with a person's perception of himself and the environment are critical to the process of communication…" (p. 27).

As I have mentioned that we sometimes find it most helpful to get a person's statement into the form of a Cause-Effect, we also recommend getting their statement into the form of a Complex-Equivalence. Remember, a Complex-Equivalence by definition defines the meaning we place to our Internal Representation. So, when someone makes a statement that "This means _____ to me" they have in essence defined the first level meaning they have placed onto their Internal Representation.

Therefore, we can take any statement a person gives us in whatever form and ask them, "What does that mean to you?" and we will chunk down on their statement towards the first level meaning they have given to their Internal Representations. If you believe they haven't chunked down specific enough, just repeat, "And, what does that mean to you?" This will direct the person to describe more in detail the meaning of their statement. And, similar to the Cause-Effect question, "How is that a problem to you?" **it prepares them for a reframe**. You can say, "Well, I know you believe it means this, but could you consider the possibility that he may mean _____ to you?" Now, of course, I have gotten ahead of myself. I just wanted to introduce you to the importance of the Meta-model. (See *Mind-Lines: Lines for Changing Minds*.)

**Examples:**

> Joe's face is red. That must mean he is angry.
> Being here means you will change.
> Going to bed early means you will be alert.
> You know the answer, so you are competent.
> Sitting in this room, you are learning many things.
> As you master these skills, you will be a better communicator.
> Keeping your eyes open like that means you'll go into trance.
> And closing your eyes means you'll go even deeper.
> That means…

## 5.  Presuppositions

By the term *presupposition*, we refer to the conceptual and linguistic assumptions that have to exist in order for a statement to make sense. By definition, we do not state our presuppositions—they operate rather as the supporting foundation or context of a given statement. In presuppositions we find the person's beliefs about life, the world, self, others, God, etc. And we all operate from specific presuppositions. So when we learn to listen for presuppositions we can hear a lot about the person's model of the world. Presuppositions function similar to Mind-Reads. They just leave out the "I know." Any non-sensory-specific language will contain presuppositions.

Presuppositions in language work covertly, indirectly, and unconsciously as we have to accept them and their assumptions in order to make sense of the communication. A presupposition can operate positively as with the fundamental Christian belief that God loves every person. And some presuppositions can impose limitations on us. Many presuppositions that limit us begin with *"why"* questions. We can also learn to listen for such terms as: *since, when, if, etc.*

The sentence: "Why don't you work harder?" presupposes that the recipient does not work hard enough. "If you only knew, you would understand my pain" presupposes the recipient does not understand the speaker's pain.

To challenge a presupposition, inquire about the assumptions in the state-ment. "What leads you to believe that I don't work hard enough? Hard enough according to what standard? "What leads you to believe that I don't know your pain?" "How specifically do you assume I need to work harder?" Or, "How would you like me to specifically understand your pain?" What presuppositions lie in this? "You have learned a lot about presuppositions." "How excited do you now feel having learned about the Meta-model and its powerful questions?" "When do you think you would best like to study and practice learning the Meta-model to become even more proficient?"

**Examples:**

> We have talked about presuppositions.
> You are learning about the Meta-model and the powerful questions the Meta-model gives us.
> If you would study and practice, you would learn the Meta-model.
> You can do this even better.
> You are changing all the time.
> How else do you **go into trance**?

You're seeing things differently now.
You'll be able to learn even more tomorrow.
You realize you have more resources than ever before.
You can easily move in the direction of your past memories.
Most of the examples of this pattern will be written here by you.
You are learning many things.

## Generalizations

### 6.   *Universal Quantifiers*

A universal quantifier refers to the set of words that make a universal generalization. They imply a state of absoluteness—of "allness." In this generalization we make one category represent a whole group. Thus we move from "Dad abused me at seven years of age," to "Men always abuse." This statement generalizes from a particular to the whole class. Generalizations have no reference point. They are intentionally vague.

Universal quantifiers consist of such words as: *all, never, every, always* and *none*. Such words do not leave room for any exceptions. By definition they express a limited mindset. The Meta-model challenge to a universal quantifier involves simply repeating the word back to the person in the form of a question. To "All men are abusers" we could respond: "All?" Another challenge involves asking if the speaker has *ever* met a man who did *not* abuse. This challenge brings out the absurdity of the universal quantifier.

**Examples:**

All Christians are hypocrites.
Every politician is a liar.
Everyone on welfare is lazy.
Nobody's perfect.
Everything is wonderful.
We are all in trance now.
There is always tomorrow.
Everybody knows this part is easy.
One can never know all there is to know.
All of the people doing this process are learning many new things.
And all the things, all the things…

### 7.   *Modal Operators*

This linguistic distinction refers to our *mode* whereby we *operate* in the world. Do we operate from a mental world of **laws** (should, must, have to);

do we operate from a world of **opportunities** (possible, possible to, can); do we operate from a world of **obligations** (ought, should); or **empowerment** (dare, want to, desire to), etc.? In other words these modal operator terms define the boundaries of our model of the world and our style of operation.

| |
|---|
| *Modal operator terms define the boundaries of our model of the world and our style of operation.* |

This suggests, as do all of the Meta-model distinctions, that we can actually learn to *hear* *people's belief systems* in their talk! NLP assumes that our language reveals and prescribes the quality and limits of our belief systems.

So words like *can* and *cannot, should* and *should not* reveal personal beliefs about what we can or cannot do in life. Now modal operators come in several categories. We have the modal operators of necessity, of possibility, impossibility, empowerment, identity, choice, etc. These modes show up in words like *can/cannot, possible/impossible, am/am not, and will/will not*, etc.

Listening for such words informs us what a client believes stands as possible or impossible in their world. "I can't change my beliefs." "I can't learn efficiently." "I can't imagine saying that." Such language not only describes their limits, it creates such limitations. Modal operators of **possibility** tell us what a person believes possible.

The Meta-model challenge to such goes: "What would happen if you did change that belief?" Or, "What stops you from doing that?"

Fritz Perls reframed "I can't..." by saying, "Don't say I can't, say I won't." If a client accepted that statement, they moved from no choice to choice, from effect of a problem to the cause of such. All of therapy has to do with putting the client *at cause*. The presupposition in the phrase, "Don't say I can't, say I won't," assumes that the client can choose.

**Necessity** words include: *must/must not, should/should not, ought/ought not, have to, need to* and *it is necessary*. These describe a model of the world that believes in necessity. Such words define some governing rule the person operates from. Often these rules limit behavior. Telling children that they *should* do their homework can induce a state of guilt (pseudo-guilt). Modal operators of necessity work wonderfully for creating such guilt. Yet if guiltiness doesn't strike you as a particularly resourceful place to come from for studying, instead of telling children that they **should** do their homework, we can tell them that they *can* do their homework. "And I *get* to help you with it."

The Meta-model challenge to a modal operator of necessity: "What would happen if you did/didn't... ?" "I *should* go to church!" Response: "What would happen if you did go?" This will elicit specific reasons why they should go to church. The question goes to the Deep Structure and facilitates the person to recover effects and outcome. It moves the client into the future. Examples: "I really should be more flexible at times like this." "I ought to go back to school." "I have to take care of her." "You should learn."

These questions come from Cartesian Logic. One can introduce this unique form of questioning by saying, "You have been thinking about this one way for quite a while and your thinking hasn't changed. May I suggest another line of thinking? (Get their agreement either verbally or non-verbally.) What would happen if you did change that belief?" etc.

Rene Pfalzgraf (1991) points out the effectiveness of utilizing a person's modal operators of necessity in motivating them:

> "Some words will be more demanding and motivating than others. If you can discover that hierarchy and then employ it, you will begin to discover that it is easier to motivate a person to do something."

Suppose someone says, "I should go back to college. I really need to get more education." Both of those sentences have a modal operator of necessity within them ("should" and "need to"). In replying, feed back the modal operator sequence in order to motivate them. "I agree with you. You *should* go back to school because we all *need* more education."

### Examples: Modal Operators of Necessity:

I really should be more flexible at times like this.
I ought to go back to school.
You should not hurry into trance just yet.
You shouldn't go into trance too quickly, now.
You must be getting this now… at some level…
I have to take care of her.
You should learn.

### Examples: Modal Operators of Possibility/Impossibility:

I can't learn.
I couldn't tell him what I think.
You could learn this now.
You could write this down… or not.
You could feel more and more peaceful.
You can change overnight.
You may hear the words of wisdom.
It's possible to learn everything easily and quickly.

You could come up with a few more examples, now.
You can learn.

## 8.   Lost Performative

When we *perform* upon our world with value judgments, we speak about important values that we believe in. But in a *Lost Performative* we have stated a value judgment while deleting the performer (speaker) of the value judgment. As a vague value judgment, a Lost Performative will push the person into the direction you wish for them to go. "You don't love me." Note that the value judgment leaves off the name of the person doing the judging but it directs attention to "love me."

"Boys shouldn't cry." "If you're going to do something, give it your best." "That is a stupid thing you just did." In these sentences the speaker has made a value judgment about something. Yet statements fail to inform us *who* said such or where the person got that value judgment.

To challenge a lost performative and restore the deleted and distorted material, ask: "Who says boys shouldn't cry?" "Who evaluates my actions as stupid?" "According to whom do you say such?" Or even more succinctly, ask, "Says who?" These questions require that the speaker access more information in the Deep Structure and identify the source of the judgments. Until we identify the source, we will lack the ability to challenge the statement's validity.

### Examples:

Oh, it's not important anyway.
It's not good to be strict.
That's too bad.
Today is a great day.
No one should judge others.
That's perfect!
It's really good that you say that.
One doesn't have to…
And, it is a good thing to wonder.

## Deletions

### 9.   Simple Deletions

A simple deletion occurs when the communicator leaves out information about a person, thing or relationship.

**Examples:**

> I am uncomfortable.
> I feel afraid.
> I am hurting.
> I feel alone.
> I don't know.

### 10. Comparative Deletions

In a comparative deletion someone makes a comparison, but deletes either the specific persons, things, or items compared or the standard by which the speaker makes the comparison. Words like *better, best, further, nearer, richer, poorer, more, less, most, least, worse, etc.,* provide cues of comparative deletions. What you compare to functions as a presupposition and the other person's unconscious mind will fill in what's missing.

"He is much better off." The challenge: "Better off than who?" "Better off according to what standard?"

**Examples:**

> He is the best student in the class.
> She is the least likely person I know to have succeeded.
> And it is more or less the right thing to do.

### 11. Lack of Referential Index or Unspecified Nouns and Verbs

By *referential index* we refer to the person or thing that does or receives the action from the verb in the statement. When a sentence lacks a referential index, it fails to specify by name, term, or phrase that it references—whom it speaks about. It fails to specify or point to a specific person or group. The pronouns (*one, it, they, people,* etc.) are unspecified. Crucial material from the Deep Structure that completes the meaning has been deleted.

Listen for words like *one, they, nobody* and *this*. "They did not come to the meeting." Here the speaker failed to specify the subject of the verb.

To challenge and recover the deleted material, we ask, "Who specifically did not come to the meeting?"

In the statement, "Those people hurt me" the noun phrase ("those people") like the unspecified verb ("hurt") lacks a referential index. So we inquire, "Who specifically hurt you?"

**Examples:**

> They don't listen to me.
> Nobody cares anymore.
> This is unheard of.
> One can, you know.

## 12. Unspecified Verb

Unspecified verbs describe vague, non-specific action. Words like *hurt*, *upset, injure, show, demonstrate, care* and *concern* certainly describe action, a process, a set of events or experiences—but they have left out so much of the specific information about the action that we cannot make a clear representation in our mind about that action. She says, "He hurt me," but we don't know if he slapped her, left her waiting at the mall, molested her, insulted the pie she baked, etc.

We recover such deleted material by asking, "How did he hurt you exactly?" "Who specifically hurt you?" If we fail to ask for the deleted information, we run the risk of inventing it in our own minds! While we may make good guesses if we know enough of the context and background, we may also make guesses that miss the other person's meaning by light years.

When we hear a sentence with an unspecified verb ("She misunderstood me"), the potential exists for much misunderstanding, because we can interpret it in many different ways. The questions will connect the person more fully to their experience. In terms of well-formedness we do not provide a sufficient enough linguistic "map" for the other person to get a clear message.

**Examples:**

> You don't care about me.
> I upset my mother.
> He doesn't show me any concern.
> I was wondering.
> If only you knew.
> You may discover.
> And you can learn this.

## Conclusion

Most sentences in our everyday languaging contain numerous Meta-model violations. As you hear them, start at the larger level violation and challenge the distortions first. Then go to the generalizations. And finally, challenge the deletions. Why? Because since every sentence has lots of deletions, if you start there, you could challenge deletions all day long. Since distortions carry the most weight and operate at a higher logical level, when we challenge them first, we get greater leverage on the person's Deep Structure.

You can now begin to use this Meta-model to enable you to get specific information in a client's Deep Structure. The questions provided by the Meta-model enable you to *chunk the person down* to details and specificity. As such, the Meta-model facilitates the uncovering of crucial information which then empowers one to expand their world-model. At the same time, the questions of the Meta-model function to essentially bring a client out of trance. To put a client in trance, we would use the reverse language patterns, and in NLP, the reverse patterns show up in a model that we call the Milton Model (see Chapter Ten).

After I (MH) first learned the Meta-model, I didn't think all that much of it. "Just simple stuff, I do that anyway." Then later at my master practitioner NLP training, Bandler talked about *everything* in NLP—every model, every process, every technique, every pattern, as having arisen from the Meta-model and to not know this model inside-out prevents one from understanding how to model. That grabbed my attention.

"How could he think of this simple model as *that powerful?*" "Why would he put that much stress and importance on it?" I didn't know. So I went back to the model and studied it "inside-out," and came away from that study with the same conviction that *to know this model gives you the ability to handle language, to not get bamboozled by language, and to challenge language instead of assuming it as real.* Later, I wrote my doctoral dissertation on *Languaging* and after exploring the foundations of General Semantics, along with several other therapy models, I added eight more pieces to the Meta-model. I finally concluded that if a person knows the Meta-model, they know the essence of good critical thinking skills and how to challenge and explore the logic of a statement.

---

**You have our permission to duplicate the following two pages of the Meta-model of Language.
I (BB) encourage my students to keep one copy on their desk and one in the shirt pocket/billfold or purse.
Refer to it often over the next year or so. You will spend your time well installing this model in your unconscious mind.**

---

## The Meta-Model of Language

| Pattern | Response | Prediction |
|---|---|---|
| **DISTORTIONS** | | |
| 1.  Nominalizations<br>Process words frozen in time<br>"We lack communication." | Turn noun back into verb<br>"Who's not communicating?"<br>"How would you like to communicate?" | Recovers the process, actions, movements, etc. |
| 2.  Mind-Reading<br>Claiming to know someone's internal state<br>"You have a problem with authority." | Question source of data.<br>"How do you know . . .?"<br>"What lets you know . . .?" | Recovers source, means<br>Discovers process |
| 3.  Cause-Effect<br>"Causation" assumed without adequate description<br>"You make me angry." | Ask about process.<br>"How does this process work?"<br>"How does what I'm doing cause you to choose to feel angry?" | Recover the mechanism that explains the cause<br><br>Recovers the choice |
| 4.  Complex Equivalence<br>Two experiences interpreted as synonymous<br>"Her frown means she's rejecting me." | Ask about the equation<br>E.B. = I.S. (External Behavior = Internal State)<br>"How do you equate her frown with feeling rejected?"<br>"Has anyone ever frowned at you that didn't reject you?" | Recovers the External Behavior and Internal State<br>Recovers Complex Equivalence<br>Counter Example |
| 5.  Presuppositions<br>"If you knew the importance of school, you would study harder." | Ask about assumptions<br>"What leads you to think that I don't know the importance of school?"<br>"How do you assume this statement holds true for me?"<br>"I don't study efficiently?" | Recover assumed ideas |
| **GENERALIZATIONS** | | |
| 6.  Universal Quantifiers<br>Universal generalizations such as all, every, never, no one, etc. | Find Counter Example<br>"All?"<br>"Never?" | Recovers exceptions, causes, details, Counter Examples |
| 7.  Modal Operators:<br>a. Modal operators of necessity/desire as in should, shouldn't, must, must not, have to, need to, it is necessary<br>"I have to take care of her."<br>b. Modal operators of possibility/impossibility as in can/can't, will/won't, may/may not, possible/ impossible<br>"I can't tell him the truth." | a. "What would happen if you did?"<br>"What would happen if you didn't?"<br>"Or?"<br><br>b "What prevents you?"<br>"What would happen if you did?" | Recovers mode of operation<br>Recovers causes |

## The Meta-Model of Language (continued)

| Pattern | Response | Prediction |
|---|---|---|
| **GENERALIZATIONS (continued)** | | |
| 8.   Lost Performative<br>Value judgments apart from originator<br>"It's bad to judge." | Seek source of statement<br>"Who says it's bad to judge?"<br>"Says who?'<br>"How do you know?" | Gathers evidence<br>Recovers source |
| **DELETIONS** | | |
| 9.   Simple Deletions<br>"I am uncomfortable." | "About what/whom?" | Recovers deletion |
| 10.  Comparative Deletion<br>As in good, better, best, worst, more, less, most, least<br>"She's a better person." | "Better than whom?'<br>"Better at what?"<br>"Compare to whom or what?" | Recovers<br>Comparative Deletions |
| 11.  Lack of Referential Index<br>Unspecified nouns and verbs—fails to specify a person or thing<br>"They don't listen to me." | "Who doesn't listen to you?" | Recovers the noun<br>or Referential Index |
| 12.  Unspecified Verbs<br>Those verbs where the statement leaves out the person doing the acting or the desired action.<br>"You don't care about me." | "How specifically do I not care about you?' | Specifies the verb |

*Figure 8:5 The Meta-model of Language*

## Extending The Meta-model

The following nine linguistic distinctions indicating ill-formedness in the mapping process along with Meta-model challenges to elicit from the speaker a more well-formed cognitive "map" come from Alfred Korzybski (1933,1994) in his classic work, *Science and Sanity*, as well as from REBT (Rational-Emotive Behavioral Therapy). The abbreviated form of this comes from the research of Michael Hall in *Languaging (1996)* and *The Secrets of Magic (1998)*.

### 1.   Identity/Identification (Id.)

Like a complex equivalence, an *identification* statement makes an equation between things on different levels of abstraction, although here the equation involves a "self" identity equation, "I am... X" "He is a... X."

"She's nothing more than a ...X!" These involve the two most dangerous forms of mapping false-to-fact (doesn't fit the territory at all), namely, "the 'is' of identification," and "the 'is' of predication." Predicating qualities even at the perceptual level ("the rose is red") fails to map the interaction of what we receive from the world and the contributions of our sense receptors (rods and cones). Predicating judgments (our evaluations, meanings) takes this to a higher level ("He is a jerk.")

This Korzybskian language distinction closely corresponds to a complex equivalence and yet it differs. For Korzybski, **identity** meant *"absolute sameness in all respects."* His "all" in this definition functions to make identity impossible. If we eliminate the "all" from the definition, then the word *"absolute"* also loses its meaning. Then we simply have "sameness in *some* respects," an acceptable concept since by it we understand "same" as "similar." The concept of similarity, in fact, would enable us to create, work with, and use generalizations, labels, categories, etc., appropriately. Yet if we alter the ideas of "absolute" and "all," that would not leave us with "identity" at all, only *similarity.*

In the world we only deal with unique individual persons, events, and things. There only exists non-identity in the world of cognitive processes. Every event stands as unique, individual, absolute, unrepeatable. No individual or event can exist as the "same" from one moment to the next.

When we engage in *identifying*, we experience a comparatively inflexible, rigid form of adaptation, low degree conditionality, and neurological necessity. This represents an animal adaptation, inadequate for modern man (p. 195). Identification frequently shows up in the **"to be" verbs** (is, am, are, was, were, be, being, been, etc.), which David Bourland, Jr. (1991) has called "the deity mode" of thinking and speaking. "This is that!" "That's how it is!"

> *When we engage in **identifying**, we experience a comparatively inflexible, rigid form of adaptation, low degree conditionality, and neurological necessity... Identification frequently shows up in the "to be" verbs (is, am, are, was, were, be, being, been, etc.)...*

In identifying, we erroneously conclude that what occurs inside our skin (that is, ideas, understandings, concepts) has objective existence. Psychologically, this leads to **projection** and then to other mental mapping mistakes: delusions, illusions, and hallucinations (pp. 456-457).

The insane and damaging "ises" include: *the "is" of identity* ("I am..." "You are..." "That is...") and *the "is" of predication* ("The apple is red"). When used as an auxiliary verb "is" ("Smith is coming") the "is" simply contributes to another verb and does not create a lot of semantic difficulties. The "is" of existence points to events and things that "stand out" in our perception.

Identification erroneously evaluates the products of our thinking-and-feeling as having objective existence. Yet ascribing such external objectivity to words causes us to map out untrue and unuseful representations. Evaluation only occurs in mind. It exists and operates only as a mental phenomenon at the level of thoughts.

The following responses enable us to challenge identifications, to de-identify and to recognize the unique distinctions of reality.

(1) **Extensionalize.** To make specific what otherwise might become falsely identified. Korzybski said that *the extensional method* deals structurally with the many definite individuals that distinguish and separate (p. 135). We can extensionalize by indexing specifics (who, when, where, how, which, etc.), by making distinctions, by hyphenating, and by E-Priming our language.

(2) **Differentiate** realities. Since "identity" never occurs in the world, by rejecting the very concept of the "is" of identity, we actually accept differences and differentiation as fundamental (pp. 93-94). Now we can begin to look for, and specify, the absolute individuality of events. *How do these things that seem similar and which you have identified differ?*

(3) **Sub-scripting** words with time-dates or space-locations (the indexing process). Such subscripting assists us in dealing with the absolute individuality of every event at every time. Since the world and ourselves consist of processes, every Smith1950 exists as quite a different person from Smith1995 (p. 263). This individualizing assists us in making distinctions. Depression1991 differs from depression1994; depressionBob differs from depressionSusan. By time-indexing we specify the date of our verbal statements. We can do the same with person-indexing, place-indexing, and even process-indexing.

(4) **Practice silence at the unspeakable levels.** A central technique for eliminating the "is" of identify involves training in recognizing "the unspeakable level of experience." In the place of repressing or suppressing,
"we teach silence on the objective level in general... Any bursting into speech is not repressed; a gesture of the hand to... the objects, or action, or happenings,

or feelings. Such a procedure has a most potent semantic effect. It gives a semantic jar; but this jar is not repression, but the realization of a most funda-mental, natural, structural fact of evaluation" (p. 481).

## 2.   *Static Words (Signal Words, One-Valued Terms)* (SW)

Like nominalizations, these terms indicate a frozen process turned into a frozen noun, and they do more. They indicate a use of such terms as if they only had one value to them. This arises from Aristotelian logic, according to Korzybski. "Whatever is, is." "Nothing can both be and not be." These terms often indicate a forgetting of the "map-territory" distinction.

Because of our tendency to *nominalize* verbs (reify processes) and to there-fore make static, definite, and absolutistic one-valued statements (p. 140), this leads us to create static expressions. These one-valued, static words and statements come across as sounding absolute and dogmatic thereby making our statements sound like pronouncements from heaven. Korzybski said that this creates a "legislative semantic mood," absolutisms, and "the deity mode."

Aristotelian logic graphically illustrates such. The law of identity, "Whatever is, is." The law of contradiction: "Nothing can both be and not be." The law of excluded middle: "Everything must either be or not be."

Use the following means to challenge and question these linguistic 'maps':

(1) **Extensionalize.** Enumerate the collection of items out of which we create the generalization. Extensionalize by dating and timing the referents. *"Point out to me specifically what you mean."*

(2) **De-infinitize the state.** Do this by identifying the stages and variables within the static over-generalized word. The extensional attitude repre-sents the only one that accords with the survival order and nervous structure (p. 173).

(3) **Ask meaning questions.** *What do you mean by... ?* Recognizing that words merely function as *vehicles* of meaning (effectively or ineffec-tively transporting meaning) enables us to remember that words exist as vehicles for our definitions. Therefore their existence operates as entirely arbitrary and optional. At the verbal level, all of our words and sentences exist only as *forms of representations* that evoke semantic reactions in our nervous system. When we realize that the objective level lies outside of our skin, then we can fully appreciate that events exist as un-speakable, absolute, and individual. Whatever we say about

anything, *those words "are" not that thing*. Words and things exist on different logical levels. Our words merely express a verbalization about things. Static words convey a false-to-fact understanding. They over-evaluate words as things and falsely ascribe an objectivity to words that they do not and cannot have. Asking, *What do you mean?* avoids ascribing our own meanings to another's words.

(4) **Develop the skill to "go meta"** to move into higher levels of abstraction. This human capacity for higher abstracting makes for sanity and prevents the semantic blockage of being stuck at a word. *What do you mean by that word? How does your use of this word contrast with X?*

## 3.  Over-/Under- Defined Terms (O/U)

Bandler and Grinder mentioned Korzybski and the role of "extensional" and "intensional" definitions in *Magic, Vol. I* (p. 56). Korzybski spoke of them also in terms of *over- and under- defined terms*. He said that we mainly **over-define terms** as we use an intensional orientation. This means moving into the world assuming that our dictionary definition of terms offers a completely satisfactory form of mapping. Hence, the gal who marries "a good husband." Without extensionalizing the specific functions, behaviors, etc., of the guy who she sees in the category of "husband," she may later discover the "territory" different from her "map"!

Korzybski asserted that we have **over-/under- defined** most terms. We over-define (or over-limit) words **by intension** when we over-trust our verbal or dictionary definition. As we over-believe in our definition of the word as "reality," we give it too much substance and concreteness. We under-define words by using too much **extension** (using too many specific facts and details) so that the generalizations become merely hypothetical.

For example, a woman finds and marries "a good husband." This conceptual linguistic reality ("a good husband") exists, totally, and absolutely **not** as something in the world, but as *a verbal definition in her mind*. If she fails to recognize this, it will set her up for disappointment and neurological shock. The same occurs with all other generalized terms that exist only in the mind. We over-trust evaluative terms (in contradistinction to sensory-based words) like beauty, ugly, good, bad, productive, useful, wonderful, exciting, traumatic, etc., and our intensional orientation itself can do us harm.

Utterances may have both extensional and intensional meanings. "Angels watch over my bed at night" certainly has several intensional meanings, but no extensional meanings.

"When we say that the statement has no extensional meaning, we are merely saying that we cannot see, touch, photograph, or in any scientific manner detect the presence of angels."

This distinction proves valuable because extensional statements have an empirical and sensory-based nature. Thus with them we can bring an argument to a close. "This room measures fifteen feet long." No matter how many guesses individuals make about the room, all discussion ceases when someone produces a tape measure.

Not so with intensional meanings. Here discussions and arguments can go on world without end. "You have decorated this room in a really nice way." This statement can provoke all kinds of disagreements, because the speaker has not based it on "sense," but based upon "non-sense" evaluations, meanings, definitions (intensional meanings). The utterance does not refer to sense data at all; so one cannot collect sense data to end the discussion. The speaker's statement does not refer primarily to the external world—but to their *internal world of evaluations*.

To question these linguistic forms of ill-formedness, we can:

(1) **Chunk down the over-defined words** of intensional statements and chunk up the under-defined words. This evokes a richer representation of the person's meaning(s) and reference(s). Ask the person for extensional evidence of their intentional meanings.

(2) **Explore** a person's presuppositions in their undefined terms. Ask, *"What does this assume? What have you presupposed in stating this?"* This gets them to put their epistemology out on the table.

### 4.   *Delusional Verbal Splits* (DVS)

I use this phrase to highlight the General Semantic (GS) emphasis on *"Elementalism."* Korzybski said that we often take reality-as-a-whole and split it up into parts (in our languaging) and then forget the "map-territory" distinction. The result: we begin to treat the "map" "elements" that we have identified as real and separate. Hence, "mind" and "body" as if you can have one without the other. "Space" and "time." Quoting Einstein, Korzybski suggested that in the territory we only have a "space-time" continuum and this introduced the field of quantum mechanics. We only have "mind-body," "thoughts-emotions," etc.

> Korzybski said that we often take reality-as-a-whole and split it up into parts (in our languaging) and then forget the "map -territory" distinction. The result: we begin to treat the "map" elements that we have identified as real and separate.

Words provide a good function as they enable us to sort, separate, divide, and categorize the ever-connected flow of processes of the world. Words split up, sort out, organize, and punctuate the flux of reality. Verbally (but not actually) we split up the world by means of our conceptual ideas. By languaging we inevitably **dichotomize** the rich interconnectedness of reality. This creates "elements" or pieces of reality. Yet, sometimes we forget that we have so slaughtered the territory and begin to believe that the elements exist as separate entities. This Korzybski called "elementalism."

In language we talk about "body" *and* "mind," "emotion" *and* "intellect," "space" *and* "time," etc. The referent of these individual words **do not exist in reality as separate elements**. They cannot exist as separate elements. Their existence involves an interconnected process. We can only split them *at the verbal level* in thinking and talking about the parts of these things. In linguistic form (mental conceptual form) we treat them as separate words. This makes them "elementalistic" and false-to-fact—not accurately repre-senting the territory.

Since we cannot actually, literally, or really separate "emotions" and "intellect," this division structurally violates the organism-as-a-whole generalization (p. 65). So with "body" and "soul," and other **verbal splittings**—by them we only confuse understanding, hamper development, and create false-to-fact ideas. An elementalistic terminology assumes a sharp division between "mind" and "senses," "percept" and "concept," etc. To challenge these elementalisms:

(1) **Hyphenate** the Verbal Delusional Split. When you catch elementalizing and dichotomizing in language, stick in *hyphens*. Korzybski said this functional process enables us to reconnect holistic processes that we can only separate verbally. "A little dash here and there may be of serious semantic importance when we deal with symbolism" (p. 289). Hence, "time-space," "mind-body," etc. Organism-as-a-whole words provide a representation that remind us of the systemic nature of the world. It reminds us of the holistic and inseparable processes with which we deal.

(2) **Question the elementalism.** *"Does X truly stand alone? What context does X occur within? Can we deal with X without also considering Y or Z?"*

## 5. Either-Or Terms and Phrases (E-O)

Another Aristotelian way of thinking involved viewing and languaging things in either-or terms, thereby create two-valued terms. Yet with most things in the world, this maps another false-to-fact distinction—leaving out the excluded middles, continua, and both-and perspectives.

When we make statements phrased in an Either-Or format, we represent the territory, and orient ourselves to that representation, as if it only offered two choices in viewing, valuing, and responding. Yet this seldom accurately represents reality.

We have created an either-or orientation and set of representations in psychology with the classic heredity/environment, nature/nurture, genetic/learning debate. Yet such false-to-fact concepts assumes that we can divide an organism's characteristics into two distinct classes: one due to heredity, the other to environment. This demonstrates the excluded middle of Aristotelian logic. It excludes any kind of inter-actionalism as a third possibility. Yet undoubtedly human experience arise from *an interaction* between genes and environment, between inherent hard-wired nature and the nurture we receive along the way. To challenge these:

(1) **Reality test the Either-Or structure.** *"Does this reflect an either-or situation? Can I discover any in-betweens, grays, or other considerations which may enter into consideration and influence my representation of this reality?"*

(2) **Explore the possibility of Both-And.** *"Could we have overlooked that in some way, at a larger frame, or in different contexts, both of these seemingly opposite responses stand as true? In what way could we consider both of these choices as accurate and useful?"*

## 6. Pseudo-Words (PW)

*Non-Referencing Words* (Masquerading Noises & Spell-Marks)

Korzybski also called these "noises" (in the auditory channel) and "spell-marks" (in the visual). Here we find linguistic "maps", but they reference nothing. Nothing exists in the actual world or in the world of logic (logical existence) to which such words can stand as true symbols.

When we use words that actually refer to nothing outside themselves, we merely make noises. What shall we say of "maps" that allude to no actual territory? We might find them interesting, even entertaining. Science fiction depends on such! But shall we find them useful to conveying accurate information or orienting ourselves to reality? No. They exist as *pseudo-words*. This makes them tricky. They look like words, they sound like words, yet they do not reference anything real—whether in the world of physics or the world of meaning and communication. These **non-refer-encing words** have no referent. These **noises** made with the mouth or **marks spelled** on paper only give that impression.

How do we tell the difference between *true and pseudo words*? What criteria do we use? By definition, for a sound or image to function as a true word it must *operate as a symbol that stands for* something other than itself. To the extent that it stands for, or refers to, something, **it serves as a true symbol,** elicits internal representations, and mentally "anchors" the referent. If it does not, it *merely stands as a noise*. It refers to nothing. Before a noise or image can function as a symbol, something must "exist" (actually or logically). If it does not, then it simply functions as *a semantic noise*, hence a meaningless sign (p. 79).

Before a noise (or a mark-sign—doing it in writing) can exist as a symbol, **something must exist**. Then the symbol can symbolize that existing thing, process, or concept. In language and "knowledge" there exists two kinds of existences. We have both *physical existence and logical existence*. So unicorns do not exist in the external world of unaided nature. They do not belong to zoology. When we apply the word unicorn to the field of zoology, we employ a pseudo-word. If we employ the word with reference to mythology or human fancy—the word there has a referent and functions meaningfully as a symbol (pp. 81-82).

Korzybski calls this a form of fraud since it literally involves "the use of *false representations*." The word *"heat"* illustrates this (Korzybski, p. 107). Grammatically, we classify the term "heat" as a substantive (noun). Yet physicists labored for centuries looking for some "substance" which would correspond to the substantive "heat." They never found it. It does not exist. Today we know that no such *thing* as "heat" exists. "Heat" refers to a manifestation of "energy" which arises as a process, or action, between processes. A verb or adverb (thermo-dynamic) more accurately represents the referent. Today we recognize that no such "substance" as "heat" exists, so we talk about **the process** of "thermo-dynamics."

What we call "heat" speaks about *our sense of temperature*, the result of energy. "Heat" speaks about a relationship between phenomena in motion. To use this non-referencing word as a word engages in *a linguistic fiction* false-to-facts. No wonder the scientists looking for "heat" found themselves ill-adjusted to reality. Here, the verbal symbolism of language did not point to anything; it had no reference. Linguistically, the word deceptively mapped a road that took people down a blind alley.

Verbal forms which have no meanings, no actual referents function as pseudo-words, a mere mechanism of our symbolism. So with *spell-marks* (noises which we can spell). They have the appearance of words, but we should not consider them words since they say nothing in a given context (pp. 137-138). In practical life, we often do not even suspect collections of noises (spell-marks) as functioning without meaning (p. 142).

As we realize that many "words" have no referent, but that we use such pseudo-words this enables us to **not** immediately "buy into" words. Many find this absolutely shocking having so long confused "map" with "territory." Yet once we make this distinction, we will shortly develop a new automatic response to words. We will first test words to make sure of them as true symbols. To challenge non-referencing words:

(1) **Reality test** the reference. Challenge pseudo-words by *referencing* them. Date and time index the referents. *"Suppose I could see-hear-feel this, what would I see or hear or feel? To what kind or dimension of reality does this word refer?"*

(2) **Explore** the possibility of the word as a non-referencing word. *"Could this word, term or phrase have no actual referent in reality, but exist as a fictional and constructed understanding? Does this linguistic symbol reference anything that has actual or logical existence?"*

## 7. *Multi-Ordinality* (MO)

These nominalizations have another quality, namely, they stand for terms that have no specific referent, hence only an over-generalized meaning, and the meaning and referent changes according to the level of abstraction or context. These then involve infinite-valued terms, hence multi-ordinal. And they have a reflexivity so that we can use them on themselves.

Multiordinal words, involving a deletion and generalization show up as words that we can use on many different levels of abstraction—hence multi-ordinal. Some exist as so multiordinal in nature that they function as an infinite-value term. These exist as among the most common terms we use in life.

"Mankind, science, mathematics, man, education, ethics, politics, religion, sanity, insanity, iron, wood, apple, object, etc." We use them not as one-valued terms for constants of some sort, but as terms with inherently infinite-valued or variable referents (pp.138-139, 433).

A majority of our terms consist of names for *infinite-valued stages of processes with a changing content*, hence multi-ordinal in nature. They represent infinite-valued variables and in principle, exist neither as true nor false, but ambiguous in meaning. Consider "love" as multiordinal. To challenge these:

(1) **Use co-ordinates.** Using co-ordinates enables us to assign single values to the variable (p. 139). We can identify **time** co-ordinates or **space** co-ordinates to contextualize the specific referent. If a word or phrase expresses ambiguity, we need to contextualize the level of abstraction. This makes the multiordinal word specific—preventing it from remaining ambiguous. These words frequently appear as nominalizations. When they do, simply de-nominalize them by recovering the hidden verb or process (p. 208).

(2) **Chunk down to the specific referents at each level of abstraction.** Here it helps to develop a behavioristic and functional set of words to map our abstracting with specific descriptions. Descriptive language order the happenings on the objective level in sensory-based terms (p. 264). Functional words enable us to translate dynamic processes into static forms and static processes into dynamic forms.

(3) **Check for reflexivity.** Can you self-reflexively turn the word back onto itself? This provides a good test for multi-ordinality. As we distinguish multi-ordinal words as those terms that can operate on many levels of abstraction, this enables us to recognize their nature and how they function in our languaging. Can you move to another level and still use the term? This question tests for multiordinality. "Do you love someone? Do you love loving them? Do you love loving love?" "Do you have a prejudice? What about a prejudice against prejudice?" "What science relates to this?" "Do you also have a science of this science?" This reflexivity test will not work with non multi-ordinal words. "What a beautiful tree!" "Suppose you had a tree of that tree?"

## 8. *Personalizing*

I draw this from the field of Cognitive Therapy and REBT, Beck (1976) and Ellis (1979) who created lists of **cognitive distortions** that govern how we filter information and perceive the world.

Two distinctions from the list of Cognitive Distortions that do not seem to fall into the Meta-model involve: **"personalizing" and "emotionalizing."** A person using these cognitive distortions would see, hear, and respond to information, events, words, etc., as if whatever occurs out there does so in a "personal" way as a statement or reflection on the person. In personalization, a person believes that they are responsible for external situations for which they could not possibly be responsible. Then they would jump to the conclusion that if they so perceive things, they should *feel* a certain way (emotionalize it). In emotional reasoning, a person believes that *because* they feel a negative emotion, *there must exist* a corresponding negative external situation.

> **Emotionalizing** refers to using one's emotions for gathering and processing information. It thereby over-values "emotions" and treats one's emotions as an information gathering mechanism rather than a reflection of one's values as one perceives things. In emotionalizing, a person reacts to things subjectively. **Personalizing** refers to perceiving things, especially the actions of others, as specifically targeted toward oneself as an attack on one's person. It refers to perceiving the world through egocentric filters that whatever happens relates to, speaks about, and references oneself.

These ways of viewing things arise, as does *identification*, from the way a child's mind work early in life—egocentrically viewing the world in terms of self, assuming the world revolves around the self, and that most communication and events by others says something personal to us or about us. It works from the assumption that if I recognize something, I have to emotionally associate into it.

Such personalizing/emotionalizing shows up in language in the personal pronouns (I, me, mine), words indicating oneself, and in implied formats.

> "Tom's making a lot of noise because he's angry *at me*."

When someone says, "Linda is ignoring me" they have selectively focused on things (also discounting and negatively filtering) that invite them to personalize. If we then can ask what that *means* to the person, they might say, "I will never have any friends." In this cause-effect statement, involving some universal quantifiers ("never," "any"), we also have another personalization, along with crystal ball mind-read of the universe!

> "What does that mean?"
> "It means I am all alone."

Personalizing not only feeds self-pity, but also "the entitlement syndrome," as well as the antisocial personality orientation. Joe typically ends work by catching a drink with the guys then going home. If he notices that the children continue playing outside or watching TV, his first thought goes, "They don't care that I've been working hard all day." If he arrives late (and doesn't call) and Becky has cleaned up the kitchen, he automatically thinks, "That bitch never fixes a decent meal for me." If he confronts her with that(!), and she doesn't respond immediately, he thinks, "She's ignoring me! How dare she!"

To challenge a personalization:

1) **Inquire** about *how* the person knows to treat it as personal rather than impersonal. "How do you know that Linda is intentionally ignoring you and doing it in order to send you a message?"

2) **Explore other possibilities**. "If Linda was just preoccupied, how would you tell the difference?"

3) **Go meta** to explore the personalization as a possible habitual meta-frame. "Do you typically read the behavior or words of others as saying something about yourself? Do you tend to be sensitive to yourself about such things?"

### 9.   *Metaphors/Metaphoring*

When we look at language at both the level of individual words and statements, we find **metaphors** everywhere. They *lurk in the corners*. They often *visit us* like *angels unawares*. At other times, we have to *smoke them out*. Most language, it seems, *operates* through the *structure* of metaphors. In fact, several theorists have proposed that all language *boils down* to metaphor. Regardless, metaphor does seem to function as an essential part of how we conceptualize—we **compare** what we know with what we seek to know and understand.

Lakoff and Johnson (1980) see metaphor as a basic process for structuring knowledge. They theorize that concrete conceptual structures form the basis for abstract thinking/talking.

> "We understand experience metaphorically when we use a Gestalt from one domain of experience to structure experience in another domain." (p. 230).

Consequently, in thinking, perceiving, understanding, and talking we constantly find, create, and use metaphors from one experience to "make sense" of another. The fundamental nature of **metaphor** "is understanding and experiencing one kind of thing in terms of another."

Analogical communication includes metaphors, analogies, similes, stories, and a great many other kinds of figurative language forms. Such language connotes and indirectly implies rather than denotes. Such language endows communication with less directness, more complexity and vagueness, and more emotional evocativeness. It describes more the language of the poet than the scientists. I say "more" because scientists also use metaphor constantly, but more as an end in itself, for its beauty and charm. To become sensitive to the metaphorical level and use of language, we need to think in terms of analogies and analogous relations. What term, sentences, and even paragraphs imply or suggest some metaphorical relation? What metaphors does the speaker use to structure their thinking and framing?

What metaphors occur in the following? "What you claim is indefensible." "She attacked the weakest point in his line of arguments." "His criticisms were right on target." "They shot down all my arguments." Since the overall frame of reference involves conflict, battle, war, we can identify such as the operating metaphors here. The speakers analogously compare the communication exchange to soldiers battling to win a war. How great this differs from another possible metaphor. "Arguing with him is like a dance." "We danced around the core issue for a long time." "The movements of our meanings whirled around with no pattern at first."

Metaphors operate like **presuppositions** in that we usually experience them at meta-levels. This makes them mostly unconscious. So when someone says, "Now I feel like I'm getting somewhere," we may not even notice the "travel" metaphor of journeying, adventuring, etc. "That was over my head" suggests a "space" metaphor to ideas and understandings.

## Thought Questions To Assist Your Learning:

1. Why do we say that the Meta-model functions as "the heart of the magic?" How does it do this?
2. Without referring back, list the thirteen distinctions of the Meta-model.
3. Where did Bandler and Grinder get the Meta-model? List the influencing and contributing factors.
4. How do you explain the Meta-model when someone asks you about it?
5. Name the three modeling or mapping processes.
6. Describe "the wheelbarrow test" that we use for nominalizations.
7. What additional distinctions has Michael Hall added to the Meta-model from Korzybski?

## Linguistics Today

Grinder and Bandler originally developed the Meta-model from the language patterns that they heard and modeled from Perls and Satir and then later from Erickson. And they did so using the tools of Transformational Grammar (TG) —hence the lengthy appendix on TG in their first book, *The Structure of Magic*. They even noted in one of their footnotes the new development in TG of Generative Semantics (p. 109, note 6).

Actually, prior to their 1975 publication, TG had suffered what Harris (1994) later called *The Linguistics Wars*. There he detailed first the wars within the field of linguistics, the rise of various "schools" of thought within TG, and finally the "death" of both Chomsky's Interpretative Grammar model (1957, 1965) and Lakoff's Generative Semantics.

Lakoff (1987) later explained why TG failed as a linguistic model in terms of the philosophical difference between a formal mathematical model-driven process and the way people actually think and process information. Earlier he and others (McCawley, Ross, etc.) had taken Noam Chomsky's original vision of ultimately finding **meaning** within the foundations of the Deep Structure and began pushing in that direction. Yet the more they moved in that direction, the more Chomsky backed off, went on the attack, and ultimately reformulated TG so that he eliminated Deep Structure as an explanatory device altogether. Increasingly he sought to explain all of the transformational rules solely in terms of Surface Structure devices.

As TG—as a linguistic model—became more and more problematic, it eventually gave way, as did Generative Semantics, to other theories and models. In the 1990s Fauconnier's (1985) space grammar which he designated mental space and Langacker's extensive two-volume work (1987, 1991) on the foundations of Cognitive Grammar, along with others, began to predominate in the field.

Where does all this leave NLP and the Meta-model? To raise this question we have to ask several other questions:

- How much does the Meta-model depend upon TG?
- To what extent does the Meta-model need the Deep and Surface Structure format of TG?

In developing the Meta-model, Bandler and Grinder obviously depended upon TG primarily for their terminology. From that field they brought over and began utilizing "modal operators, nominalizations, universals," etc.

## The Meta-Model — Extended

| Patterns/distinctions | Response/challenges | Predictions/results |
| --- | --- | --- |
| 1.    Identification (Id.) "He is a democrat."  "She is a jerk." | How specifically does he identify with the term "democrat?" In what way? Upon what basis do you evaluate her using the term "jerk?" | Recovers the process of identification or prediction. Invites one to create new generalizations. |
| 2.    Static Words (SW) "Science says that . . ." | What science specifically? Science according to whose model or theory? Science at what time? | Recovers the deleted details. |
| 3.    Over/Under Defined Terms (O/U) "I married him because I thought he would make a good husband." | What behaviors and responses would make a "good" husband for you? What references do you use for the word "husband?" | Recovers the extensional facts about the terms used. |
| 4.    Delusional Verbal Splits (DVS) "My mind has nothing to do with this depression." | How can you have "mind" apart from "body" or "body" apart from "mind?" | Recovers the split that someone has created verbally in language. |
| 5.    Either-Or Phrases (E-O) "If I don't make this relationship work, it proves my incompetence." | So you have no other alternative except total success or failure? You can't imagine any intermediate steps or stages? | Recovers the continuum deleted by the Either-Or structure. |
| 6.    Pseudo-Words (PW) "And that makes him a failure." | What do you mean by "failure" as a word that modifies a person? | Challenges a map that uses words that have no real referent. |
| 7.    Multi-Ordinality (M) "What do you think of your self?" | On what level of abstraction do you refer to "self?" "Self" can have many different meanings, depending on context and usage— how do you mean it? | Recovers the level of abstraction that the speaker operates from. Specifies the context and order. |
| 8.    Personalizing (Per.) "He does that just to irritate me." | How do you know his intentions? How do you know to take these actions in a personal way? | Challenges process of personalizing. |
| 9.    Metaphors (Mp) "That reminds me of the time when John . . ." | How does this story relate to the point you want to make? | Recovers the isomorphic relationship between the story and the person's concepts. |

Interesting enough, however, as the model developed, they (and especially their initial disciples) moved further and further away from the usage of such terms in TG. In fact, no subsequent author ever repeated the TG appendix and no NLP trainer ever spent any significant time teaching Transformational Grammar as such.

In fact, some of the same confusions that led Chomsky to drop the use of "Deep Structure" in linguistics occurred in the field of NLP. These revolved around the connections of "deep" signifying greater or more significant "meaning." This usage began showing up in some NLP literature. And also this highlights what the Meta-model depends upon—namely, a logical-level system.

Not surprisingly, Alfred Korzybski (1933, 1994) offered precisely this in his model of the "levels of abstraction." He constructed this from his studies of neurology and it refers to the fact that the nervous system abstracts first at the sense-receptor level, thereby transforming the energy manifestations of the world into various neurological translations. But the nervous system doesn't stop there. It then abstracts again from the cell activation at the end receptors as it transforms and transmutes those "information" forms into bio-electric impulses which it sends to the central nervous center and brain. It next abstracts from those products as it translates the impulses using various neuro-transmitter chemicals, and so it goes.

The Meta-model assumes this kind of levels of abstraction—that what we say in our surface expressions arises from "abstracting", summarizing, and synthesizing at a lower level, etc. In this, the Meta-model does not have a marriage with TG—only an affair. In the fling, it only appropriated the language of linguistics and the idea of levels of information processing.

In Cognitive Grammar today we see new developments that actually fit the NLP model of representations, logical levels, frames and contexts much better than TG ever did. In Langacker's (1991) work, *Image, Metaphor, and Concept*, he speaks about internal representing of information/language in terms of "mental images," metaphors, and conceptual categories or domains. For a fuller description of this, see Michael Hall (1998) *The Secrets of Magic*.

# Chapter 9

## Hypnosis Part I

## The Misunderstood Nature
## Of So-Called "Hypnosis"

*Using Language To Create Neuro-Linguistic "Realities"*

**What you can expect to learn in this chapter:**

*   What hypnosis really means
*   How hypnosis functions at its core
*   A number of everyday trances we all experience
*   How to access and anchor hypnotic states
*   Empowering things we can do with hypnosis

> *A hypnotist hypnotizes by... **saying words**.
> Pretty incredible, wouldn't you say?*

Previously, we hinted that "hypnosis" functions as *a form of communication* and a state that arises from a certain type of language processing. What do we mean by that? In this chapter, we will define what we mean by this term and offer some understandings of the phenomenon.

## Defining Hypnosis

When we finally boil down what a hypnotist actually does—what do we have? What medium does a hypnotist use to affect the minds-emotions, bodies, and nervous systems of those who cooperate with the process? They *simply say words*. Think about that. A hypnotist hypnotizes by... *saying words.* Pretty incredible, wouldn't you say? **"Just saying words."** So how does that work? **How** can the saying of words "hypnotize?"

> As a more formal definition, "hypnosis" literally means "sleep" and refers to "being asleep **to** the outside world" **because** a person has totally focused on something in their inside world.

As a more formal definition, "hypnosis" literally means "sleep" and refers to "being asleep *to* the outside world" *because* a person has totally focused on something in their inside world. They have inwardly focused on some memory, idea, thought, representation, feeling, person, etc. Yet this definition poorly identifies the experience, and has led to lots of misunderstandings. It describes things accurately only to this extent: *to someone viewing* the hypnotized person *from* the outside, it often looks like the person has gone into a kind of sleep. The person seems to have gone into a trance—which means, they do not seem present, but off somewhere else, lost in their thoughts, zoned out. When this happens in everyday life, we wave our hand in front of their face and say, "Hello? Anyone home?" "Earth to John!"

But this only partially describes the experience. When someone goes on some internal journey in their thoughts—and "space out" external stimuli (the "hypnosis" experience), on the inside—in their sense and feel of the experience—they seem *more awake and more alive and more in control of themselves* than ever.

Perhaps the word "trance" works a bit more usefully. It speaks about *the "transition"* that we make from one state of mind to another. Communication professionals, psychologists, and hypnotists have distinguished a dozen different kinds of mental states that we sometimes call "the hypnotic state." For instance, consider the highway trance. I (MH) always *trance-out* when I drive the 430 miles across the state of Kansas on Interstate 70. I can never stay sufficiently alert, so much in sensory awareness (up time), that I don't "go inside" and visit more interesting places in my mind.

Before going further we ask you to put all of your previous associations, definitions, and experiences with these terms on hold. You may have all of those anchored to such things as the occult, mind manipulation, drug trips, stage showmanship, etc. Such *mis*informed linkages will only keep you ignorant about the true significance of "hypnosis," as a form of communication and human consciousness, as we shall show.

Rest assured also that the meanings we give to these terms and our use of the terms in no way have any association with those kinds of popular ideas. If you like to use more comfortable, everyday parlance for these concepts, you might use one of these as a substitute: "not paying attention," "daydreaming," "twilight before going in and out of sleep every night and morning," "lost in deep thought," or "focused inside."

Also, in NLP, we do not use formal hypnotic inductions. Rather we informally utilize *the natural trans-derivational search* (TDS, see Chapter Thirteen) *transitioning processes* that occur when the human mind makes meaning of language. This means that a listener's mind always and inevitably *"goes inside"* and uses its stored logic (learnings, history, and experiences) to make sense of things. Hypnosis as such does not necessarily operate in opposition to reason or volitional control. Actually, it accesses such!

The value of all this? Once we understand the true nature of a hypnotic trance we will begin to realize how people naturally use it destructively to create dysfunctional problems. We say that a person "isn't thinking," "seems under a spell," "act as if out of control," "has gone crazy," as they compulsively act against their own values. In other words, a great deal of our work with "trance" and "hypnosis" will involve bringing people (ourselves included!) *out of old trance states—de-hypnotizing!*

> *Medically speaking, hypnotic trance occurs during the theta level of sleep when our brain neuro-transmitter chemical acetylcholine dominates instead of norepinephrine.*

Medically speaking, hypnotic trance occurs during the theta level of sleep when our brain neuro-transmitter chemical acetylcholine dominates instead of norepinephrine. When this happens, we tend to pay more attention to internal information in stored patterns in the brain such as memories, instead of sensory input from the environment. Many people typically report that their visual images are more vivid, and that they have a decreasing ability to direct their attention, as most people typically report when they are dreaming.

More recent research about how to take charge of one's dreaming and how to induce lucid dreaming, as well as anthropological studies of cultures who put a lot of emphasis on dreams, suggests that the subjective sense of having less ability to direct attention may simply indicate the lack of training, not some innate trait. Obviously people can misuse and abuse every powerful model, insight, and technology (human or mechanical). Yet *the abuse* of an item does not, in and of itself, argue against *a proper use* of it.

Having defined hypnosis as a trance experience, we should make a disclaimer that almost all of what we see on television and in the movies about hypnosis does *not* present it accurately at all. Sure, it makes for a great story. And it can scare the hell out of people about someone "controlling their mind," or making them do things against their will. But none of that represents anything real about hypnosis. It stands on a par with the starship Enterprise going beyond the speed of light, warp-1 through warp-9. Pure science fiction!

| *We cannot make people do anything with hypnosis that violates their morals or values.* |

We can say the same for "stage hypnosis"— entertainment, pure and simple. Further, there exist all kinds of tricks that facilitate that kind of mental and visual sleight of hand which create illusions and misperceptions. The truth about what the hypnotic state can and cannot do boils down to this: *we cannot make people do anything with hypnosis that violates their morals or values*. It just does not work that way! In recent years, scientific experiments on hypnosis have sought to discover the limits of suggestions and hypnotic "control." The results have indicated that hypnosis just does not work in a way that overpowers human consciousness. Milton Erickson once commented that *if we could control people* through hypnosis a lot fewer sick and neurotic people would exist! You can't make them do things against their will—not even get better! Hypnotism merely enables us to focus on something important to the exclusion of the unimportant.

What can this phenomenon of "hypnosis" do? What value does it have? Primarily we can use various trance states to enable us to *activate our innate powers and forces of mind and body*. Because the experience can facilitate greater mental concentration (in fact, this chiefly characterizes the hypnotic state), we can use this high level of inward focus and concentration to activate our resources. Hypnosis simply describes **an intense meditative state** wherein our entire mind focuses on one thing. It functions as a state wherein a person can say, "This one thing I do..." We see this exemplified when an athlete "psyches" themselves before an event.

Using our innate potential, we can access healing forces within the body, slow our breathing and heart rates, slow our bleeding, reduce pain, and many other things that normally (in our normal waking state) we cannot do. There exists nothing mystical, magical, or occult about this. It simply describes one of the ways we humans exist as "wonderfully and marvelously made."

So "hypnosis" refers to a natural process of consciousness that occurs everyday to everybody. Whenever consciousness ceases to see-hear-and-feel what exists immediately present in our external environment, we have "tranced" (transitioned) out and gone somewhere else, into some internal, trance-like state. We may be "thinking deeply," concentrating on something important, just relaxing our mind, meditating, praying, "not thinking of anything in particular," daydreaming, etc. We may have gone inside our mind to create a vision of what we want to accomplish sometime in the future.

The fact that we seldom label such states as "hypnotic" only serves to blind us to the regularity and commonality of this experience. It also blinds us to how easily and quickly we go in and out of altered states.

> *A healthy and enhancing use of hypnosis **empowers one to feel more in control of oneself**, not less.*

The disinformation of the erroneous paradigm says that in hypnosis someone else "controls" your mind. No! Nothing could stand as further from the truth. In fact, the opposite occurs. Many who first experience the trance state discount it as not hypnosis for this very reason. "But I remember everything that I thought and felt." "I felt so focused and so much in control of my experiencing." A healthy and enhancing use of hypnosis *empowers one to feel more in control of oneself*, not less.

In hypnosis, you can always resist. You can resist as much as you can in the waking state. You can resist the induction. You can also resist any specific instructions or suggestions that don't fit for you. In fact, people always ultimately discover that when something does not fit, it causes them to break state and "come out."

This popping out of state, this breaking of state, also explains why most everyday communication that involves a hypnotic nature is of *a very poor quality* to it. It poorly paces or matches the individual's reality and so poorly maintains the hypnotic state. This describes precisely what a good hypnotist learns to do. In the everyday hypnotic communication that occurs, the recipients of our words receive a mixture of words that fit and those that don't. When we continually mismatch their inner reality of values, beliefs, morals, etc., they pop out of that state.

> *Hypnosis **opens us up to new learnings** and new formulations.*

The hypnotic state works powerfully to allow us to manage consciousness as it enables us to access more receptive and suggestible states. What value does this serve? By accessing a comfortable and relaxed state and moving into a more responsive state to ideas and suggestions, *it opens us up to new learnings* and new formulations. We feel more highly responsive and open to the ideas that we want to run our programs. It enables us to get beyond our own defenses, barriers, and limitations! This then allows us to *program in* the ideas, affirmations and even beliefs that we want installed. We like thinking of it as merely another change-tool for renewing the mind so that we can transform "personality."

Dr. Ernest Rossi (1988) wrote,

> "The hypnotized person remains the same person. Their behavior is altered by the trance state, but even so, that altered behavior derives from the life experiences of the patient and not from the therapist. At the most the therapist can influence only the manner of self-expression.

> "The induction and maintenance of a trance serve to provide a special psychological state in which patients can re-associate and reorganize their inner psychological complexities and utilize their own capacities in a manner in accord with their own experiential life. Hypnosis does not change people nor does it alter their past experiential life. It serves to permit them to learn more about themselves and to express themselves more adequately." (pp. 14-15)

So *the meaning* of "hypnosis" refers to a "sleep-like state" of an intense and strong inward focus created primarily by trance inducing words. These words send us inward so that we go on a TDS (trans-derivational search) for meaning. Thus the power of words ultimately (and only) arises from *our attribution of meaning* to them. We do this by "going inward" to our internal "library of references" that we have built up over the years in our "memory" files where we code our understandings, values, beliefs, etc. All of this simply describes one of the powers within personality—the power to attribute meaning to things and to have an internal world—also a sign of "spirit" in our personality.

## The Conscious/Unconscious Mind

Much of NLP, and especially Time-Line processes, requires that we have a working knowledge about our "parts" and that part of mind that we call "the unconscious mind." (Again, remember, this merely offers us a way to talk about processes and phenomena—a "map," not the "territory"!)

Sometimes we use the term "parts" to refer to unwanted and uncontrollable behaviors and the neurology that produces these behaviors. Such "part(s)" result largely from Significant Emotional Experience(s) of Pain— (SEEP). How does this relate to "the unconscious mind?" Before proceeding, we want to provide a discussion of this and how it relates to the "trance" process. Again, don't treat these concepts (conscious, unconscious, trance, hypnosis) as "things" or as literal. We use them accommodatively because we have found them useful—just as we find talking about the sun "rising" and "setting" as useful. We know better than that!

We have moved out of the Middle Ages—we don't buy the Ptolemaic Model of the Universe—and yet we still talk about the sun rising and setting. We do so accommodatively. *From our perspective* "on the planet" the terms work. So with these other terms.

The dictionary defines *conscious* as "having awareness of one's own existence and environment." This conforms to our use of the word. We use *consciousness* to refer to our awareness of internal or external stimulus. Roughly two million bits of information per second come into the human nervous system. To maintain sanity, our mind filters out most of this stimuli. Miller (1956) discovered that we typically can only handle seven plus or minus two bits of information at a time.

To illustrate how we delete most information, notice that a moment ago you had deleted your awareness of your big toe, front teeth, etc. This shows a distinction between what we can consciously maintain awareness of and how much more lies in our unconscious mind.

Imagine your whole mind as a room. The part you experience as "conscious" represents a flashlight shining in this dark room. As you shine on things in that room, you see and bring awareness of its contents—so with our conscious awareness. We see, at any moment in time, only a small part of what we know. We describe our consciousness as that natural neurological process whereby we can see, hear, and know and therefore choose. Obviously, the words *consciousness* and *unconsciousness* only exist as metaphors. We cannot locate them in the brain. These words enable us to talk about brain functions, not actual substances. "The 'map' is not the 'territory'"—never!

*Consciousness* in NLP describes our level of awareness that we code in the rep system. An item in memory represents itself in a combination of pictures, sounds, feelings, tastes, smells and words. Such representations move into consciousness when a signal or stimulus crosses our awareness threshold. When an external or internal stimulus stimulates a memory, the memory moves into consciousness through some modality. The interaction between the intensity of the external stimulus and the internal neurological state determines whether or not a representation becomes conscious. We therefore assume that our primary rep system will have the strongest signal. Our consciousness will therefore represent itself essentially in our primary rep system (see Dilts, 1983).

> **Unconscious behavior arises from stimuli within a particular representational system low in intensity.**

*Unconscious behavior* arises from stimuli within a particular rep system low in intensity. This representation will occur in one of our lesser developed rep systems. The person will not have awareness of the stimulus. In this way, much (if not most) of our behavior operates at unconscious levels. We breathe, move, remember, reason, etc., unconsciously. Usually, we only have awareness of the *content* of an idea, not all of the internal processes that make it possible. It works similarly to the output of a TV or computer monitor—we only see and notice the external end-results, not the processes.

We may have to process new information repeatedly in consciousness in order for this new learning to become automatic, part of us. In learning to drive an automobile, we consciously work the switch, gas pedal, break, steering wheel, etc., until we can drive *without thinking*(!). The new learning comes to feel as "second nature," "intuitive" (an "in"-knowing), or "unconscious." In NLP, we describe this as moving the learning from the primary rep system to a non-primary system. The behavior "fires off" whenever we need to drive a car. We don't have to run the "driving a car" program with our conscious minds. We can take consciousness and go somewhere else! Our response, at that point, operates automatically. It runs from an unconscious level. Amazing, don't you think? Do you drive by maintaining an image of how to drive the car while driving? No. Your "program" for driving lies in some unconscious part of your "mind." (And someone says this just evolved? We don't think so.)

Our unconscious (part of the) mind references that vast amount of information not in awareness. As neurologists have probed the human brain with electrodes, people experience no feelings of pain because we have no pain receptors there. A patient can stay *awake* during such probing. In probing the brain, people have reported recalling events that happened early in their lives. A person may recall memories as a child. In describing these memories, they may even adopt a child's voice. They had stored these memories in some unconscious part of their brain and the probing activates the memory and brings it to consciousness.

Such experiments inform us that our mind records so much of what happens, and records our emotional response as well. Neuro-scientists and cognitive scientists speculate that the brain especially records those events that we make while in an intense emotional state.

In using the term *unconscious*, we mean "not conscious." Whether we can or cannot develop consciousness of it—that describes another issue. Some facets of brain functioning seem to completely lie outside of our ability to access. Other facets we can access—if we seek to and learn skills for accessing.

Sigmund Freud used this term *and* loaded it with many false ideas. He treated and labeled the unconscious *"the id."* For Freud, this "id" contained our sexual desires and primitive drives for aggression, competition, violence, etc. He also believed that these drives operated *apart from* our control (not a very enhancing belief!). As he gave the term such meanings, he left a stigma on the idea of the unconscious—as something to fear, dread, and avoid. Not so with NLP. We look upon the unconscious facet of "mind" as a gift and therefore a friend, not a foe. We would more accurately describe this phenom-enon as "other-than-conscious", signifying simply that which we do not now have awareness about.

> *In NLP we look upon the unconscious facet of "mind" as a gift and therefore a friend, not a foe.*

Given this, the majority of our experiences lie outside of conscious aware-ness. The conscious part (the content) of our communication is but a fraction of the total message. When we try to communicate exclusively through conscious processes, we reduce our ability to communicate. In this other-than-conscious model of mind, we view our conscious mind as a gift from the unconscious. So as a gift of the unconscious, the conscious mind works best when it has the full resources of the unconscious mind.

We have found that many times a client will give a quick response when asked, "What do you want?" Then, after further exploration, the client discovers that they really did not want that. They wanted it in their conscious mind (perhaps they thought that they "should" want it), but later, as they get in touch with some of their less conscious values and beliefs, they discover some of their more authentic wants. In this, their unconscious mind provides them more truth (about themselves) than their conscious mind.

This shouldn't surprise us. After all, our unconscious mind takes care of us. We certainly don't run our heart, lungs, kidneys, glands, immune system, etc., *consciously*. Creation has given us two nervous systems—a central nervous system and the autonomic nervous system, and the function of the autonomic nervous system is to keep us breathing, sleeping, waking, moving, thinking, etc. And a therapist will seek to accomplish various changes to create long-term and lasting change at these unconscious levels.

## Altered States And Trance

Given that our unconscious mind contains vast reservoirs of knowledge and experiences, we need to learn how to tap into this reservoir. Regrettably, many people let this reservoir go largely untapped. Though most of our behavior functions unconsciously, we just let it run—thinking (erroneously) we can't effect it. This shows up in how we language ourselves. We do something and then regret having done it. So we say, "I couldn't help myself. It just came out! I felt as if something else controlled me." All too often when we do that, we use it as *an excuse*—an excuse to *not* really deal with the problem. By not knowing its source, its true nature, and how to get to its origin—we seem to have no way to effectively deal with it.

### OK, OK, Give Us The Patterns!

*How* specifically does NLP and Time-Line processes provide tools for uncovering these unconscious parts? By utilizing trance as an altered state, as a state of mind-and-emotions (relaxed, safe, open, comfortable, receptive, expectant, etc.) that enables us to function effectively and directly at the unconscious level. It gives

> *Trance is an altered state, as a state of mind-and-emotions (relaxed, safe, open, comfortable, receptive, expectant, etc.) that enables us to function effectively and directly at the unconscious level.*

us access to that part of our mind for storing and coding our habitual patterns—it refers to nothing more than that, nothing mysterious, occult, demonic.

Now another factor about the conscious mind—if you have limiting beliefs wherein you fear yourself, you fear your emotions, you fear your experiences, you fear what you might do, you fear what you might feel if you do wrong, etc. (again, all Meta-states of pain!), you thereby train your brain to become a master at keeping unconscious parts repressed. Think about it. We have a level of consciousness that radically differentiates us from all of the animals—*so that we can wake up to reality and live consciously.*

But if we *fear* or hate consciousness, if we don't know how to handle it, if we anger at it, guilt over it, etc., then we condemn ourselves with our active consciousness. The solution to this problem? To repress awareness. To shove moral values into the unconscious, to deny reality, to repress the truth, etc. When we do so, we condemn ourselves to darkness, to living life on the surface, to living with a seething world of unresolved issues inside, to psychosomatic illnesses, etc. Not a pretty picture, huh?

If the conscious mind, by such limiting beliefs, can become *the master of repression*, then how can we undo repression (un-repress)? What tools provide us with a way to open ourselves up to the unpleasantries that we often form and store inside? Obviously, we have to make an approach— and it takes a lot of self-esteem and self-dignity, safety, and assurance to face such internal "demons."

## Trancing Ourselves To Face The Inner Darkness

> *Once occupied, the conscious mind permits the unconscious mind to provide it with information.*

The beauty of trance lies in how this state enables us to focus completely, in our conscious mind, and experience a total occupation with something. Once occupied, the conscious mind permits the unconscious mind to provide it information. Thus, anything that allows you to function internally at the unconscious level causes trance.

Actually *we all* go in and out of trance several times every minute/hour. Trance simply describes the ability that we have to keep us from going insane. Without trance, we would see and hear and process every word and stimulus around us! By trance we develop an intense focus on something and shut out other things. *Daydreaming* offers an excellent example of trance. Have you ever driven several miles and not remembered passing certain landmarks? Or, have you ever started out driving to a familiar place only to end up somewhere else? Once you came to yourself, you wondered how you got there? Welcome to tranceland!

In contact sports, injured athletes sometimes become totally unaware of their injuries until afterwards. They concentrated so intensely on the game that they remained unaware of the injury... of the pain. Trance.

Soldiers sometimes report of getting injured in battle and yet not feeling the pain until afterwards. Their conscious mind became so concentrated on the battle that they had no awareness of pain. They also had entered into a trance.

These examples, in fact, describe hypnotic pain control. In NLP, we think of hypnosis or trance as simply a form of intense concentration and therefore a shift of consciousness. Biofeedback operates as a trance. What does a person learn in biofeedback training? To focus intently on their body functions, especially their autonomic functions. With the use of monitoring instruments, the patient monitors how their consciousness effects or controls their body (breathing, temperature, blood pressure—things we once thought that we could never learn to control). Using the external feedback processes, the patient learns to control their blood pressure and heart rate and they do so by the trance phenomenon of concentrating on some "thought" that then lowers pressure and reduces the rate. When they do this, they have accessed a deep trance. Nothing mysterious or occult— but a part of the wonder of our world. In fact, many of the stress reduction techniques on the market today base their effectiveness on trance.

> *We can even plot trance on the EEG (electroencephalogram).*

We can even plot trance on the EEG (electroencephalogram). The EEG divides among four different wave lengths: beta (12-25 Hz), alpha (9-12 Hz), theta (5-8 Hz) and delta (0-4 Hz). When the EEG prints out beta waves, this indicates active thinking in the brain. Alpha waves indicate relaxation. Theta waves mean a trance state. When one falls asleep the EEG print out will show delta waves.

## The Feeling Of Trance

What does it feel like? Most people thoroughly enjoy getting into a trance simply because it feels so good. On the EEG, trance lies below relaxation. Actually, trance describes a deep state of relaxation, comfort, focus, control, etc.

Trance, as a receptive and internally focused state, can greatly enable a therapist or communicator to communicate ideas. Since the recipient will have accessed a most receptive state—relaxed, open, thoughtful about the ideas—it empowers him or her to take what makes sense and make it a deep part of one's reality. Now could anybody find that useful?

Further, given that the unconscious mind, once open and accessible, tends to accept suggestions uncritically, when we have rapport with someone, their focus will more easily follow and receive our communications. So we say, we have *en-tranced* them with our words and stories.

> *Trance also greatly helps to move the critical and argumentative conscious mind out of the way.*

Trance also greatly helps to move the critical and argumentative conscious mind out of the way. Our conscious mind tends to operate in a highly egotistical way. It wants to have its way! When it doesn't get its way, it goes on the warpath. It then may block out communication from others, from your unconscious mind, from useful and creative ideas, etc. Not exactly a smart thing for the "mind" to do!

Trance enables us to nudge the conscious mind out of the way so it doesn't intrude with defenses, cynicism, etc. Then we can hear the wisdom and concern of our unconscious mind. Then as our conscious mind realizes the value and power of the unconscious mind, it can even consciously communicate and cooperate with it. Here Time-Line and other relaxation and NLP processes can help us tremendously to bring healing to people.

Consider the hypnotic effects of stories and metaphors. A therapist who uses therapeutic metaphors designs them to have an isomorphic (similar) structure to the client's experience. Because of the similarity, their unconscious mind can interpret the metaphor in relation to their own needs. The client will take what they hear and represent it in terms of their own experience.

When we read or hear a story or metaphor, our conscious mind occupies itself with the details of the story—the content. But at unconscious levels, our deeper mind interprets and hears a story behind the story and it goes to work applying its lessons. Sometimes we can recognize this when we or another says, "I just don't know why, but that story really touched something deep inside me." By occupying our conscious mind with the unrelated story, the therapist/communicator can thereby put us in trance in order to get to our unconscious mind with his message.

In Time-Line and other NLP processes, we deal primarily with unconscious behaviors. In reframing these behaviors, we first establish a communication with the part producing the unwanted behavior. We then tap into other parts (the creative part, for example) that can produce alternative behaviors. All of these parts will lie prima-

> *Our challenge as therapists will involve getting the person's conscious mind out of the way so we can assist them in fixing problems stored and coded in the unconscious mind.*

rily at the unconscious level. Establishing communication with these unconscious parts requires trance. Our challenge as therapists will involve getting the person's conscious mind out of the way so we can assist them in fixing problems stored and coded in the unconscious mind. Indeed, most clients experience their distress precisely because their conscious mind has gotten *out of rapport* with their unconscious mind. Trance simply enables us to re-establish such rapport.

When people ask me (MH), "Where did you first learn hypnosis?" I say, "At church!" When I later sought out additional training, I already had the skills of a good hypnotic subject—I could take that trip inward and create wild and wonderful worlds, ideas, abstractions, etc., in my mind! I also already had the art of casting a spell with words. I just had never thought of it that way (a new frame of reference)! Nor did I have the art very refined.

Stories, as a form of hypnosis, "sneak around our left brain mental blocks. Stories inform us indirectly, which means the static of cognitive dissonance is avoided to a great extent." Stories feed the imagination and right hemisphere of the brain with pictures and dramas (Hall, 1985, pp. 151-155).

If we naturally use stories to so define ourselves, then by hearing and experiencing new stories we can redefine ourselves. This describes the psychodynamic power within any story from a piece of gossip, to a movie, a fairytale, a life script, etc. What story would you like to begin to use which would make your life bigger, better, and grander?

## "Hypnosis" As Poetry

If you believe that "real men don't read poetry," skip this section. But if you have an appreciation for the wonder and magic of poetry, then it probably will not surprise you to realize that poetry and poetic language patterns function in an inherently hypnotic way.

The language causes ideas to take a back seat to emotions, moods, states, and experiences. The experience becomes central. Poetry evokes us to do more right-brain thinking than left. Thus, the content of *what* they say (trees clapping their hands in joy) doesn't have as much importance as the manner of *how* they say it. Here a literalist truly goes astray, for we cannot take this language literally without erring!

Poetry calls us to deep emotions and therefore enables us to do the emotional work of grief, anxiety, anger, joy, calm, excitement, etc. This kind of hypnotic literature can change a person. It provides one with an opportunity for catharsis, for cleansing, and for renewal of vision.

## Defining The Conscious/Unconscious Facets Of Mind

Bandler and Grinder (1979)—edited by Steve Andreas—wrote the following in *Frogs Into Princes:*

> "Don't get caught by the words 'conscious' and 'unconscious.' They are not real. They are just a way of describing events that is useful in the context called therapeutic change. 'Conscious' is defined as whatever you are aware of at a moment in time. 'Unconscious' is everything else." (p. 37)

In thinking about these terms and using them to help us to effectively navigate the territory of human awareness, being *"conscious"* provides the more focused definition while *"unconsciousness"* conveys a very broad labeling. Here it stands for "everything else!" Accordingly, we need to distinguish between various kinds of *unconscious awareness*. Thus, minimally we have at least the following facets of *the unconscious mind:*

1)  Consciousness that has become unconscious
2)  The autonomic nervous system that remains "out of conscious awareness"
3)  Subconscious information—below the threshold level for consciousness
4)  The forgotten mind
5)  The repressed mind
6)  The Meta-levels of awareness

### 1.   When Consciousness Goes Unconscious

George Miller (1956) wrote his classic paper, "The magic Number 7+/-2", at the beginning of the Cognitive Psychology Movement. This distinction enables us to recognize our cognitive *information processing* in terms of "chunking."

Thus we say that we order and structure information in terms of 5-to-9 "chunks" of information at a time. We all did this when we first learned the alphabet. We went to school and saw the **"A a"** on the blackboard as a "chunk" of information that the teacher wanted us to learn. When we got that one down, in terms of visual and auditory recognition, and had progressed to kinesthetic reproduction (actually writing it)—a major task in those days!—then we went on to **"B b."** Eventually we got numerous "chunks" represented and stored ... and as this *habituated*, it became less and less *at the front of consciousness*. In other words, it became more and more *in the back of the mind*. And as it did, it became increasingly *less-conscious*.

As we keep learning the alphabet, we kept adding "chunks." Eventually we got up to the 5-to-9 "chunks" of information limit (A/a to I/i). But then another process kicked in. As our "chunks" habituated—they began to "clump" (another technical term?!) together so that "A/a, B/b, C/c" became a "chunk." Then, "E/e, F/f, G/g" became a chunk, etc. Eventually, the entire list of 26-letters became *one chunk*. And after that all of those learnings themselves (clumping, chunking, and how to chunk!) became one *unconscious* chunk.

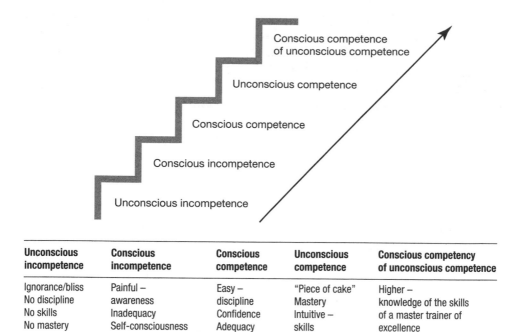

| Unconscious incompetence | Conscious incompetence | Conscious competence | Unconscious competence | Conscious competency of unconscious competence |
|---|---|---|---|---|
| Ignorance/bliss | Painful – | Easy – | "Piece of cake" | Higher – |
| No discipline | awareness | discipline | Mastery | knowledge of the skills |
| No skills | Inadequacy | Confidence | Intuitive – | of a master trainer of |
| No mastery | Self-consciousness | Adequacy | skills | excellence |
| | Unskilled | Growing – | Habitual | |
| | No mastery | mastery | Programmed | |
| | "Hard" | Skillful | | |
| | "Difficult" | | | |

*Figure 9:1 Levels of Learning*

In other words, "chunks" grow. They *clump together* to form larger and larger self-contained sequences of *anchored,* or linked-together, pieces of information that then function as single units. In this way we move through the conscious/unconscious levels of learning:

1) *Unconscious incompetence*—incompetent *and* ignorant of it!

2) *Conscious incompetence*—intelligent enough to recognize our incompetence!

3) *Conscious competence*—learnings that develops more and more skill and understanding.

4) *Unconscious competence*—the learnings clump together and drop from the front of the mind, go to the back of the mind, and then "out" of conscious awareness.

5) *Conscious competence of unconscious competence*—the trainer's (or expert's) state of mind that allows him or her to teach and train others in a skill by having conscious access to unconscious materials.

This developmental process from unconsciousness to consciousness describes the stages of **the learning process.** It indicates that when we learn something consciously, and over-learn it so that it *habituates* in our neurology, it becomes "installed" in what we call an "unconscious part of the mind." At this point, we truly and deeply "know" our stuff! When our learnings reach this stage, they comprise our **in-tuitions**. This term literally describes our "in"—"knowings." We have an *intuitive knowing* about the subject. For instance, we *intuitively know* how to drive, how to skate, how to read, how to do mathematics, how to play the guitar, etc. As an aside, Daniel Dennett (1991) says that we better describe the "unconscious driving" phenomenon as "a case of rolling consciousness with swift memory loss." (p. 137)

This also illustrates one "royal road" to the unconscious—*conscious learning*. We can *put things into our unconscious mind* via learning and over-learning.

## 2. The "Unconscious Mind" Of The Autonomic Nervous System

One facet of "the unconscious mind" (or facet of "mind") involves the "mind" (intelligence) of our autonomic nervous system. This "mind" keeps our heart beating, regulates our neuro-transmitters, hormones, neurological bio-chemistry, governs our breathing, internal organs of digestion, endocrine and immune systems, etc. This "mind" obviously receives *input* from outside the body about temperature, pressure, oxygen, smells, gravity, balance (the vestibular system), etc. In response to such "messages" (information), it *processes* that information in terms of its internal own needs and wants. Then it *acts upon that information* in its outputs in neurological responses and behaviors. It does all of this apart from any of the human *symbolic systems* (whether of propositional or non-propositional language, music, mathematics, etc.).

And yet, while we have begun to learn some of the mechanisms that allow us entry into this more "hard-wired" part of human neurology and experience, this world runs primarily in an *unconscious way*. Or, we could say, our "unconscious mind" runs it.

We now know that by directing and activating the right hemisphere of the brain to vividly experience and feel images, scenarios, and metaphors, we "hypnotically" produce such an inwardly focused concentration that it activates autonomic nervous system processes. From this we can control blood pressure, the experience of pain, heart rate, etc.

We also have a "genetic mind" as Noam Chomsky pointed out in his classic research in linguistics that defeated the Behaviorist Model of Skinner. We do not and cannot learn language as merely a stimulus-response, associative conditioning. Rather we have some kind of a language generator and language acquisition mechanism within us that comes as part of our species heritage. This allows us to unconsciously produce word-strings and to understand word-strings—even those that we have never heard before.

## 3.   The Subconscious "Mind"

Another facet of our *unconscious consciousness* involves that information that exists *below* the threshold level, and therefore *prior to* consciousness. The *signal value* of this information occurs below a level that we can "sense" consciously. Robert Dilts described such facets in *Roots of NLP* (1983). Here occurs such *sub*conscious elements as light outside the ultraviolet electromagnetic range that our eyes can see, sounds/vibrations beyond what our ears can hear, etc.

The existence of a "mind" within our Mind that can over-hear (so to speak) data from the outside and which does not *emerge* into consciousness— speaks about a second "royal road" to the unconscious part of mind. Namely, it speaks about **apart-from-consciousness learning.** Many things seem to get into this part of "mind" *without* going through consciousness. We pick up tidbits of information, and little side-pieces of data. Such information gets in "unaware." Here we *learn* but don't know *that* we learn—let alone *what* we learn.

What kind of information specifically gets in in this manner? We believe that what gets in is structured as embedded commands, tonal shifts, connotations, suggestions, presuppositions, meta-level framing, etc.

Such "learning" seems to operate as a *spill-over effect* from being alive. That is, we pick up on things, but don't "know" (consciously) that we do. We especially recognize this in our dreams. Frequently we will *incorporate* the sound of water, an alarm clock, someone speaking, a dog barking, etc., from the outside—but continue dreaming all the while *making that stimulus a part of the dream.* Once, while lost in thought while rocking in a chair—I (MH) suddenly "woke up" from the reverie to notice that I had somehow unconsciously synchronized my rocking with some background music.

In NLP, the idea of *overloading consciousness* has received a lot of press. Some have taken this idea of overloading and used it in their trainings. They even advertise their approach as such. "We overload consciousness so that once you get to overload, everything else just slides right into the unconscious mind—immediately giving you unconscious competence."

For us, this idea has some problematic features. If **overloading** works that well and in that way—why don't we set up elementary, middle, and high schools so that the kids go for 12-hour days? Why don't we have the teacher lecture at them for 4 hours without a break, get them to overload— then everything afterwards will "just slide right in" and they'll "have it"? Why don't we do that? Does it work for you to get overloaded—do you suddenly become a "mean, green, learning machine?"

It just doesn't work like that, does it? The assumption driving that idea just doesn't hold up under scrutiny. Typically, the majority of learning goes through the conscious mind that does the work of incorporating, imple- menting, applying, relating, etc. What we have here involves some empty hype that does not serve NLP well.

Apparently "the spill-over effect" does *not* send lots of data into the human system nor even the best data. How much of these bits and pieces get in? And how do we then process it in ways that serve us well?

### 4. The Forgotten "Mind"

We call *unconscious* the "mind" within us where we store all of our memories and prior experiences. In the 1950s, Penfield and other researchers discovered that electrical stimulation of various parts of the brain triggered automatic recall of long forgotten experiences. These "recalls" did not merely involve the "data" in a pure or cold form, but a seeming *re-experiencing* of the information. At that time, they concluded that *everything* we ever experience gets recorded and stored somewhere.

Later research studies, however, questioned this universal quantifier. Theorists eventually concluded that while *much* of what we experience does get recorded, not *everything* does. We do not record in "memory" what we do not attend or pay attention to. Our "not-knowing" of that informa- tion does not mean that "it is unconscious." It may mean that we didn't encode it in the first place. Thus just because someone has a "dark area" on their Time-Line does **not** *necessarily* mean that they have experienced some trauma. They may have just not encoded anything of significance during that period. Or they may have lost interest in it so that it slipped away.

Further, we can and do *forget things*. We can lose memory of previous learnings, experiences, conversations, etc. Just go through old boxes of reports and notes that you wrote when you attended school twenty or thirty years ago. Or read journal writings of everyday conversations, experiences, and happenings from five years ago—and experience the surprise of not even recognizing much of it. Not only has it become *unconscious*, it has become unconscious *and inaccessible*.

I (MH) did this recently with old notes I came across that I made from some calculus, trigonometry, and advanced mathematics classes. Not only had I forgotten that I had taken such notes—I couldn't even recall the learnings in a way that could make sense of the information. "What in the world do these formulas mean? I can't believe that I once knew this stuff!"

## 5. The Repressed "Mind"

While Sigmund Freud did **not** invent or initiate the idea of *the unconscious mind*, he certainly popularized it. And as he did, he made it a part of Twentieth Century knowledge and parlance. Accordingly, he spoke about the *pre-conscious, the conscious, and the sub-conscious*. By the latter, he referred to the part of "mind" that we push-down and repress. He theorized that as we use various defense mechanisms, we build barriers against consciousness. We do not *want* to know what is in our unconscious. We *fear* knowing (this structure operates as a meta-state). So as our "ego" (the "reality principle" as he called it) can't handle certain information, it suppresses, represses, denies, projects, etc. It develops an attitude (has an agenda) *against* knowing.

Freud looked upon this less-than-healthy facet of the unconscious as the place of repressed negative emotions, rampant and tabooed sexual fantasies, and deep genetically-oriented urges or "instincts" like his postulated "death instinct."

To Freud's genius, he developed numerous methods for recovering *the repressed unconscious material*:

1) Free-floating associative thinking: lie quietly and just notice whatever intrudes into consciousness, let it come, don't push it away or down, let it come and say so.

2) Dream welcoming, recording, and analyzing: notice the images and presentations that your unconscious mind offers you in dreams. Commit yourself to recording the dreams, then later pull apart the dream's manifest content and latent content.

3) Catch and notice "Freudian slips." Catch the unconscious mis-statements that arise which frequently indicate thoughts and awareness in the other-than-conscious mind. Then inquire whether it indicates any "agenda" against some knowledge.

With regard to this facet of unconsciousness, Milton Erickson (1976) said, "Your patients will be your patients because they are out of rapport with their unconscious mind." (p. 276). This suggests that *true mental health* involves a good balance and rapport between the conscious and the uncon-scious "parts" of Mind. We develop what we call "unconscious parts," "bitter roots," and other internal incongruencies because in some way, one part of the mind has gotten out of harmony with another part. The Mind no longer operates as whole and integrated.

## 6. *Meta-levels Of Awareness*

Another facet of Mind that becomes *unconscious* and that then exhibits the power and nature of *unconsciousness* occurs in the Meta-levels of conscious-ness. This refers to those *frames of reference* that we construct as we move through life—those frames that we then use as our Meta-level referencing system. This includes such subjective mental-emotional phenomena as beliefs, values, criteria, "rules," domains of knowledge, conceptual under-standings, etc.

As we learn things, they not only become *unconscious* but many begin to operate at a level meta to regular everyday primary level consciousness. These become our Meta-programs, our Meta-states, our Meta-level domains of knowledge. We can certainly bring these *meaning* (semantic) structures into consciousness—but typically they operate as simply the frames of reference within which we live and function—as our presupposi-tional reality.

A **conscious thought** thus involves not only an *awareness of* something—but also a higher level awareness: awareness *of the awareness* of something. I can drive with *awareness* of streets, people, traffic signals, etc., but unless I have *awareness* of that awareness, it seems (and so we say), that we're driving *unconsciously*. Rosenthal ("Why Are Verbally Expressed Thoughts Conscious?", 1990, as quoted in Dennett, 1991) says that what distinguishes a conscious state from a non-conscious state involves the straightforward property of having "a higher-order accompanying thought that is about the state in question."

## An NLP Pattern For Working With The Unconscious Mind

### *The Six-Step Reframe*[12] *Extended*

1) **Get Rapport.** The first step involves establishing rapport with that part. When a person explains the problem, match, mirror and pace them during their description. This enables us to establish rapport with the part. We can start by *using unspecified verbs* in establishing this communication with the part—words like "communicate" and "check out." Such words will encourage the part to speak in its own rep system. As that part then begins to speak, we can match its predicates. It then becomes important for us to remember that parts will frequently use a rep system different from what the conscious mind uses. So, note if, when a client accesses the unconscious part, their language reflects a different rep system. If so, then match the rep system of the part.

2) **Establish Communication Signals.** Next, we need to assist the client in establishing conscious communication with their unconscious part if the problem lies outside of conscious control. If a client could or can consciously control the behavior, let them. Yet the majority of times, people come for help precisely because they have an internal conflict between conscious desires and unconscious behaviors which they cannot control. Frequently, the unconscious mind will know far more about a person's need than does their conscious mind. So their unconscious mind will also frequently know far more about the client's needs than we do. So the wise therapist will concern themself with the unconscious mind.

When a person says, "I want to stop gaining weight," they announce therein that they have tried consciously to stop over-eating, but have failed. Consciously, they have run out of options. Our job? To go straight to the location of the problem—how they have mapped out their reality and stored it in their unconscious mind. *To discover the positive intent of the part* that causes the problem, we need to talk to it. So communicating with that part enables us to discover its positive intent for the person. Once we discover this, we can assist in empowering the client to find alternative behaviors that work much better.

3) **Engage The Unconscious With Questions/Statements.** Now we can formally establish communication with the part. Working from the assumption that all behavior has value and use in some context, we accept the part as attempting to do something important. This helps in establishing communication with it.

"I respect that you have this part of you that does this behavior that you dislike and no longer find useful" (thus we interpersonally Meta-state the person). "This behavior has some value or significance to you; you have done it for a long time. And you also can begin to believe that it does something of value for you—even if you don't know the specifics of its value... And you also have consciously come to a place where you dislike these results and wish it would **stop creating problems for you**. And right now, I do not know its positive intent for you... And from your response, you probably don't either. And yet, wouldn't you like to know? So let's engage this powerful part of you and see if it will *tell us what it seeks to do for you that you can value*. So as we establish communication with it, we must just find that this part has wanted, perhaps for many years, to communicate with you. And I wonder how you would feel about that, now? So now we can provide it that chance."

## 4) Sensitize The Client To Their Own Unconscious Signals.

"And as you *go inside* and ask it a question, you can then allow yourself to pay close attention to any internal feelings, images or sounds that occur in response. And you don't have to influence these responses in any way. This part of you that generates the behavior will communicate, as it does, and you can just comfortably notice... how it responds. Just ask that part, 'Will this part of me responsible for generating this behavior communicate with me in consciousness and *effectively tell me its positive intention?*'"

We can keep the part separated from the behavior if we speak of "the part that generates this behavior" rather than "the (name of the behavior) part." In reframing, we must exercise care to get the positive intent of the part. This intent will differ from the behavior as "criticism" (behavior) differs from "trying to straighten things out," "trying to correct something I view as a problem" (intention). Therefore, as we word our statements and questions, we take care to speak of the two as separate.

As the person hears our words and then echoes them within, we need to pay careful attention for shifts or changes in their physiology/ neurology. Here we calibrate to see if we can detect the person's unconscious autonomic nervous system responding. Often we will observe changes in the person *as we describe the question!* We will get responses non-verbal signals from the person before the person even has such awareness. Here we watch for changes in breathing, twitches of muscles in fingers, a shrugging of the shoulders, color changes in the face, etc. These all offer us possible unconscious signals—external signals of the unconscious.

Sometimes a client will notice an internal feeling, voice, or picture—treat this as an unconscious signal. It differs only in that it exists as an internal signal.

5) **Establish Yes/No Signals**. Once we get signals from the unconscious, we can use them to ask specific questions that can generate yes/no responses. If you have an internal signal, say, "Just so that I clearly understand you and so that I can appreciate your purpose better, if this truly represents 'yes' please increase this signal... and if this truly represents a 'no,' please let it decrease." Recycle through this until you feel confident about these signals. "Will this part or internal state that generates this behavior increase this 'yes' signal so that I know that you truly mean 'yes'." "And for this 'no' signal that involves the decreasing of the brightness, decrease it even more if I truly understand this as your 'no' signal."

We ask a yes/no question on that order and we will usually get a "sense of yes" or a "sense of no." Our internal picture might grow brighter for "yes," or closer, more colorful, etc. Our internal voice may sound louder, quick, or a different tone for "no." Our internal kinesthetic sensation may get warmer or cooler for "yes," tighter and more tense for "no."

On the outside, we might notice a "yes" head nod or a stopping of the head nod for "no." Sometimes the unconscious responses will show up in that obvious a way. Or we may see more tension in the facial muscles for "no," and more relaxation for "yes."

6) **Apologize To This Part**. If neither you nor the person can seem to detect an unconscious response—assume that the part *won't* talk to you. It is refusing. What does that mean? It probably feels offended and unappreciated.

"As you go inside, you may begin to realize that the way you have talked to this part of you over the years(!) has probably hurt its feelings so that it doesn't feel validated or appreciated, and that has arisen because you just didn't know that it sought, in some way or other, to do something of value for you... but as you now begin to understand that... you can apologize to it in just the right way so that it knows that you now want to make up with it and make it a friend because as long as you stay at odds with this facet of yourself and it with you, it only keeps you stuck ..."

Having done this, recycle back to setting up Yes/No Signals.

7) **Discover Its Positive Intent**. With the yes/no signals, have the person go inside and pose a question. "Would you allow me to know in consciousness what you seek to accomplish for me that I can deem as a positive value as you produce this behavior?" If we get a "yes," have it inform the person of its positive intention. If you get a "no," ask the person, "Will you allow yourself, just now, to go ahead and trust that your unconscious has some well-intentioned and positive purpose for you, even though it won't tell you that purpose right now?"

8) **Access The Creative Part**. Access the part that creates, innovates, comes up with new and wild ideas—and anchor it. Now ask the part that runs the unwanted behavior to communicate its positive intention to this creative part and for each time the creative part generates a new behavior that would work as good as or better than the old behavior, let it give you a "yes" signal.

9) **Future Pace The Change**. As the person goes in, have them ask that part, "Will you now allow yourself to take responsibility to use one of these three new behaviors in the appropriate contexts?" Again, let your unconscious mind identify the cues that will trigger the new choices and to experience fully what it feels like to effortlessly and automatically have one of those new choices available in that context.

10) **Check For Ecology**. And as you go in again, ask, "Does any part of me object to having one of these three new alternatives rather than the old behavior?"

## So How Does "Hypnosis" Work?

"Hypnosis" works by using words that engage someone's mind to "go inward" to make meaning out of your languaging. Underlying "hypnosis" we have hypnotic language patterns. This refers to those words and word structures that "hypnotize" and "entrance" people. In doing this, *nominalizations* take the cake as "trancy" language (relationship, self-esteem, satisfaction, motivation, relaxation)! These "verbs turned into nouns" have lost their immediate referent, vaguely describe the process and so, as a result, a listener has to "go inside" and do a TDS to their referent index to identify what that word stands for.

These *trance inducing words* facilitate the hypnotizing process—unless the person goes into "uptime" and Meta-models the words. Indexing such words with the Meta-model challenges essentially *de-hypnotizes*. How? By getting you to "come up" (uptime) rather than going down (downtime).

When I (MH) engage in hypnotic processes with clients, I know that my main stock of linguistic tools lies in these trance words.

> "And you can now allow yourself to rest comfortably in the growing knowledge that you are going to experience a deepening relaxation that can, and will, enable you to release some of your untapped potentials so that you can begin to function in a much more useful way in your everyday life so that your effectiveness will increase in a way that both your conscious and your unconscious mind will find pleasing and acceptable."

Don't you like that? Did you *experience* those words as you read them? Or, did you read them analytically? Check it out. Give yourself the chance to notice how your mind processes such words and "makes sense" of such. All "hypnosis" refers to, after all, involves how we can *turn inward* and access conceptual awarenesses within our spirit. It shifts us from the outside to the inside. O'Connor and Seymour (1990) described this "downtime" nature of hypnosis:

> "Trance is a state where you are highly motivated to learn from your unconscious in an inner directed way. It is not a passive state, nor are you under another's influence. There is co-operation between client and therapist, the client's response letting the therapist know what to do next." (p. 119)

> "Abstract words, by their very nature, have a strong hypnotic effect since to 'make sense' of them you have to go inside to your world of meanings (ideas, understandings, beliefs, etc.) and access or create conceptual references. And by going inward to your world of abstraction (which you can easily do with your eyes wide-open) you develop an inward focus." (Hall, 1994)

> "Creatively using such linguistic vagueness enables you to speak in hypnotic language patterns. To stimulate a mind (yours or others) with nominalizations, unspecified nouns and verbs, etc., invites the recipient to use those fluffy statements to do a TDS and to create, out of their own meanings, the experiences, states, emotions, etc., which your words allude to. In this process, linguistic vagueness sounds exceedingly meaningful. That's because the listener is 'making sense' of your words by going inside and incorporating them with their own learnings and understandings. This is how hypnotic language patterns work." (Hall, 1994c, p. 8)

Besides nominalizations, *any word that makes an abstract evaluation of something* works hypnotically in the mind. NLP makes a distinction between **sensory-based words** and **evaluative words**—a distinction that points us to the land of hypnotic language. After all, language references "realities" we cannot see, hear, taste, sense or smell. Evaluative realities of one's meanings, beliefs, and values *do not exist in the world outside the* human nervous system, but inside. They exist as abstractions—neuro-semantic abstractions.

So anytime we communicate *evaluative meanings* (to self or others) we engage a hypnotic process. We deal with internal abstractions. To "make sense" of this, others have to take an inward focus. This explains why we Americans don't typically hallucinate concrete nouns—people, places, and things. We hallucinate pseudo-nouns—nominalizations and evaluations. We move into the world "seeing" disrespect, rudeness, laziness, and insult, we "hear" guilt-trips and irresponsibility, we "feel" put down. Do you know the ideas, judgments and understandings you go around hallucinating? In Chapter Ten we now move into the language patterns that induce trance.

## Thought Questions To Assist Your Learning:

1. What have you learned about hypnosis from this chapter?
2. What mechanisms primarily drive hypnosis?
3. Name six everyday trances that you experience.
4. What characteristics of the hypnotic state make it such a useful tool in working with consciousness?
5. Identify the process that you use to access a relaxed, inwardly focused state.

# Chapter 10

## Hypnosis Part II

## The Milton Model

*Specific Language Patterns For Artful Vagueness*

**What you can expect to learn in this chapter:**

- The meaning and content of the Milton model
- How and why we say it reverses the Meta-model
- Specific language patterns for inducing trance
- The skill of using artfully vague language

### The Milton Model

After developing the Meta-model, Bandler and Grinder met Milton Erickson, a world-renowned medical hypnotherapist and founder of the American Society for Clinical Hypnosis. Grinder reported that Erickson provided him with the single greatest model he has ever used (O'Connor and Seymour, 1990, p. 119). Erickson opened an entire new area of thought in therapy and communication. From their study of Erickson, they soon after published *Patterns of Hypnotic Techniques of Milton H. Erickson Volume I* (1975). Later, with Judith DeLozier, they published *Volume 2* (1977). Bandler and Grinder learned from Erickson the value of trance and altered states in therapy.

Many of the NLP presuppositions come from Erickson's work. He respected the client's unconscious mind, believed that positive intention drives all behaviors, that individuals make best choices available to them, that people have the resources within to make their desired changes, etc. Much of the rapport building techniques of NLP come from Erickson's genius at building and maintaining rapport (pacing and leading).

As the Meta-model *steps down to specifics* to recover distorted, generalized, and deleted materials, this takes us *out of trance*. The Milton Model conversely *chunks up* to make new generalizations, deletions, and distortions. Rather than go for specific information, it steps up to general information—to the big picture. The Milton model *mirrors in reverse* the Meta-model (Figure 10:1).

"Chunking up" questioning dissociates the Problem State towards their higher level (meta) resources. You will find the source for healing "up there."

*In Trance*

General – Chunk up – Big picture

Questions: What is this an example of?
For what purpose…?
What is your intention?
What does having this give you that is more important?

**The Milton Model**

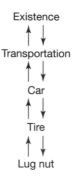

Existence

Transportation

Car

Tire

Lug nut

**The Meta Model**

*Out of Trance*

Specific – Details – Chunk down

Questions: What are examples of this?
What specifically?
Any Meta-model question

*Figure 10:1  Chunking up/Chunking down*

> *The Milton model **mirrors in reverse** the Meta-model*

Expect to find lots of distortions, generalizations, and deletions in this model. Here we intentionally use language to give the client room to fill in the pieces. We provide an open frame with little context so that the client's unconscious mind will activate an internal search. General language inherently induces one to go into a trance on this search. So the language patterns within the Milton model facilitates this process.

Because the Milton model mirrors in reverse the Meta-model, we put a person in trance *by using the Meta-model violations.* Here we do not ask questions—questions invite the mind to come up (into uptime). The following illustrates creatively using Meta-model violations to induce a trance state:

> *Because the Milton model mirrors in reverse the Meta-model, we put a person in trance **by using the Meta-model violations**.*

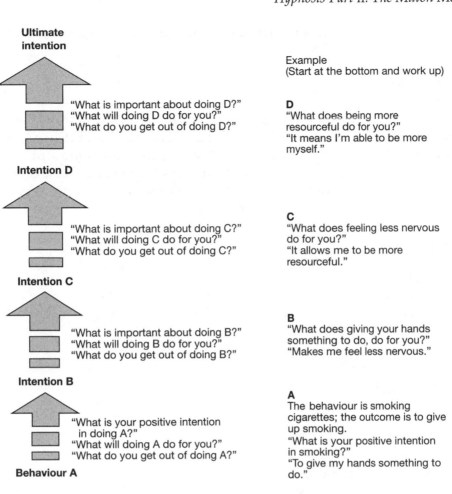

(Young, 1999)

*Figure 10:2  Chunking up—Another Format*

"I know (mind read) that you have begun to gain new learnings (nominalization) about a great many subjects (unspecified noun) of significance to you. And, it is a good thing to learn (lost performative), to really learn... For, as you gain new learnings (presupposition), you have already begun to change (cause-effect) and I don't know how you feel that, now... but you can. And, the fact that you have begun to change in ever so slight ways means that healing (complex equivalence) has begun. And you might experience these changes (presuppositions) by how you feel or just by how you talk to yourself. Since you have begun to make changes (nominalization), that means all (universal quantifier) other areas needing healing can begin to change (entire sentence— a complex equivalence.). And you can change (modal operator of possibility and unspecified verb), as you should (modal operator of necessity). It is more or less the right thing to do (lost performative), that is to change (comparative deletion)."

In addition to these Meta-model categories, the Milton model offers other categories as listed below:

## 1. Tag Questions

You can displace resistance from a statement by placing a question after the statement, can't you? The question added at the end draws the conscious mind's attention thereby allowing the other information in the sentence to go directly into the unconscious mind. "It is OK for me to do that, isn't it?" Tag questions "tamp down" the suggestion contained at the front part of the sentence into the unconscious mind.

**Examples:**[13]

>Isn't it?
>Have you?
>You know?
>Won't you?
>Can't you?
>Aren't you/we?
>That's right?
>Don't you know?
>Didn't I?
>Couldn't you?
>Will you?
>And you can, can you not?

## 2. Pacing Current Experience

A powerful means of building rapport and inducing trance involves pacing the client's current experience by simply making statements that "agree with and have similarity with" their ongoing experience. Pacing current experience associates the person into an internal focus.

>"You can feel yourself sitting in your chair or lying down... And, as you read this material, you continue to breathe in and out at first quickly and then as you *take a deep breath* you can become more relaxed, won't you, now? The sounds in the room and those that you may hear outside, and the words on the page means that you can go deeper and still deeper into trance."

Of course, noticing the sounds in the room has nothing to do with relaxation *unless* you link the two. So as we talked to your unconscious mind, it could say,

"Yes, now that you mention it, I do hear sounds and I can take a deep breath and of course, this makes the next statement about going into a trance much more believable."

## Examples:

You hear my voice.
We are in this group.
You will enjoy it more.
As you notice each blink of your eyes.
As you sit here now you can hear external sounds. ...
And you can hear internal sounds...
You can experience being bathed by the light...
As you continue breathing in and out...
You can experience yourself going deeper and deeper into trance.

## 3. Double Binds

"And you can go into a trance now or ten minutes from now and I don't know which you'll do ..." If your unconscious mind accepted the presupposition of that sentence, you will either have already entered a trance or you will shortly. Double binds have an unspoken presupposition contained within the sentence. Parents seem to have a natural talent at communicating double binds. "John, when will you do your homework? Before this TV program comes on or as soon as it ends?" "Now that you have entered a trance, which arm do you wish to lift?" "Do you wish for your right arm to raise or your left?" Asking which hand the image will come out on (in the Visual Squash) illustrates an example of a double bind.

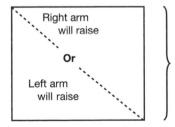

*Figure 10:3 A Double Bind*

## Examples:

Do you want to begin now, or later?
As you dream, or upon awakening. . . .

Either before, or after, leaving this room . . . .
When you go to bed you will either dream, or not.
Will you begin to change now or after this session?
Would you like to quit smoking today or tomorrow?
Would you like to buy the car now, or test drive it first?
You either will or you won't (followed by an unspecified verb).
Take all the time you need to finish up in the next five minutes.
You can change as quickly or as slowly as you want to now.
If you don't write at least one more double bind in the space below
    now, you will either think of one automatically very soon, or else
    wonder when the next one will come to mind, so you can write it
    down then.

### 4. Conversational Postulate

A conversational postulate takes the form of a "modal operator" question which is actually a command to do something. The answer requires a yes or no response. However, that question seems to bypass the conscious mind and create within the unconsciousness a desire to do something about the statement. A classic example: "Can you close the door?" Instead of responding with a "yes" or "no," most of us respond by simply closing the door. Such questions avoid authoritarianism.

**Examples:**

Can you imagine this?
Will you just let go now?
Can you picture doing this?
Can you see what I am saying?
Can you reach that level now?
Would it be all right to feel this good?
Do you know that you know it already?
Could you open your mind for a moment?
How easily do you think you can do this?
Can you remember to be kind to yourself?
Does this sound like it will work for you?
Do you feel prepared to sign the contract now?
Do you think you can make the changes you want?
Would you like... to just sit here... and relax now?
Wouldn't you like to just drift into that peaceful state?
Would you mind writing down a couple more conversational postu-
    lates here?

## 5. Extended Quotes

Susan said that she heard Dave say that Tad James said, "I heard Richard say that NLP offers some of the most powerful, if not the most powerful, tools for personal change available today. And, these tools locate themselves within your unconscious mind. In fact, you have access to them at the unconscious level. Once your conscious mind and unconscious mind gain rapport with each other then you will have total access to those resources." Many speakers make extensive use of quotes. The use of quotations takes the attention away from the speaker and serves to displace the conscious mind so the information can go into the unconscious mind. The listener accesses a trance by focusing on the quotation as it facilitates an inward focus. Extended quotes play off our need to make sense out of statements.

**Examples:**

> Last year, in San Diego, John Grinder was telling us about
> > this African drummer who asked Judy if she had heard the
> > > village chief say how easy it is to generate extended quotes.

> Last year, I met a woman who said she knew a man
> > who had mentioned
> > > that his father told him...

> Bob said that in a training four years ago,
> > he had told the story about when
> > > Richard Bandler was quoting
> > > > Virginia Satir, who used to say
> > > > > that...

> I was speaking with a friend the other day, who told me of a
> > conversation she had had with a therapist who told her
> > > about a session he'd had with a client who said...

> When I went to Charlotte, North Carolina the other day
> > with Sam and Doris, one of them told a story about
> > > when his mother would sit down and explain to
> > > > the children how father had said...

> The other day, a participant in the training told me that her husband
> > said Bob had told him to ask you to write a couple of extended
> > > quotes down right here.

### 6. *Selectional Restriction Violation*

A selectional restriction violation describes an ill-formed sentence which ascribes feelings to an animal or some inanimate object. "Have you ever thought about your pen, typewriter, or word processor? Just think how many notes it has taken over the years. How many, I wonder? It knows more than even you know." "What about giving your chair some thought? Don't you know it gets tired? After all, it has carried your weight for a long time, hasn't it?"

**Examples:**

> My rock said...
> The walls have ears.
> That nail hurt my tire.
> Flowers like to be picked.
> My car knows how to get here.
> Put the noise down in your toe.
> What did your actions say to you?
> Could you open your mind for a moment
>     and just listen to what the butterfly has to tell you?
> Because the words have power of their own.
> The cat doesn't care about the furniture's outrage from the scratching.
> As he picked up the spoon, the Jell-O trembled with fear.
> And if your pen told us all the things it has learned.
> My car loves to go fast when the road beckons.
> Do trees cry when they drop their leaves?
> Sometimes the cookies just call to you.
> Do you know what the pen thought?
> These walls can tell such stories.
> Your pen knows how to write selectional restriction violations very
>     easily, if you will just lead it to the lines below now.

In Bandler's Weight Loss Transcript he utilizes the following **Selectional Restriction Violations:**

"The furnace inside you ..." This refers to the metabolism of the body.

"I want to talk to that part of you... or your unconscious."

"And this is what he installs in people..."

"And your brain goes brrrrrrr..."

"The box of Godiva chocolates calls out to you."

## 7. Phonological Ambiguities

Many words have different meanings but sound the same. "Your nose/ knows the truth of this." "You can be hear/here anytime you wish." Such language distracts the conscious mind. The client will go into trance while trying to sort out the ambiguities.

**Examples:**

> you're/your
> there/their
> here/hear
> son/sun
> bare/bear bottoms
> there's no "their" in there
> He reddened as he read in it.
> You are the one who has won.
> After all you have learned from the tapes.
> And here today as you hear your unconscious mind....
> You can trust **you're unconscious** mind **now.**

## 8. Syntactic Ambiguity

Syntactic ambiguity exists when we cannot immediately determine from the immediate context the function (syntactic) of a word. For instance, "Hurting people can feel difficult." Does that sentence mean that when you meet hurting people they can make this difficult for us emotionally, or does it mean that engaging in the behavior of hurting people feels like a difficult problem? We can construct syntactic ambiguities by using *a verb* plus *"-ing."* Then you construct a sentence so that it lacks clarity about whether the "-ing" word functions as an adjective or as a verb.

**Examples:**

> running water
> shooting stars
> babbling brook
> Hypnotizing hypnotists can be tricky.

## 9. Scope Ambiguity

Scope ambiguity exists when you cannot determine by context how much one portion of a sentence applies to another portion. "The organization consists of healthy men and women." Do we mean to imply that just the men have the quality of "health" or do we mean to include the women as healthy as well? You can construct Scope Ambiguity by adding an "-ing" on a verb and put an "and" between the objects.

**Example:**

> Your deep breathing and trance…
> Hearing Bob and John…
> Yesterday I was driving my car with tennis shoes on.
> I was riding my horse with blue jeans on.

## 10. Punctuation Ambiguity

There exist three kinds of punctuation ambiguities. The first involve **run-on sentences**. "I want you to notice your hand me the book." "On your arm I see a watch yourself go into trance." The second form involves **improper pauses**. This form of sentence involves times when you begin a …. uh… sentence and you never quite… uh… finish the… sentence. This causes a forced mind reading and becomes highly trance inducing. Newscaster, Paul Harvey, does this in a marvelous way when he says, "… good… day." The third type of punctuation ambiguity involves an **incomplete sentence**. In this form you begin a sentence and you never quite… You then go on to another sentence with a totally different thought.

**Examples (run-on sentences):**

> Let me take your hand me the pen.
> See the butterfly drifting over the hilltop is a beautiful valley.
> She has freckles on her butt I like her anyway.

**Examples (improper pauses):**

> My wife left me… to go to Texas.
> I was looking for my tie… into this thought.
> If you hear any ambiguities, it's all right to write them right here.

## 11. Utilization

Erickson utilized utilization to its fullest potential. He used everything the client said. He used every sound and incident in the room. In one of my (BB) trainings a wall chart fell off the wall. Tad James said, "And old concepts are falling away." Once when I used hypnosis with a client, I had a relaxation tape playing. Suddenly the tape finished. I knew that in a short moment that the tape player would make a click as it cut off. So, I said, "In just a moment you will hear a click. And, when you do, that means you will let go of the pain totally and completely." In a brief moment the player clicked and the client's body jumped as the emotion totally released.

**Examples:**

> Client: "I don't think I know."
> Practitioner: "That's right, you don't think **you know**."

> Client: "I can't be hypnotized."
> Practitioner: "That's right. You can't **be hypnotized yet**."

> Client: "I'm not sold."
> Salesman: "That's right, because you haven't asked the one question yet that will let you be sold."

## 12. *Embedded Commands*

Erickson worked as a master at giving the unconscious mind directions through embedded commands. He would *mark out* such *words* that he wanted to go into the unconscious mind. To give such commands and mark out words, we have to both lower our tone and raise the volume of the voice. "**It is possible for you** to instruct a client's unconscious mind through embedded commands **to get well, now**." Say, did you *get the command* from the marked out words? When you have a client dissociated above their Time-Line, this offers a wonderful opportunity to *send embedded commands* to the unconscious mind. When using Time-Line processes, the client will have then entered into a rather deep trance.

## 13. *Analogue Marking*

Erickson would **mark out** the words that he wanted to go into the unconscious mind. **Marking out** refers to emphasizing specific words or phrases by altering tonality. In giving these commands and marking out words, both lower your tone and raise the volume of your voice. **It is possible for you** to instruct a client's unconscious mind through embedded commands **to get well, now.** Did you get the command from the marked out words?

## 14. *Spell Out Words*

John Burton says that by spelling out key words we draw attention to the word we are spelling out. This induces trance. And, you **k-n-o-w** that spelling out words does induce trance, doesn't it?

### 15. *Linkage Language*

This refers to the verbal process of describing (pacing) observable and verifiable behavior in the listener. Then, by using a "linking word," the speaker goes on to describe (leading) the desired behavior. Different people, of course, respond differently to each pattern. Linkage language involves the process of utilization connected to specific linking words.

### a.   *Conjunctions*

Use a conjunction such as "and" to link observable behavior and desired experience. The conjunction links the pacing statement to the leading statement. ("X" and "Y"). Example: "As you sit there, breathing and reading this document and you can begin to breathe more deeply and become more relaxed." The purpose here involves linking the pacing statement to the leading statement so that the latter seems to follow logically from the former. Thus, the linkage collapses information boundaries to enhance the sense of continuity. Additional pacing statements further enhances the effect ("X" and "X" and "X" and "Y"). Examples: "As you sit in your chair (pacing) and read this paper (pacing) and I communicate to you (pacing) and you can breathe deeply and relax more thoroughly (leading)."

### b.   *Disjunction*

Using the contrasting or negative form of conjunctions can also sometimes achieve the same results. ("X" and "X" and "X" but "Y"). Examples: "I don't know whether you prefer to continue gazing at this paper (pacing), or, whether you'd like to look elsewhere (pacing), or whether you'd like to breathe deeper (pacing), but I do know that your conscious can develop a trance that will fit nicely your present needs (leading)."

### c.   *Adverbial Clauses or Implied Causatives*

Causatives often exist as "time" words that imply that one event inevitably functions as linked in time with, or caused by the other. Key implied causatives include: (1) *Since* "X" then "Y." *Since* you are now breathing deeper, you can begin to relax even more. (2) *When* "X" then "Y." *When* you settle comfortably into that chair, you can allow your eyes to slowly close. (3) *While* "X" then "Y." *While* you remember that very special time and place, you can comfortably begin to develop that trance. (4) *After* "X" then "Y." *After* you have become very comfortable, you can begin to allow your trance to develop. (5) Other implied causatives words include: *often, as, before, during, following* and *throughout*.

To familiarize yourself with these language patterns, write down five sentences for each. Include the Meta-Model violations as well in your exercise. You will find these skills most helpful in all areas of communication and highly useful in public speaking.

## Conclusion

"Hypnosis" and trance describes nothing new, odd, occult, strange or mysterious. Our consciousness can "come up" (uptime) and "go down" (downtime). And when it goes down inside—we enter into another world, the inner world of meaning, belief, concepts—a world of spirit where we create our neuro-semantic reality.

Nor can we escape from this. We can only effectively develop awareness and understanding of this and how it plays out in communication in everyday life so that we can have more choice and control over it. When we do that, then we can choose our hypnotists well. Then we can know when to "go into trance" and when to come out! Then we will not allow ourselves to unknowingly or unconsciously receive the onslaught of the bad suggestions that some people forever put out. Then we can know how to dehypnotize ourselves from the dysfunctional negative suggestions left over (in our heads) from childhood. Then we can take a proactive stance in communicating positive and enhancing suggestions for ourselves and others. This empowers us in communicating professionally and consciously.

### Summary Of Milton Model Language

*Milton Model Language Patterns Using Meta-Model Violations*

1. Mind Reading
2. Lost Performative
3. Cause-Effect
4. Complex Equivalence
5. Presuppositions
6. Universal Quantifiers
7. Modal Operators of Necessity
8. Modal Operators of Possibility
9. Nominalizations
10. Unspecified Verbs
11. Simple Deletions
12. Lack of Referential Index
13. Comparative Deletions

*Milton Model Continued*

14. Tag Questions
15. Pacing Current Experience
16. Double Binds
17. Conversational Postulate
18. Extended Quotes

19. Selectional Restriction Violation
20. Phonological Ambiguities
21. Syntactic Ambiguity
22. Punctuation Ambiguity
23. Utilization
24. Embedded Commands
25. Spelling Out Words

*Linkage Language*

25. Conjunctions "X" and "Y"
26. Disjunctions "X" and "X" and "X" but "Y"
27. Adverbial Clauses (implied causatives)
    a.  Since "X" then "Y"
    b.  When "X" then "Y"
    c.  While "X" then "Y"
    d.  After "X" then "Y"

## Steps In Communicating

1.  Determine your Well-Formed Outcome

2.  Build rapport and test

3.  Gather information with the Meta-Model

4.  Use Milton Model language patterns to:
    a.  Induce trance.
    b.  Directionalize language towards outcome.
    c.  Deliver embedded commands toward outcome.

## Thought Questions To Assist Your Learning:

1.  What do we mean by the "Milton model"?
2   Describe what the phrase "artful vagueness" means?
3   How does the Milton model operate in a reverse way to the Meta-model?
4.  Which distinction within the Milton model did you discover you already have in your language repertoire?
5.  Which distinction(s) would you like to become really skilled at? Why?

# Chapter 11

## Hypnosis Part III

## Story, Metaphor, Analogy
### (Derived from Hall & Bodenhamer, 1997d)

**What you can expect to learn in this chapter:**

- The role of "story" or metaphor as a hypnotic pattern
- How to use storytelling to induce trances
- The power of metaphors to bring about changes
- How to re-story your own life

> *Robert Dilts (1976) has defined a metaphor as "a figure of speech in which something is spoken of as if it were another."*

Robert Dilts (1976) has defined a metaphor as "a figure of speech in which something is spoken of as if it were another." (p. 74) The word "metaphor" itself literally means "to carry over." Thus by means of a metaphor, we carry over or transfer a message to another person's mind. The listener interprets the framework or structure of the metaphor and interprets them in the framework of their own experience(s).

Yet because we put the message in the frame of an unrelated story, the story typically bypasses the conscious mind and thereby allows the unconscious mind to receive it. A well-designed metaphor as a set of mind-lines that conversationally changes beliefs, must have *a similar structure* to the person's experience. This similarity at the structural level, in fact, works to invite the unconscious mind to interpret it in relation to one's own needs. The term *isomorphic* describes this.

> *As a communication device, story, metaphor, and narratives also present a far less threatening style than does direct advice.*

As a communication device, story, metaphor, and narratives also present a far less threatening style than does direct advice. What explains this? It occurs, in part, because we veil our intended message in the metaphor.

Further, as a multi-level device, we can use story to communicate on numerous levels at the same time. Milton Erickson's genius centered in this. He would use metaphors to communicate with both the conscious and unconscious facets of mind simultaneously. In this way, he provided the conscious mind with a fun and entertaining message while simultaneously he would address deeper concerns using the structure of the story. The surface story primarily keeps the conscious mind occupied. The deeper (or higher) structural message then "carries over" to the unconscious mind through the story's similarities. Accordingly, we primarily use stories and metaphors in hypnosis.

Theoretically, the Meta-model of language explains that metaphor works by presenting a Surface Structure of meaning using the surface statements that comprise the story's content. At this level we *just hear a story*. Yet at the same time, the Deep Structure of meaning activates our TDS to find references in our own library of references which then connect us to the story at that level. Yet this primarily occurs outside of conscious awareness. We unconsciously make connections.

Sometimes this process can bring about deep healing at these out-of-consciousness levels. When such healing occurs, we engage in a "submodality mapping across." The story operates as a meta-level to our lower level autonomic nervous system processing.

As with the other reframing patterns that we have mentioned, metaphors function directly on our mental internal representations. The languaging of metaphors introduces new strategies, meanings, states, ideas, etc., to the lower level belief meanings. The only difference: it operates apart from conscious awareness. Here we use story and narrative as *"as if"* formats to try on new meanings.

Did you have any idea that story, metaphor, narrative, poetry, etc., could have involved such depth or complexity? On the surface, a story seems so simple. Yet the transformative power of a story does not lie on the surface, but under the surface. The three major components involved in the nature and processes of a story include:

---

*Major Components of a Metaphor*

1. *Trans-derivational Searches*
2. *Displacing Referential Indexes (Symbolism)*
3. *Isomorphism*

---

## Trans-derivational Searches

The TDS (or trans-derivational search) refers to the neuro-linguistic process whereby when we hear symbols (words, language, etc.), to make meaning of the symbols, we *go in* and access our memory banks, our library of references, our internal references. We search inside. (Think about TDS as *Travel Down* in *Side!*).

| |
|---|
| *Language always exists **meta** to experience.* |

Whenever we **describe** an experience, we move from the actual experience to *a description of the experience*. We have moved from the territory, to our *"map"* of the "territory." Now our language, as a description or symbolic verbal representation of the experience, moves us into the neuro-semantic dimension of reality. At this level, the experience *only* exists as **an internal mental representation.** It does not involve external reality and so does not have that kind of reality to it. It only exists as our internal paradigm or model of the world.

This means that language always exists *meta* to experience. It operates at a higher level of abstraction than the internal representation to which it refers. So for language to "work" it must elicit and evoke inside of us sensory-based representations. We experience the meaningfulness of language when the words (as symbols) trigger us to see, hear, feel, smell, taste, touch, etc, the referents on the screen of our mind.

What does the word "car" evoke in terms of sensory-based representations? Does it evoke for you a black Pontiac as it does for me (BB)? Probably not. That reference describes the result of my TDS. Where did your TDS take you? A Toyota, of course (MH)!

What does the word "dog" evoke? Where does your TDS take you? I (BB) have an internal representation of a black Cocker Spaniel. What kind of dog did you find in your library of references?

We make sense of language in this way. We understand by searching through our internalized and stored experiences for visual, auditory, kinesthetic, olfactory and/or gustatory sensations that correspond to the language symbols we use and hear. This explains how language (all language) operates metaphorically.

| |
|---|
| *All language operates metaphorically.* |

Now we call this process of associating the language we hear with our own internal representation(s) a "trans-derivational search" (TDS). When we go from the Surface Structure language of a metaphor to the Deep Structure, we make our internal search. So when we listen to a story or metaphor, our brain and nervous system makes an unconscious TDS to connect the metaphor with our model of the world. Count on metaphors doing this. Count on stories activating listeners to search their "memory banks" to make sense of things using their model of the world.

## Displacing Referential Indexes

Obviously working with story, narrative, and metaphor involves *symbolism*. A symbol refers to any object, situation, or character that becomes an anchor for certain responses. Many everyday metaphors take the form of, "I once knew a person who..." The symbolic link here? The word "person." Further links will arise from the similarities within the story. Such symbolic links exemplifies the concept of "displacement of referential indices."

This means that whenever someone talks about their experience, but does so with enough vagueness (artfully vague!), we then, as listeners, hear the story in terms of our own experiences. Come on, you know you do this! And when we do, we have shifted or displaced the referential index. (But don't worry, the mind police won't arrest you for this!) When we do this we have begun to listen sympathetically and experientially to the story. Doing this empowers the story to affect us and "speak to us."

Making these referential index shifts occurs all the time. We all do it many times everyday. And it also occurs at both conscious and unconscious levels. We distort our sensory representations, we switch the referential index, we enter into the story, and the story casts its spell. Then its magic happens. No wonder the old term for story is **spell!**

> *Storying, narrating, metaphoring, etc., encourages the switching of referential indices.*

Storying, narrating, metaphoring, etc., encourages the switching of referential indices. This invites the *"as if" quality* of stories which then begins to work in our minds and bodies. And when it does— suddenly we feel transported to another time, another place, into another body, etc. The spell has *entranced* us. We lose track of time, place, self, environment, etc., as we go zooming off into new and different worlds and realities.

Then, once inside the story, an animal, another person, even inanimate objects transform and take on special meanings. They frequently take on powerful symbolic representations for us. And in the story, we become *storied*. Themes, plots, sub-plots, dramas, comedies, tragedies, victories, heroic journey, etc., define, describe, limit, and/or free us. White and Epston (1990) have, in fact, recently developed an entirely new therapy model from this marvelous phenomenon. Of course, the parables of Jesus came before White and Epston. And two NLP people, Freedman and Combs (1990, 1996) have further contributed to Narrative Therapy.

## Isomorphism

The basic component that drives the power of story or metaphor to transform meaning and change **the formula** arises from the story sharing a similar structure to our life and experiences.

> *The basic component that drives the power of story or metaphor to transform meaning and change the formula arises from the story sharing a similar structure to our life and experiences. We call this similarity of structure, an **isomorphic** structure.*

We call this similarity of structure, an *isomorphic* structure. Characters, events, emotions, dramas, etc., in the story relate and correspond to similar formats in our lives. This makes the story meaningful to us.

Isomorphism, as the similarity in structure, also explains how and why we can so easily, even unconsciously, use the story to shift our referential index. Dilts has offered this explanation:

> *Isomorphisms describes the brain's ability to incorporate information about behavior from one class to another similar class.*

"Isomorphism involves the formal similarities between representations of different responses... Individuals can learn much about the possibilities of their own behavior by considering the operation of other systems. Imagining that you are a bird in a certain situation, as opposed to a lion, will open up and abolish many different avenues of response... In general, symbols will identify the structural aspects of the metaphor, while isomorphisms will deal with the relational or syntactic components.

The neural network of the brain constantly generalizes information making learning possible. Isomorphisms describes the brain's ability to incorporate information about behavior from one class to another similar class. This is cross class learning."

David Gordon gives an excellent example of choosing isomorphic relationships in developing a metaphor for family therapy.[14] This does not represent a completed metaphor, but gives an example of how to choose isomorphic characters for metaphorical construction.

The specific selections of the objects, situations and/or characters of the metaphor does not really matter. What matters in metaphor creation concerns how the symbols relate or inter-relate to the needs of the client. In real life the characters undoubtedly refer to actual people in the person's life. In constructing your metaphor, you can use animals, animated objects, people, situations or a combination. The rule, however, states that they must relate isomorphically to the client's needs. Consider the following example:

| Actual Situation | Metaphor |
|---|---|
| Father | Captain |
| Mother | 1st Mate |
| Son | Cabin Boy |
| Family | Boat crew |
| Father rarely home | Captain often shut-up in cabin |
| Son gets into trouble | Cabin boy sets the wrong sails |
| Mother covers for son | 1st mate corrects him and tries to reset sails before captain sees |
| Father finds out, becomes furious and leaves | Captain finds out, furious no one told him and retires to his cabin. |
| No resolution | No resolution |
| Problem recycles | Problem recycles until... resolution |

Milton H. Erickson gives an account of how he used this process while working with a couple having marital difficulties over their sexual behavior. Erickson talked to the couple about their eating habits. He found that their eating habits paralleled the individual sexual behaviors that were causing the difficulty. The husband was a meat-and-potatoes man and liked to head right for the main course, while the wife liked to linger over appetizers and delicacies. For their therapy, Erickson had them plan a meal together in which they both were able to attain satisfaction. The couple, of course, had no idea of the significance of the event, but were pleasantly surprised to find that their sex life improved dramatically afterwards.[15]

Now, I ask you, "What medical term do you believe describes the major sexual dysfunction in their sex life for this metaphor to have worked"? A metaphor which satisfies the similar structural components and becomes isomorphic with the problem situation can not only deliver effective therapy, it may also provide a complete therapy. Erickson turned to the use of metaphors almost entirely in his later years.

> *A metaphor which satisfies the similar structural components and becomes isomorphic with the problem situation can not only deliver effective therapy, it may also provide a complete therapy.*

## Transforming Meaning Using Metaphor

Using the language forms of metaphor, analogy, story, etc., enables us to conversationally reframe. Consider the following one-line stories.

1. "A river runs to the ocean as fast as it can."

2. "The water held captive behind a dam still yearns for the sea."

3. "A friend of mine always complained about her husband being late. But then after he died, she often thought about him and wished that he would just be late."

4. "I once had a friend who always complained about the high cost of clothes for his teenage daughter. He complained and complained. Then, one day his daughter died in an accident. Now when he thinks about spending money on clothes for her—he wishes he had that opportunity."

5. "If a surgeon is late for dinner because he's saving someone's life, does that mean he doesn't care?"

6. "It's like spitting into the wind."

To story someone with a narrative or metaphor, think about what a particular problem, issue, concern reminds you of. What is this like? More frequently than not, we do our best *lateral thinking* when we stop thinking about a problem and think about something else (especially when relaxing, kicking back, and enjoying ourselves) and then all of a sudden, presto, an idea pops into consciousness that we then relate to the problem.

In Narrative Therapy, we use **externalization** as a central eliciting process. This refers to externalizing a problem, situation, theme, idea, emotion, etc. By separating person from behavior (and all other functions and productions—especially thoughts and emotions) we underscore another central theme in narrative, namely:

> *The person is not the problem;*
> *The problem is the problem.*

Thus, as we externalize, we change our thinking and emoting about our life story, our thoughts and emotions, etc. This invites another story—a Preferred Story that we can build out of unique outcomes and sparkling moments.

> How has Anger sabotaged your success this week?
> When did the Rages invite you to enter back into that story?
> So Sneaky Pee pulled one on you when you went to stay at your best friend's house, huh? And I bet you do really like to get back at Sneaky Pee so he doesn't embarrass you like that again.
> What tactics have you found that Wimping-Out uses to trick you into giving up? How have you stood up to Wimping-Out?

## Connecting Present State With The Desired State

Present State in NLP defines the condition of the client exhibiting undesirable behavior. By Desired State we mean the outcome the client desires for themselves. We must pay careful attention in making the client's desired state conform to the Well-Formed Outcome Model. The purpose of your metaphor (and all NLP therapy) is to move the client from Present State to Desired State.

> *The bridge between the problem (Present State) and the successful outcome (Desired State) involves both pacing and leading.*

In order to move the client from their Present State to their Desired State, we build a bridge between the two. The bridge between the problem (Present State) and the successful outcome (Desired State) involves both pacing and leading.

## Pacing

Pacing describes an essential element in bringing about change. Pacing describes the process whereby the therapist enters into the client's model of the world and joins him/her in that world view. In pacing the client, use the client's own language, topic(s) and story(ies).

In the example given above, Erickson used food as a metaphor for the couple's marital problems. So, if a client who suffers from marital dishar-mony gets into a lengthy discussion that centers around the preparation and eating of food, the therapist can ask themself the question, "Are they talking about food or problems in their marriage?"

Always listen for the story behind the story. Within the structure of your client's stories, you will often discover a metaphor for something else. And, their metaphors may provide a framework for you to devise therapeutic metaphors. In such cases, the therapist paces the client by adopting the client's language, topic(s) and/or metaphors. In the example of the prepa-ration and eating of food equating marital conflict, Erickson paced their story and fed it back to them in the form of a metaphor that contributed to their healing.

## Leading

Once you have paced the client, your responsibility as the therapist moves to leading the client through metaphoric symbolism to the client's desired outcome. Importantly, this does not mean that you necessarily solve the client's problem. Again, the metaphor may or may not work. The metaphor provides a model that we can use to facilitate change. And, sometimes the metaphor itself lacks sufficient correspondence to produce change.

> *A metaphor's content non-specificity provides choice for the client.*

A metaphor's content non-specificity provides choice for the client. The client's unconscious mind may choose to accept or reject the metaphor. Often the client's uncon-scious mind may accept parts of the metaphor and reject other parts. Sometimes the metaphor may have an impact on areas within the client's life that you have not targeted directly. Learn to appreciate the unconscious mind's ability to direct the healing to the most needed areas. Erickson trusted his own unconscious mind as well as his clients'. Indeed, much of Erickson's power rested on his total accept-ance of the unconscious mind's ability to do best for the client.

Any area within the client's life that the metaphor may represent has poten-tial for change. Therefore, the client's unconscious mind may generalize the metaphor to other areas of the client's life that lie analogous to the issue(s) presented through the metaphor.

All language operates as metaphor. Actually all language provides a doorway into the problem they desire your assistance in changing. As stated earlier, often the client will give you a metaphor through someone else's story or even a similarly disconnected story. They will do this rather than describe the problem. Pacing the client means you enter their model of the world. This model of therapy does not force unconscious material into the client's conscious mind. Rather, you as the therapist work with the client's metaphors. That describes what Erickson did by picking up on the relationship of the food metaphor with the marital problem in the example above.

> *Because human neurology can organize itself isomorphically, parallels among neurological representations arise. The brain functions far more through structural relationships via the representational systems than it does through content.*

Because human neurology can organize itself isomorphically, parallels among neurological representations arise. The isomorphic relationship of planning and enjoying a meal carried over into the couple's sexual activity. The brain functions far more through structural relationships via the rep system than it does through content. Indeed, content means very little compared to the rep system structure. You will remember that with the exception of maintaining body functions, the brain can only do six things at the representational level: make pictures, create sounds, have feelings, smell, taste and create words. The parallel between the isomorphic relationship of the metaphor with the neurological representations (pictures, sounds, feelings, smells, tastes and words) give metaphors their power to bring about change. Thus, any experience processed by a person will obviously parallel representations from other areas of their life. Pacing the client means that you allow the metaphor to work in accordance to the client's unconscious mind. This allows for clean and elegant therapy.

After pacing the client, the therapist leads the client through use of the metaphor to resolution of their problem. Again, this does not say we solve the client's problem. The metaphor may or may not work. Like all NLP techniques, metaphors simply provide another tool in your therapeutic toolbox. By design, a metaphor offers the client a strategy that will lead them to resolution if their unconscious mind chooses to accept the metaphor. Erickson led the couple to resolution through the food metaphor. Once they successfully prepared and enjoyed a meal, they isomorphically related this accomplishment into their sex life. Erickson led them through the metaphor to resolution.

## Utilizing Reframing Within Metaphors

Reframing provides a technique of changing problems into resources. A key NLP presupposition states that all meaning operates as context-dependent.

Context determines to a large extent the meaning of everything we say, think or hear. When doing reframing, what we first view as a problem becomes the basis for a resource. Reframing serves as a vital component in using metaphors for therapeutic resolution. The metaphor provides an excellent frame for reframing.

> *The metaphor provides an excellent frame for reframing.*

## Unspecified Verbs, Nominalizations, Embedded Commands & Analogue Marking

Metaphors provide context for a most effective use of delivering reframes. Metaphors also provide the context for effective utilization of some language patterns you have already learned. Metaphors provide the context through which the use of unspecified verbs, nominalizations, embedded commands and analogue marking take on more effectiveness in delivery. We will review these patterns. A metaphor by nature induces a mild trance within the client. Milton model language patterns enhance this process. Thus, the wise therapist will incorporate Milton model language within the structure of their metaphor.

> *A metaphor by nature induces a mild trance within the client. Milton model language patterns enhance this process.*

### Unspecified verbs

Unspecified verbs are those verbs where the speaker or writer leaves out the details of the action. David Gordon illustrates:

1) John went into the closet.

2) John crept up to the closet, gently opened the door, then jumped in, head first, using his feet to slam the door behind him.

You will note that the second sentence gives specific details of how John got into the closet. Although John chose a ridiculous way to get into the closet, you have a much greater description of how he got in the closet. The first sentence, on the other hand, gives little detail and permits the client to interpret for themselves as to how they got into or would get into a closet.[16] In metaphorical description, the more you leave to the client's unconscious mind for interpretation, the better. For that reason, unspecified verbs give you a tool to assist the client into trance.

## Nominalizations

Nominalizations provide an excellent addition to therapeutic metaphors. You will recall that nominalizations describe those process words turned into a noun. A nominalization takes a process and freezes it. If you cannot see, hear, smell, or taste an noun, it indicates a nominalization. If you cannot put it in a wheelbarrow, you have the classic NLP description of a nominalization. If you fill in the blank below with the word and it makes sense you probably have a nominalization: "An ongoing _____." Nominalizations delete large amounts of information. Consider the statement, "I am in a poor relationship." Here we have a nominalization, the word "relationship." You cannot see, hear, smell or taste a "relationship." Nor can you place a "relationship" into a wheelbarrow. Changing the verb "relating" into the noun "relationship" nominalizes the verb. Other examples of nominalizations we hear come in words like *education, illness, respect, discipline, friendship, decision, love, fear, strategy* and *sensation*. Unless you want to hypnotize, nominalizing our experiences does not prove very helpful. However, nominalizing experiences in therapy may prove very helpful because nominalizations initiate trans-derivational searches. Because nominalizations delete massive amounts of information, they force the listener to go inside, search for connective meaning and supply their own meanings. The "going inside" describes a trans-derivational search. Consider the sentence, "Ralph has a friendship." Do you see the nominalization here? "Friendship." The process of acting friendly has become frozen into "friendship." This sentence, within a metaphor, invites a client to initiate a trans-derivational search and apply their own meaning for "friendship." Using nominalizations in metaphors gives the client the opportunity to de-nominalize the word, that is, turn the nominalization back into a process of their own choosing.

## Embedded Commands

Embedded commands provide another tool from the Milton model that proves extremely useful in delivering a therapeutic metaphor. Erickson demonstrated his expertise as a master at giving the unconscious mind directions through embedded commands. To form embedded commands, insert the client's name in a sentence to draw the client's attention to what follows. Suppose you desire for a client to "let go" some negative feelings. Within your metaphor you may speak of someone who lets some negative emotions go. In your metaphor you could say something like this: "And just like he let his emotions go, Ralph, **let those emotions go, now!**"

Erickson also **marked out** such words that he wanted to go into the unconscious mind. **Marking out** refers to emphasizing specific words or phrases by altering your tonality. In giving these commands and marking out words, both lower your tone and raise the volume of your voice. **You can instruct** a person's unconscious mind through embedded commands **to get well, now.** (Did you get the command from the marked out words?) In a therapeutic metaphor incidents, concepts and/or characters provide the isomorphic tools which provide the essential elements of the metaphor. Marking these elements out draws the client's conscious and/or unconscious mind to them.

## Summary—The Attractiveness of Metaphors

1.  Metaphors speak to the unconscious mind.

2.  A metaphor suggests solutions to problems in a way that invites a client to enjoy solving their own problem. The client makes a movie of the metaphor and the movie in turn does the healing.

3.  People identify themselves in the metaphor.

4.  Metaphors help control the therapeutic relationship.

5.  You can embed directives within the metaphor.

6.  Metaphors decrease resistance.

7.  Metaphors provide an excellent frame for reframing. In the story of the metaphor, reframe their problem.

8.  Metaphors build ego-strength. When people hear a story about how other people solved their problems, they can identify with it and feel good about it.

9.  When you use metaphors in your communications, you model a great way to communicate.

10. Metaphors provide a wonderful way to remind others of their own resources and to assist them in tapping those resources.

11. Metaphors assist people in desensitizing them from their fears. Metaphors provide another tool of dissociation.

12. Metaphor descriptions stimulate much more interest than most forms of communication. They immediately garner focus.

13. Metaphors provide much less threat than do directives.

14. Metaphors provide opportunity for flexibility.

15. Metaphors provide an exceptional tool for building rapport.

16. Metaphors provide a non-manipulative form of communication.

17. The listener must go inside to their own experience to make sense out of the story. Metaphors provide one of the easiest ways to get to Deep Structure.

## Boiler Factory Metaphor

One time, when Milton Erickson was a student, he was walking down the street in his town and he saw somewhere across the street a rather large building and there was this noise coming from across the street from this building. And he looked up and he saw a sign on the building and it said 'So and So' boiler factory. Now I don't know if you know this, but in those days they used to make boilers to heat the hotels that were rather large. In fact, imagine a boiler the size of this room and the sheets of steel this thick, or maybe this thick, going up like this around the outside and then along the top a seam with one rivet every two feet or two rivets every foot or maybe three rivets every so much space. Rivet around the edges like this to seal in the uh... pressure inside.

And Erickson, being curious, said there is something over there to learn, so he went across the street and even as he crossed the street the noise was louder and he got to the boiler factory and he went **inside** the boiler factory. When he got **inside**, he said the noise was horrendous. I mean people were going back and forth riveting the rivets, you know, along the thing and the plates of steel. And the men taking the steel off of... And, he saw all these workers going back and forth. And, they **were communicating** clearly to each other, but he couldn't hear them... inside the boiler factory. So, he got curious about that. And, he said, I think there is something to learn here. So, he stopped one of the workers and he said, "Can you get me the boss? I want you to ask the boss to **come outside**. I need to have a conversation with the boss."

So the boss **came outside** and Erickson said, "I am a student and I am interested in learning how to learn and I would like to sleep here for the evening." And, the boss said, OK. So Erickson went home and got his pillow and his blanket... went back to the boiler factory. And, he said when **he got inside** once again the noise was horrendous, it was like, the riveting going on, steel coming out, and he said he found, after a while, a very quiet place over in the corner and he laid out his pillow and his blanket. But even so... I mean he was out of the way of the workers, but even so, the noise was horrendous... And, he said around about midnight he managed to take all the noise and put it out of his mind and then he fell asleep.

## Metaphor Analysis

What does this metaphor talk about and what does it do? Here, Milton Erickson, as he walks down the street, sees something across the street and he moves closer to it. What does that do structurally? Structurally, he dissociates. He goes across the street and walks up and goes, "Now this is interesting." So we zoom in. Not only does it zoom us in, but when he goes inside does he associate or dissociate? He associates when he goes inside. Now, what does he hear over there? He dissociates. What does he hear? Noise comes from the boiler factory. This provides for an internal auditory tonal. So, he hears noise coming from the boiler factory.

Now, he walks across the street, looks up, sees the sign and goes inside. When he gets inside, what happens? So much noise comes from inside he cannot think. The metaphor provides a direct correspondence or isomorphic relationship to what goes on inside people's heads sometimes. By my gesturing (moving arms around), I make this training room the boiler factory. Thus we take everyone and close them inside this room, that is, the boiler factory. We take rivets and put them down the side to make sure that each person trances inside this particular space (the training room). Thus, this metaphor sets up the room as an enclosed learning space and a safe place for people to be.

So Erickson goes inside the boiler factory. He looks around and what goes on? People communicate inside but he can't hear them. What is that? Unaware of his unconscious mind, so he says, "Gee, I think there is something to learn here." Again, we have a direct correspondence to what goes on inside this class. What does he say? Since he has found something to learn here, he has decided the importance of communicating with the unconscious mind so he says, "Can you get me the boss? I want you to ask the boss to come outside." And, the boss came outside. And, Erickson said that he would like to sleep in the boiler factory for the evening. So, he goes home, gets his pillow and blanket, finds a quite place in the corner and falls asleep. That implies a trance, right? Now, what does he do just before he falls asleep? He says he managed to take all the noise and put it out of his mind. We use a visual anchor by taking our hands, boxing up all the noise and placing it outside. Thus, this seemingly innocent metaphor has within its structure much about setting up a classroom (or a client) for learning.

And, I bet it has even more to do with… your unconscious mind knows what else it has to do with, doesn't it? This provides an excellent metaphor for installing a learning state. I (BB) learned it from Tad James.

## Constructing A Metaphor

The major purpose of a metaphor is to pace and lead a client's behavior through a story. In constructing your metaphor, keep in mind the following:

1.  Displace the referential index from the client to some character in the story.

2.  Pace the client's problem by establishing behaviors and events between the characters in the story that are similar to those in the client's situation.

3.  Use the context of the story to access resources from within the client.

4.  Finish the story such that a sequence of events occurs in which the characters in the story resolve the conflict and achieve the desired outcome.

## The Mother Of All NLP

I learned from John Overdurf the "Mother of all NLP" model and have found it most useful both in doing therapy and in teaching NLP. In analyzing the patterns of NLP, you will find that the patterns walk the client through the steps of this model. It also provides a super framework for building your metaphor.

1.  **Associate the Client to the Problem.**
2.  **Dissociate the Client from the Problem.**
3.  **Discover Client Resources and Associate Client to their Resources.**
4.  **Associate Resources to Problem.**
5.  **Future Pace Resources.**

## The Basic Steps In Generating A Metaphor

1.  **Identify the sequence of behaviors and/or events in question.** This could range from a conflict between internal parts, to a physical illness, to problematic inter-relationships between the client and parents, a boss or a spouse.

2.  **Identify the desired new outcomes and choices.** In NLP we communicate with an outcome in mind. Metaphors provide a rather unique way of doing this. Hold in your mind a visual construct of your outcome and let that outcome drive your unconscious mind in generating a metaphor for the client.

3.  **Displace the referential indices.** Map over all nouns (objects and elements) to establish the characters in the story. The characters may consist of anything, animate or inanimate, from rocks to forest creatures to cowboys to books, etc. What you choose as characters has no importance so long as you preserve the character relationship. Very often you may want to use characters from well known fairy tales and myths.

4.  **Establish an isomorphism between the client's situation and behavior, and the situation and behaviors of the characters in the story—map over all verbs (relations and interactions).** Assign behavioral traits, such as strategies and representational characteristics, which parallel those in the client's present situation (that is, pace the client's situation with the story).

5.  **Access and establish new resources in terms of the characters and events in the story.** You can do this within the framework of a reframing of the re-accessing of forgotten resources. You may choose to keep the actual content of the resource ambiguous allowing the client's unconscious processes to choose the appropriate one.

6.  **Use ambiguities and direct quotes to break up sequences in the story should you detect resistance to the story.** Conscious understanding does not, of course, necessarily interfere with the metaphoric process.

7.  **Keep your resolution as ambiguous as necessary to allow the client's unconscious processes to make the appropriate changes.**

8.  **Provide a future pace if possible.**

## Metaphor Exercises

### I. Building Associations

The basis of therapeutic metaphors lies in similarity. The person(s), object(s) and/or things in the metaphor exist as structurally similar (isomorphic) to the client's model of the world. The similarity rests in the items themselves, in the relationships between those items and other items, in the presuppositions behind the items or in the effect those items have on the client. The following exercise attempts to channel your thinking to that of isomorphic thinking. This type thinking obviously provides the basic essentials in metaphor construction.

1.  Divide into triads.

2.  "A" plays the therapist. "B" plays the client. And "C" plays the role of the meta-person.

3.  "B" thinks of a category such as an actor, politician, sports figure or some other famous person.

4.  "A" asks clue questions like: "If "B" became a part of nature, what would "B" become?" Or, "If "B" became a car, what kind, color, etc, would "B" become?" "If "B" became a piece of furniture, what piece would "B" become?" Some of the questions may not produce helpful clues. Some may produce great ones. For example, if the politician were Jerry Ford, the car question would elicit a great response. If he were George Bush, the nature question would give it away.

5.  "C" assists "A" in asking questions.

6.  Do a round robin.

7.  The purpose of this exercise encourages "B" to give short metaphors to help "A" and "C" guess correctly, for "A" and "C" to try to find similarities, and for everyone to learn to think associatively or isomorphically.

## II. Likeness

1.  Divide into triads.

2.  "A" makes a very *general statement* (large chunk) such as: "Seminars are like _____" (or "Life/Marriage/Church/School is like _____ ).

3.  "B" spontaneously and quickly fills in the blank with something very specific (small chunk) such as "*a river*". (A bathtub, a banquet, a woman, a man, a party, etc.) So the statement now reads: "Seminars are like a *river*."

4.  "A" now declares the first similarity that pops into their head, no matter how foolish or bizarre it may sound. "They just go on and on," or "Sometimes they get mighty deep," or "Sometimes the waters get muddy," or "Some of them are pretty fishy."

5.  Do a round robin.

## III. *Therapeutic Metaphor*

1.  "A" shares (or role plays) a problem with "B" and "C" but does *not* discuss a solution. "A" takes 5 minutes to develop the story (or problem) they will tell. If you choose a role-play, make sure you have your story well rehearsed and that you tell it congruently, complete with non-verbal signals.

2.  After listening to the story, "B" and "C" take 15 minutes to develop a therapeutic metaphor guessing at an adequate and reasonable solution. During this time, each "A" will go to a different group, and sit in on the development of the metaphor by a different "B" and "C." "A" has freedom to make any suggestions that provides assistance. "B" and "C" make careful ecological checks, deleting any potentially unpleasant material or any possible misunderstanding their client ("A") might make.

3.  In 15 minutes, "A" returns to their original group. The "B" in each group delivers the metaphor using "A's" preferred language patterns, vocal patterns, gestures, analogic markings, etc. The outcome of the exercise paces the present state and leads to the desired outcome.

4.  As "B" delivers the metaphor, "C" watches for "A's" non-verbal signs of responding to "B's" metaphor. "C" pays particular attention to "A's" non-verbal shifts indicating unconscious agreement, understanding, (or non-agreement/misunderstanding).

5.  All parties debrief by sharing information about the exercise. "A" shares internal state changes that occurred while hearing the metaphor. "A" shares which parts of the metaphor were most and least effective. "B" shares their observations while delivering the metaphor. "C" shares all meta-observations.

4.  Do a round robin.

## Thought Questions To Assist Your Learning:

1.  How does "story" or metaphor operate as a "hypnotic" language pattern?
2.  Define a metaphor.
3.  Name the three major components of a metaphor.
4.  Explain how and why we say that all language operates metaphorically.
5.  In metaphoric designing and use, why does isomorphism play such a crucial role?
6.  What does it mean to pace and lead in the context of communicating a metaphor?

# Chapter 12

## Satir Categories

*Adding Variety To Your Communication*

**What you can expect to learn in this chapter:**

- The five categories of communication developed by Satir
- How to use the categories for recognizing patterns

Until she died in 1980, Virginia Satir served as one of the world's foremost family therapists. She wrote and lectured extensively throughout her career. Today she has disciples in many disciplines, in many countries who use her techniques to heal dysfunctional families. She was an excellent choice for Richard Bandler and John Grinder to model in their initial development of NLP.

### The Categories

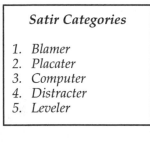

*Satir Categories*

1. *Blamer*
2. *Placater*
3. *Computer*
4. *Distracter*
5. *Leveler*

Virginia Satir noticed that people tend to consistently use one of five different language behaviors. She labeled these five patterns: *Blamer, Placater, Computer, Distracter* and *Leveler*. These categories describe large chunk styles of communication, which give reliable information about people's preferences in how they tend to converse with others.

The *Blamer* usually looks for somebody else to place responsibility on for things going wrong. The blamer projects their feelings and thoughts towards other people. Some refer to them as skunks, for they always spray people with their language. They use stiff gestures and usually point their fingers at the other person. Universal quantifiers, complex equivalences and lost performatives provide the blamer with invaluable tools in their quest to "let 'em have it"! Unless the blamer chooses to change, they will usually find themselves very alone.

*The Blamer Position*

*The Placater Position*

*The Computer Position*

*The Distracter Position*

The **Placater** in some ways mirrors the blamer in that they want the blame placed elsewhere. However, they try to shift responsibility in such a manner so as that others will perceive them as nice. A Placater may even accept the blame for everything. The Placater utilizes the Meta-model violations of cause and effect, unspecified verbs and modal operators. Unlike the Blamer, the Placater does not use forceful language or threatening gestures. The Placater operates more like a turtle than a skunk. Instead of spraying the other person, the Placater will draw into their own shell. They try to trigger guilt in you with the "poor little me" attitude. The statement, "How come I care about the world and nobody cares about me?" summarizes the feelings of the Placater.

The **Computer** type uses language that hides emotions. Their defense lies in their never giving themselves away. They mirror Mr. Spock of Star Trek: logical, always under control, unemotional, etc. The Computer type appears like Mr. Cool. Some may say they have a cold and unfeeling personality. In marriage and other close relationships, the spouse or significant other to a Computer may very well experience them as cold and aloof. This often causes many problems. Often they live dissociated. The Computer type uses words as buffers. They give many "you" messages. Often they will deflect responsibility by saying, "One must conclude..." Listen for the Meta-Model violations of lost performatives, nominalizations and deleted referential indexes in identifying the computer. Most bureaucrats and accountants function like the Computer type.

The **Distracter** at one moment will appear as a Blamer. At another moment they will give off the characteristics of a Placater. Then they will switch to the Computer type. They just jump from one mode of behavior to another, hence the name Distracter. They cause confusion and their mouths run in high-gear overdrive. They use lost performatives, generalizations and deleted referential indexes.

The **Leveler** does not have many distinguishing characteristics. The major characteristic of a Leveler comes out in the absence of any of the other Satir categories. A Leveler comes across as factual and congruent. You can rely on what a Leveler says as true to their perception. The physiology and language display the congruency of the Leveler. The one negative thing we can say

*The Leveler Position*

about a Leveler concerns the challenge that many people do not want to know the truth. This will lead them to respond negatively to the Leveler.

By observing body language, you can usually identify the Satir category in use. The Blamer often uses posture, breathing and gestures that correspond to a visual Person. They point their fingers a lot with the finger and palm down. The Placater matches the kinesthetic. Often their palms turn up as if to say, "Please." The Computer mirrors the auditory digital. Often the Computer will stand with their arms crossed. The Distracter will take on the physiology of all the above as they switch from one mode to another.

After spending a good deal of time with a person, you will identify their preferred Satir category. When under stress, we usually give away our preferred category. So, have your sensory acuity attuned when gathering information from a stressed person. Do not jump to a quick conclusion concerning someone's preferred Satir category. Listen and watch over a period of time before forming your conclusion. As situations and contexts change, our use of Satir categories may very well change. In all probability, you operate from a different Satir category *when under stress* then when utterly relaxed.

## Pacing Satir Categories

In pacing Satir categories, as a rule, you do not match as with predicate matching. If you match the Satir category, you will break rapport and enhance whatever mode they use. Satir herself always recommended that you mismatch except when with a leveler. As mentioned in the chapter on building rapport, you can match the physiology and volume of an angry Blamer, but do not match their threatening tonality and words. To answer a Blamer with Blamer leads to an argument. Placating a Placater leads to a whining contest. Distracting with a Distracter will lead to chaos. Matching a Computer type with a Computer type may work, but the conversation will sound stale and cerebral. Most committee leaders lead meetings in the Computer mode, and therefore come across as boring and, therefore, unproductive. This leaves only one Satir category that you can safely match, the Leveler.

How do you use Satir categories in communication? First go to the Computer mode if you do not know what to do. Computers take no risks but they also communicate little substance. This response will give you time to decide what to do. Always avoid the Distracter mode. Operating from the Distracter mode tends to cause others to perceive that you have serious personality problems.

Satir suggested that there is often incongruency between what a person's physiology communicates and what one actually feels inside. A Blamer may have a stiff and pointing finger and at the same time have a judgmental and confident attitude. However, such a position may very well cover up a feeling of loneliness and lack of success. A Placater may say with their posture that they experience helplessness, but inside they may feel worthless. On the outside the Computer may seem calm and collective, but inside they may feel uncomfortable and vulnerable. The Distracter may sound and act like a scatterbrain, but they may actually feel unbalanced and unloved.

Stress almost inevitably pushes us out of leveling and into one of the other categories. Most people have learned to feel comfortable in a preferred Satir category. However, that may provide a poor means of coping because it reduces rather than expands a person's choices. Under stress, we need all available means of communication. By going to our preferred Satir category, we limit our response to others. We need access to a rich variety of ways of responding when under stress. A wise communicator will develop proficiency in the use of all the categories.

> *We need access to a rich variety of responses when under stress. A wise communicator will develop proficiency in the use of all the categories.*

## Exercise

### Satir Categories (3 people)

1. "A" role plays a fourteen-year-old teenager who wishes to go on a date. "B", the parent, has just said, "No. You know that the rules around here say that you must turn sixteen before you date." "A" responds, "Why can't I go? You don't trust me. All my friends at my age date. Their parents trust them, but you don't trust me. I will never, never forgive you for this!"

2. "B" replies using each of the Satir categories in turn. At the end of each response, "C" helps "A" and "B" process their thinking and feelings during the various replies. Pay particular attention how different replies will access different internal states each time in "A" and "B." As "B" replies by matching "A's" words with appropriate posture, tone, gestures, facial expression, etc.

## Example Of Replies:

**BLAMER:** "I am fed up with listening to that kind of talk. You know the rules around here. I have told you since you were a child that you will never date until you are sixteen. You never listen to me. I am the parent and you are the child. As long as you live in this house and eat at my table, you will always do what I tell you to do. Just keep it up and I won't let you date until you are eighteen!"

**PLACATER:** "Now, honey, please don't act like that. I do trust you. You make me feel so bad when you talk to me like that. I am having PMS today and I may have been a little harsh. I don't want to be mean. I sincerely wish to be a good parent. Please don't be angry with me. It hurts me when you are angry with me. Forgive me, please."

**COMPUTER:** "You may think that I am the only parent who exercises responsibility by not letting their children date before sixteen. However, I know for a fact that other parents have the same rule. In any case, I am not responsible for other parent's children. I am responsible for you and I accept responsibility for determining when you are mature enough to date. Studies prove that most teens are too immature to date alone until they are at least sixteen. And I was fourteen once, you know. As a responsible parent, I am concerned about your welfare. Would you have me be any other way? Forgive ness is yours to give. Responsibility as a parent is mine. And, because I love you, I choose not to let you date alone until you are sixteen. Any further discussion will be fruitless. Therefore, our discussion is complete."

**DISTRACTOR:** "What do you mean I do not trust you? You make me so mad. You hurt me so much when you act this way. You know, honey, that I wish to give you as much latitude as possible. I desire for you to grow into a responsible adult. In order for you to do this, I understand that I must allow you freedom. However, I must make decisions based on what I believe is your present level of maturity. Oh, you aggravate me so much when you tell me I don't trust you. You know better than that. Please don't tell me that I don't trust you. You make me feel like I am some kind of a tyrant. However, one must realize how easy it is to make a bad decision based on hormones and not reason. And, you have heard about AIDS haven't you?"

**LEVELLER:** "Honey, I love you very much. Whether I say, 'yes' or 'no' does not change that. In this situation, I believe 'no' is the answer love would give. Thus, the answer is 'no!'"

## Satir Categories In Public Speaking

> *The Satir categories provide invaluable tools to the public*
> *speaker. Learning to use all the categories will help you*
> *establish rapport with everyone in the audience.*

The Satir categories provide invaluable tools to the public speaker. Learning to use all the categories will help you establish rapport with everyone in the audience. Put on the tone and physiology of each of the categories during the course of your speech. Use Blamer when you want to make a strong point. Having served as a preacher for many years, I (BB) have great confidence in my ability as a Blamer. Many times I went overboard with it. Lots of people get tired of having a guilt trip laid on them. So, when engaged in public speaking, use wisdom in how often you utilize the Blamer mode. Use placater for sympathy. Use Computer to garner the perception as dissociated and logical. Use Distracter for fun and to grab the audience. Use Leveler for candor and to convince the audience. Run through these categories at will and you can put people through an incredible set of states.

## Thought Questions to Assist Your Learning:

1.  How would you use all five Satir categories in expanding your own communication style?
2.  What use or value do you see in knowing, recognizing and using these categories?

# Part Three

*The NLP Neurology Model*

# *Chapter 13*

## Anchoring: Managing Neurology

*Speaking The Silent Language*

**What you can expect to learn in this chapter:**

- The NLP user-friendly form of Pavlovian conditioning
- How to "anchor" experiences and states
- Numerous things to do with the anchoring process
- Patterns of transformation using anchoring

I (BB) grew up in the rural mountains of North Carolina. My father thought and behaved like a typical mountain man. He sternly disciplined us. While he did not physically abuse, he expected and received the behavior he wanted. To this day I can still remember that special look he would give when my behavior did not meet his expectations. When I saw *that* look, I knew that wisdom lay in immediately changing my behavior! The consequence for not changing my behavior—a trip behind the corncrib and a special visitation of a branch. A nearby bush had narrow branches that felt like leather when dad wrapped them around my backside. So, when dad gave that special look, I immediately responded. He had me *anchored to that look.*

- Following the success of the allied forces in Desert Storm many felt a sense of pride in victory—so when we saw an American flag widely displayed it re-induced those feelings every time.

- When we drive down the road and approach a rectangular box with three lights on it, we notice on the top the red light, yellow in the center and green on the bottom. When the light changes to yellow, we slow down. When the light changes to red, without thinking, our foot leaves the gas pedal and touches the brakes.

- Before the death of his wife, Joe went to church regularly. But since having her funeral at his church, he hasn't returned to church. When he even thinks about going back to church, he creates a mental image of his wife's casket at the front of the church. This image brings on a sense of overwhelming grief and he begins to sob. So, in an attempt to lessen the grief, Joe stopped going to his church.

## The Stimulus-Response Concept

What do all of these experiences have in common? In each of these *something elicited* memories, feelings and behavior. This stimulus-response reaction goes back to the early Russian psychologist, Ivan Pavlov, and his experiments with unconditioned and conditioned responses. As Pavlov studied dogs, he discovered that they would salivate upon seeing, smelling, and tasting meat. He added the sound of a bell or a tuning fork when he gave the dogs the meat. After a few repetitions of conditioning, he would only sound the bell or tuning fork to elicit their salivation response. This became foundational in behavioral psychology and learning theory.

Bandler and Grinder discovered *a "user-friendly" use of conditioned responses* (classical conditioning) as they recognized that they could use the triggering stimulus (the anchor) as a mechanism for moving "experiences" around in time and space.

> *In NLP, anchoring refers to the natural process by which any element of an experience (any sensory modality component) can recreate (re-evoke) the entire experience.*

Because much of our "learning" follows this model, we also get various internal/external responses (thoughts-feelings, states, behaviors, etc.) *linked to* or connected to various stimuli—some of which lie outside of awareness. In NLP, anchoring refers to the natural process by which any element of an experience (any sensory modality component) can recreate (re-evoke) the entire experience. And, inasmuch as individual skills result from the development and sequencing of rep systems, stimuli that evoke any part of the representation will often trigger the entire experience.

Since anchoring occurs all the time, it actually represents nothing new. Normally, we just do not notice it. Perhaps we don't have a model (conceptual schema) for thinking about it. So it occurs—but occurs *outside* of our conscious awareness. This very fact itself makes it such a powerful communication mechanism—one that we can now learn to use more systematically and strategically.

One of the highlights of my life (BB) consisted in receiving my Doctor of Ministry Degree from Southeastern Baptist Theological Seminary. In my memory of that experience I can vividly *see* the splendor of the chapel, the packed auditorium, the march of the professors down the aisle at the opening of the ceremony. As I do, I *feel the feelings* that I had then. They come back. Each professor wore the robes and hoods of their respective institution and discipline. The *sounds* of the large pipe organ reverberated through the building. I recall hearing Dr. Elmo Scoggin giving the address.

To those receiving the doctor's degree, Dr. Scoggin said, "My father told me when I received my doctor's degree, 'Son, that doctor's degree is like a curl on a pig's tail. It is mighty pretty but it ain't worth nothing.'" The day's highlight came when President Randall Lolley placed the hood around my neck. Today when I wear the robe to conduct a wedding, the very sight of it *re-evokes that whole experience*. The robe acts as an anchor for the entire experience. Even the sound of a pipe organ can recall the experience.

> *An anchor refers to an internal or external representation that triggers another representation.*

## What Do We Mean By "An Anchor"?

An anchor refers to an internal or external representation that triggers another representation. The external sight of the doctoral robe or the sound of the pipe organ re-triggered my thoughts-feelings about that experience. The sight of the robe triggered the entire memory with all the internal representations of the memory. If the memory contains all the rep systems, we call that *a 4-tuple*. Why 4-tuple and not 5-tuple? We do that by combining the olfactory and gustatory rep systems into one. So, the term "4-tuple" refers to VAKO with "O" combining both olfactory and gustatory rep systems. Any one of these representations when triggered will cause the recall of the entire memory. Dilts (1983) noted,

> "This process happens as a result of the synaptic and electric interference patterns created during neural processing." (p. 25)

Anchors fill our lives. Now, while behavioral psychologists tend to think that all our behavior results from conditioned responses, in NLP we view life as a combination of conditioned reflexes and consciously chosen anchors.

We can see anchors all around us. We have already mentioned some. Yet anchors include every rep system. Auditory anchors include: "Winston taste good like a _____." Though that commercial played twenty years ago, people over thirty probably hear the rest of the sentence ("...cigarette should.") in their heads.

We have a great many *auditory anchors* within church buildings and services: the joy of hearing a church bell, the smell of a sanctuary, the pastor intoning, "Let us pray," a tune of a favorite hymn. Radio and television producers know the power of such anchors. So they fill up hours of listening pleasure with "Golden Oldies." Advertisers also make good use of auditory anchors.

Recently while out driving with my wife (BB), we had driven a short distance when she noted that she had forgotten to fasten her seat belt. "Do you ever forget to fasten the belt when you drive?" I asked. "No, I only forget when I sit on the passenger's side." Suddenly she became aware that her body had kinesthetic and visual anchors *to the driver's seat*. How? The pressure of the seat when she sat in the driver's seat, the sight of things from that position, etc. She didn't have the same kinesthetics or visuals on the passenger's side. Whenever she sat in the driver's seat, the visual and kinesthetic anchors fired (triggered) and her arm automatically reached for the seat belt. However, when she sat in the passenger's side, she often forgot to fasten the seat belt. The passenger seat did not provide her with anchors for fastening the seat belt. This indicates the specificity of many anchors—and their unconscious nature.

## Warning: "Negative Anchors Present"

Do negative anchors get established in our lives as well? Yes. Consider a family receiving friends at the funeral home. If the wife's mother died and many friends come to pay their respects, while the wife grieves, person after person comes by and hugs her. Unconsciously the touch of a hug can get linked to the feeling of grief.

So, days or months later when her husband suddenly hugs her, inexplicably she suddenly feels like crying! Grief floods over her. She had accessed a state—at unawares—and so her conscious mind might spend some time trying to figure out the content of her negative feelings about her husband! As such, she develops a negative conditioning *to his touch.* Now the older psychologies would have us go back looking for traumas, stuck places in the developmental process, and Greek mythologies that explain unconscious processes. Actually we just have a case of an accidental anchor. So cleaning up negative anchors and teaching couples how to set positive anchors becomes an essential facet of good relating. Anchoring as conditioning presents the therapist with a practical tool for change. Bandler and Grinder (1979) said that approximately 90% of what we do in therapy involves changing the "kinesthetic responses that people have to auditory and visual stimuli." (p. 85)

> *Bandler and Grinder (1979) said that approximately 90% of what we do in therapy involves changing the "kinesthetic responses that people have to auditory and visual stimuli."*

## Anchoring Forgiveness

A former church member called me (BB) about one of his co-workers (Jim) who had emotionally suffered a great blow of having his wife of fourteen years leave him. In two weeks of her leaving, Jim lost seventeen pounds. Emotional pain afflicted him intensely. I had him think about "time" (using some Time-Line processes) along with some anchoring to get him out of the emotional distress so that he could cope with his reality better. Like all of us, Jim had made some mistakes in his past—mistakes that he used to feel guilty about. As a Christian, Jim believed that Jesus had forgiven him, yet Jim had not forgiven himself.

When I questioned Jim concerning the forgiveness of Christ, I anchored the state of forgiveness by touching him on his knee. I then asked Jim to "go back in his life" on his Time-Line to a time before he made those mistakes. As he did, I fired the anchor so that he could experience that sense of forgiveness with regard to those specific events. Then, while holding the anchor on his knee, I asked him to come forward through time bringing that sense of forgiveness with him... As a result, this anchoring of this spiritual resource (forgiveness) provided Jim the means of experiencing the forgiveness of Christ with regard to those mistakes.

## Consciously Anchoring In Therapy

*First anchors last because they set the frame.*

At first I (BB) used anchoring sparingly in therapy. However, with time and practice I now use anchoring regularly (primarily verbal and tonal anchors). I didn't realize its power at first because of its simplicity. Actually, we inevitably set and fire off anchors all the time. One cannot live without doing so. NLP simply makes us aware of the process. Knowing the neuro-linguistic process of anchoring explains how "first impressions form lasting impressions." First anchors last because they set the frame. Awareness of setting anchors in others and ourselves gives us the ability to control the process. We can then set anchors that serve ourselves and others well, bring out our best, and create a context for openness and learning.

*A properly set anchor will get an immediate response and demonstrate the NLP presupposition of one-trial learning.*

Although anchoring originated with Pavlov's theory of stimulus-response, the two conceptual processes do differ at points. Stimulus-response generally requires additional reinforcement. With anchoring, we can usually create a linkage on the first attempt. In the stimulus-response model we reinforce the desired behavior through positive conditioning over time. This may take the form of praise, a smile, a pat on the back or any stimulus that encourages a behavior. The reinforcement will continue until the person makes the desired behavior a habitual part of their lives. This process takes time. Generally an external behavior program internalizes into an internal state through repeating it for twenty or thirty days. Then the behavior operates automatically and unconsciously. On the other hand, a properly set anchor will get an immediate response and demonstrate the NLP presupposition of one-trial learning.

Every time we communicate or send messages, we *anchor representations*. We use words (sound and/or visual symbols—signals) to *represent* something else and to evoke thoughts, representations, ideas, memories, values, etc. Sensory-based words quickly elicit their referents. "The thirty pound dog with a brown coat stood eighteen inches off the ground, sopping wet from the rain and smelling like it had slept the night in a garbage pit, and there it stood shaking itself in my living room!"

We call that *verbal anchoring*. Here we use words to induce or evoke in another person various images, sounds, sensations, smells, and feelings. All effective communicators use anchoring, although they usually do so without knowing precisely how the process works. Good storytellers more consciously pair certain messages or experiences with certain tones of voices. They anchor states, experiences and representations.

## Developing The Art Of Anchoring Effectively

When we systematically and precisely anchor, we can elicit desired behavior and states immediately in response to the new stimulus. Use the following procedures to establish anchors quickly and proficiently.

As an overview of *the anchoring process*: first determine and identify the current state, calibrate to the qualities, signals, and indicators of the state. Then attach some VAKO stimulus to the state. After setting the anchor, break state and then test to see if the stimulus can re-elicit that state (see below). Next, elicit some desired state, get a good full sensory description of it. Attach a new stimulus. Break state and test.

> *We stack anchors by anchoring several similar states on the same place.*

States and/or experiences that need reinforcement probably involve a Meta-state rather than just a primary state. Such states involve a layering of logical levels so that you essentially build not only a program of thoughts-and-emotions about something, but thoughts-and-emotions about those thoughts-and-emotions. In this case, you can reinforce an anchor through stacking anchors. We stack anchors by anchoring several similar states on the same place.

You may choose to change an anchor or erase one. A stronger kinesthetic anchor can "erase" a weaker one. The wife who became negatively anchored at the funeral home may erase that anchor by a more powerful positive anchor so that it "collapses" and cannot function as it did.

## Four Keys To Anchoring

---

### Four Keys to Anchoring

1. Use a **unique** place to anchor
2. Set the anchor at the moment of the state's highest **intensity**
3. Make the anchor as **discrete** and **pure** as possible.
4. Precisely **time** the anchor.

---

Unlike stimulus-response, anchoring can occur as a one-time learning experience. Anchoring can sometimes last years or even a lifetime. When certain conditions occur at the time of anchoring (a very intense state, a very unique stimulus, a most effective linking), then the process needs to occur only once to become permanent. Earlier we mentioned the jingle— "Winston tastes good like a..."? Did that stimulus *anchor* you to go "cigarette should?" How long has that anchor lasted? The four keys of effective anchoring include:

### 1. Uniqueness: Use A Unique Place To Anchor

In setting an anchor, select a unique stimulus for the anchor. This explains why just shaking someone's hand doesn't usually work for anchoring, as it is a generalized behavior. People shake hands frequently, with many different people, and in different ways. Otherwise whoever established the first anchor would have forever set the "meaning/significance" of a handshake every time thereafter! The handshake would forever trigger the person to go into that state! Actually, a handshake lacks enough uniqueness to even set an anchor. Conversely, the more unique the location, the better. This gives an anchor more of a chance to get set and to last.

The more *unique* the stimulus, the better the anchor. When anchoring kinesthetically, pay attention to where, the size of that place, amount of pressure applied, length of time you touch, etc. Choose a location you can easily return to with precision. Avoid anchoring with reference to a person's clothing—clothing moves, gets changed frequently, and thus will change its position with respect to the body.

When self-anchoring, choose a stimulus that you can do comfortably. Select a unique anchor, something that you do not commonly do. For instance, squeezing your earlobe or placing your thumb and little finger together. For kinesthetic anchors, select rarely touched places on your body. I (BB) created a relaxation anchor by squeezing my thumb together with my little finger. Creating an anchor in a unique place enables it to endure much longer.

Concerning reinforcing anchors, Dilts (1983) noted that reinforcement of an anchor tends to increase its effectiveness. However, the effectiveness of an anchor comes from the initial quality of the experience.

> *"Stacking" anchors refers to putting additional resourceful states on top of an anchored resourceful state.*

*"Stacking" anchors* refers to putting additional resourceful states on top of an anchored resourceful state. This makes the anchor more powerful in eliciting a strong positive state. One can also *refresh anchors*. Periodically, I refresh my relaxation anchor. While deeply relaxed, I press my left thumb on my left little finger to reinforce my relaxation anchor.

## 2. Intensity: Set The Anchor At The Moment Of The State's Highest Intensity

We create an anchor by applying a stimulus at the time one experiences *an intense state*. This ties the anchor to the state. Anchors operate state-dependently. This means their operation and functioning depends upon their state of mind-and-body that a person experiences when setting the anchor and re-firing it later.

The "intensity" of a state refers to how strong, emotional, vivid, big, etc., that state feels on the inside. Suppose you want to anchor a resource state in a client. You ask them to remember a time when they felt resourceful. "Think about a time when you felt like you could conquer the world!" As they access the state, it becomes intense if they fully associate into it so they experience it *as if* there again—seeing what they saw, hearing what they heard, and feeling what they felt—fully.

People vary in the amount of time it takes to change internal states, as well as how intensely they experience their states. Some change states quickly and instantly! Tracking them necessitates a lot of calibration and sensory awareness.

Recall an experience that occurred six months to a year ago. Allow yourself to begin to see yourself in the experience and notice, that as you see yourself (your younger you of that time) in the memory, you now have a dissociated memory of it. Now step into that movie and experience it fully from the inside. With this you experience it as if *in* the experience. Dissociation removes most of the emotion of an experience. Many NLP techniques use the mental-emotional ability of associating and dissociating. Although dissociation offers powerful effects, when we seek to anchor a state, we want an associated state.

> When anchoring a state, we will get a more powerful effect with an associated state than with a dissociated state.

Once a person associates into a resourceful state, use your sensory acuity to calibrate to them as they go into a different state. Notice the changes in face color, skin and muscle tone, and breathing. Then apply the anchor at the time when they most intensely experience the state. Doing so neurologically links the state and the anchor. Mind-body inevitably work together. Anchoring works because when we fire the anchor, we access the anchored state. The nerves associated with the anchor connect neurologically to those neurons that contain the remembered state.

### 3. Purity: Make The Anchor As Discrete As Possible.

"Purity" for an anchor means that it has no competing experiences. When accessing the desired state, elicit the resource experience in such a way as to not elicit contaminating, competing thoughts-and-emotions. Avoid inquiring about two different experiences. "Purity" refers to the distinctness of a state.

Allow no contradictory or contrary internal dialogues to go on while recalling the state. It will distract you in an unuseful direction. Use your internal languaging to amplify the desired state you seek. An intense remembered state will have no competing experiences to weaken the state's intensity. If you elicit a reference experience in its simplest, purest form— this insures against not contaminating the desired state.

When anchoring, use your sensory acuity skills to notice when the person associates fully into the intense state. Invite the person to remember the state several times—this will help them to focus. When you see them reach a peak in their experience, set your anchor.

## 4. Precision: Precisely Time The Anchor

For precision in anchoring, aim to identify and utilize the proper timing, namely, when you see the state reaching its maximum intensity of neuro-logical response—apply the anchor. After the state seems to peak, and to decline in intensity, release the anchor. Let go of the anchor as the state releases so as to *not* anchor a "reducing response"(!) or a shift to another state. Holding the anchor too long may contaminate the anchor if the person accesses another state. When I observe the intensity level increasing in someone, I lightly apply the anchor. As the state intensifies, I increase the pressure on my anchor. When the state begins to weaken, I immediately let go of the anchor. How long do you hold the anchor? The time will vary from between five to twenty-five seconds (Figure 13:1). Your sensory acuity skills will inform you as to how long you apply the anchor.

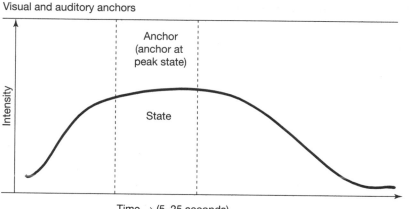

Visual and auditory anchors

Anchor
(anchor at
peak state)

State

Intensity

Time → (5–25 seconds)

*Figure 13:1 Precision Anchoring*

To *set* auditory anchors use particular words or sounds. We often use the word "relax" to anchor in a state of relaxation and speak that word with a relaxing tone of voice. We say "relax" with a low and soft voice. In this way both the word and tone establish an auditory anchor for relaxation.

Other sounds can anchor a state: a cough, the snap of the fingers, or the click of a pen—any auditory stimuli. This works well with groups. And usually you not only have a sound but a particular "face," expression, posture, etc., that adds a visual anchor. When a person or group experiences the desired state, raise your hand and cough. Whenever you desire the same state in the person or group, repeat the same procedure. Part of the secret will lie in replicating the procedure precisely. This will fire the anchor to recall the same state.

## Five Steps To Anchoring

---

### *Five Steps to Anchoring*

1. *Establish rapport.*
2. *Explain the process (Set the frame).*
3. *Elicit and anchor the desired state.*
4. *Interrupt the state (Break state).*
5. *Test the anchor by firing it.*

---

Anchoring involves performing a series of steps. Follow these steps and develop the ability of anchoring as an effective tool for improving life and accessing resources. We can use anchoring to interrupt people in negative states to bring them out. Negative states predominate whenever we experience lots of pain. To heal that situation, we can address the negative emotional states using anchoring.

Anchoring alone will not heal clinical states such as clinical depression. For more complex and layered experiences we will need to bring other processes and interventions to bear. And yet, anchoring will play a role even in those interventions.

### 1.   *Establish Rapport*

Mirror and match the person's physiology, tonality and predicates to enter into their world. This will help them feel comfortable and trusting with the processes.

### 2.   *Explain The Process*

Even though we can use just auditory or visual anchors, we will get the best results by redundantly using anchors in every system. Visual and auditory anchors operate in a more covert way than kinesthetic anchors. And because they usually function in out-of-conscious awareness, we do not need to explain the process.

When using kinesthetic anchors, I (BB) always inform the client. When I use kinesthetic anchors, I first ask the client's permission to sit close to them and touch them. Why? Because many visual people do not like someone "crowding their space" when you sit close to them. They prefer to have more room so they can see things going on around them. Therefore, I always ask permission to sit close to them and always receive such permission. I explain the purpose of touching them on the top of the knee or the hand. If you do this unannounced with some people... Well, you get the picture!

## 3. Elicit And Anchor The Desired Experience (Positive Or Negative)

As we assist someone in recalling a desired state or a negative emotional experience, we want to assist them in re-experiencing a strong, intense, and "pure" experience. In working with positive states, we want the internal experience to feel intense—intensely motivated, excited, competent, resourceful, etc. We ask, "Have you ever experienced certainty?" "Yes." "Good, so now allow yourself, now, to begin to remember a time and a place when you experienced that sense of certainty— when specifically did that occur? What did you see at that time? And where?"

As we help the person to specify time, place, persons, and specific facets of the memory, they will become more and more focused on a specific event. Many Gestalt-thinkers (those who have the Meta-program of general sorting), will have flashes of sights, sounds, and sensations from numerous experiences.

*Keep in mind that a key to anchoring involves the person having accessed an intense state and getting fully associated into it.* A person associates into a state by seeing, hearing, and feeling the state *as if* they have re-entered the experience. They look at the details with their own eyes, hear through their own ears, etc. Their association into the experience enables them, neuro-logically, to relive it in the present moment.

Good focusing questioning will facilitate their association into the experi-ence. To think in terms of *focusing questions,* incorporate the 4-tuple model into your elicitation. The 4-tuple summarizes the major rep system (VAKO). In using the 4-tuple to help a person associate into a desired state, elicit from them representations in each system and anchor each as they become intensely aware of it. By asking the following questions, the person will associate more into the experience. In doing this, you essentially build a stacking anchor (The $^e$ and $^i$ refer to external and internal representations).

$V^e$  Do you see clearly things going on around you while you recall the experience of motivation?

$V^i$  As you recall this feeling of motivation, do you yet notice any pictures?

$A^e$  How well do you hear things happening around you?

$A^e$  What does your own voice sound like as you recall this experience of motivation?

$A^{di}$  Do you have any internal dialogue?

$K^i$  How do you feel now as you begin to relive that memory?

$K^e$  What external body feelings or awarenesses do you have?

$K^i$  As you notice your breathing, where does it come from—high or low in the chest?

K$^i$   How fast do you breathe as you experience this state?
O      Do you remember any special odors or tastes in this motivating experience?

By asking a client to recall an experience from all of these perspectives, it brings to their awareness specific qualities, and as they re-create the representations, they associate back into that state. If you stack these anchors, each on top of the other, you will end up with a strong recreation of the experience—with a strong anchor for motivation or any other desired state.

### 4.   Interrupt The State So The Person Breaks State

After establishing the anchor, stop the process. Break state. Say or do anything that has nothing to do with the process. This will interrupt and separate the person from that state of mind-emotions. Even standing up and moving around will break the state. Now ask them to "clear the screen" of their mind. Ask them to take a deep breath (taking a deep breath will usually change their physiology and hence their state). Change the subject for a moment.

### 5.   Test The Anchor By Firing It

If you used the knee to anchor motivation, touch the same place in just the way as you did when you established the anchor. Touching in the precise spot and with the precise pressure provides neurology the same stimulus associated with the resourceful state. Using your sensory acuity skills, calibrate to their responses. If their face, physiology, breathing, muscle tone, etc., indicates the motivation state (and they confirm it), then you know you have established a good anchor. When you fire the anchor, their motivation state should return without them needing to "think" about it.

If you do not see anything that looks like the motivation state, take that as feedback, inquire about the person's internal state of thoughts-and-feelings. Since anchoring functions as a non-verbal form of communication (signal/symbol sending), like verbal communication—*we never know what we have communicated.* Until we see, notice, and inquire of the person concerning their internal state of thoughts-emotions, memories, fantasies, beliefs, values, etc., we never know what message we have sent or what state we have anchored. So feel free to inquire. Where did their mind and emotions go? What Trans-derivational Search did they make? Wherever they went and whatever information they processed during the anchoring—you anchored *that!*

Once in a workshop in front of twenty people I (MH) asked a lady permission to access and anchor a state of assertive firmness on her knee—when I did touch her knee, before she could "help" it, my touch anchored in thoughts-and-emotions of older memories from someone molesting her! She gave some subtle signs (!)—slapping my hand away, adopting a look of terror on her face, forcefully sitting up straight, muscles taut, breathing hard. "Where did you just go... inside... what memories, thoughts-and-emotions, awarenesses suddenly came upon you?" I asked a moment later.

After she explained, I simply noted, "So you already have an anchor there, huh?" "Yes, Sir." "And a mighty powerful one from what I could see!" "I guess so." "Let's try another place for an anchor." With her agreement, she gave me her right arm and I put two fingers on her forearm. Once we had a strong resourceful experience anchored there, we rehearsed it half a dozen times to demonstrate to the group, and for her own self-validation. Then touching first her forearm, I said, "And when you feel this...fully and completely ...knowing that this assertive firmness empowers you to stay true to your values, your beliefs, your God-given dignity...and you can ...how does it weaken and nullify this..." (and I touched her knee anchor).

She showed little response. "I feel like I don't know what to think or feel. I kind of feel the old feelings, but..."

We call that process *the collapsing of anchors*. So get a good anchor. Keep checking with the person for confirmation of their internal experience. Use feedback for learning and for enriching the experience. Keep rehearsing through the anchoring process.

## Exercises

### I.   *Anchoring States 1*

*(triads)*

1.   **"A" instructs "B" to recall a specific time when "B" felt highly motivated. (Or "B" may wish to choose some other positive state.)**

2.   **"A" establishes with "B" where "A" will apply the anchor.**

3.   **"A" associates "B" into the desired state for anchoring and applies the anchor.** Both "A" and "C" calibrate to "B's" experience of the desired state. "A" follows the four keys to anchoring:
     i.   Choose a unique place to set the anchor.
     ii.  Set the anchor at the point of peak intensity.

    iii. Make sure you have a pure state, that is, make sure that "B" does not have an internal dialogue going on or experience any competing experiences.

    iv. Use proper timing when applying the anchor, i.e., when "B's" desired state begins to build and hold from 5 to 25 seconds until the state begins to weaken.

4. **"A" directs "B" to break state by "clearing the screen," changing breathing and/or changing the subject.**

5. **"A" tests "B's" anchor by reaching over and firing the anchor. Both "A" and "C" calibrate "B's" response to see if "B" recalls the desired state.**

## II. Anchoring States 2

*(Four people)*

1. **"A" accesses and anchors three different states in "B" (e.g., joy, sense of competence, frustration, hope, nice surprise, accomplishment, anger, etc.). "A" anchors these states on "B's" back so that "D" cannot see the anchor. Note: Make the anchors several inches apart since the nerves on the back supply large areas, and anchor three quite different states such as anger, joy and accomplishment.**

2. **Test each anchor, allowing "D" to see the response (to calibrate), but not the location of the anchor.** During this time, "C" (Meta-person) monitors the process to make sure "A" sets each anchor cleanly, and getting good responses.

3. **"A" sets off each anchor, one at a time, with "D" identifying which state "A" elicits from "B" (# 1, # 2, or # 3).** The exercise continues until "D" guesses four or five in a row. Should the anchors not seem to hold firmly, "A" may go back and reset them.

## III. Anchoring And The Trans-derivational Search

*(triads)*

Kinesthetic anchoring provides an excellent tool for initiating a Trans-derivational Search. I (BB) have found this especially true for the more kinesthetically oriented person. While leading a client in age regression in the search for the root cause of a Problem State, use a kinesthetic anchor to inaugurate and continue the search. Follow this procedure:

1. **"A" asks "B" to "Think of a Problem State you would like to discover the root cause of."** For the purpose of this exercise, I suggest that "B" not choose a particularly strong Problem State. In this exercise we want to uncover the root cause but not attempt to heal it. That will come later.

2. **"A" leads "B" to associate into a particularly strong memory of that Problem State.** Using your sensory acuity skills, "A" anchors in "B's" Problem State.

3. **Using Milton Model language patterns, "A" directs "B" back in time to their earliest memory of this problem. All through the Trans-derivational Search, "A" holds the anchor.** "A" may say something like this: "Now, as you are feeling this problem, I want you to go back in time to other memories when you had this problem. You may wish to imagine that your history is like a photo album. And, as you feel this experience, you will begin to see pictures of other memories when you experienced this feeling. Just allow these memories to unfold like flipping back through your very own photo album of your life history. The uncovering of one memory will cause other memories to come up. Just let it happen."

4. **"A" continues holding "B's" anchor as long as "B" searches their memory bank.** "B" will inform "A" when they have found the root cause of their problem or when no other memories surface.

   **WARNING:** Should "B" get into some real heavy memories, "A" leads "B" to break state. "A" will lead "B" to stand up, breathe deeply and look up. You will find other techniques more appropriate for working on resolving more deep-seated problems later in this manual.

4. **Do a round robin.**

## IV. *Trans-derivational Search Limiting Feelings—Good For Anxiety*

*(triads)*

A "universal experience" involves those feelings that nearly all members of the human race experience, hence "universal." These involve those feelings that limit us (disappointments, grief, loss, etc.) as well as those that greatly enhance life (surprise at something new and exciting, etc.) The following exercise utilizes the concept of anchoring and the Trans-derivational Search (TDS) to eliminate these limiting feelings:

1. **"A" directs "B" to recall a recent experience of feeling positive about learning, being motivated or just excited about life. As "B" remembers and associates into that particular memory, "A" anchors the state kinesthetically.**

2. **"A" directs "B" through use of the kinesthetic anchor to recall at least three other memories when they felt this positive state.** As "A" holds the anchor, "A" says to "B,"

   "Now use the feelings of this experience to go back in your history until you arrive at a younger age when you experienced these same feelings of feeling ready to learn (motivated or excited) in a very productive way."

   -or-

   "Just relax and allow your unconscious mind to sort through similar learning (motivating, exciting) experiences to surprise and delight you by reminding you of an earlier time that included these good feelings."

   -or-

   "That's right, enjoy that good learning (motivating, exciting) experience and re-experience those good feelings. Then, whenever you feel ready, let those feelings guide you back through your past history to an earlier time to find another good experience with those same enjoyable feelings."

   Continue with this process until "B" has recalled and identified three such positive experiences. All the while "A" holds the anchor making sure "B" fully associates into each remembered experience. Release the anchor after they fully access their positive state.

3. **"A" now directs "B" to future pace these resources into a future time when "B" imagines needing those resources.** "A" asks "B" to identify a time in the future when normally they would experience limitations by some unconscious feeling.

   "A" in present time fires "B's" resource anchor and directs "B," "Now, that you experience all these positive resources, while remaining associated, I want you to move into that imaginary time in the future, only this time you face that time with all these resources. And, notice how you now respond with all these powerful resources."

4. **Round robin**

## V.  Uptime Self Anchor

Sometimes we need awareness of what goes on around us. In those times we need to direct our attention away from ourselves to our surroundings. When counseling someone, teaching or making a sale, we need to be aware of our surroundings at all times. Or, consider sitting before someone who is interviewing you for a new job. In the interview, would focusing on the person interviewing you prove helpful? When the occasion calls for our focus to direct externally, the following self-anchor will immediately recall that state:

1.  **Find a quiet place.** Go to your favorite place when you desire quiet. This place could exist inside or outside. Once there, sit down, relax and enjoy the world.

2.  **As you observe your surroundings, practice going inside and coming back out (in your self-awareness). Continue doing this until you become fully aware of what it feels like to focus on your external environment.** Begin to notice each rep system by trying to access each channel. You can plug up your ears to help you to concentrate on seeing more clearly. Or, you can cover your eyes to allow yourself to focus on hearing better. Eliminate internal pictures or internal dialogues as far as possible. Focus your concentration on the world around you.
    a.  Notice what you feel. Feel the edges, surfaces, textures, hardness, etc., of the objects around you. Notice the feelings of the things you touch, sit on, the feelings of your skin, etc.

    b.  Notice what you see. Notice any movements or stillness, colors, shades, tones, distance comparisons, and light patterns. Use both detailed and wide-angled viewing.

    c.  Notice what you hear. Listen for the difference in tones, pitches, and the texture of sounds. Note the location of the sounds. If other people are around, listen for the pitch and tempo of their voices. Listen to your breath coming in and going out.

    d.  Notice what you smell. Do the odors smell sharp or subtle? Do you sense the odors close by or far off?

    e.  Notice anything you taste, including changes within your mouth.

3.  **As you become fully aware of what you notice, set an anchor on the back of your left hand with your right finger(s).** Plant the anchor only

as firmly as you have accessed each rep system. Place the anchor for seeing on top of the anchor for feeling. And, place the anchor for hearing on top of both of them. In this way, you stack your anchor.

4.  **Now fire off the anchor so that it activates all the rep systems simultaneously. Focus your attention totally outside. Do not make internal pictures, dialogues or other feelings.**

5.  **Now, break state by changing your breathing and clearing your screen.**

6.  **Once you have broken state, reach over and fire your anchor.** If your attention automatically and fully turns outside, without any conscious effort, you have a clean and powerful anchor. You now experience "uptime." If not, repeat the above steps.

## VI. *In-time Self Anchor*

You may have need to go inside an experience yourself. An important person in history encouraged this. Jesus said, "You shall love your neighbor as yourself."[17] Jesus says that loving ourselves provides a prerequisite to loving others. You can't love your neighbor until you have a healthy love for yourself. Establishing an in-time anchor will assist you in loving yourself. You can also use this procedure with your favorite spiritual imagery to develop your prayer and meditational life. As with the uptime anchor, do this exercise alone.

1.  **Find a quiet, comfortable place where you can sit or lie down alone for a while.**

2.  **Begin to allow your attention to turn inward.** Do this until you are no longer aware of any surrounding noises, feelings or sights around you. You may wish to close your eyes. If you process mainly auditorily, earplugs may prove helpful. Begin to notice each of your internal rep systems and:
    a.  **Notice your internal feelings.** Notice the difference between the feelings of the location of your internal organs. Notice what emotions you experience. Remember how things feel with your hands—smooth, rough, hot, cold. You may fantasize and make up things to feel.

    b.  **Notice how things look in your mind.** Through your mind's eye, look at details of things you have seen and places you have experienced. Notice the differences between things you have seen and things you have only imagined. Notice how you tell the difference, in your mind, between the things you have really seen and the things you only imagine.

c.   **Notice and listen to any internal voices.** Remember conversations and music. Make up more conversations. Make up sounds you have never heard.

d.   **Imagine smells and tastes.** Remember odors you have experienced and tastes you have enjoyed. Now imagine some you have never experienced.

3.   **As you become more fully aware of what you notice, set a self-anchor.** Set the anchor on the back of your right hand with the finger(s) of your left hand. As you more fully access each rep system of perception, more firmly plant the anchor. Put the anchor for internal seeing right on top of the one for feeling, and the one for hearing right on top of those.

4.   **Begin to access all internal systems at the same time by firing off the anchor.**
a.   Remember an experience and access what you felt, saw, heard, etc., from that one situation.

- OR -

b.   Within each rep system choose a different experience to pay attention to.  For example, see one thing, hear another, feel something else, and smell/taste something that has nothing to do with the others. You may have a wild experience doing this.

5.   **Repeat the process until all you have to do to focus internally (fully and automatically without any conscious effort) involves reaching over and touching the spot on the back of your right hand. We call this "in-time" or "downtime."**

*With these two anchors, you now have the means to both quickly, cleanly, almost automatically, either get outside yourself to more effectively notice the world around you, or go inside to monitor those things going on within you.*

## VII. *Circle Of Excellence Exercise*

This exercise uses the technology of anchoring to increase your state of resourcefulness in problem situations. The procedure as given uses primarily the visual rep system and secondarily the auditory rep system. The exercise requires at least two people. This version is for three. You may also do this procedure on yourself. "A" serves as the operator. "B" role plays the client and "C" serves as the observer.

1.  **"B" selects a situation or context where the current behavior does not provide the desired outcome.** "B" makes a snapshot (single frame) of the problematic situation or context. "A" coordinates the above and observes "B's" physical shift in and out of the experience.

2.  **"A" has "B" break state by clearing the screen and changing breathing patterns.**

3.  **"A" asks "B" what resources they have available and have used in the past, which could adequately overcome the Problem State or situation if applied.** "A" discovers from "B" the resources "B" possesses which when "B" applies to the problem situation or context, the situation would reflect their full potential. "A" calibrates "B" closely, noting specific physical shifts associated with each resource presented. "A" facilitates "B" in selecting those resources "B" thinks would have allowed them to have met their objective in the problematic situation were they present and available to them.

4.  **"A" has "B" pick an identified area on the floor on which "B" looks at.** "A" helps "B" to see themselves demonstrating each of the resources (from specific past reference experiences) one at a time, until "B" has seen all of them on the spot selected. "A" overlaps each experience to add the auditory and kinesthetic components of each resource for "B" to insure full representation of the experience.

5.  **"A" has "B" step into the circle (identified area on the floor) to experience fully those resources in their "Circle of Excellence."** Do one resource at a time. You visually stack a resource anchor.

6.  **"C" monitors the exercise format, insuring that "A" and "B" remain on track.** Also, "C" observes to insure "B" has a complete set of Resource States. "C" demands excellence of the exercise at all times.

7.  **After "B" programs the "Circle of Excellence," "A" takes "B" back to the chair or original standing position.** "A" then instructs "B" that

upon hearing their handclap, "B" will immediately move to the "Circle of Excellence." If "B" hesitates into their "Circle of Excellence" move, "A" will nudge "B's" arm to move them into their "Circle of Excellence." Once "B" experiences their "Circle of Excellence," they step out of the circle.

8. **"A" then asks "B" to remember the problematic behavior or situation.** As soon as "B" begins to shift physically to what "A" saw before, "A" claps their hands (nudge if necessary) and makes sure "B" goes directly into their "Circle of Excellence." "A" then instructs "B" to experience fully these added resources in that situation noticing *ALL* of the changes and effects that "B" experiences, noting what happens. While "B" remains in the circle, "A" requests "B" to review how other people involved respond to "B" with new resources.

**Note:** Since most resources will function "Meta" to the problem, I (BB) have found it most useful to utilize the language from the Meta-state model in assisting the client in the integration process. Say to "B" as "B" experiences their Circle of Excellence, "Bring Resource 1 (name the resource) to bear on the problem (name the problem)." Repeat this language with each resource.

9. **"A" has "B" step out of the circle and asks "B" if he or she got what he or she wanted.** If yes, proceed to the next step. If no, change, add and delete if necessary the resources by recycling to step three.

10. **"A" then instructs "B" to go from the starting position (chair or standing) to the "Circle of Excellence" again.** This time "B" moves into the circle without "A" clapping the hands or giving nudges.

11. **"A" future paces the experience for "B."** "A" has "B" select a situation or context in the next two weeks identical or similar to the problem situation. After selection, "A" facilitates "B's" experiencing that by moving "B" associated into a future event. Check for satisfaction from "B" that this new experience provides an excellent example of their full new potential.

12. **Do a round robin so each participant has an opportunity to experience their "Circle of Excellence."**

## VIII.    *Collapsing Anchors: Integrating Parts*

During my (BB) practitioner training, I volunteered for a demonstration of an NLP technique called "collapsing anchors." The trainer, Gene Rooney, wanted a participant who had experienced a negative state and desired help. A few months before the seminar, I had resigned a ten-year pastorate. I experienced much grief. Along with the grief came some strong negative feelings that needed neutralizing. Gene's interest seemed not in the content, though I shared some of the content with the group. Most of the participants served as ministers as well. As I accessed the negative state, Gene anchored the state on my left knee. He followed all the proper procedures of anchoring, including testing. Gene then began to ask me to recall a positive resourceful state. Gene anchored that state on my right knee. He had me recall several of these positive states. With each of the positive states, he stacked the positive anchor on my right knee.

Gene's purpose involved establishing a positive anchor sufficient in collapsing or overcoming the negative anchor. On a scale from one to ten, he had me rate the strength of the negative state. I said that I had a ten. With each positive state, he had me rate them in relation to the strength of the negative state. As he stacked the positive states on my right knee, I would give each a rating. Gene kept on adding these states until the total exceeded ten. Once he convinced himself that the positive anchor had become stronger than the negative, he fired both anchors simultaneously. My mind went into a state of confusion. I experienced all kinds of weird feelings. My eyes went all over the place. When I settled down, Gene took his finger off the negative anchor. He left his finger on my positive anchor for about five seconds. Then, he lifted his finger from the positive anchor. The procedure left me in a positive state. Interestingly, the pain I had felt when I volunteered had greatly diminished. I could still remember that I had a painful experience. And I am sure that I will suffer such feelings again—but not from that experience. For me, collapsing anchors really worked and gave me new choices.

*Exercise*

Suppose you have two opposing states anchored in two different locations and both fire simultaneously. What would happen when you fire both anchors? Imagine each state as being a different psychological part. With both anchored and fired simultaneously, the negative state will collapse into the stronger positive state. And, of course, should you experience the negative state as stronger than the positive state, the positive state will collapse into the negative state. It does not seem possible for the nervous system to engage two mutually incompatible states at the same time. So, the nervous system creates new patterns as old patterns break. To collapse anchors, you anchor an unwanted negative state. Then you anchor in a more powerful positive state (by stacking anchors if necessary) and collapse the negative state into the positive state.

1.  **Establish rapport with your client.**

2.  **Identify the negative state you desire to eliminate.**

3.  **Identify the positive state(s) necessary to overcome the negative state.** You may need to stack several positive states on the same place in order to obtain a powerful enough positive state to overcome the negative state. A good way to do this involves asking the client on a scale of 1 to 10 to rate the power of the negative state. Then, as you stack your positive states, ask the client to rate each state you stack in order to obtain a number at least two numbers higher than the negative state.

4.  **Anchor the positive state.** Follow the four steps in setting a good anchor:
    a.  Have the client recall and associate into the positive state(s).
    b.  Provide a specific stimulus at the peak of the client's experience.
    c.  Change the person's state.
    d.  Set off the anchor and test.

    Calibrate the positive state.

5.  **Anchor the negative state.** Follow the procedure in step # 4. Calibrate the negative state.

6.  **Take the person through each state in turn, using the anchors alternatively, saying something like this, "So you will find some times when you feel 'negative' (fire the negative anchor) and in these situations you would rather feel 'positive' (fire the positive anchor)." Repeat this a number of times without breaking state between them.**

7.  **Fire both anchors at the same time.** Say to "B" as you fire the resource anchor and then fire the Problem State anchor, "What happens when you bring to bear (name the positive state) on the (name the Problem State)?" Hold the two simultaneously. Watch the person's physiology carefully. You will probably see signs of change and confusion. Usually their eyes will go around and around and from side to side as the brain completes the integration.

    **Note:** By bringing the positive state to bear on the Problem State, you in effect Meta-state the Problem State with the positive state. Utilizing Meta-state language will enhance integration. Any time you take a higher level thought and merge that thought with a lower level thought, you perform what we refer to as "Meta-stating." In NLP, we seek to discover resources in order to reframe Problem States into Resource States. Resource States must function at a higher level of abstraction than the problem in order to reframe the Problem State into a resourceful state. Therefore, by definition, all Resource States function as Meta-states or higher level concepts. When we say, "Bring that resource thought to bear on the Problem State" we simply mean to merge those two thoughts together in such away as to reframe the Problem State with the resources of the Resource State. Thus, when we anchor in a Problem State and then we anchor in a Resource State, by firing them both at the same time, we cause the brain to process both concepts at the same time. The two concepts merge and the greater concept will reframe the lesser—we thus Meta-state the lesser concept (hopefully the Problem State) with the greater concept (the Resource State).

8.  **Once the client settles down, release the negative anchor first. Hold the positive anchor for approximately five more seconds.**

9.  **Test your work by either asking the client to access the Problem State or by firing the negative anchor.** You should see the person go into a state somewhere between the two different states. Or, if you had an especially strong positive anchor, they will go immediately into the positive state.

10. **Future pace by asking the client to think of some situation in the near future where they probably would have felt negatively before the collapsed anchor.** Ask them to run through it in their imagination while you calibrate their state. If you do not have satisfaction with their state or if they appear still unhappy, discover from the client the resources they need in order to overcome that negative state, and then repeat the procedure.

### IX. *Change Personal History*

This pattern offers you a way to recode your past in such a way that it no longer serves as a reference in your library of understandings for feeling bad, for defining yourself in negative ways, etc. Now you can use such memories as resources, for learnings, and for moving into the future with a positive attitude and faith.

*The Pattern*

1.  **Access a problematic memory**. Access and elicit from a person a problematic, unwanted, or unpleasant feeling. As you do, establish a good anchor for this state. Calibrate to this state in the person.

2.   **Do a Transderivational Search (TDS).** Utilize this anchor to assist the person in finding a previous experience when this same feeling occurred. Using the anchor in doing a TDS back to earlier experiences when they first created the state. Whenever you note the person re-experiencing the same negative state, calibrate to it, have the person stop and re-anchor it. Ask, "At what age did you have this experience? How old do you feel with these thoughts-and-feelings?"

3.   **Continue the TDS.** Continue using the anchor and have the person go back through their sense of time to find three to six similar experiences of this negative state. Each time request their age.

4.   **Break state.** Have them return to the present. "Now what specific resource would you need in that past situation for you to have felt better and coped more effectively?" Elicit and anchor this Resource State.

5.   **Collapse anchor.** Now have the person return to the earliest experience as you fire off the negative state anchor while simultaneously firing off the resource anchor. As you do ask, "What would that past memory feel like when you know you *have this resource* with you back then, now?" "How would this resource make that past different?" Then have the person come up through history, stopping at each past experience with the resource anchor so that their history begins changing, so that each experience becomes satisfying.

6.   **Trouble-shooting.** If the person has difficulty changing the past experience, bring them back to the present and elicit and anchor more resources so that their resource anchor becomes stacked with resources.

7.   **Break state.** Once they have changed all of the past experiences, have the person break state. After a little bit, have them think about that problematic feeling, or unwanted feeling.

8.   **Test.** What happens? Have the memories changed? In what way? Does the person have a sense of having the resource where previously they had the Problem State (# 1)?

9.   **Future pace.** Finally, have them think about similar experiences that may occur in the future.

*X. Change Personal History—Through The Eyes Of The Meta-state Model*

1.  **Identify the Problem (Primary State).** Think about a time and place in your history that still troubles you.
    a.  How do you know it generates a "problem" for you?
    b.  When you step into that memory—what emotion arises? What meanings?
    c.  Step out of the Problem State.

2.  **Take an Observer's Viewpoint of that Experience (Meta-state).**
    a.  Float above your Time-Line (dissociate)—go back to the event of the problem and observe and witness the problem from a Meta-position.
    b.  See that younger you going through that particular event.
    c.  If you have difficulty staying dissociated—put an imaginary screen (like a piece of Plexiglas) at the Meta-level between the dissociated "you" and the "you" in the event.

3.  **Gather Learnings from the Observer Position (Meta-state).**
    a.  What resources did that younger you need?
    b.  What resources did the others in the event need?
    c.  Identify the needed resources.

4.  **Come Back to the Present and Access Resources.**
    a.  Access and anchor each and every needed resource.
    b.  Amplify and test the anchors for the resources.

5.  **From the Observer Position, Transfer Resources (Meta-state).**
    a.  Give the younger you each resource and let the event play out with that resource. See yourself giving the younger you the added resources. Observe the event playing out with that resource intact.
    b.  Give others in the movie those resources they need.
    c.  Run an **Ecology Check**.
        •  Does it provide better closure?
        •  Does it enhance life?
        •  Does it give you a more useable "map"?

6.  **Associate into Resource State (# 5 above).**

7.  **Come Forward Associated Through Your History with the Added Resources.**
    a.  Bring the added resources up through the Time-Line of your history through each subsequent year of your life enhancing and enriching your Time-Line.
    b.  Let the added resources transform everything.

## XI. *Collapsing Visual Anchors: Overcoming Doubt*

In his NLP training seminars, Tad James takes his participants through an exercise in overcoming doubt.[18] James does this to prepare them mentally to break a pine board. The exercise serves as a powerful utilization of the concept of parts integration. You can do the exercise by yourself. If you are left-handed, then substitute left for right throughout.

1.  Stand for this exercise. Take both of your hands and put them out in front of you. Close your eyes, and recall a time when you felt totally powerful. As you recall that time, step right into your body, feel what you felt, hear what you heard, see what you saw. Now, take all that feeling of **feeling totally powerful** and bring it up through your body. Make an image of it and put it in your right hand.

2.  OK, clear the screen. Now I want you to remember a time when you **felt totally loved**. Allow that love to envelop you. Associate fully into that experience by seeing what you saw and hearing what you heard. Take all that love and make an image of it. Open up your right hand and put it into your hand. Then close your hand. Again, clear the screen.

3.  I would like for you to remember a time **when you couldn't fail**... a time when you knew you had it all. Remember a time when you knew you could have all you wanted. As you recall that time, step right into your body. Look through your own eyes, hear what you heard, see what you saw, feel what you felt. Associate fully into that time when you knew you could have it all. Feel that experience of feeling totally powerful in knowing that you could have all you want. Take all that energy and bring it up through your body. Make an image of it and put it right into your right hand. Close your right hand over that.

4.  Now clear the screen. Remember a time when you were **really energetic**. Select a time when you had a whole lot of energy. You felt so energetic. You had all the energy you could ever need to do whatever you wanted to do. Step right into your body, see what you saw, hear what you heard, feel and what you felt. Take all that energy and pull it up through you. Make an image of it and put it in your right hand. Close your right hand over that. Just hold that in your right hand.

5.  Now, remember a humorous time, a time when you were **laughing uncontrollably.** Step right into your body and see what you saw, hear what you heard and feel what you felt. Now take all that laughter and

good feeling and make an image of it. Put that image in your right hand and hold it there.

6.   Now open your right hand and look at the shape of all that energy, power and good feeling. Look at the color. Look at the size. What would it say to you if it spoke to you? Hold it up to your ear and hear what it has to say. What sounds does it make? Now notice how good it feels. Notice the size, the weight and the texture of all that energy. Now close your right hand lovingly over this.

7.   Do you have any doubts about your becoming the person you want to become? Make an image of those doubts and put them in your left hand (or right hand if you are left-handed). Take whatever doubts that you may have and place them in your left hand. Listen to what they say to you. Feel the feelings of all those doubts.

8.   Now take the good stuff in your primary hand and pour it into your other hand and make a noise while you do it. Continue pouring the energy hand into the doubtful hand until they become the same. Look at them until they get to become the same color, size, shape and texture. When they become exactly the same, then once more recall a time when you felt totally powerful, totally loved, and a time when you could have it all. Put them all right into your primary hand and close your hand lovingly around it and squeeze your hand. You can now recall those feelings any time you want.

## XII. *Chaining Anchors*

What do you do when the desired state becomes so far away from the present state that integration will not happen with the collapse anchor procedure? In some situations the desired state appears so far away from the present state that the two-step process of collapsing anchors will not work. Moving from a stuck state to a state of motivation could possibly provide an example. For some people, motivation seems too far away from stuck for integration to happen. Stuck will not chain through to motivation. Neurologically, stuck will not integrate with motivation. Chaining anchors is the answer. In this process, we place other states between the two.

I (BB) use the knuckles for this procedure. You may choose to use the back of the hand or the arm. The process involves selecting states that will step or chain the person from the present state to the desired state. I will use stuck to motivation as an example. Stuck state represents the present state. Motivation represents the desired state. However, the desired change provides too great of a change for a two-step process of collapsing anchors.

So the answer lies in designing several steps to get the person from stuck to motivation. You anchor each state including the present state and the desired state. I have listed below the steps to the process. I will explain the process as we go through the steps. You can do this exercise with two people. A three-person exercise works best.

1.   **Establish rapport with the client.**

2.   **Explain to the client that you will touch them for the purpose of anchoring.**

3.   **Identify the Problem State.** For sake of illustration, we will use a stuck state as the Problem State.

4.   **Identify the end state.** We desire motivation as an end state.

5.   **Design your chain.** Crucial to the success of this procedure involves the designing of the chain. Your choice of the state that will get the person off of stuck will determine the effectiveness of the procedure. Ask the client, "Recall the last time you got off of stuck. How did you do it?" If they cannot recall a time they got off stuck, ask them to imagine what it would take. Ask the person what motivates them. For some people, moving "away from" something motivates them. In NLP we call these people "away from" people. Their direction filter (a direction filter is a Meta-program or a neurological filter) moves away from what they do not want. You will need to choose a negative state like fear to get them out of the stuck state. This first step must function as a major driver for the individual.

Other people will move "towards" what they want as their direction filter. Being drawn towards something or someone motivates them. For this person you need to choose a state like desire or passion to get them off stuck. Question the person until you lead them to tell you what will get them off stuck. For the sake of illustration, we will say that our demonstration subject functions as an "away from" person. Fear is a motivator in their life. Thus, we will choose fear as the first step to get them off stuck.

After choosing the first step we begin to design the remainder of the chain. How many steps does a chain require? The answer is: as many as it takes! Usually three to six steps will do the job. The client will let you know. I (BB) write the present state down and then leave a space and write down the desired state. I then let the client look at it and decide how to fill in the middle.

a.   Present State (stuck)
b.   Intermediate state # 1 (fear)
c.   Intermediate state # 2 (calm)
d.   Intermediate state # 3 (security)
e.   Intermediate state # 4 (pressure)
f.   Desired state # 5 (motivation)

In the above design I inserted some possible states that would get an "away from" person off stuck to motivation. Notice that pressure exemplifies a negative state but provides a powerful motivator for an away from person. In questioning the individual, calibrate each step. Using your sensory acuity skills, you can determine if each step follows congruently from the former. The person will tell you both verbally and non-verbally.

6.   **Elicit and anchor each state separately.** After designing your chain, elicit and anchor each state. Include the present state and desired state. Follow the procedures of proper anchoring. Make sure to test each anchor. You may wish to stack your anchors.

7.   **You have now become ready to fire the anchors.** This step offers a crucial step in this process. In order to chain or link the anchors, you must fire them correctly. First, fire present state anchor (stuck). Have your finger over the intermediate state # 1 (fear). Once the present state peaks, release that anchor and fire intermediate state # 1 anchor. Do not fire them at the same time. Doing this collapses the anchors. You do not want to do this in chaining anchors.

8.   **Do a break state by having the client clear their screen, breathe deeply, etc.**

9.   **After chaining from the present state to intermediate state # 1, test your chain.** You test by firing the present state anchor. If your chaining works, the client should go into the stuck state then into the intermediate state # 1 of fear.

10.  **Do a break state by having the client clear their screen, breathe deeply, etc.**

11.  **Now, fire present state anchor (stuck), observe client go into stuck and then into intermediate state # 1 (fear). When the client goes into intermediate state # 1 (fear), then you fire intermediate state # 2 (calm) at the peak of fear.**

12.  **Do a break state.**

13. **Test your chain.** Fire the present state anchor. Your client should chain from "stuck" to "fear" to "calm."

14. **Do a break state.**

15. **Fire the present state anchor (stuck).** You will see "stuck," then "fear," then "calm." When "calm" peaks, you fire intermediate state # 3 ("security"). Do a break state and test.

16. **Repeat on each state through the desired state of motivation.**

The successful completion of this procedure will give the client a choice of whether to function in a "stuck" state or "motivated" state. The event that triggered stuck can now trigger motivation. The client now functions at choice. A person who has choice will most often choose to live not in a "stuck" state but a state of "motivation."

After reading this chapter, you will probably agree with me that knowledge of anchoring provides a useful tool. What kind of anchors does our behavior produce? Do we have negative anchors that need collapsing? Do you have negative anchors in your marriage that need collapsing? Does a particular tone of voice that you use anger your spouse? What kind of responses do you get from your children? You can anchor positive behavior in your children. Whenever you desire positive behavior from them, fire the anchor. The process offers a simple tool in state control. Whenever they behave in a way you desire, anchor that behavior in any rep system or a combination of the three. I (BB) do not have any children. However, I have an eleven-year-old niece who adores me. I anchored a positive anchor on the side of her arm. Every time I fired the anchor, she gave me a strange look and shaped up.

The uses of anchoring for pastors and teachers provide endless examples. I always stood on the right side of the pulpit whenever I spoke of commitment and decision. If my subject matter was somewhat negative, I stood on the left side of the pulpit. Guess which side of the pulpit I stood when I invited people to come forward to the altar as a sign of their public commitment? You may observe evangelists doing this. However, I (BB) doubt that they realize they do this.

Have you ever followed a popular speaker? You walked to the podium in fear and trembling. You may ask yourself, "How can I follow that presentation?" Not only can you follow him, you can have immediate rapport with the audience. Observe what anchors the speaker uses. Notice their gestures. Observe their posture and where they stand on the platform. Do they use audio-visual aids? Steal their anchors. They will not know how you gain such immediate rapport with the audience unless they understand NLP.

## XIII. *Visual And Auditory Anchors: Stage Anchoring*

How do you set visual or auditory anchors? In setting auditory anchors you may use particular words or sounds. For instance, I (BB) often use the word "relax" to anchor in a state of relaxation in a client. Not only do I use the word, I also use a particular voice tone. I say the word with a low and soft voice. Therefore, both the word and tone of voice establish an auditory anchor for relaxation in the client. You can also use a cough, snap of the fingers or the click of a pen for an auditory anchor. This works well with groups. A cough provides not only an auditory anchor, but it also provides a visual anchor. When the person or group gets into the desired state, raise your hand and cough. Whenever you desire the same state in the person or group, repeat the same procedure. Repeat the procedure exactly. This will fire the anchor and recall the same state or behavior.

I use the "thumbs up" sign as a visual anchor. Often I will couple the thumbs up sign with some positive statement like "I can do all things . . ." at the same time I give the thumbs up sign. By doing this, I establish both an auditory and visual anchor. I use the "thumbs up" anchor with my students. Any time I wish to challenge my students to move out into action, I will fire this anchor. I call this procedure "stage anchoring." The "thumbs up" anchor works the same way as the positioning of the minister's body on the pulpit area in anchoring in a certain state with the congregation (see above).

**Note:** A salesman could ask a customer to recall a previous major purchase and describe it. As the customer describes the purchase, the customer will have to mentally go through their buying strategy. Once the customer gets to the point in their strategy of actually purchasing the product, the salesman should set an anchor. After the salesman determines the customer's need for his product, and has explained his product, he can fire the anchor at the time of his closing. This will place the customer back into the state of purchasing a product at the point of closure.

In setting stage anchors, anchor desired states for the audience to your particular positions on the stage. Also, when anchoring a state in an audience, put on that state by physiologically and tonally getting in the state yourself. Then, when you wish to re-create a state in an audience, reposition yourself on the same spot on the stage where you originally set the anchor. And place yourself into the same physiology and tonality of the state you wish to re-create. This procedure will evoke from the audience the previously anchored state.

You can also create a series of stage anchors. For example, suppose you desired to move an audience from apathy to excitement. Because we measure a great distance from apathy to excitement, you will become more successful by creating a series of stages to the desired outcome. This procedure provides the same model as the previous procedure of chaining anchors. The only difference lies in the fact that on stage you use visual and auditory anchors rather than kinesthetic anchors. The challenge becomes to devise a state that will bring the audience out of apathy for the first step. Intense curiosity may accomplish bringing the audience out of apathy. Then, ask yourself what would the next state on the way to excitement become? What about a state of becoming challenged? Would this move the audience towards excitement? Yes, it probably would. Now, do we need another state between challenge and excitement? For good measure, let's put one in. A step between challenge and excitement could become expectation. So, our chain from apathy to excitement would look like this:

**Step one: Apathy**

**Step two: Intense curiosity**

**Step three: Challenge**

**Step four: Expectation**

**Step five: Excitement**

In moving the audience from apathy to excitement, you will chain these anchors. So, first, select a spot on the stage and anchor in the state of apathy. Be sure to put yourself into the state by exemplifying the physiology and tonality of the state of apathy. Next, select another spot on the stage and anchor in the state of intense curiosity. Exemplify curiosity by placing yourself into the state of intense curiosity. Follow this procedure with each of the five states. After setting these anchors, chain through them two or three times. In short order you will move the audience through the chain by simply placing yourself in the five positions on the stage. Don't you find this exciting?

## XIV.    *Collapsing Anchors: The Advanced Visual Squash Pattern*

This pattern offers a way to bring about an integration of parts in conflict. When you have two conflicting internal representations, these differing representations set up differing programs for believing, perceiving, emoting, and behaving. They run incompatible neurological patterns. This pattern will bring about an integration of these two models of the world.

*The Pattern*

1. **Identify the inner conflict.** Identify and separate parts. "You have a part responsible for "X," do you not?" Give each a name or label, and notice the internal representation of each part.

2. **Now allow a visual image of each part to form and, as they do, place each part in each hand.** For instance, put your Playful part in the right hand and your Work/Business part in your left hand.

3. **Separate intention from behavior.** Reframe each part by finding what they deem as valuable and worthy of appreciation about each part. (This alters the frame by allowing the person to become aware of the positive intention or purpose of each part.)

4. **Establish communication.** Ask each part what resources does the other part have that would become useful in assisting it to function even more effectively? How could this playful part work in a useful way for you? How could this work part serve you? In most cases the part will respond with a verbal, visual or kinesthetic response. Listen for a verbal response. "Now that you know that these two parts have the same positive intent at a higher level, what resources does each part have that the other could use?" Start with the more positive part. "Now transfer that resource to the other part... notice how this part begins to look and feel differently."

5. **Imagine what a part would look like, sound like, feel like which has the combined resources of each part.** Allow this third image to form in the center of the other two images as it takes on more and more of the valuable qualities of the other two parts.

6. **Now allow a series of visual images to form that represent the transition (metamorphosis) from each part until it forms the representation you have of that center image.**

7. **Next, ask the person doing this to begin to** *bring their hands together* **while simultaneously having the internal images begin to merge (or collapse) so that the third image remains.**

8.  **Finally, tell the person to** *take the integrated image inside.* Reach out in front of you to this integrated image that contains the values of both of these parts and bring it into yourself.

9.  **Test.** Think about the conflict situation. What happens? How do you feel? What's different? What has shifted?

## Conclusion

Words do not comprise the only symbol system for communicating with ourselves and each other. Non-verbal communication is also a "language" whereby we can (and do) communicate. Whether or not we communicate *consciously* and *intentionally* is another issue. Using the understandings in behavioral psychology, learning theory, and classical conditioning, NLP has provided a language, a model, and numerous human "technologies" for understanding this whole dimension of communication.

Now we can begin to examine the "anchors" and "anchoring processes" in our lives and in the lives of those with whom we live and work. We can examine them for the "messages" and neuro-semantic states that they induce. We can also now develop more skill and consciousness in our everyday use of anchors—understanding how we do it one-on-one with loved ones and with an entire audience in public speaking.

## Thought Questions to Assist Your Learning:

1.  What does "anchoring" mean?
2.  How did Pavlov discover the process of anchoring and what did he call it?
3.  List the four keys to anchoring.
4.  How do you "set an anchor?"
5.  What experiences did you have in using anchors in the various exercises?
6.  What does it mean to collapse an anchor?
7.  How does it fit with the subject of integrating parts?
8.  When you thought about anchoring in the context of public speaking or presenting—what did you learn?

# Chapter 14

## Focusing On Submodalities

**What you can expect to learn in this chapter:**

- An explanation of submodalities
- New insights about the secrets of submodalities
- Specific therapeutic interventions utilizing submodalities
- Submodality exploration exercise
- The "cure" for headaches and other uncomfortable feelings
- Mapping across with submodalities
- Time-line submodalities
- Godiva Chocolate pattern
- The Swish Pattern
- Belief formation change pattern
- Grief/Loss pattern

Have you ever heard someone say, "I feel pretty dull today"? Consider the meaning of the phrase, "I hear you loud and clear." We hear such metaphorical sayings constantly. Until the discoveries of NLP, most of us considered them as just metaphors and therefore as symbols carrying little meaning. However, with the insights of NLP, we now know that such metaphors frequently offer **literal descriptions of the speaker's internal representation**. More often than we sometimes realize, our brains take such statements and "make sense" of them at a literal level. And, as part of this process, the notion of **submodalities** provides us with one of the basic ways of how our brain-nervous system functions and how it *programs* us for our emotions, behaviors, skills, etc.

> *And, as part of this process, the notion of submodalities provide us with one of the basic ways of how our brain-nervous system functions and how it **programs** us for our emotions, behaviors, skills, etc.*

We have described three primary ways of "thinking." Namely, we think through the three primary modes of pictures, sounds, and feelings. "Thinking" also occurs via smell, taste, and the meta-representational system of words. Primarily, however, we formulate our internal representations in pictures, sounds, and/or feelings. Given this, the *domain of submodalities* enables us to discover further distinctions in our internal representations.

Recall a pleasant experience.

*Visually:* You have a picture, don't you? Now, do you see that picture in color or black-and-white? Does that picture appear to you as three dimensional or flat like a photograph? Do you see yourself in the picture (dissociated) or do you look through your own eyes (associated)? Does the picture have a frame around it or do you see it as a panoramic photograph? Do you see it as a movie or still picture? Do you see the picture far off or close? Does the picture look bright or dark or in-between? Is it in focus or do you see it out of focus? Where have you located the picture? Do you see it up to your left, or right, or straight ahead in front of you? Where do you see the picture?

*Auditorily:* Does the memory have sounds? Does it sound loud or soft? Does the tone come to you as soft or harsh? Does it sound full or thin (timbre)? What direction does the sound come to you from? Does the sound move fast or slowly? Is it clear or dull? Do you hear it in stereo or mono?

*Kinesthetically:* Does the memory have any sensations within it? How intensely do these feelings present themselves to you? Do you experience the feeling as having a texture? If it had weight, how heavy would it be? If the feeling had shape, what shape does it possess? What would it register on a thermometer? Where in your body do you experience the feeling(s)?

> *Submodalities comprise the building blocks of the representational system.*

In NLP we refer to these **quality** distinctions in the internal representation as **submodalities**. The rep system includes the VAK modalities. With the term submodalities, it sounds like we will find *sub*-distinctions. Yet, as we have already studied in Chapter One, this does not accurately describe the situation. These **qualities or properties** of the representations comprise the building blocks of our internal representational system, but not at a sub-level. Certainly, the internal representation of all experiences involve submodalities. Wyatt Woodsmall has noted,

> "If the mind/body is capable of making any distinction, then it must have some way of making that distinction; and the way it in fact does so is by differences in the submodalities by which the alternatives of the distinction are internally represented."[19]

The human brain determines the parameters of our experiences by means of these submodality properties (plus the word meanings we give them). Within the brain we represent all of our experiences, emotions, and even beliefs using submodalities. Over two millennia ago a wise man said, "For as he thinks within himself, so he is."[20] Thus, our brain processes information using submodalities plus the word meanings we give our representations to create our realities. This in turn gives rise to our emotions, which determines our behavior. At both the primary level of representation and at meta-levels, we have various qualities (submodalities) in our representational codings.

The distinctions given in the example of the pleasant experience present but just a few of the submodalities in each rep system. However, they only provide the key ones. Figure 14:1 provides a more complete list of submodalities.

## Different Kinds Of Submodalities

In looking at the submodalities, you will note *a distinction* even within the submodalities. Consider the visual submodalities. What difference do you notice between a picture appearing in color or black-and-white and a picture appearing far off or close?

This difference comes from the fact that a picture will appear *either* in black-and-white *or* in color. We don't (and can't) create pictures with some in-between coding. (Not all NLP trainers agree with this conclusion. They believe that all submodalities fit into the analogue category.) However, as for a picture appearing far off or close, a visual image may occur at any place along a continuum in-between. The picture may appear fifteen feet away or ten feet away or right in front of your nose.

> A *digital* submodality operates like a light switch: either on or off. A submodality that can vary over a continuum we define as an *analogue* submodality.

Thus, some submodalities function like in a way similar to a light switch: it operates in either an "on" or an "off" position. For instance, a picture may have movement in it or remain still. It cannot do both. This type of submodality we refer to as **a digital submodality**. A submodality that can vary over a continuum we define as **an analogue submodality**. "Location" provides an example of an analogue submodality. Typically we learn to develop a fuller appreciation of submodalities after we have learned to change them and notice the alteration it makes in our experience. When an event happens, that event exists as a fact of history. We cannot change the fact that it occurred. However, today we respond, not to the fact of history, but to our *memory* of that event. So while we may not change history, we can change how we internally represent and perceive a memory.

When we make a perceptual change by giving our internal representations new meanings, we also change the submodality structure of that internal representation. Likewise, when we make a change with submodality shifts, we will always activate a higher level frame that we have given a higher level meaning. So, we can make perceptual shifts both with words (through reframing) and with submodalities (through mapping across). In either case, for a shift to happen, we must "move" the problem state into a higher level frame (desired state) in order for the shift to take place and to remain.

> *While we may not change history, we can change*
> *how we internally represent and perceive a memory.*

Consider something that causes you anger. As you recall that experience, you probably have a picture of the stimulus that sets off the anger. Does the picture appear in color or black-and-white? Do you see it in 3D or flat? Do you see yourself in the picture (dissociated) or do you see all the events of that memory through your own eyes (associated)? As a rule, dissociating yourself from a memory removes much, if not all, of the emotion. Do you have a panoramic picture or does it have a frame around it? Does the picture have movement in it or not? How far away do you see the picture? Does it appear bright or dark, in focus or out of focus? Where do you see the picture in reference to yourself now?

> *When we explore and identify the differences between the submodalities of*
> *one image and another we call that a **contrastive analysis**.*

Now think of something about which you feel totally calm and relaxed. Think of any external stimulus to which you typically respond with a calm gentleness so that you breathe deeper and fuller and all your muscles relax their tensions. Allow yourself to see a picture of that stimulus. Now, elicit the same submodalities of this second picture of relaxation as you did with anger. You will discover some differences. We call this a *contrastive analysis*. Here we have explored and identified **the differences** between the submodalities of opposite primary states: anger and relaxation.

So for an intervention, take the image of anger and put it in the same submodalities of gentle and calm relaxation. If the picture of anger appeared in black-and-white and relaxation appeared in color, take the picture of anger and put it in color. Changing the submodalities of anger into the submodalities of relaxation will typically cause a change in how you feel about that particular state. Your state of anger will feel more calm, gentle, and positive. You end up with "relaxed anger" (that's right!)

In this instance, we did not change anything except the internal represen-tation of anger. The content of the memory remained the same. Truly, "as a man thinks within himself, so is he." And this demonstrates the power of submodalities.

> *A meta-level phenomenon* **does not** *shift with indiscriminate submodality mapping across.*

In this illustration, we worked with phenomena at the primary level (the anger). We did not use meta-level phenomena like beliefs, dis-beliefs, understanding, etc. Higher meta-level (abstract) phenomena **do not** shift with indiscriminate submodality mapping across. The meaning frame for relaxation is at a higher level of abstraction than the primary level of anger. For most people, when you shift "anger" into "relaxation, i.e., bring "relaxation" to bear on "anger," you will experience a shift.

If you do not experience a calming of your anger, then your anger must exist at a higher level than your relaxed state. You have given your anger a great deal more meaning (meta-levels). If you had this experience, ask yourself, "What is the purpose of my anger?" Keep asking that until you step up to a higher level frame that you can use to modulate your anger. For instance, as I (BB) processed some old anger I asked myself, "Bob what was the purpose of that anger?" The reply came back (from the back of my mind), "To justify its existence." "Well then, Bob, what was the purpose of justifying the existence of your anger?" This answer flashed from the back of my mind, "I am right!" "And, Bob, what was the purpose of your being right?" "So that I am considered by others as a person of worth." Whoa! That won't work. Anger never gives me a sense of personal worth. What does? My higher spiritual beliefs give me a sense of worth. So, I can shift my anger "up" into my spiritual representation of Jesus or I can bring Jesus to bear on my anger and guess what happens to the anger? It just dimin-ishes away.

> *The process of changing the submodalities of one image into the submodalities of another image we refer to as submodality mapping across.*

In changing internal representation through submodality changes, you will discover that some submodalities produce more change than others do. For instance, in moving the picture of confusion into the picture of certainty, you may have discovered that changing the location changed other submodalities as well. The process of changing the submodalities of one image into the submodalities of another image we refer to as submodality *mapping across*. In *mapping across*, usually two or three submodalities will change other submodalities (location does that for me as it does for many). When this happens, you have a *critical* submodality or, as some say, **a driver submodality**. In changing one experience into another through submodality mapping across, we use the drivers to make that change. This demonstrates one of the uses of doing contrastive analysis on various experiences.

> *In **mapping across**, usually two or three submodalities will change other submodalities. When this happens, you have a **critical** submodality or as some say, a **driver** submodality.*

Again, while you cannot change historical events in your life that have resulted in much pain happening to you, you can change your internal representation of your memory. And, by changing the internal representation, you can change how you feel about it. And by changing how you feel, you change your responses to similar events. Thus running our internal representation of events and memories empowers us to control our feelings about things. Rep systems, eye accessing cues and submodalities are key elements in how we structure our subjective experiences. We also need to consider how we sequence our internal representations as we engage in thinking and behaving. The sequencing of our rep systems in the production of thought and behavior we call **strategies.**

> *Representational systems, eye accessing cues and submodalities provide key elements in how we structure our subjective experiences. Another building block of subjective experience concerns **the sequencing** of these key elements into thought and behavior. The sequencing of our representational systems in the production of thought and behavior we call strategies.*

### Figure 14:1 Submodalities Checklist

| Visual | 1 | 2 | 3 | 4 |
|---|---|---|---|---|
| Black-&-White or Color? | | | | |
| Near or Far? | | | | |
| Bright or Dim? | | | | |
| Location? | | | | |
| Size of Picture? | | | | |
| Associated/Dissociated? | | | | |
| Focused or Defocused? | | | | |
| Focus (Changing/Steady) | | | | |

| | | | | |
|---|---|---|---|---|
| Framed or Panoramic? | | | | |
| Movie or Still? | | | | |
| Movie-Fast/Normal/Slow | | | | |
| Amount of Contrast | | | | |
| 3D or Flat? | | | | |
| Angle Viewed From | | | | |
| # of Pictures (Shift?) | | | | |

**Auditory**

| | | | | |
|---|---|---|---|---|
| Location | | | | |
| Direction | | | | |
| Internal or External? | | | | |
| Loud or Soft? | | | | |
| Fast or Slow? | | | | |
| High or Low? (Pitch) | | | | |
| Tonality | | | | |
| Timbre | | | | |
| Pauses | | | | |
| Cadence | | | | |
| Duration | | | | |
| Uniqueness of Sound | | | | |

**Kinesthetic**

| | | | | |
|---|---|---|---|---|
| Location | | | | |
| Size | | | | |
| Shape | | | | |
| Intensity | | | | |
| Steady | | | | |
| Movement/Duration | | | | |
| Vibration | | | | |
| Pressure/Heat? | | | | |
| Weight | | | | |

---

For a more thorough treatment of how Meta-levels and Meta-states affect submodalities see *The Structure Of Excellence: Unmasking The Meta-levels Of "Submodalities"* (Hall and Bodenhamer, 1999, Empowerment Technologies, Grand Jct, CO, USA).

---

## Therapeutic Interventions Using Submodalities

## Exercises

*I. Submodality Exploration Exercise*

*(triads)*

Take one submodality at a time from the list on the previous page and at the same time each person uses it to change an experience (a primary level experience) as a joint research project. Briefly share your experiences with each other before going on to try another submodality. I suggest that you choose a visual submodality such as location, size and/or brightness. If you happen to work with a Meta-level experience, the process may not work. If it does happen to work, pay special attention to what submodality **quality** worked. Then explore it from a Meta-level analysis. What higher level resource thought (a Meta-state) caused it to shift?

Change only one submodality at a time to find out how it changes the impact of the experience. As you do, stay alert to ecology concerns! This exercise, by design, leads you into the exploration only of submodalities. Interventions come later with additional exercises. If a shift causes unpleasantness or brings up objections, respect that and explore something else. Notice the following:

1) Do any other submodalities shift along with it?

2) Does your feeling change, in either intensity or quality?

3) Ask yourself, "In what context might this submodality shift provide a more useful behavior"? How could I use this to make my life better?"

4) Try some Auditory and Kinesthetic (tactile [external] and proprioceptive [internal]) distinctions as well as visual ones.

## II.  *"The Cure" For Headaches And Other Uncomfortable Feelings*[21]

1.  Rank the headache from 1 to 10. This initiates the process of dissociation. It provides a standard for comparison. It enables the subject to "chunk down" the headache into parts. And, it allows the subject to constantly experience reinforcement by the success they have when they reduce the headache, that is, from a 7 to a 6.

2.  Represent the headache by making a picture or a movie in your mind. This step serves to dissociate the headache as well as translate it into concrete rather than a general form. The subject begins to control their headache rather than it controlling them.

3.  If the picture has movement that causes pain, you may want to ask the subject to alter the movement. Suppose the subject experiences their headache as hammer blows. Ask the subject to suggest something that will reduce the impact of the hammer blows like imagining pillows being placed under the hammer blows. Ask the subject, "What number would you place on your headache now?"

4.  Change the color of the headache so that it reduces from a _____ to a _____. This simple submodality procedure often produces and effective change.

5.  Project the picture of your headache on a movie screen and reduce the size of the picture until your headache measures only a 3. Since the size of the picture usually provides a powerful submodality driver, save this for the moment of reducing a bigger chunk of the headache. If the subject has difficulty, introduce a double dissociation by having the subject rise above themselves in the theater seat and watch themselves watch themselves on the screen with the headache.

6.  Reduce the size of the picture on the screen until it becomes a small balloon. Let the balloon start to rise. As it reaches the clouds your headache will reduce to a 1.

7.  Now watch the balloon fade in the clouds. When you can no longer see the balloon you will have only the faintest memory of your headache.

If you noticed, many of the steps in this process take a **quality** of representation (a submodality) and use it as a meta-level frame. You take dissociation (the color blue, the sense of coolness, etc.) and bring it to bear on the primary level experience—the headache.

You may use this procedure on unwanted feelings such as anger, depression and desiring to eat. Familiarize the subject with the procedure using it as a headache cure. Then, allow the headache cure to become a metaphor for removing their unwanted feelings. Ask them to visualize the feeling they want to get rid of existing in some form within the balloon. Next, lead them to visualize those feelings leaving the balloon slowly one by one. Last, speed up the process until it takes no more time than you could say, "Zap!"

### III. *Mapping Across With Submodalities*

*(triads)*

1.  "B" thinks of a Problem State and an appropriate Resource State that "B" believe presents an adequate enough resource to overcome the Problem State. "A" asks of "B," "Think of a context in which you feel stuck or in some way not as resourceful as you want to feel." "A" calibrates "B's" state. Once "B" accesses the Problem State and "A" calibrates "B," "A" says to "B," "Now think of a time when you had a Resource State that you believe would have provided assistance in this stuck context." "A" makes sure from "B" that the resource has the characteristics that "B" needs in the Problem State. "A" calibrates with "B."

2.  "A" identifies from "B" the differences between the visual, auditory and kinesthetic submodalities of the Problem State and the Resource State. "A" writes down the submodalities of each image making a note of the differences between them (contrastive analysis). Do this without "B" giving any content and you will find this much easier. When a client gets into content, they have left process. Remember that change takes place at the process level. "A" will record the submodalities of both states on the submodality checklist.

    "A" asks of "B," "How do you experience the Problem State as different from the Resource State?" Let "B" give the submodality differences that they observe. Then, you can ask for other submodalities. Have "B" hold both images simultaneously in their mind.

3.  Mapping Across: "A" says to "B," "Now, think of the Problem State and the Resource State simultaneously. Keeping the same content in the Problem State, I will ask you to change the way you experience the content of the Problem State. Take the submodalities of the Problem State and apply them to the Resource State." First, use the visual submodalities and then the auditory submodalities if necessary. Only use the kinesthetic submodalities should they be important to "B."

Move one submodality at a time. After "A" directs "B" in changing one submodality, "A" asks "B" if other submodalities changed. If other submodalities changed, "A" places an asterisk beside that submodality as being a driver or critical submodality. Put the submodality back in its original position. We will make the shift after testing each submodality.

"B" uses hypnotic language patterns from the Milton-model. "A" leads "B" with such language as "You can allow the black-and-white picture to become color and as you change the color this will allow you to move the image of the Problem State into the same location as the Resource State, etc."

4.  Submodality mapping across: Using the drivers that "A" has identified in # 3 above, "A" leads "B" to shift the Problem State into the submodalities of the Resource State.

5.  Test: "A" asks "B," "Do you now feel resourceful in this context?" If either non-verbally or verbally they indicate that they don't yet have the resource fully available, ask them to now compare the "almost Resource State" to the "Resource State" and identify any submodalities that differ. Map across with these submodalities until "B" accesses a fully resourceful state (still keeping the same "problem" content).

6.  Future Pace: "A" says to "B," "Imagine yourself sometime in the near future in a similar context. Notice how you now experience that state with these added resources." "A" calibrates "B's" nonverbal response. Wait a few minutes while talking about something else (breaking state), and then test again by asking about the problem content or context.

## Time-Line Submodalities

> *The effectiveness of the techniques of Time-Line Therapy™ premises upon the visual submodality of location.*

Time-Line Therapy™ has found its place among effective NLP therapeutic interventions. Thus, understanding how we code our "Time-Lines" provides an effective learning tool for the NLP Practitioner. This exercise in Time-Line Submodalities will serve to introduce you *to the concept* of "time" as a line.

Time-Line Therapy™ premises upon the visual submodality of location, which we then use as a meta-frame.

## How Your Brain Tells Time

Remember, in NLP we focus primarily on process or structure, not content. So we ask the question, "How does our brain understand time?" What goes on inside our head that enables us to know the difference between the past, the present and the future? How do we know the order of events from the past? The brain must do something or we could not separate events in our lives. One clue lies in the very way we talk about time:

"I see it in front of me."

"I am stuck back there and I can't get out."

"I look forward to seeing you."

Such statements are spatial metaphors about the concept of time and offer a description about how we make sense of "concepts" by using metaphors. The spatial metaphor for time enables us to "locate" time in relation to our bodies in space.

Try this experiment. Think of something you do on a regular basis. You may wish to think of driving to work or brushing your teeth. Remember a time about five years ago that you did this. Of course, you probably cannot recall a specific time. However, imagine a time five years ago when you probably performed that activity. Now, remember doing this same thing two years ago. Once you have done that, recall doing this thing last week. OK, good. Imagine doing the same thing in the present. Now, imagine doing it next week, two years hence and then five years from now.

As you recalled and imagined doing this thing, you probably had a series of pictures in your mind. As you look at those pictures again, what differences do you notice in the submodalities?

Does each picture appear in color or black-and-white?
Does each picture have movement or not?
Does each picture appear as a 3D or flat picture?
Do you see yourself in each picture or do you look through your own eyes?
Does each picture have a frame around it or do they appear as a panoramic image?
How bright do the pictures appear? Does the brightness get brighter or darker the further back in time you go?
How far off do you see each picture?
As you look at each picture, how do they vary as far as to focus?
Where do you see each picture in your field of vision?

The way we code time allows our brains to conceptually distinguish the "past" from the "present" and the "future." It also allows us to know how long ago in the past that memory belongs. And, we can also distinguish the past from the present, and the past from the future, and also know how far that future is into the future. We are not usually consciously aware of doing this. Your unconscious mind remembers the location of your memories. Tad James in his Time-Line Therapy™ trainings asks this question: "When you woke up this morning, how did you know to be you?" We know because we have a collection of memories that when we look in a mirror, we compare what we see with the past memories of what we look like and we say, "Yes, that's me." In NLP we call this collection of memories the Time-Line. Our sense of having an historical identity is a Meta-level frame of reference.

In Time-Lining, the location of the pictures provides a crucial component. Most people code and store "time" in a linear manner. In listing the submodalities of your Time-Line,

> *The brain must choose an analogue submodality to code the variations of time.*

did you notice the importance of location? This speaks about the spatial metaphor that you use for "time." Coding "time" using location is the brain's primary way of representing time sequentially.

> *Coding "time" using location is the brain's primary way of representing time sequentially.*

Because of the spatial metaphor of a line for "time," we primarily use the visual submodality of location in our coding and storing of "time." We code chronological distance in time in terms of size and/or distance. Brightness and intensity also indicate other aspects of time. We have "faded memories," a "dim or murky past," or a "bright future."

Auditory submodalities do not allow for simultaneous access of memories. The imprecision of the kinesthetic submodalities tend to eliminate for most people any usefulness in time storage. We can represent far more information visually than we can using the auditory or kinesthetic systems. Of course, each person has their own way of storing time. Thus, one system does not have precedence over the other. However, the way you store time does have consequences. What would happen if your past appeared directly in front of you? Your memories appearing directly in front of you would tend to drive your state and behavior.

Bill came to me in a state of depression. One year earlier his girlfriend had dumped him. In working with Bill, I discovered that the picture of her leaving him was directly in front of his face. I used several interventions with Bill. The major change resulted from Bill moving the image from in front of his face to behind his head.

## IV. Time-Line Submodalities

*(triad)*

1.  **"B" picks an activity they do quite often.** Pick an example like going to work, brushing your teeth, eating lunch, etc.

2.  **"A" leads "B" to think of several specific instances in which they did the activity.** (If "B" has difficulty eliciting specific memories, then "B" should simply imagine when they did these particular activities.)
    a.   a year ago
    b.   a week ago
    c.   yesterday
    d.   today
    e.   tomorrow
    f.   next week
    g.   next year

3.  **"A" elicits from "B" the varying submodalities of each of the memories.** For this exercise, check all three major rep systems. Pay close attention to such things as each picture's location, associated/dissociated, distance, size, clarity, internal dialogue, etc.

    "B" will have some way they internally accesses these pictures in order to tell one from the other since the content remains the same. How do they know one picture comes from the past, another from the present and another from the future? How do they know the difference between the far past and the near past?

4.  **Do a round robin.**

5.  **Debrief by sharing your similarities and differences.**

6.  Experiment with your personal time-sorts to see how that changes experiences. Suppose you associate into your past memories and disso-ciated in your future pictures, what would happen if you reversed these? Or, suppose your future appears on the left and your past appears on the right, what would happen if you reversed these? What effect does switching a picture make? Play with other submodalities. **When you finish experimenting, put everything back as it originally appeared.**

## V. Godiva Chocolate Pattern

Apathy describes a feeling most of us struggle with at one time or the other. Suppose you desire to do something that you know you need to do but presently you do not wish to do. And even though you need to do it, or you feel you must do it, because you don't enjoy doing it, you prevent yourself from doing this particular task. Richard Bandler developed a submodality change pattern that he calls the Godiva Chocolate Pattern that will help you change your feelings from apathy to desire. Wanting to (desire, compulsion) and not wanting to (apathy) do something can be conceived of as operating as primary level experiences. This makes it easy to shift these experiences with a submodality mapping across.

1. **"B" begins by thinking about something they have enthusiasm or a compulsion about.** This procedure gets its name from the way some people compel themselves over eating chocolate. Utilize all three rep systems in the image.

2. **"B" thinks of something they have to do or needs to do so that "B" might as well enjoy doing it.** The decision must be congruent with the total system. "B" chooses something that "B" not only needs to do but wants to do. "B" checks their ecology by asking if there any parts object to "B's" enjoying carrying out this decision enthusiastically.

3. **"A" leads "B" in the formation of this decision (# 2) in their mind. Then, "A" asks "B" to open up a small hole right in the middle of the image.**

4. **"A" leads "B" to form an image of # 1 right behind # 2.** "B" will see a small portion of # 1 through the hole of # 2.

5. **Now "A" leads "B" to allow the little hole to open up but only AS RAPIDLY as "B" needs to get a full feeling response to # 1.** Then "A" directs "B" to allow the hole to close but NO FASTER than "B" can KEEP the feelings generated by experiencing # 1.

6. **"A" directs "B" to repeat the process done in # 5 three or four more times.** "B" performs these repetitions rapidly. Do a break state between each repetition. Make certain that the feelings of # 1 attach to # 2.

7. **"A" asks "B" to look at # 2 and experience the feelings of # 1 simultaneously.**

8. **Do a round robin.**

## VI. *The Swish Pattern*

The Swish Pattern provides a tool to exchange memories or to replace the visual of deleted memories. In his book *Using Your Brain For A Change*[22] Bandler describes a procedure for the purpose of working on specific behaviors that the client may not want anymore. The pattern has proven effective in eliminating unwanted habits. It also provides an extremely effective means in the removal of negative images and their replacement with positive images. The Swish Pattern equips the NLP Practitioner with an effective tool in generating new responses. Such work results in positive behavioral changes.

This procedure generates a new direction for the person to take their brain in. The Swish Pattern has two basic elements:

1) A chain that leads from the cue for the Problem State toward the desired state.

2) A motivation piece, utilizing a dissociated self-image with compelling submodalities.

We will cover the outline of the general model for The Swish Pattern here.

1. **Identify a specific behavior that you wish to change.** The procedure has proven effective with nail-biting, over-eating and, on occasion, smoking. It works best with changing minor habits. Would you like to respond differently to someone than how you presently respond?

2. **Determine the definite cue that triggers the unwanted response.** How do you know when to do the unwanted behavior? Do you experience a feeling, sound or a picture? If you had to teach someone how to do this, what would you tell them to do? If the cue comes from outside you, get an image of exactly what you see. Associate into the experience. If working on biting nails, it may involve seeing your hand moving up to your mouth. As with most NLP techniques, The Swish Pattern works better with visual images. However, auditory and kinesthetic cues will work. Discover the submodalities of the cue.

   **Follow this line of questioning:**

   a) "When do you do the unwanted behavior?" (This puts the person into the appropriate context, so that it will create a context for answering the next question.)

b) "What do you see/hear/feel that makes you want to do the unwanted behavior?" If they don't know, and you can't find out, you can pick a cue that you know has to exist for the behavior to run, such as seeing your hand come up to your face as in the case of biting nails.

c) "Make a large, bright, associated image of what you see just before the unwanted behavior begins." Calibrate to the client's nonverbal external behavior.

d) "Now set this picture aside briefly."

3. **Form an image of having your outcome.**

   **Ask the following questions:**

   a) "How would you see yourself with the desired change?"

   b) "What would you look like if you did not do the unwanted behavior?"

   c) "How would you look if you did the desired behavior?"

   d) "Make a dissociated picture." Remember, in NLP you associate into present state and dissociate in the desired state. In an associated picture you already have the feeling of accomplishing your desired outcome. Thus, an associated picture will not motivate you. The picture must offer a compelling and desirable image. The more desirable the desired state appears, the more likely The Swish Pattern will work.

4. **Have you created an ecological desired state?** Run your desired state through the well-formed outcome model.

   a) Have you stated it positively?

   b) Describe it in sensory-based language.

   c) Have you designed a self-initiated and self-controlled desired state?

   d) Will your desired state fit in all contexts of your life?

   e) Have you maintained appropriate secondary gain?

f)  What resources will you need?

g)  Have you designed an ecological desired state appropriate for your total system? Does any part of you disagree with you having this state?

**Ask the following questions:**

a)  "Have you stated your outcome positively?"

b)  "What will you see, hear and feel when you have your outcome?"

c)  "Does your desired state depend on you and on you alone?"

d)  "Where, when, how and with whom do I want this outcome? Do you want this outcome all the time, in all places and without any limitations?"

e)  "What would you lose if you accomplished your outcome?"

f)  "What do you have now, and what do you need to get your outcome?"

g)  "How will having this outcome affect the lives of those around you?"

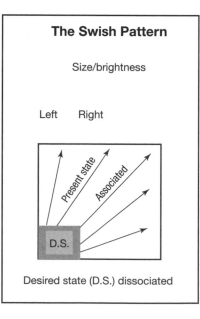

*Figure 14:2 The Swish Pattern I—Using Size/Brightness*

5.  **Swish the images using size and brightness.** Take the cue picture and make it bright and large. Make sure you associate into the cue picture. **Say to the client,** "Close your eyes and see in front of you a big bright, associated image of your present state (where you are now). In the lower left corner of the cue picture, place a small, dark and dissociated picture of the desired image [see Figure 14:2]. Now, take the large bright picture and quickly make it small and dark. At the same time, make the small dark desired image large and bright. Do this very quickly. Remember, the brain learns fast." As the client does this procedure, make a s-w-i-i-i-s-s-s-h-h-h-ing sound to assist the change. Clear the screen. Repeat this procedure at least five times.

6.  **Future pace by testing for results.** Ask the client to think of the cue that triggered the undesired behavior. If it produces the new image, you have completed the process. If it doesn't, go to the next step.

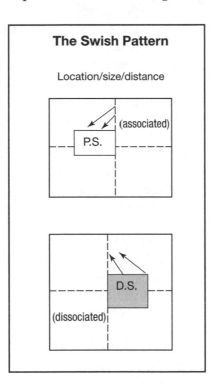

*Figure 14:3 The Swish Pattern II—Using Location/Size/Distance*

7.  **Swishing the images using distance.** If size and brightness do not work, distance could provide the driver. You may wish to test for certainty. Follow the same procedure as above. Only, instead of using the small dark picture in the corner, you swish from distance. Lead the client in taking the cue picture of the unwanted behavior and zooming

it out on the horizon until it becomes a black dot. Place a small, dark and dissociated picture of the desired outcome on the horizon. Then lead the client to zoom in with the desired behavior from the horizon. Lead the client in doing this real fast. Repeat five or six times and test. (See Figure 14:3)

## Beliefs

*What we hold as true or not true* powerfully determines our behavior. Indeed, our beliefs present a major driving force of our lives. If you believe you can accomplish something, you probably will. If you believe you cannot accomplish a particular task, the odds pile up against you that you won't.

> *A belief involves a generalization about a relationship between experiences.*

A belief involves a generalization about experiences, about relationships between experiences, and about the meaning of experiences. Suppose you failed at a particular task. From that moment on you may believe you will always fail at a similar task. Thus, you have generalized by connecting your first failure at a task to always failing at similar tasks.

Increasingly, the medical community has begun to appreciate the role of beliefs in recovery. One hundred cancer patients in a particular study had been diagnosed with terminal cancer. Ten to twelve years later, the researchers found them still living. They had received different treatments. Some had standard medical treatments, surgery, chemotherapy, and radiation. Some had received non-medical treatments like acupuncture. Others received treatment through special diets and nutrition. Others turned to psychology and religion. Some received no treatment. The reporter that interviewed these people discovered that they all had one thing in common: *They all believed that their treatment would work for them.* In each case the patient worked from the generalization that the particular therapy would cure cancer. And because they believed it would, it did. They generalized from the agent of cure to the actual physiological cure, using submodalities, and through neuro-transmitters and the immune system. ***Our brain knows what we believe, what we doubt and what we don't believe by the structure of our internal representation—and this sometimes involves submodality differences.*** We will look closer at this phenomenon in the belief change exercise.

> *Our brain knows what we believe, what we doubt and what we don't believe by the structure of our internal representation—and this sometimes involves submodality differences.*

You have probably heard of **the placebo effect.** In the placebo effect the experimenter gives the subject a non-active drug, typically a sugar pill. Yet the experimenter gives the subject such in a way so that they believe that they have received the real thing. An interesting phenomenon happens. Roughly one third of the time a placebo will work as effectively as the real drug. Some studies indicate that placebos work as well as morphine in 54% of the cases. Indeed, in drug trials, experimenters know to always take the placebo effect into consideration because of this well documented phenomenon.

Robert Dilts has written:

> A man even did a study in the other direction, where he took people who responded to placebos and people who didn't and he gave them real drugs. He gave them drugs for pain such as morphine, and it turned out that the placebo responders responded effectively to morphine over 95% of the time. The other people responded to the morphine 46% of the time. That was roughly a 50% difference, which shows you that even real drugs may require belief to be effective in some cases.
>
> Placebos have even been shown to have an effect in cancer treatment. In fact, in one study they gave people "placebo chemotherapy" and a third of the patients lost all their hair.
>
> The most effective electroshock machine in the state of California was supposedly one that hadn't worked for three years. They gave people a general anaesthetic before they put them on the machine, so mental patients thought they got electroshocks even though they didn't. And that worked better than giving them the actual shock treatment.[23]

Yes, beliefs play a very important role in both our behavior and our health. We installed most, but obviously not all, of our core beliefs during childhood. Parents, peers, teachers, and the media help form our beliefs even before we have reached an age where we have enough maturity regarding awareness or choice about which beliefs we want and which we don't want.

*Can we change beliefs that we choose now not to have and that in some way limit us?* Yes, NLP provides the technologies necessary to unlearn or change old unwanted beliefs and create new ones. In this practitioner course we will study one technology of submodality "mapping across" in changing unwanted beliefs.

## VII. Belief Formation Change Pattern

*How* does your brain know the difference between what it believes and accepts as true and what it believes as false? *How* does your brain know the difference among belief, unbelief, disbelief, and doubt?

Traditionally in NLP we thought that the answer involved *submodality distinctions*. Accordingly, Bandler and others developed a couple of versions of using submodalities shifts and "mapping over" processes for the purpose of changing beliefs. More recently, Hall (1997, 1998) and Bodenhamer, *The Structure of Excellence* (1999) have called this into question.

Beliefs certainly do have their own individual codings. Yet these structural codings do **not** occur merely at the representational level. This explains how you can **think** about a **belief** and even represent it fully, completely, compelling, etc., and still **not believe it.** This actually presents an incredible and amazing thing. We can **think** without **believing.**

Therefore **believing** must involve *something more* than just representations. It must involve another piece of awareness—some particular kind of thinking **about** the first thoughts.

What we have discovered about **beliefs** boils down to this: to believe, a person must begin with a thought—a representation about something or another. It may involve a way of representing the existence of something, the relationship between one thing and another (a cause-effect structure), the significance and value of something (a meaning construction), the identity of something (identity beliefs), what one presupposes and assumes about the world (ontological and presuppositional beliefs), etc. After a person constructs one of these mapping processes—he or she must **affirm it as true.** Without the meta-level **affirmation of truth** *about* the representation—one does not have a "belief." One only has a "thought," one merely has a set of representations.

With this understanding regarding the structural nature of beliefs—to transform or change a belief we have to **disconfirm** the truth or validity or usefulness of the representation. We can do this by *reframing* the ideas and representations using the Meta-model. We can also do it by finding *counter-examples* to the idea. This frees up "space" in our mental world to then construct another idea or concept that we can affirm as a belief.

NLP offers several techniques for changing beliefs. The early models base themselves entirely on the technique of submodality *"mapping across."* We have found that more often than not, people do *not* get the results that they wanted. When a person does find that a particular submodality mapping across worked—it usually does so because it enabled the person to deframe the old reality structure and thereby provided opportunity for another belief to get installed.

*Information Gathering And Preparation:*

1. **Identify the old unwanted belief: "A" asks "B" to think of a belief that the person wishes he or she did not have.** "B" thinks of a belief that limits them in some way, or has undesirable consequences. "A" elicits the submodalities of "B's" unwanted belief. "A" asks "B": "How do you represent this belief in your internal experience?" For this exercise use the visual submodalities of color/black-&-white, movie/ still, 3D/flat, frame/panoramic, associated/dissociated, bright/dark, in focus/out of focus, far off/close and location. After eliciting these visual submodalities, "A" asks "B" if the auditory or kinesthetic submodalities present seem important. If they do, elicit them. "B" lists these submodalities on the top left side of a blank sheet of paper.

   Next, write down *the language* of the belief. How does the person express the idea or concept that limits and that creates various difficulties? What *concept* does this belief address? What *kind of a belief* does it represent: existence, ontology, cause-effect, meaning, etc.?

2. **Think of something you doubt and feel unsure of: "Now think of something that you doubt. You feel unsure about its truth or its untruth. You just don't know. It may be, it may not be. You do not have certainty about it but doubt it."** Elicit the submodalities of this experience of doubt and un-sureness. "How do you represent this doubt in your internal experience?" List the submodalities on the top right of the sheet of paper. List them beside the submodalities of *the unwanted belief* (# 1) in the same order.

   Identify also *the language* of the doubt or feelings of being unsure. How do you express this to yourself?

3. **Run a Contrastive Analysis:** Now run a contrastive analysis on these two experiences: belief and doubt. Mark with an asterisk (*) those submodalities that differ. Identify how the languaging of the two also differs.

4. **Test the Structures: Test each of the submodality differences that you have marked with an asterisk (*) between belief and doubt. Do this**

**to find out which ones provide the most effect in changing you from believing in the thought to doubting it.** After testing one submodality, "A" directs "B" in changing it back to the way it originally appeared before testing each one.

5. **Identify the New Desired Belief**: "What new belief would you like to have in place of the old limiting belief that you have come to dislike?" Run a well-formed outcome on "B's" new belief to make sure that they have it well-formed. For example, check that "B" has stated this belief in positive terms without negations. Especially identify *the language* of the new enhancing belief.

   Example: "I can learn to change in response to feedback," rather than "I won't be unable to change what I do." Elicit the submodalities for this new belief. "How do you represent this belief so that it feels desirable, compelling, and real in your internal experience?" List the submodalities on the bottom left side of the sheet of paper. Also, make sure that "B" thinks of the new belief in terms of an ability or process, rather than having already achieved a desired goal.

6. **Identify the Structure of a Strong belief:** Ask "B" to think of something that they believe without a shadow of doubt, like "The sun will come up tomorrow." "Mom loves me." "God loves me." Elicit the submodalities of this unquestioned belief. "How do you represent this strong belief in your internal experience?" Lists the submodalities on the bottom right side of the sheet beside the submodalities of *the desired belief* (# 5) in the same order. Calibrate to "B" for future testing.

   Make sure that "B" specifies and languages this new belief in a way that feels strong, solid, real, and compelling.

7. **Run another Contrastive Analysis:** Contrast the new desired belief (# 5) and the solid unquestioned belief (# 6). List the visual, auditory, and kinesthetic submodalities as well as the language of each. Mark with an asterisk (*) those submodalities and language formats that differ.

8. **Test the Structures:** Test each of the submodality differences that you have marked with an asterisk (*) between *the new desired belief* (# 5) and *the solid and unquestionable belief* (# 6) to find out which ones provide the most effect in changing the new desired belief into the unquestioned belief. After testing one submodality, ask the person to change it back to the way it originally appeared before testing each one.

*Belief Change Process:*

9. **Turn the Undesired belief into Doubt:** Using one or more of the most powerful submodality drivers that you discovered in # 4, direct "B" to change the undesired belief to the submodalities of doubt. Have him or her language the old thought, "Maybe it is so, but maybe it is not. I don't know. I feel very unsure about it."

10. **Turn the New desired belief into a Solid and Unquestioned belief:** Using one or more of the most powerful submodality drivers that you discovered in # 8, direct the person to change the new desired belief (# 5) to the submodalities of the solid and unquestioned belief (# 6). As you do this, invite the person to use their language of validation, solidness, and unquestionableness to set the frame for the idea or concept that they want to use as their operating belief.

11. **Test the Structures:** You have two ways to test. First, ask "B" to think of the new desired belief. As the person does, calibrate to "B" to check that he or she has the physiology of the solid and unquestioned belief.

    Second, elicit the submodalities of "B's" new desired belief. The new belief should now have the same submodalities and language patterns as "B's" solid and unquestioned belief (# 6). If not exactly the same, "A" directs "B" in adjusting the new desired belief into the same submodalities and languaging as the true belief.

12. **Future Pacing:** "Now, go out into the future associated into an imaginary time when before this change you would have felt tempted to behave in response to the old undesired belief and notice how you now respond with the new belief." Calibrate to "B's" responses.

## VIII.    *The Grief/Loss Pattern*[24]

*Part I*

1. **Identify a "Loss" (absence/emptiness):** "A" asks "B" to think of an actual loss such as a loss from death or divorce. Or "A" can ask of "B" to think of a potential loss such as a valued person who has a terminal illness. If "B" chooses the potential loss, this will take the form of "pregrieving" which provides a useful coping response to a possible future loss. "A" should make sure "B's" representation consists of what "B" valued and did not want to lose, not the person after they died or divorced. The Andreas' state: "It's what you *valued* and now miss that leads to grieving—the child's laughter and play, special qualities,

future promises, etc." If "B" just sees the ill child or a coffin, ask, "How do you know you lost something valuable?" or "How do you know this has significant value worth grieving over?" Follow this line of questioning until "B" thinks of some valued experience, not its negation. This piece plays an extremely important role in this pattern. The grief pattern will not work without it.

2.  **Identify the Structure of "Loss."** "A" asks "B": "How do you represent this person—the loss of this person—in your internal experience?" For this exercise use the visual submodalities of color/black-&-white, movie/still, 3D/flat, frame/panoramic, associated/dissociated, bright/dark, in focus/out of focus, far off/close and location. After eliciting these visual submodalities, "A" asks "B" if the auditory or kinesthetic submodalities seem significant and important. If they do, elicit them. "B" lists these submodalities on the top left side of a blank sheet of paper.

    The structure of loss will involve, in some way or another, a sense of emptiness. The person will attempt to represent the person, thing, experience, value, etc., and will then "ghostify" it in some way so as to create the meaning—"not really here anymore."

3.  **Get the Structure of Presence and Fullness (resource person):** "A" ask "B" to think of a significant person who has died or who through some other incident no longer lives in "B's" vicinity but when "B" recalls them "B" no longer experiences loss. "B" selects a person that at the time of the death or loss they experienced some grief but when they recall them now they experience a presence or fullness as if the lost person seems "still with you in some way." "B" experiences this person as a resource for them in some way.

    Sometimes the person may draw a blank and seem incapable of identifying such a resource. In this case, ask the client to think of a person that they typically have available to them but who does not live in their vicinity at this moment. A child living somewhere else may provide a resource. Or, I may ask the person to recall a special schoolteacher who still lives, but lives elsewhere. *This person will serve so long as the client experiences the person as a present resource.*

    **"A" elicits the submodalities of "B's" resource person. "A" asks "B," "How do you represent this resource person in your internal experience?"** "B" lists these submodalities on the top right of the sheet of paper. List them beside the submodalities of the unwanted belief (# 1) in the same order.

4.  **Run a Contrastive Analysis:** Contrast these two experiences (# 1 and # 2). Mark with an asterisk (*) those submodalities that differ. Also note what the person says about each and identify the specific languaging of this.

5.  **Test the Structures:** "A" directs "B" in testing each of the submodality differences (marked with an *) between # 1 and # 2 to find out which ones provide the most powerful in changing grief/loss to presence/fullness. After testing one submodality, "A" directs "B" in changing it back to the way it originally appeared before testing each one.

6.  **Run an Ecology check:** "A" asks "B," "Does any part of you object to your experiencing person # 1 like you do person # 2? Would any of your family members object if you stopped grieving now?" Satisfy any objecting parts through reframing. For instance, should "B" say that they would not honor the deceased if they did not grieve, you could reframe by asking, "What better way to honor this person than by joyfully carrying this person in your heart for the rest of your life and by drawing on the resources they have given you for a fuller life for yourself?"

7.  **Map the Submodality Differences from One to the Other:** Using the submodality drivers discovered in # 4, "A" directs "B" in changing the experience of loss (# 1) into one of presence/fullness (# 2). Usually the content of the representation will remain the same. However, at times the content may need adjusting in order to match the structure of the present experience. Also map across what the person says about the loss when they have come to terms with it and accept it fully.

8.  **Testing:** "A" directs "B," "Think of the "loss" experience now. Does it feel like a resource to you in the same way as the original "fullness" experience?" "A" checks "B's" submodalities for the former loss experience. They should appear the same as the presence/fullness experience. Sometimes they may not have the exact submodalities. In such cases, use those differences to complete the change.

*Part II*

In Part I, you utilized submodality "mapping across" to transform an experience of a past loss into a present resource. In Part II, you will direct the client in seeking out replacement experiences now and in the future to replace the experiences with the person whom they have lost. This provides a future pace designed to insure that the person gets on with their lives.

1. **Access the valued experience:** "A" asks "B" to take the valued experience of the person that you just transformed from a loss into fullness, and represent it in whatever way seems natural and easiest for you now. Imagine a blank movie screen in front of you. Place the image of the person at one side of that screen."

2. **Identify resources:** "A" says to "B," "I know that this person meant a great deal to you. And, that this person has given you much that will enhance your life now and in the future. Get a representation (image) of how that person's gifts of resources, qualities and values will assist you now and in the future. Place that image at the other side of the screen." "A" paces "B." Sometimes the client will take a few minutes and will need a little coaching to get this image. "A" recalls some of the qualities, values and resources that "B" gave to them in previous conversation, and points these out to "B" to assist them in forming this image.

3. **Ecology check:** "A" asks "B," "Does any part of you object to making these experiences or directions a part of your future? Would anyone else in your life have any objections to this?" Adjust this representation and/or reframe to satisfy any/all objecting parts before continuing.

4. **Installation in the future:** "A" directs "B," "Now, take those resources, qualities and values that this person has given to you with you into your future **and notice what form these resources take and how they assist you in living your life with other people.**" "A" may suggest to "B" to imagine a series of images unfolding out in the future of "B's" drawing upon these resources to greatly enhance their lives. These representations should look attractive and convincing, but they should not construct too specific images. They should look somewhat vague and unclear, allowing for a variety of possibilities. For most clients, this produces a very valuable experience.

## Thought Questions To Assist Your Learning:

1. Describe the difference between a digital and analogue submodality.
2. If you wanted to know the critical or driving submodalities of someone, how would you go about discovering them?
3. What does it mean to "map across" using submodalities?
4. What submodalities did you find most critical in your "time" representations?
5. How do submodalities explain the Swish Pattern?
6. What problems does the term "submodalities" have within it?
7. What words or terms have we suggested as more accurate and productive for "submodality?"
8. How do submodalities work in making changes?

# *Part Four*

*Advanced Neuro-Linguistic
Programming Modeling*

# *Chapter 15*

## Strategies

*Part I—Identifying The Pieces Of Subjectivity*


"The 'map' is not the 'territory'."
(Korzybski, 1933)

(**Note:** This material edited from Chapter One of
Michael Hall's *NLP: Going Meta Into Logical Levels*, 1997).


**What you can expect to learn in this chapter:**

- NLP "strategies" as ways to track down where brains go.
- How to use representational system (rep system) language as strategy language.
- How to elicit and unpack a strategy.
- How to interrupt, design and redesign a strategy.
- How to install a strategy.

As *"the study of the structure of subjectivity,"* NLP encompasses three most influential and essential components involved in experience: neurology, language, and programming. Let's review. *Neuro-Linguistic Programming* therefore describes the dynamics between mind-body and how they interact as a system to generate our neuro-linguistic "model of the world." From that interaction come our emotions, behaviors, communications, etc.

*Neurology* describes how our bodies contribute to creating our "states" and the behaviors that come out of those states. *Linguistics* describes how we represent the external world inside our mind-body through various symbolic systems (words, sentences, metaphors, gestures, mathematics, music, art, etc.). *Programming* describes those formats, processes, technologies, paradigms, etc., by which we organize our neuro-linguistics in useful ways.

Part I of this chapter presents *the NLP Model* in order to provide the foundation of this study. Here you will find *the aspects of subjectivity* which NLP identifies, and which comprise the essence of genius of this model of human neuro-linguistics. In Part II we extend this to provide a summary of the NLP *strategy model*. In Part III we provide step-by-step directions in doing strategy work with the Decision Strategy, Spelling Strategy, Motivation Strategy and the Learning Strategy.

## NLP—A Model Of Models

The NLP model arose originally as an experiment in *modeling* examples of human excellence. The linguist (John Grinder) and the computer programmer (Richard Bandler) combined their resources to look at the therapeutic skills which Virginia Satir and Fritz Perls demonstrated in communicating with clients. From that original modeling Bandler and Grinder (1975) created *an explicit model* of the implicit models Satir and Perls were using to guide their responses, behavior, language, etc. Bandler and Grinder called this model-about-a-model "a *Meta-model* of language in therapy." Thus began NLP.

Bandler and Grinder both came from backgrounds that equipped them to think in terms of breaking down complex behaviors and linguistic patterns into smaller chunks. They eventually found these pieces of subjectivity in the sensory rep systems. Thus they used the sensory modes of awareness (visual, auditory, kinesthetic, olfactory, and gustatory) as the building blocks of subjectivity.

> *Using a neuro-linguistic "bio-computer" model of the brain they assumed that it was possible to program its information processing system. What they wanted to know was how the internal structure of these sequences of representational sensory systems could give rise to high quality behaviors. This gave rise to the strategy model.*

They then were able to find sequences in these elements by asking, "How does this work?" "How does a piece of subjectivity (e.g. therapeutic communication, motivation to get up in the morning, staying resourceful in the face of negative feedback, etc.) work?" "What goes first, then second, then third?" Using a neuro-linguistic "bio-computer" model of the brain they assumed that it was possible to program its information processing system. What they wanted to know was how the internal structure of these sequences of representational sensory systems could give rise to high quality behaviors. This gave rise to the strategy model.

## The Philosophy/Epistemology Of NLP

NLP represents a constructivistic epistemology based upon the ideas first articulated by Immanuel Kant and then expanded by General Semantics (GS). *Epistemology* is about what we know, how we know what we know, and how we know that we know. NLP takes as part of its epistemology the quote from Alfred Korzybski (1933/1994), "The 'map' is not the 'territory'."

*What* we know and experience "inside" ourselves (human "subjectivity") differs radically from what exists "outside" (that is, the "territory"). What we know and experience within functions as a "map" relating to a "territory"—it may *represent* the territory, accord to it, reflect it, symbolize it—but it does not exist *as* the territory. These two phenomena ("map" and "territory") exist on different levels (superficially called the "subjective" and "objective" levels of experience). This means, as Dilts, Bandler, Grinder, and DeLozier (1980) wrote, that we do not operate directly on the world.

> "Rather, we operate through coded interpretations of the environment as received and experienced in our sensory rep system—through sights, sound, smell, taste and feeling. Information about our internal universe (as well as our internal states) is received, organized, consolidated and transmitted through an internal system of neural pathways that culminate in the brain— our central processing bio-computer. This information is then transformed through internal processing strategies that each individual has learned." (pp. 3-4).

> We operate directly, not upon the world, but upon **our** **"maps" of the world**. *The models that we build to cope with the world require that we identify and represent two things: 1) a set of structural elements and 2) a syntax.*

We operate directly, not upon the world, but upon *our "maps" of the world.* The models that we build to cope with the world require that we identify and represent two things: 1) a set of structural elements and 2) a syntax. The structural elements comprise the building blocks and the syntax the set of rules or directions that describe how we can put the building blocks together.

As an constructivist epistemology, NLP shares with Western scientific models its grounding in the realm of sensory experience and transforming environmental variables into decision variables. As such, it focuses more on *form* than content, and it differs from such models by including the observer into the model.

NLP adopts a systems approach to mind-body as it explores how the brain creates (or constructs) internal representations (IR) that thereby generate our state of consciousness. Our mind-body, culture, language, etc., form a complex system in which no part operates in isolation from the other parts.

*Constructivism* here refers to the fact that we do not deal with the territory (first-level reality), but only with *the internal reality* that we construct.

Korzybski argued first for a correspondence model of truth, namely, that our model should have a correspondence with the territory. Secondly, he argued for a pragmatic model of truth, that we need a model that will enable us to navigate effectively even if the "map" may not correspond with accuracy.

## The Components Of Subjectivity

> *The brain uses its senses (sensory modalities) to form its **modes** of awareness.*

We begin then with the sensory rep system, which makes explicit that we think in see-hear-feel-smell-taste terms. Through our sensory apparatus mechanisms (eyes, ears, internal sensations, tactile feelings), we input data from the outside. Then we *"think"* using these see-hear-feel forms to "represent" what we have seen, heard, felt, etc. The brain uses its senses (sensory modalities) to form its *modes* of awareness. We cannot think without these basic modes. These components comprise the very form of our thoughts as distinct from their content. We process information in sensory channels. For notation purposes, NLP notates these rep systems as:

V — Visual (images, pictures)
A — Auditory (sounds, tones)
$A_t$ — Auditory tonal (sounds)
K — Kinesthetics (tactile and internal sensations of the body)
0 — Olfactory (smell)
G — Gustatory (taste)
M — Motor movements

These rep systems can refer to *external* or *internal* sources of data, hence sometimes we notate this by adding an *e* or *i* as in $V^i$ (visual internal). These rep systems can also refer to *remembered information* stored inside neurologically ($^r$) or *constructed in the imagination* ($^c$).

r —Remembered information (VAK)
c —Constructed information (VAK)
i —Internal source of information (TDS, Trans-derivational Search)
e — External source of information (uptime, sensory awareness)

Then to denote that we have a Meta-Representational System, words and language, we use the notation:

$A_d$ —Auditory Digital (the language system, words, self-talk)

Via these *rep systems* we *present* to ourselves *again* ("re", hence *"representation"*) the information. Our thinking follows from, and builds upon, our external sensory modalities (the VAK plus language). By these "tools" we sketch personal "maps" of the world to navigate life. Most of us *favor* one rep system over the others and we may, in fact, over-use it to the neglect of the others.

These rep systems function as the building blocks of behavior. We make mental distinctions using categories and classes. Each sensory modality has specific qualities, which are the properties of representational systems. These qualities are traditionally called *submodalities* in NLP. We prefer to call them "modality qualities" or "representational distinctions." They provide the brain specific information for sorting and coding experience. Even though we usually do not experience submodalities consciously, we can easily make them conscious by simply becoming aware of them. This awareness enables us to alter the submodality structure of the experience.

**Key Visual Submodalities:**

__ Brightness
__ Focus
__ Color
__ Size
__ Distance
__ Contrast
__ Movement
__ Direction
__ Foreground/Background
__ Location

**Key Auditory Submodalities:**

__ Pitch
__ Continuous or Interrupted (Digital/Tonal)
__ Associated/Dissociated
__ Tempo
__ Volume
__ Rhythm
__ Duration
__ Distance
__ Clarity

**Key Kinesthetic Submodalities:**

__ Pressure
__ Location
__ Extent
__ Shape
__ Texture
__ Temperature
__ Movement
__ Duration
__ Intensity
__ Frequency

> *Ultimately we format or program our behavior, skills, and competencies through the process of combining and sequencing these neural system representations.*

We then format or program our behavior, skills, and competencies using the process of combining and sequencing these neural system representations. Our processing of input stimuli occurs through a sequence of internal representations, which we call "a strategy." Thus, in *strategy work* we focus on the processes of unpacking and repackaging behavior into efficient and communicable sequences. In this way we can format new and better ways of functioning.

## "Map"-Making: Creating "Maps" For Charting The Territory

Bandler and Grinder suggest that we use *three modeling processes* to create our internal 'maps' of the world (our "programs"). These processes are deletion, generalization, and distortion, and they specify how we abstract or summarize from the territory and transform them into a representational "map." These involve three processes:

### Deletion

We delete because we cannot possibly process all of the billions of bits of information that impinge upon our nervous system at any given moment. Such would overwhelm us. Nor do we have the sensory apparatus to input all available data. Our eyes scan only a very narrow part of the light spectrum. Our ears receive only a very narrow band of sound wave frequencies. Thus we do not deal with reality directly, but indirectly— through our brain and nervous system. We only register a small portion of the sights, sounds, sensations, smells and tastes do come in. In this way, our brain protects us by selectively attending to items. This deleting function only becomes problematic when we delete essential or important items of information.

Huxley (1954) describes the function of the brain and nervous system as designed

> "to protect us from being overwhelmed and confused by this mass of largely useless and irrelevant knowledge, by shutting out most of what we should otherwise perceive or remember at any moment... To make biological survival possible, Mind at Large has to be funneled through *the reducing valve of the brain and nervous system*. What comes out at the other end is a measly trickle of the kind of consciousness which will help us to stay alive on the surface of this particular planet." (p. 23, emphasis added).

He later describe our experience of "the world of reduced awareness" as expressed and "petrified" by language (p. 24).

> *Miller (1956), in a classic paper, asserted that consciousness has a limit of 7+/-2 chunks of information.*

Miller (1956), in a classic paper, asserted that consciousness has a limit of 7+/-2 chunks of information. This severely limits our learnings and us. So we have to habitualize perception, learnings, "programs" so that our "unconscious" mind runs them. When we habitually repeat a certain mental pattern it drops out of conscious awareness as we store it unconsciously. This model treats *consciousness* as "an emergent property of neural system activity." A representation attains consciousness only when it reaches a certain level of intensity. Given consciousness limitations of 7+/-2 chunks of information at a time (a "chunk" in consciousness refers to a patterning in experience we haven't yet made unconscious), when it achieves the status of a TOTE, it drops out of consciousness, leaving consciousness free to attend other things.

## Generalization

With the over-abundance of data, we generalize to summarize patterns. We create generalizations to simplify the world by categorizing, organizing, abstracting, and making higher level learnings. We generalize by putting items of similar function, structure, nature, etc., into categories. We look for Gestalts of meaning, configurations of significance, and synthesis of information so as to build generalizations. We look for patterns and when we find an experience repeating over time, we often jump to the conclusion that we have a pattern. This saves us time and trouble so we don't have to constantly face the world anew. We generalize to give the world order and meaning, based on our ability to notice patterns, of similar syntax, context, form, and significance.

## Distortion

As we build our models we inescapably distort things by deleting and generalizing data. We experience the territory through our perceptual filters. Once we install our programs, our "thoughts" (rep system) move to a higher logical level as beliefs, values, and attitudes (higher level distortions). When we "see" potentials in something, we distort. When we impose meaning or value on some item—we distort. We don't evaluate this modeling process as good or bad in itself, but simply the way our nervous system handles and organizes data. Thus "color" does not exist out there in the world, but inside our nervous system.

> *Every form of distortion (e.g. beliefs, values, and perceptions) "organizes" us.*

Every form of distortion (e.g. beliefs, values, perceptions) "organizes" us. Eventually the format of the distortion will *psychologically organize* our very "being" or personality (the way we think, perceive, feel, value, believe, and act). In other words, our "maps" have a reflexivity to them such that they form us in their image. The beliefs and values that result from our "map"-making induce us into our "states of consciousness" which, in turn, define, identify, motivate, and order us. This creates our particular form of "personality." (Hall and Bodenhamer, 1997b).

## Modeling That Creates Strategy "Maps"

> *What results from deleting, generalizing, and distorting? An internal "map" of the world—a paradigm. We construct this "map" in order to navigate reality.*

What results from deleting, generalizing, and distorting? *An internal "map" of the world—a paradigm.* We construct this "map" in order to navigate reality. This explains how very intelligent people can engage in stupid behavior. They have an internal "map" that demands it! Their "map" "programs" or controls their perceptions, behaviors, communications, skills, states, etc. If their "map" causes them to delete something essential, to generalize a principle, rule, belief, decision too quickly, to distort too much, those programs (strategies) can organize and motivate them in unproductive ways.

We describe these processes and learnings as *strategies*. As we "run our brain" and nervous system in structured and organized ways, deleting, generalizing, distorting, etc., our brain gets into the habit of "going to the same place." It develops a strategy or sequence of rep systems to generate its experiences. For this reason we say that every experience has an internal structure. Even disorganized states such as madness, confusion, stress, procrastination, etc., have a governing, specific, sensory blueprint.

> *All behavior (learning, remembering, motivation, making a choice, communicating, changing, etc.) results from systematically ordered sequences of sensory representations.*

Strategies simply provide a formal description of what we do inside our head and nervous system to generate some particular behavior, whether it consist of thoughts, emotions, beliefs, values, states, skills, experiences, communication, etc. All behavior (learning, remembering, motivation, making a choice, communicating, changing, etc.) results from systematically ordered sequences of sensory representations.

## Conclusion

This basic introduction to the component pieces that make up "mind," "personality," and human subjectivity, provides the necessary ingredients for our behaviors. Our next concern is to focus on how these ingredients come together and blend to create our "subjectivity."

*Part II—The NLP Strategy Model*

## Tracking Down Consciousness

Consciousness goes places. You can count on that! And in our thoughts, emotions, neurology, behaviors, we sometimes feel as if the stream of consciousness rushes us along its currents. We get up in the morning minding our own business (or someone else's!) and then all of a sudden, a thought flashes across consciousness thereby activating our memories so that, inwardly, we travel to another time and place... and find ourselves feeling strong and familiar emotions!

> *Phenomenologically, we experience "consciousness" on the inside in terms of the "senses" that we originally used to input information.*

How can we *track down* the steps and places that consciousness takes us? The pieces of subjectivity—the *coding* "thoughts" in terms of *the sensory systems* and submodality qualities—give us a content on which to focus. We need to watch our internal "screen of consciousness" and pay attention to our *coding*. Because if every behavior and experience has a structure, then the explanation of (and key to) any behavior lies in its *code.* Phenomenologically, we experience "consciousness" on the inside in terms of the "senses" that we originally used to input information.

If these internal rep systems comprised the *ingredients* that we throw in and mix around to create all of our "experiences" including our thinking, thinking style, emotions, behaviors, "personality," etc., then how do these ingredients relate to each other? What relationships govern their order, sequence, amount, timing, etc.? Describing this takes us into the next realm of NLP—strategies. But before we get there, I want to ask a historical question. How did NLP come up with this strategy model for tracking down the flow and movement of consciousness in the first place?

## "Once Upon A Time There Was A Stimulus-Response Model..."

When modern psychology began at the turn of the twentieth century, several new models of "mind" and "personality" vied for acceptance.

Wilhelm Wundt in Germany and his American popularizer, Titchner, presented a theoretical model that *almost* invented NLP with their emphasis on the sensory systems. But Wundt hated application and thought of anything clinical as below him—so he worked to keep his model entirely theoretical. For Wundt and Structuralism, psychology ought to operate as a "science of mind." Today we find many facets of his model subsumed within other psychologies.

Sigmund Freud in Vienna mixed "the hard science" of medicine with the very "soft" art of mythology and mesmerism to create psychoanalysis. His model started with a wild, primitive, out-of-control Id full of sexual, aggressive, hateful, rebellious, etc. forces, and to that Id, he postulated two other entities—a conscious ego "mind" that brings "the reality principle" to bear upon it hoping to restrain the wild primitive urges; and the superego. Then as the super-ego consciousness gets more and more programmed with the rules of home, of culture, of society, of work, etc., it brings more restraint upon the irrational and totally selfish inner Id. For Freud and psychoanalysts and even the neo-analysts, psychology should function as the "science of the unconscious."

John Watson and the behaviorists had a different idea. They suggested that the inner "black box" of "mind" or "consciousness" didn't matter in terms of building a scientific discipline of psychology. So they completely refocused psychology. They designated it as "the science of behavior." As they prevailed more and more in influence throughout the 1920s, 30s, 40s, and into the 50s, Behaviorism or Learning Theory popularized the S-R Theory of human subjectivity.

Stimulus-Response (S-R) theory sought to explain human functioning *exclusively* in terms of conditioning. "This stimulus sets off that response." "This eating disorder originated from that particular conditioning at such-and-such a date." Relying heavily upon the original work of Pavlov in Russia, this model found two tremendously effectively popularizers in John Watson at the beginning of the century and B.F. Skinner in the middle of the century. Miller, Galanter, and Pribram (1960) wrote,

> "Sir Charles Sherrington and Ivan Petrovitch Pavlov are the two men who are probably most responsible for confirming the psychologist's image of man as a bundle of S-R reflexes." (p. 23).

## "And Then The S-R Grew Up Into A TOTE"

Then came the information age of computers, cybernetic systems, the cognitive revolution of George Miller et al. Many famous psychologists within Behaviorism (e.g. Edward Tolman) began increasingly arguing for an Intervening Variable between S-R. Tolman (1948) wrote in "Cognitive Maps In Rats and Men," in *Psychological Review*:

> "[The brain] is far more like a map control room than it is like an old-fashioned exchange. The stimuli, which are allowed in, are not connected by just simple one-to-one switches to the outgoing responses. Rather, the incoming impulses are usually worked over and elaborated in the central control room into *a tentative, cognitive-like map of the environment*. And it is this tentative map, indicating routes and paths and environmental relationships, which finally determines what responses, if any, the animal will finally release." (emphasis added).

Noam Chomsky's (1956) classic reply to Skinner about the source and nature of "language" within human consciousness delivered a death blow to Behaviorism. Then came Miller, Galanter, and Pribram's (1960) analysis of *Plans and the Structure of Behavior.*

Going beyond the simple behaviorist Stimulus-Response model and the reflex arc, they utilized their newly developed *TOTE model* (TOTE). This model provided a flow-chart for tracking human subjectivity from stimulus through internal "processing" in terms of the human responses of *Testing* the stimulus against internal models (plans, expectations, thoughts, ideas, paradigms), *Operating* either on the stimulus to alter it or one's internal map to alter it, *Testing* for congruency or the lack of it, and then *Exiting* the program.

> *The S-R model as well as the TOTE model describe **the process of modeling**.*

The S-R model as well as the TOTE model describes *the process of modeling*. It starts with some stimulus in some present state and tracks the process of getting to some new, different, and better response that leaves one in a more desired state. Thus:

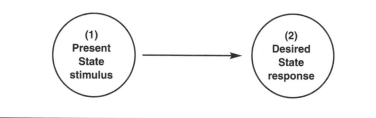

(3) **The resources needed to move from Present State to Desired State**

*Figure 15:1  The TOTE Model*

> *The TOTE model updated the S-R model of the reflex arc primarily by incorporating **feedback and outcome**.*

The TOTE model updated the S-R model of the reflex arc primarily by incorporating *feedback and outcome*.

It also offered a formal format of internal processing sequence triggered by a stimulus. *Tests* referred to the conditions that the *operation* had to meet before the response would occur. In *feedback phase*, the system operates to change some aspect of the stimulus or of person's internal state to satisfy the test. Dilts, et al (1980) illustrate the working of a TOTE in tuning in a radio station (see Figure 15:2).

> "When you adjust the volume dial on your radio or stereo, you continually test the sound volume by listening to it. If the volume is too low, you operate by turning the knob clockwise. If you overshoot and the volume becomes too loud, you operate by turning the knob counterclockwise to reduce the intensity of the sound. When you have adjusted the amplifier to the appropriate volume, you exit from the 'volume-adjusting' TOTE and settle into your comfortable armchair to continue reading."

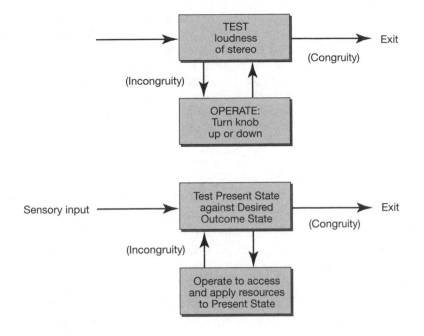

The TOTE model presupposes that we can achieve behavioral excellence through having:
1.  a future goal in mind;
2.  senory and behavioral evidence that indicates the achieving of the goal; and
3.  a range of operations, procedures or choices with which to accomplish the goal.

(Dilts, 1980)

### Figure 15:2  Dilts' TOTE Model

"What do the arrows represent? What could flow along them from one box to another? We shall discuss three alternatives: energy, information, and control." (p. 27)

They discussed this *information* according to the method of measuring information that Norbert Wiener and Claude Shannon developed. Then they discussed the concept of "control" and wrote about information as "a set of instructions" controlling responses or behavior.

"It is the notion that what flows over the arrows... is an intangible something called *control*. The arrows may indicate only succession. This concept appears most frequently in the discussion of computing machines, where the control of the machine's operations passes from one instructions to another, successively, as the machine proceeds to execute the list of instructions that comprise the program it has been given.

Imagine you look up a particular topic in a book. You open the book to the index and find the topic. As you look up each page reference in turn, your behavior can be described as under the control of that list of numbers, and control is transferred from one number to the next as you proceed through the list. The transfer of control could be symbolized by drawing arrows from one page number to the next, but the arrows would have a meaning quite different from the two meanings mentioned previously." (p. 30).

Operating in *the test stage* reveals congruity or incongruity. If incongruity shows up, the process will *loop back* to the test. If congruity shows up, it *exits*. This model demonstrates the importance of continually applying resources to present state to achieve new outcome state. Success comes from repeatedly testing present states against desired outcomes; accessing and applying resources until the two states attain congruence.

The TOTE model presupposes that we can achieve behavioral excellence through having 1) a future goal in mind, 2) sensory and behavioral evidence that indicates the achieving of the goal, and 3) a range of operations, procedures or choices with which to accomplish reaching the goal.

## Then NLP Enriched The TOTE Model And Created "Strategies"

The co-founders of NLP derive their strategy model from the *TOTE* (Test-Operate-Test-Exit) model of the cognitive psychologists Miller, Galanter, and Pribram who presented it as a more complete elaboration of the old S-R model. The TOTE provided the basic format for describing a specific sequence of behavior as it described a sequence of activities that consolidates into a functional unit of behavior that typically executes below the threshold of consciousness.

Designating this process a mental strategy, Dilts, Bandler, Grinder, and DeLozier (1980) articulated the NLP model with the template of the TOTE. As they did this they enriched and extended the TOTE to include the pieces of subjectivity that they had discovered: sensory rep system, submodalities, eye accessing cues, and linguistic predicates, etc. By these pieces one could learn to unpack an unconscious strategy, anchor the elements together, and reframe its meanings, and thereby design and install a strategy. They thought that this would provide a fully articulated model for modeling excellence.

NLP refined the TOTE model by specifying how we do our *testing and operating* in terms of rep system and submodalities. By stating that the test conditions and the operation stages took place actually through the rep system, they provided an even greater refinement to the model. In doing so,

> *NLP refined the TOTE model by specifying how we do our **testing and operating** in terms of rep system and submodalities.*

it offered more refined methods for working with a TOTE. For instance, a person could compare external/ internal visual remembered ($V^e/V^i$) to test something. "Does this spelling look like the way I remembered that it should look?" Or one could do it in the kinesthetic system ($K^e/K^i$) or in the auditory ($A^e/A^i$). The experience of congruence (which leads to exiting a program), and incongruence (which keeps us inside a program) also shows up as represented through one of the rep systems.

In this model, a *test* may take place between two internally stored or generated representations. Tests may involve tests of the intensity, size, color, etc., of a representation. A person may require that a certain sensation, sound, or sight reach a certain threshold value before it produces a sufficient signal to exit.

Further, since we generally prefer one rep system over another, *rep system primacy* reveals how we may use our most highly valued rep system in performing tests and operations, even when it doesn't work well and so creates difficulties and limitations. This more refined model revealed that effectiveness often simply involves learning to match the appropriate rep system to the task (that is, visual rep system to spelling, auditory to music). In fact, the goal of TOTE and rep system analysis inherently involves *finding the most appropriate rep system for the TOTE steps* that will lead to the outcome. In this way, we can learn to use all of our rep system as resources for learning and performing.

> *The goal of TOTE and rep system analysis inherently involves **finding the most appropriate rep system for the TOTE steps** that will lead to the outcome.*

We sort spelling strategies into visual ones and phonetic ones. A phonetic strategy goes: $A^e$? $A^i/A^e$. Yet since visual coding of the English language does not follow phonetic rules, people with visual strategy consistently perform much better in spelling. The sounding-out strategy works very well for oral reading presentations, but not for spelling. The visual strategy goes:

$$A^e \rightarrow V^c \rightarrow K^{i+ \text{ or } -} \rightarrow \text{Exit} (A^e \text{ or } K^e)$$

*Figure 15:3 Spelling TOTE*

(First, you hear the sound of a word by someone saying, "Spell _____." Then you run the first test by constructing a Visually Remembered check. If it feels right for the second Test you then Exit by spelling the word out loud or writing it out. If it feels wrong, loop back to recall another visual image.)

## Using "Strategy Analysis" To Track Down Where A Brain Goes

As a summary of strategies, Dilts, Bandler, Grinder, DeLozier (1980) wrote,

> "All of our overt behavior is controlled by internal processing strategies. Each of you has a particular set of strategies for motivating yourself out of bed in the morning, for delegating job responsibilities to employees, for learning and teaching, for conducting business negotiations, and so on." (p. 26).

> *We analyze a strategy by breaking its structure (the TOTE) into its components of representations and discovering its order (sequence) for that particular activity.*

We analyze a strategy by breaking its structure (the TOTE) into its components of representations and discovering its order (sequence) for that particular activity. In doing this we "track" where a brain goes (representationally) to create its neurological experiences. The TOTE model informs us that in doing so we perform tests on input, operate on it, perhaps loop around in retesting, and eventually exit the "program."

> *Metaphorically, we can think of **representations** as the digits on a telephone that we push when we want to call someone.*

Metaphorically, we can think of *representations* as the digits on a telephone that we push when we want to call someone. To reach our desired party, we have to punch in certain signals (the numbers) and do so in a certain sequence. Similarly, sequencing our internal representations leads to various outcomes depending on what signals we punch in and the order in which we do that. If we punch in a sequence of representational activity (seeing this, hear that, feeling this, etc.) that leads to accessing mental-emotional resources, then we have the structure of that experience.

By the same token, we *mis-strategize* inappropriate information. Other problems can arise in our strategies: we may develop inflexibility, over-generalize our strategies, get stuck in them as in troublesome behaviors like phobic responses, losing temper, jumping to conclusions, or mis-strategize tune into inappropriate information in another rep system.

## Mastering "The Strategies Model"

Tracking down where a brain goes to create its experiences presupposes numerous skills. Inasmuch as a strategy identifies where the brain goes, and how it responds along the way, to produce its results, to identify strategies we minimally need the ability to:

> *identify* the strategy,
> *elicit* the strategy,
> *interrupt or alter* the strategy,
> *design* new strategies or *redesign* old ones,
> *install* the strategy,
> or *utilize* it in a different context.

These skills also presuppose awareness and sensitivity to the signs and cues that indicate the operation of a strategy. We need to be skillful in managing the strategy that we elicit via anchoring, reframing, pacing, etc. We need to be able to compare and analyze between strategies in order to improve their design.

> *When we unpack a strategy we start to make conscious the pieces that make it up.*

When we unpack a strategy we start to make conscious the pieces that make it up. When a behavior has attained the status of a TOTE, its signal level lies below consciousness so that we no longer know explicitly the details of each step. It therefore requires much skill and practice to make these unconscious strategies explicit. Even the person displaying the strategy will not consciously know the steps. The NLP model entails applying the art of calibrating to accessing cues, sensory specific predicates, etc.

## Strategy Elicitation

When we want the recipe for a delicious dish and how to cook, we need specific information about the elements, their amounts, the order, etc. The same holds with getting the structure of subjective experiences.

1) **Establish a positive frame for rapport**. "You do that very well, teach me how to do that." "Suppose I lived your life for a day, how would I do this?"

2) **Access the state.** The person needs to associate fully and congruently with the skill or state. To fully elicit their strategy, take the person back to the place where the behavior naturally occurs. This lets the context, with its natural anchors (sitting at a keyboard) elicit the response.

Or we can elicit the state by reproducing a portion of the context (tonality, gestures, play-acting, etc.).

3) **Intensify the state.** In elicitation, the more of the state we evoke, the better.

4) **Explore the "how."** "How do you make this?" If the person has consciousness of their strategy, they will tell you. If not, expect them to demonstrate it. Eliciting involves good questioning techniques that evokes a person to carry out a task that requires the strategy.

"Have you ever experienced a time when you really felt motivated to do something? "When did that last occur when you felt really motivated?" "What does that feel like when you felt exceptionally creative?" "Have you ever gotten into a situation where you felt very creative?" Accessing questions involve a person recalling an experience. "What did it feel like? How did you do it? When do you feel best able to do it? What do you need to do it? What happens as you do it? When did that last occur?"

Such questions encourage a person to "go inside" to their memory banks and access their personal history. Doing this *Trans-derivational Search* (TDS) to our reference experiences not only serves as the way we all make sense of things and deal with stimuli, but also how we use such to re-create states and experience. We can also use this TDS process to assist someone to go back through "time" to recover the full experience.

5) **Calibrate from an uptime state.** Being fully alert and open to the person's external cues enables us to calibrate to the state as we watch the person demonstrate the strategy. People typically demonstrate as they talk about problems, outcomes, or experiences (the mind-body systemic response). Our attentiveness to such "instant replays" enables us to note how they cycle through the sequence of representations that lead to their response.

6) **Ask them to exaggerate.** If we don't get the strategy, invite the person to exaggerate some small portion of the strategy. Exaggerating one step in a strategy may also access other representations linked to it synesthetically.

7) **Stay Meta to the content.** Remember that strategies operate as purely formal structures.

In NLP we typically focus on eliciting *excellence* rather than pathology in human experience. We elicit resourceful experiences (creativity, motivation, remembering, decision, conviction, confidence, etc.). This is what you say:

"As you remember a time when you experienced all your full resources and potential as a person, go back to that occasion, now, so that you re-experience that event fully and completely."

General and basic elicitation question include:

## Trigger questions:

"How do you know when to begin the process of...?
 (motivation, deciding, learning)
"What lets you know you feel ready to...?"

## Operation questions:

"What do you do first?
"What happens as you begin?"
"What do you do when you don't feel sure that you have reached your
 goal?"

## Test questions:

"What comparison do you make?
"How do you know when you have satisfied your criteria?"

## Choice point questions:

"What lets you know you have finished?"
"What lets you know you should move on to something else? "
"What lets you know you have not succeeded at this?"
"How do you know you've ended your process?"

If we think about the learning strategy, then once we ask a person to think about a time or situation wherein they learned something extremely well with ease and competence, then we can ask the following:

## Operations questions:

"What happens as you learn something?
"What do you do as you prepare to learn something?"
"What steps do you go through to learn something quickly?"
"What do you do when you don't feel sure that you have met your
 criteria?"

**Test questions:**

> "What demonstrates that you have successfully learned something quickly?"
> "How do you know when you have learned something quickly?"
> "How do you test whether you have achieved your desired outcome?"

**Decision Point questions:**

> "How do you know when you have successfully learned easily and effectively?"
> "What lets you know that you have not yet finished learning something?"
> "What lets you know that you feel ready to move on to something else?"
> "When you don't feel sure you have successfully learned something, what lets you know that?"

Suppose we want to track the brain-body (neuro-linguistics) of someone who completes a task generally considered unpleasant and discover their strategy. Begin by asking generally, "How do you get yourself to do an unpleasant task like cleaning the toilet, taking out the garbage, doing taxes, etc." Then invite them to access that state. "Think of a time when you motivated yourself to do something that you didn't want to do. How did you do that? What pictures, voices, and messages, etc., did you use to motivate yourself to do something you found unpleasant?"

One man I interviewed would look at the situation externally and make a constructed image of seeing himself carrying out the proposed behavior and then quickly fast-forward the movie to the end where he sees the desired results. He would get a positive feeling of muscle tension and increasing warmth as he watched this internal movie. He would then hear a voice saying, "Just do it" in a matter-of-fact tonality. When he heard that voice, he would simply rise and execute the behavior.

$$V^e \to V^c \ldots V^{c\ -m-}\ K^+ \to A^{dt} \to \text{Exit}$$

Let's track down your brain activity as it codes and creates a sense of anxiety, stress, and de-motivation about getting up for work. One man said, "I tell myself that I can rest for a few more minutes, and I do. As time passes, my picture of arriving at work late gets bigger and closer and brighter. It stays the same picture, but when it becomes big enough, I have to get out of bed to stop the bad feelings."

$$A^d \to V^i/V^i/V^i/ \to K \to \text{Exit}$$

## Unpacking Strategies As They Flash By

One problem involved in unpacking strategies that we want to model, modify, or utilize—they zoom by! So how can we identify the appropriate steps in the sequence if they go so fast? This holds especially true for those that have achieved the status of an unconscious TOTE. To identify each step we must either increase our abilities to observe rapid and minute behavioral changes or slow the process down by asking good questions. "What happened first that allowed you to respond so creatively in that situation?" "What do you do first when you motivate yourself?" Keep asking until you find the initial external stimulus that triggers the strategy. "What happens just before that?"

> *To identify each step we must either increase our abilities to observe rapid and minute behavioral changes or slow the process down by asking good questions.*

1) **Unpack strategies in terms of predicates.** We tend to reveal our preferred rep system (seeing, hearing, feeling, etc) in the kind of language predicates we use. These predicate words are adjectives, verbs, adverbs and other descriptive words that identify what we assert (or predicate). We can also listen for *predicate combinations indicating synesthesia patterns.* "That looks uncomfortable" (V-K). "It sounds like colorful place" (A-V). "Don't look at me with that tone of voice" (V-A). "It sounded frightening" (A-K). By *going Meta* to this content we can note its form and structure.

2) **Unpack strategies in terms of accessing cues.** Most of our communication takes place on the unconscious level. We are usually unaware of the vast majority of representations that pass through our neurological systems as we cycle through our strategies. Yet all behavior indicates our internal neurological processes and therefore carries information about them. We are able to decode this form of communication as we gather information.

3) **Unpack by asking logical questions.** Does the strategy make logical sense? If a person seems to jump steps in the process, ask backing-up questions to get to the beginning of the strategy. "What happened first that allowed you to feel motivated in that situation?" Back up. "What did you do before that?" "What stimulated that?" Eventually we find the initial external stimulus that triggered the strategy and thus the step-by-step process.

## 4) Unpack using the Strategy Notational System.

"I hear alarm clock, then look at it as I turn it off. Then I lie down again and feel how comfortable bed is. Eventually an internal voice says, 'If you stay here, you'll go to sleep and be late.' So I make a picture of a time when I was late for work. I then feel bad and I say to myself, 'It will be worse next time,' and make a bigger picture of what will happen if late again and feel worse. When the bad feeling is strong enough, I get up." Then we notate it as follows:

$$A^e \rightarrow V^e \rightarrow K^{e+i} \rightarrow A^{id} \rightarrow V^{i-} \rightarrow K^{i-} \text{ (loop)} \rightarrow \text{Exit}$$
$$\text{Loop back}$$

"I picture all the things that I am going to do during the day and feel good about them. The pleasant pictures then 'pulls me out of bed.' If have to do something unpleasant, I think about how wonderful it will be when it is done."

$$V^{i+}/V^{i+}/V^{i+} \rightarrow K^{i+} \rightarrow A^{id,+} \rightarrow \text{Exit}$$

"I feel a sensation of warmth and say to myself, 'I have to get up.' This voice is in a calm, easy tone. As voice speeds up, it becomes more clear and distinct, and I become more alert."

$$K^{i+} \rightarrow A^{itd}/A^{itd}/ \rightarrow \text{Exit}$$

(Analogue increase in volume/pitch)

> *Many times we can redesign better tests and operations in our strategies by simply making sure that we have all of the rep system components represented.*

## Designing Strategies

Some strategies just don't work very well or could work a lot better if streamlined in some way, or if we added additional resources. Many times we can redesign better tests and operations in our strategies by simply making sure that we have all of the rep system components represented.

What do you hear around you?
What does it sound like?
What do you hear inside your head?
What do you see around you?

Describe the tone in your internal dialogue...
What internal pictures do you see?
How do you feel internally?
What qualities do these pictures have?
What do you smell?
What body awareness do you have tactilely or externally?
What tastes do you experience in this?

> *Strategizing involves sending the brain in productive directions. It describes the process of organizing representational components in certain sequences to create the desired outcome. This skill is more important than intelligence in achieving outcomes.*

Strategizing involves sending the brain in productive directions. It describes the process of organizing representational components in certain sequences to create the desired outcome. This skill is more important than intelligence in achieving outcomes.

We can learn about our styles of thinking and responding by becoming aware the steps in our strategies that lie between the original stimulus and the resulting behavior. Then we will have more choices about how to respond and how to change a strategy program. In this way we will get to know the structure of our subjective experience. And this will enable us to track down what our brain does, which modality it is using, the resources it calling upon, etc. For example, response styles could include: congruent, incongruent; polarity (reversal in content; Meta ("about"); hidden (unseen); passive, aggressive; immediate and delayed.

## *Designing New And Better Strategies*

The strategy model enables us to actually design custom-made strategies for achieving specific outcomes. In *strategy design* we create desired outcomes, trouble-shoot problems, streamline cumbersome and inefficient strategies, limit strategies that we use too generally, re-contextualize others to appropriate contexts, install appropriate tests, etc. We need to have well-formed strategies. For example: making sure that we have all the necessary tests and operations.

> *We need to have well-formed strategies. For example: making sure that we have all the necessary tests and operations.*

To redesign the maladaptive strategy of someone in too much downtime, we build in more external checks. For someone fearful of public speaking, we design in a strategy step wherein they access a state of relaxation, comfort, self-humor, etc. In such design work, we build in context markers and decision points that control the neuro-linguistic processes. Design work enables us to create cues for different contexts.

When we use strategies for *modeling*, we find someone who already has the ability to achieve the outcome and simply identify and use that strategy *as a model*. If a person has a good strategy for reading and criticizing literature, but not for generating it, we don't want to model that for creating literature.

When we *tailor a strategy* for a specific task and person, we must first determine the kinds of discriminations we need. Which rep system will we need for gathering information? Do we have the needed rep system? Do we need to break a synesthesia pattern or divert it so it doesn't interfere? How much rehearsal will we need to practice with the new sequence?

A *well-formed strategy* involves knowing:

- **The kind of information (for input, feedback) that we need and in which rep system.**

- **What kind of tests, distinctions, generalizations, associations we need to make in processing that information.**

- **What specific operations and outputs we need to achieve the outcome.**

- **The most efficient and effective sequence for testing and operating.**

- **An explicit representation of the designed outcome.**

  Without specifically identifying an outcome when we "operate" and compare the representation of present state with desired state, the strategy will break down. This explains our need for representations of the outcome. "What do you want? How will you know if you've changed...?

- **If you have designed an ecological strategy.**

  "Will this violate personal or organizational ecology?" We make sure the strategy doesn't conflict with other strategies. In so working with human subjectivity, we will want to discover what "important reasons why" a person hasn't yet achieve an outcome. The person's

Meta-outcomes provide their behavior in terms of some general goals (preservation, survival, growth, protection, betterment, adaptation).

- **If you have utilized the Visual, Auditory and Kinesthetic components of the rep system.**
  If you have utilized both an internal and an external check, using all the rep systems, this will reduce the probability of looping, for example, getting stuck with no way of exiting.

## Utilizing Strategies

The meaning of an experience depends partly on our outcome within a given context. If we can use our creativity to transform obstacles into resources, we thereby expand our choices and behavioral repertoire.

One major use of strategy work is with modeling someone's language strategies. This means that we have to unpack a sequence of thinking, deciding, or perceiving, etc., into steps using rep systems. If we then use that same sequence back to them, we will automatically be pacing them. We are thus developing such a strong rapport that they will find it difficult to resist our communication.

For example, if we notice that someone has a decision-making strategy that involves seeing then talking to themselves about it until it creates certain feelings ($V \rightarrow A^{id} \rightarrow K^i \rightarrow Exit$) then we could use that sequence to organize our communication to them. Doing this matches their form. We ask the person to picture clearly our idea, suggest some internal talk, and some feelings that this will likely generate.

> *By so packaging our information so that it mirrors the individual's thinking processes, we make our communications maximally congruent to the person's model of the world.*

We can also pace non-verbally by directing the person to the appropriate eye accessing positions. By so packaging our information so that it mirrors the individual's thinking processes, we make our communications maximally congruent to the person's model of the world.

If people cannot but respond to their own internal processes, then entering their world, identifying their strategies for buying, deciding, feeling motivated, feeling resourceful, acting in a pro-active way, etc., increases our effectiveness. It assists in managing, communicating, relating, understanding, etc. We no longer have to move through the world assuming or *imposing* our strategies for motivation, decision, belief, etc., on others. Once we have discovered their preferences we can fit our communication to their model. In a psychotherapy context, we will be more effective in understanding how to help the client make the changes they desire. To motivate another, we find and use the person's motivational strategy. To communicate, we find their strategy for understanding. To manage, we find their strategy for trust. To sell, we find their strategy for decision, valuing, planning, etc.

## Installation Of Strategies

We can *install* a strategy by anchoring, by rehearsing strategy pieces (new dialogue lines, gestures, facial expressions, etc.), by vicarious experiences (role-play), and by creating altered states and experiences. By installing we get the strategy to function naturally and automatically, as an intact unit (a chunk) so that each step automatically ties into the next.

**(1) Installing through anchoring** involves anchoring a representation or state and inserting the steps of the strategy as the person rehearses the strategy sequence. Anchoring helps us "walk" a person through it. When we anchor a sequence, we wire it to some contextual stimuli. Elicit the steps of the strategy through questioning and observation and then anchor each step with the same anchor. For example, we have someone access their motivation strategy. "Think of a time when you felt really motivated..." and then anchor that experience. Later, we can fire off that anchor in a new context so the person re-accesses that strategy sequence for motivation in that new context.

Synesthesia patterns automatically carry through on their own processes once initiated. For example: a person with a phobia of water can see a body of water and immediately have a phobic reaction. They see ($V^e$) water and feel ($K^I$) fear. We symbolize that phobia as $V^e/K^I$. A synesthesia has two component rep systems with the first rep system triggering immediately the second rep system. We anchor these synethesias and then tie them into other situations. This can streamline an inappropriately long strategy and thereby avoid loops.

One man had a cumbersome and inefficient decision-making strategy. He would spend days in deliberation and put off decisions until he had passed up key opportunities. Then he would feel agitated and angry with himself for wasting so much time. In redesigning the strategy, he considered "the possibility of missing opportunities and wasting time" ($A^d/K^-$) at an earlier point. The question, "What does it feel like at the end of your strategy when you realized the value of wasted time and missed opportunities?" helped him install it. This streamlined his strategy as it provided the needed motivation to decide earlier. He used it as a resource by checking his time schedule and using his negative feelings as a decision point.

**(2) Instructions create new representational steps to install a new strategy.** Since words work as anchors and can anchor a new strategy, we can install a strategy by "giving instructions."

**(3) A hands-on approach to installing a strategy is to rehearse the new way of doing things.** Simply ask someone to practice each representational step until they feel comfortable with it. To develop the visual system, we can practice holding up an image, making mental snapshot of it, then closing our eyes and seeing it inside, etc. Eventually we will develop the ability to create and hold an internal visual image in our mind's eye.

**(4) Game-playing rehearsal.** By making a "game" of reading words in the air, this puts more emphasis on the form than on the content, or their past negative experiences. Have the person learn where to look, where to put their head and eyes, when to use feelings, when to use pictures, etc. By framing the process as a game, the rehearsal can feel more like dancing and playing than learning, spelling, or whatever. Typically this makes the learning easier and less stressful.

**(5) Rehearsing synesthesia patterns** offers another powerful method for installing sequences of rep systems independent of content. Certain synesthesia patterns will feel unfamiliar and underdeveloped.

A/K: As you listen to the words in your head, pay attention to any body sensations that occur. Identify one set, then listen to the words again and allow another feeling to emerge. Continue doing this until you have seven different feelings.

K/A: Pick the feeling most appropriate to the words pronounced internally and from that feeling generate seven sounds. "Get in touch with that feeling and allow it to turn into a sound." Pick one of the sounds, and let it generate an internal visual image.

We can install via overlapping accessing cues. *V-K overlap*: "Look down and to the right, defocus your eyes, breathe high, and shallow, and *now* create picture." Repeat this process until the transition feels smooth and easy, then anchor it.

**(6) Interrupting strategies.** Sometimes we have to interrupt a strategy that has a well-beaten or ingrained path. We can interrupt by overloading— by giving them more information than they can handle. A naturally occurring overload is a noisy place where we "can't hear ourselves think." In the same way that a person may feel so good (or bad) that they don't know what to do or say, as when they are overcome by an emotion, so they can be "overwhelmed by beauty," or "knocked out" by smell. Overloading interrupts their strategy, thereby preventing it from completing its cycle.

> *We interrupt or **divert** a strategy by using some input to shift the representational sequence away from the habitual sequence.*

We interrupt or *divert* a strategy by using some input to shift the representational sequence away from the habitual sequence. When lost in thought and noise overrides sequence and draws us away. Stopping or blocking accessing cues provides a direct and powerful way of interrupting strategy (i.e. like waving hands in front of someone's face while they attempt to visualize!). You can typically interrupt a depressive strategy by asking the person feeling depressed to sit up straight, hold their head up high, to take in a full breath, to throw their shoulders back, to open their eyes wide and to smile. The typical depressive posture and breathing pattern tends to perpetuate the feeling of depression. If they are slumped over, their head is accessing the kinesthetic, thereby preventing them from seeing or talking themselves into a better state! We may also spin out a strategy. We do this by feeding the output of the strategy back into the strategy.

A man with an obligation strategy felt that he "should" do something if he could see himself doing something. We spin his strategy out by having him see himself not doing it. In effect, by seeing himself not doing what he wants to stop doing he does the opposite and therefore "spins himself out" of the old strategy. At least, he will learn that he knows how not to do the old strategy which is a step in the right direction. Each of these techniques for interrupting strategies aims to stop the sequence in the middle, thus giving us an opportunity to redesign and install a better one.

---

**Hall, Michael, *NLP: Going Meta Into Logical Levels* (1997). Seventeen years after NLP Volume I formulated the NLP Strategies Model (1980) —*get the rest of the story* and take the next step in the ongoing study of the structure of subjective experience *by adding logical levels*. An overview of ten Logical Level systems in NLP and other levels erroneously labeled "Logical Levels." Entire chapter devoted to the models developed by three seminal scholars on logical levels: Korzybski, Bateson and Dilts.**

---

*Part 3—More On Strategies*[25]

## Strategy Elicitation

1. Get yourself into an uptime state.
2. Establish rapport.
3. Identify the strategy you wish to work with.
4. Help the person back into the experience (fully associated and congruent. Anchor the state. Speak in present time to maintain the state.)
5. Write down the steps you observe in proper sequence.
6. Notice all accessing cues to track the process of the strategy. (Maintain alertness to eye movements, auditory markings, breathing patterns, gestures, etc.).
7. Backtrack when necessary to get to previous steps.
8. Ask basic questions:

    "How do you _____?" (decide, motivate, etc.).
    "How do you know when it's time to start?"
    "What happens first?"
    "And then?"
    "What happens just before that?"
    "How do you know what to do next?"
    "How do you know you have finished?"
    "Teach me to do it like you do."

9. Check to see if the evolving sequence flows logically.
10. Make sure you elicit and not install each stage. (Use neutral predicates.)
11. Make sure the person answers the question you ask.
12. Get as much detail as you need.
13. Watch for loops (recurring sequences that do not make progress).
14. Ask for the same strategy in a different context and check for duplication of the new sequence.

## Example: Eliciting Decision Strategy

*Context Setting:*

1. Re-experience a time when you made a good decision easily.
2. Imagine some future time or likely situation in which you need to make a strong decision. What would you do?
3. What takes place (what happens) when you decide something?

*Test Questions:*

1. Where did you first think about deciding?

2. How do you know when to decide?
3. What first thing lets you know to begin deciding?
   **Warning**: If you ask, "What do you *see* when you begin?" You may install a strategy rather than eliciting it.
4. What's the first thing you must do in order to decide something?

### Operate Questions:

1. What do you do when you prepare to decide something?
2. How do you know its time to try alternatives?
3. How do you know you have several options?
4. How do you generate alternatives?
5. What steps do you go through to decide something?

### Test Questions:

1. How do you know when you have decided something? What criteria do you use in deciding?
2. How do you test your alternatives?
3. How do you know you prefer one option more than another?
4. What do you have to satisfy for you to know you have the right alternative and the time to decide?

### Exit Questions:

1. What lets you know when you when you haven't yet finished deciding?
2. How do you know when you've made your choice?
3. How do you know you've decided?
4. What lets you know you have successfully decided?

## Strategy Elicitation Through Backtracking

You can elicit a strategy by simply backtracking from a recent decision. Follow this line of questioning:

1. "How did you know you had decided?" (Exit Question)

   Sample Answers: "Well, I just felt it in my gut." ($K^i$)
   Or, "It was just crystal clear." ($V^c/V^r$)
   Or, "It just clicked in." ($A^c/A^r$)
2. Backtrack: "What did you need to satisfy before you could decide?" (Test Question)

Sample Answers: "I looked at all my options." ($V^c/V^r$)
"I just wrote out all the pros and cons." ($A^c/A^r$) or ($V^c/V^r$) or ($K^e/K^i$).

3.  Backtrack: "How did you know what your options were?" (Operate Question)

    Sample Answers: "I talked to a lot of people." ($A^e$)
    "I read up on the subject." ($V^e$) or ($A^r/A^e$)

4.  Backtrack: "How did you know when you needed to decide something?" (Test or Trigger Question)

    Sample Answers: "My boss told me to make up my mind." ($A^e$)
    "I could see that I was at a crossroads." ($V^c/V^r/V^e$)
    "I was too uncomfortable with things the way they were." ($K^i$)

## Potential Problems People May Have With Their Decision Strategy[26]

1.  **Problems knowing the time has arrived to decide:**
    a.  Not enough internal dialogue saying, "This isn't working."
    b.  Not enough pictures of current situation, pictures "fuzzy", or picture of the "road forking," etc.
    c.  Internal negative K (feeling badly about current problem, or not enough association).

2.  **Problems generating alternatives:**
    a.  No visual construct.
    b.  Constructing options but not visualizing outcomes with them.
    c.  Not enough options to choose from (too much "this or that").

3.  **Problems evaluating alternatives:**
    a.  Options not represented in all systems, which makes evaluation difficult.
    b.  No external checks to get necessary data. (Others' responses, etc.)
    c.  Not enough data gathered to make good decisions.
    d.  Criteria not appropriate to context or not prioritized.
    e.  Inappropriate or irrelevant criteria chosen for making the selection.
    f.  Each option considered in a vacuum and not in comparison or contrast with the others.
    g.  Same criteria used for every type decision... too rigid and narrow.
    h.  Same criteria used across time for similar decisions... criteria not revised according to new data or different circumstances.

Remember the importance involved in the words chosen in structuring the questions. Poor wording can prevent you from getting the correct information instead of assisting you. Avoid moving your body or hands in a way that distracts the client instead of allowing them to go inside. Quiet observation is far more productive than talking to the subject too much. Phrase your questions well, then be silent so they can "go inside" to do the Transderivational Search necessary to come up with the information.

As you ask people to "Think of a time when...?" and you ask the various questions about their sequencing, the accessing cues become your clues as to sequencing of their strategy. The eye movements and predicates provide particularly helpful tools. These "beamers" will tell you the order in which the representation systems happen. For instance, in a three part V-A-K strategy, you should be able to see (usually), three distinct eye movements. Cycling through the strategy may take some time for some people and only a second or two for others.

Eliciting strategies takes a lot of practice. However, it becomes easier after you have been doing it for a while. If you feel a little overwhelmed in the exercises, that's OK. You may find it easy to elicit strategies; help someone who finds it difficult.

## Pointers In Elicitation

1. Use all the cues you get during elicitation.
2. Use repetition, that is, check them out.
3. Notice the non-verbal cues, specifically eye patterns and gestures.
4. Go for information in all rep systems.
5. Pay attention to the non-verbal information, such as marking out, tonality, etc.
6. Be sure to watch and listen for a strategy rather than installing one.
7. Use-counter examples (i.e. say something that you know they will disagree with, and check if they disagree) to help avoid installing anything.
8. Check for logical sequence.
9. Pay close attention: Does the person answer the question you ask? Keep asking it until you get the answer.
10. Write down what you get only after you are sure you have it.
11. How much detailed (content) information you obtain has little importance. You want to gather process/structure information.
12. Seek contrast, i.e. "Did you do anything else?"

# Exercises

## I.  The Spelling Strategy

*4 person group—1 hour*

1.  "A" serves as the teacher. "B" and "C" role play as students. "D" serves as the Meta-person. "A" asks "B" and "C" which one considers themselves good or poor spellers.

2.  "A" with "D's" assistance determines the eye patterns for "B" and "C." "B" and "C" may volunteer this information.

3.  Begin with the better speller, "B" or "C." You may need to test this out by asking for the spelling of several words. As you do, notice closely that "B" and "C" will demonstrate everything (eye patterns, predicate usage) you'll be asking for later.

    "A" asks "B" (the better speller) what happens in their head when someone ask them to spell a word. You have a choice here of two ways to proceed. (1) "A" asks "B" to go back to a time when they were spelling a difficult word. (2) Or, "A" just asks "B" to spell some difficult words like "phenomenology," "psychoneurology," "triglyceride" or "caterwaul." "B" will demonstrate the operate phase of their strategy.

    **Note:** You already know when the TOTE begins for spelling. It begins with the $A^e$ (The word called out by the teacher in the classroom). It would begin with $A^i$ for someone writing.

    If "B" can describe for you what they do as they do it, you will have both observation and their understanding. Trust your observation in preference to their understanding. They may not know what they actually do. What they do and what they say they do may very well provide contradictory information. Always believe non-verbal over verbal feedback.

4.  Ask "B" to repeat the spelling several times. You may wish to have "B" do this with several different words.

5.  "A" and "D" collaborate. Did they see and hear the same things (eye movements, predicates, and other "beamers")? Once you agree on what the strategy seems to be, ask the following questions to yourself:

a.   At what point does the strategy begin? (**Test**) With spelling it will start with the hearing of the word. In other strategies it may start with something else.

b.   What steps constitute the **Operation** phase? Does it seem to function logically? Does the strategy make sense to you? Would this strategy work for most people? "A" may need to question "B" to insure they have the correct strategy.

For instance, after they hear the word to be spelled, what do they then do? All the best spellers seem to: A$^e$ (hear the word); V$^{ir}$ (remember how they saw it before); K (familiarity or not).

c.   What makes up the second **Test**? For most good spellers it will usually be another K which tells the person that they spelled the word correctly.

d.   Finally, what provides the **Exit**? It might consist of A$^{id}$ - "Go for it", or "That's it." One good speller didn't exit until the word takes on a red glow in his mental imagery (V$^i$).

6.   Now "A" does the same for "C" (the poorer speller).

7.   "A" compares the strategies. You already know whose strategy works better. Now see if you can determine why. Does "C" leave out some necessary step... or add some unnecessary or confusing ones? Some very poor spellers will leave out a whole modality or will get caught in a "loop." (Example: Spelling purely auditorily, one might try to spell the word, feel bad, say "No, that doesn't sound right," try again, etc.)

8.   After figuring out where and why "C's" strategy doesn't work, have them try "B's" strategy to see how it works for them. Try it yourself. Even though we allow for different ways of accomplishing things, and even while there's not just one way to do things, some universals usually exist. If something works very well for one person, it will probably work at least fairly well for others as well.

9.   When "C" feels good about the new strategy, anchor and future pace.

10. Round robin

## II. Decision Strategy

*3 Person Group—1 hour*

1. "A" asks "B" to pick a specific decision they made. Have "B" choose a fairly simple decision, such as deciding what to wear today, or, choosing what to eat for lunch, or for dinner that evening. ("A" observes "B" closely as "B" decides on a decision. "A" may very well see a quick demonstration of "B's" decision strategy.)

2. "A" assists "B" in going back (associated) into the decision-making moment. "B" doesn't just recall the event but actually associates into the time of the decision.

   **Note:** "A," in helping "B," will find it helpful to use the present tense to pace "B's" being in the decision process. Example: "And as you look at the menu to begin selecting dinner, what do you do then?" At each step, if you "feed forward," you ask the question, "And, *now* what do you do?" Their response will usually elicit their next step in the deciding process. To "Backtrack" you would ask: "And, what did you do just before you gave the waiter your order?" or "How did you know to give the waiter your order?"

3. As "A" proceeds with the elicitation, make notes. Watch eye cues. Listen for predicates (all "beamers"). Pick out the key elements of the TOTE by using the Test, Operate, Text, Exit questions given below.

   **Note:** "A" decides ahead of time which single question to ask "B." **Do not** ask all the questions at once. Ask one question and observe and listen to "B." If that question does not elicit "B's" strategy, then go to the next question under each heading of the TOTE.

   **First Test:**
   > How do you know to begin deciding? (or that it is time to decide?)
   > Where were you when you decided?
   > What is the first thing that lets you know to decide?
   > What is the first thing you do to decide?

   **Operate:**
   > How do you gather data and/or generate alternatives?
   > How do you know you have choices?
   > How do you know it is time to try thinking of new alternatives?
   > How do you know you have several options?
   > What steps do you go through to decide something?

**Second Test:**

How do you test your alternatives?

How do you know whether you like or dislike an option?

How do you know that you prefer one option to another?

What do you have to satisfy for yourself to know you have the right alternative?

**Exit:**

How do you know you've decided?

How do you know the time to choose has arrived?

How do you know you have not decided?

What let's you know you are not yet through deciding?

**Note:** In any decision process you need several things:
- A trigger or tip-off that it's time to decide.
- A way to think about the possible alternatives.
- A way to test or evaluate the choices.
- A way to make your final selection of your alternatives.

4. Have "B" run through a few other simple decisions made recently and notice the strategy. It should match your previous discoveries. You might consider having them run through a decision non-verbally with you watching just the "beamers."

5. Round robin

6. Experiment with someone else's strategy. If it works well for them, does it work for you? If they have trouble with decisions, do you become indecisive using their strategy? What might be a needed additional step (or deleted step) to enhance their strategy? Discuss it fully, then have them try it.

### III. Motivation Strategy

*3 Person Group—1 hour*

1. "A" asks "B" to pick something about which they were very well motivated and were successful. Get specific information about what, when, where.

2. "A" assists "B" in re-experiencing that motivation.

3. "A" elicits "B's" motivation strategy.

**First test:**
>How do you know it is time to motivate yourself?
>What must you do first to motivate yourself?
>What experience lets you know that you are motivated?

**Operate:**
>What steps do you go through to motivate yourself?
>How do you go through the alternatives of being motivated a lot, some, not so much, not at all?

**Second test:**
>What criteria do you utilize for picking an alternative or different level of motivation?
>What do you have to satisfy for you to know its time to be motivated?

**Exit:**
>How do you know you're motivated?

4. Test your work. "A" picks any trivial behavior that "B" can do ecologically (stand up, cross room, pick up a book, etc.) and runs it through the motivation strategy. For example: Say "B's" motivation strategy looks like this: $V^{ic} \rightarrow A^{id} \rightarrow K$ (See the job completed, say to self, "Boy, I'll be glad to get that over with," and feel pleased. Then "B" does the activity.) So now "A" will say to "B", "Please look at that book over there and imagine that you're picking it up. Say to yourself, 'Gee, I'm really doing this well', and imagine feeling extremely pleased about picking it up, as you proceed to do so."

5. Round robin

## IV. *Learning Strategy*

*3 Person Group—1 hour*

1. "B" picks a time when they learned something well and easily.

2. "A" assists "B" in fully accessing this associated experience. (As "B" does this, "A" anchors the good feeling that comes from this successful learning experience.)

3. "A" elicits "B's" strategy:

**First test:**
> How do you know the time has arrived to learn something?
> What do you need to think or do to know you have opened up for learning?
> How do you know the opportunity to learn something has arrived?

**Operate:**
> What steps do you go through to actively and effectively learn?
> What smaller steps do you utilize in learning effectively?
> How do you know what things to do to learn?

**Second test:**
> What must you satisfy to know you are learning?
> How do you know you actually experience learning?
> What kind of comparisons do you use to measure your learning?
> What serves as proof to you that you have learned something?

**Exit:**
> How do you know when learning has taken place?
> How do you know when this particular learning has finished?

4. Round robin

5. Try out someone else's learning strategy to discover how it works for you.

**Note:** Good learning strategies have several common components:[27]

1. The person has good, positive feelings about learning.

   For example: excitement, eagerness, willingness, etc. These feelings can result from $V^c$ (seeing self learning, growing, etc.), or $A^{id}$ "Isn't this exciting. I can learn this. I want to know this." A good learning strategy will have some *motivation* in it.

2. The person avoids feelings of being overloaded or overwhelmed by *chunking* down the whole task. One way to do this involves having an ($A^{id}$) component that says, "How can I divide this up into pieces I can manage," or a series of pictures of smaller pieces ($V^c$). Thus a learning strategy will contain a little bit of a *decision* strategy.

   In addition, good learners understand that confusion is usually a part of the learning process. "Not knowing" means the data has not yet been fully sorted out. Good learners expect to experience confusion sometimes.

However, unlike poor learners who get stuck inside battling the confusion, good learners just set the confused material aside for a while and get ready for the next piece or chunk of data. The poor learner "feels bad" about what he doesn't understand. Good learners feel excited or fascinated or challenged about what they yet have to learn.

3.   An efficient learning strategy will also have a good feedback system to help make corrections. Depending on the task, it might contain an $A^e$ for a music student, $V^e$ for a student painter, or $V^e$, $K^P$, $A^e$ for an athlete shooting free-throws ($V^e$ = seeing basket over the ball; $K^P$ = feel of body and arm moving "in the groove;" $A^e$ = sound of ball swishing through the net.)

4.   Appropriate comparisons to other good learners provide important feedback. To compare yourself with your past learnings or to others in a class of students may very well provide you with invaluable material for your learning strategy. Find out how they learn and model their learning strategy. Or, remember a time when you did learn, and elicit your strategy from that experience.

5.   One of the Exit questions looked like this: "How do you know when this particular learning has finished?" This question has important implications. Some people chunk very small and *Exit* so soon that they do not learn much. Some chunk so large that they never *Exit* and never feel as though they have learned anything. The first may feel good but not know as much as they think they do. The second may have learned a great deal but never feel competent. Once the good learner decides to *Exit*, they can immediately think about when, where, with whom, and how they will use what they have learned.

## Thought Questions To Assist Your Learning:

1.   What does "modeling" mean in NLP?
2.   What map-making processes do we need to always take into consideration when working with strategies?
3.   Who invented the TOTE model?
4.   How does NLP enrich the TOTE model?
5.   How do you elicit a strategy? Name the steps in the process.
6.   Describe how you would go about unpacking a strategy.
7.   Which installation process (anchoring, repetition, etc.) do you recognize as something you already do?
8.   Which installation process would you like to develop?

# *Chapter 16*

## An Introduction To Time-Lining

**What you can expect to learn in this chapter:**

- How we code "Time" using NLP.
- What we mean by "Time-Line."
- How to use a Time-Line to transform experience.
- Numerous applications of Time-Lining Processes.
- Kinds of "Time."

> *The strength of Time-Lining lies in its ability to direct the participant in reframing old and no longer useful thinking patterns.*

How much do the frames we set, especially in our childhood, affect our adult lives? I (BB) believe that many of the conceptual filters that we utilize as adults, started early in our lives. The problems arise when old thinking patterns no longer serve us. The strength of Time-Lining lies in its ability to direct the participant in reframing old and no longer useful thinking patterns.

Time-Lining and the tools of NLP allow the therapist to help the client heal painful memories using the client's own resources. Once these painful memories receive healing, the client can now forgive mother and father and anyone else who has harmed them. Our belief is that a total healing results only after forgiveness happens.

Remember that in NLP we concern ourselves primarily with process rather than content. In Time-Lining we ask, "How does our brain code time?" What goes on inside our head that enables us to know the difference between the past, the present and the future? How do we know the order of events from the past? The brain must have some way of coding time, or else we would not be able to distinguish separate events in our lives. There are clues in the sayings and metaphors we have about time: "I see a bright future in front of me," "I am stuck back in the past, and can't see my way forward," "I am looking forward to seeing you." Such languaging indicates that we see past, present and future events in spatial terms, in directions around us.

In the submodality section we covered this thoroughly. We give it here as a review. Try this experiment. Think of something you do on a regular basis. You may wish to think of driving to work or brushing your teeth. Remember a time about five years ago that you did this. Of course, you probably cannot recall a specific time. However, imagine a time five years ago when you probably performed that activity. Now, remember doing this same thing two years ago. Once you have done that, recall doing this thing last week. OK, good. Imagine doing the same thing in the present. Now, imagine doing it next week, two years hence and then five years from now.

As you recalled and imagined doing this thing, you probably had a series of pictures in your mind. As you look at those pictures again, what differences do you notice in the submodalities? Compare and contrast those several pictures asking yourself the following questions:

• Does each picture appear in color or black-and-white?
• Does each picture have movement or not?
• Does each picture appear as a 3D or flat picture?
• Do you see yourself in each picture or do you look through your own eyes?
• Does each picture have a frame around it or do they appear as a panoramic image?
• How bright do the pictures appear? Does the brightness get brighter or darker the further back in time you go?
• How far off do you see each picture?
• As you look at each picture, are they in focus or out of focus? Does this differ for "older" and "newer" pictures?
• Where do you see each picture in your field of vision? Note how the "older" pictures differ from the "newer" pictures.

> *This submodality coding allows the brain to distinguish between the past, present and future.*

This submodality coding allows the brain to distinguish between the past, present and future. This activity of the brain allows you to know if you look at a memory from the past and how far in the past. And, this activity allows you to distinguish the past from the present and future. This ability is a process of the unconscious mind. Your unconscious mind codes your memories in such a way that they are located in time. In NLP we call this collection of memories the Time-Line. Indeed, you may find it a useful convention to have all your memories arranged in a line.

Tad James in his Time-Line Therapy™ trainings asks this question: "When you woke up this morning, how did you know to be you?" We know because we have a collection of memories of what we look like, sound like, feel like, etc.

> *As we usually conceive of time as flowing, or moving, we need to code it using a metaphor, which also has this characteristic/quality.*

Time-Lining presupposes that we have the pictures of our memories ordered in a linear fashion. As we usually conceive of time as flowing, or moving, we need to code it using a metaphor, which also has this character-istic/quality. Most people store time as some kind of line, either straight, curved, bent, or folded. When you listed the submodalities of your Time-Line, did you notice the spatial arrangement? Could you join up the individual memories to form a continuous line? We call this line your Time-Line.

Using the "time is a line" metaphor means that we are primarily paying attention to the visual submodalities, such as color, bright-ness, size, distance or location. The critical factor (submodality) is usually distance. A distant memory is one that happened long ago. The greater the perceived distance, then the farther away in time the memory. Other visual qualities will also indicate age, and

> *Using the "time is a line" metaphor means that we are primarily paying attention to the visual submodalities, such as color, brightness, size, distance or location. The critical factor (submodality) is usually distance.*

whether something is in the past or the future. Some people find that brightness or focus is also significant in knowing how "far away" in time a memory is. Some people have a dark or "murky" past, and often the future is seen as "bright" and it may appear unfocused, or very small on the horizon. It is also worth noting whether you see time as moving—"Time is an ever-flowing river," or whether you are moving in time on your "journey through life."

Auditory submodalities do not allow us to access memories simultane-ously. Kinesthetic submodalities are usually too imprecise. However, some people do have time coded this way and they usually find that it doesn't work very well! In that case, have them to switch using more visual coding, as the visual metaphor of a line they can see is far more useful when it comes to finding, reviewing, and "changing" memories.

Each person has his own way of storing time. One way does not provide a more correct way and the other an incorrect way to store time. However, the way you store time does have consequences. What would happen if your past were directly in front of you? Would you not drive yourself from your past memories? Bill came to me in a state of depression. One year earlier his girlfriend had dumped him. In working with Bill, I discovered that the picture of her leaving him lay directly in front of his face. I used several interventions with Bill. The depression disappeared when Bill ended up moving the image from in front of his face to behind his head.

If a person's vision for their future lies behind them, will they have self-motivation in attaining their vision? No, self-motivation will barely exist if at all because their future lies behind them. The most useful orientation is having the future in front of us. It is unlikely that pictures, which we have behind us, are going to be motivating—for the unconscious mind says, "Hey! The past is behind me, so that picture has little relevance for the future."

On the other hand, what will your chances of attaining your goals be like if your vision for yourself lies in front of you and appears big and bright? If bigness and brightness function as critical submodalities for you, you will be far more motivated to attain your goals. An old proverb says, "Where there is no vision, the people perish."[28] Time-Lining teaches us how to realize the truth of that verse.

## Anglo-European And Arabic Time

Does your primary interest lie in what happens *now* or in the future? Does the future even concern you? As a minister, I (BB) used to live in frustration with those people who lived only for the moment. How could they not count the cost? At the same time, I envied them because they appeared to enjoy the present moment more than I did. NLP taught me that people view time differently. The problem concerned neurology and not spirituality.

Tad James in the book *Time-Line Therapy™ And The Basis Of Personality* speaks of the difference between Anglo-European time and Arabic time.[29] Anglo-European time comes to us as a product of the Industrial Revolution. Assembly-line work required that workers arrive on time. The assembly line required time structured as linear. At each successive stage of construction, the worker placed a specific part on the equipment being manufactured. Anglo-European time describes time as one event happening after another. Time is perceived in a linear fashion and the events in time stretch out like as on an assembly-line.

In contrast, in Arabic time everything is happening at once. Whereas a person characterized by the Anglo-European concept of time will arrive on time, for someone operating with the Arabic concept of time, time does not matter. If they don't show up today, then tomorrow will do just as well! People from the Islamic countries and areas of the world with warm climates seem to function primarily in Arabic time. They live for the moment. Time for them happens *now* and not at their next appointment. These people can handle several matters simultaneously.

A few years ago my (BB) wife and I visited a missionary friend of ours in Martinique. Martinique is a French Island in the Southern Caribbean area. It is nothing for a committee meeting to start an hour or so after the scheduled time. And if someone told you that they would arrive at your home at 3:00 pm, they might arrive by 5:00 pm and think nothing of it. I went into a state of cultural shock. A person who thinks this way will rarely plan beyond two weeks. An exception would be when for their work, or for some extremely important matter, they were forced to plan ahead. You will find in the United States both the Anglo-European and the Arabic understandings of time. If, for example, the wife is operating in the Anglo-European mode of time while the husband is operating in the Arabic mode, it would not be suprising if there was conflict in their marriage: the wife is planning to save money for the future, and the husband wants to spend it, *now*!

## Determining Your Personal Time-Line

How do you know which time frame you function from? Your internal submodality codings of time determine which time frame you operate from. Pause for a moment and do the following experiment: Recall an event that happened to you six months or a year ago. Pay particular attention to which direction that image of the memory comes to you. The image may be inside or outside your head. It may appear up or down, right or left. Take your finger and point in the direction of that image. Get an image of five years ago. Note where you see that. Continue going back in time getting images from ten years ago, fifteen years ago, etc., all the way back to early childhood. Note the location of each image.

Now, do the same thing for the future. Imagine something that will probably happen in the next six months to one year, two years, five years, etc. Pay particular attention to which direction the image comes to you. Take your finger and point in the direction. This image appears in a different place from your past image, doesn't it? Your future usually appears in the opposite direction from your past, although for some people it may appear in the same direction. I (BB) have found the past and the future appear in a similar direction but at different distances.

You may need to close your eyes for this. Having located your past and future images, now get an image in your mind of the present. Where do you locate the present? Note that your "present" appears in a different location from does your past and future images. For most people this is how your brain distinguishes time. And if you were to join up all the individual memories (and that includes the past and future "memories") you will have your personal Time-Line. Now, if you could not do that, don't worry. Just keep reading.

## Difficulty Eliciting The Time-Line

For many people, just asking them to point in the direction of their past and future will be sufficient for eliciting their Time-Line. However, if that does not work for you, you may need to practice seeing visual images of your memories. Earlier we asked you to recall a series of events that you do regularly. You recalled doing this in the past and in the future. Did you find that easy to do? If you were able to do that, then the series of pictures from your past and into your future represents your Time-Line. I have had clients to say, "I can get the pictures but they are not as clear as if I were looking at them." Most people have this experience, and it is a good thing they do, because it means they can tell when they are in uptime, and when they are remembering. A useful distinction! We do not want the clarity of the recalled image to be the same as actuality. Using this technique of recalling a series of events at various ages provides an effective tool in eliciting the Time-Line. You can ask clients to recall happy events over a period of years. Try it for yourself.

You still don't know the location of your Time-Line? Don't worry. Let us pretend. Just suppose you did know the location of your Time-Line. Ask your unconscious mind to take control of your finger. Your unconscious mind knows which finger on which hand to point in the direction of your past. If you knew the location of your past, what direction would you point? Once your unconscious mind points to the past, thank the unconscious mind. Now, unconscious mind, in which direction do I locate future? Allow your unconscious mind to point your finger in the direction of your future.

You still don't know the location of your Time-Line? Don't worry. You haven't joined the odd-ball club. I have elicited many Time-Lines. Numerous clients respond immediately when I asked them to point in the direction of their Time-Lines. I (BB) have had only one failure.

My friend Randy has difficulty making pictures in his head. Randy represents primarily kinesthetically. So, I had Randy place his Time-Line on the floor. I asked Randy to imagine his Time-Line on the floor and about ten or fifteen feet long. Randy then placed his memories on the Time-Line. "Randy, with your Time-Line on the floor, which end represents your past and which end represents your future?" He told me which end represented his past and which end represented his future. Next I had Randy walk his Time-Line. I always try to force a visual representation. However, you may very well be one of those who has difficulty doing so. Walking your Time-Line offers an option.

May I give you a warning? Do you remember association and dissociation? A major key to the effectiveness of Time-Line centers in that it dissociates the person from their memories. Walking the Time-Line discourages this. The client easily associates into each memory. However, NLP offers steps in teaching the client to dissociate when walking the Time-Line.[30] Dissociation from the memory gives Time-Lining its power in letting go of the emotional hurt through reframing.

> *In eliciting a Time-Line, pay more attention to the process of remembering.*

In eliciting a Time-Line, pay more attention to the process of remembering. Ask for the memory and not the content. When people start describing the content of the memory, you know they have moved into content and not the image of the memory. Lead them to focus on the memory, that is, the location of the recalled image.

## Parts Reframe

Do you still having difficulty seeing your Time-Line? If that happens, you may have a conceptual part of you that objects to your seeing your Time-Line. This part may have the purpose of protecting you from some memory or memories in the past. Regrettably, many people have experienced a difficult childhood. These painful memories lie buried deep in the unconscious mind. Your protective part keeps these memories hidden from the conscious mind. Sometimes the conscious mind creates unconscious parts to repress painful memories so as to consciously, but not realistically, deal with them. Thank the part for protecting you all those years. Assure the part that you have now reached the age and wisdom where you can accept those painful memories in order to deal with and transform them. Tell the part that you have other ways of protecting yourself. Assure that part that it will not be destroyed and the purpose to us is to allow it to accomplish its highest intent for you. Get in touch with this part that no doubt believes it is protecting you and ask it its intent/purpose for you. When you get an answer, ask it what that answer's intent/purpose consists of for you. Continue asking this question until you get an intent/purpose that will give you permission to go back and clean up the old memories. I assure you, if you continue stepping up with the highest intent/purpose question, you will get a positive response. And, this positive response will give you permission to discover your Time-Line and ultimately reframe (heal) the problem as you discover new resources.

## Through Time And In Time

Did your images for the past, present and future all appear in front of you? If they did, you function as a "Through Time" person. Your Time-Line stretches from right to left, or it may be up and down, or even be at an angle or a V. Any combination may occur. The pictures comprising your Time-Line, however, will all appear somewhere out in front of you. A "Through Time" person usually operates in the Anglo-European mode of time. If you locate some of your Time-Line images behind you, so that the line passes through your body, then you probably operate in the Arabic mode of time, as an "In Time" person (See Figure 16:1).

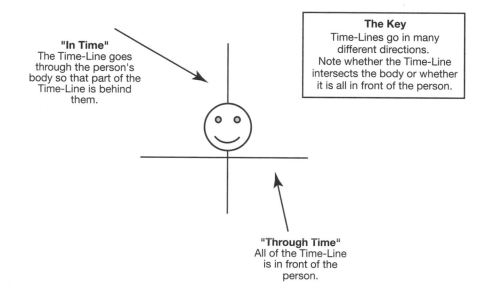

**Figure 16:1** *Through Time and In Time*

| A person's Time-Line affects a person's personality. |
|---|

A person's Time-Line affects a person's personality. (See Hall & Bodenhamer, *Figuring Out People: Design Engineering with Meta-Programs*, 1997.) As mentioned earlier, your Time-Line may go in any direction. The Time-Line may appear as a straight line or it may appear as a spiral or a loop. You may function Through Time or In Time. Through Time people usually dissociate from their memories. They see themselves in their memories. Because all of their Time-Line lies in front of them, time often has high value. These people have difficulty in wasting time. A Through Time person will want to get their money's worth.

You may be familiar with the Myers-Briggs psychological instrument. A Through Time person scores as a Judger on the Myers-Briggs. A Through Time Judger loves organization. They will do things step by step. They love procedure. Time operates always at the conscious level. You can count on Through Time people to show up on time for an appointment. They carry pocket calendars and love them. A Through Time person loves goals and sets them regularly. They need closure. A Through Time person will say, "Let's decide *now* and keep on keeping on."

---

> A ***Through Time*** *person scores as a Judger on the Myers-Briggs.*
> *An* ***In Time*** *person compares to the Perceiver on the Myers-Briggs.*

---

An In Time person compares to the Perceiver on the Myers-Briggs. Remember, if any part of a person's Time-Line is behind them, they function as In Time. An In Time person usually has their past behind them. On the other hand, a Through Time person sees their past in front of them (usually to the left). Because of that the past may haunt the Through Time person more than it does an In Time person. Each one has its own value.

An In Time person has difficulty, however, in letting go of emotions. Unlike the Through Time person, the In Time person has a tendency to associate into their memories. They look through their own eyes at the past. Because of this, they feel the past as if it happens *now*. Time-Lining provides a godsend for an In Time person. For Time-Lining allows them to dissociate from their past, reframe their problem and let go of the emotions.

On the Myers-Briggs, the In Time person tests out as a Perceiver. Organization is not a characteristic of an In Time person. A Perceiver lives in the *now*. They live for and enjoy the moment. Because an In Time person lives in the *now*, they make great lovers. Time does not seem very important to them. On the other hand, a Through Time person has difficulty living in the *now*. A Through Time person has the past and the future as well as the *now* always present. Remember, a Through Time person's Time-Line always exists totally in front of them.

An In Time person is always present and desires to enjoy it, *now*. A favorite expression of an In Time person could be: "Be here *now*." Living in a constant state of association, In Time people may have a different problem each week. An In Time person can recall and re-experience any memory or state they wish whenever they wish. In Time people have difficulty punching a time clock and being on time for appointments. Because they live so in the moment, they may forget the next appointment. As to

Organizers and To Do Lists, they will have low importance to an In Time person. Oh, they may use them to make a living, but don't expect them to like them. As a Perceiver, they function opposite to the Judger. The In Time person does not want immediate closure; they wish to keep their options open. In Time people adjust to life as life presents itself.

Can one function from both Through Time and In Time characteristics? Yes, most definitely. You may display behavior of both in different contexts. The purpose of NLP is to increase choice. Some people operate healthily in both modes of time.

Once in a while you will run into a person who has difficulty accessing a single memory. This may happen because similar memories are clustered together. Though I cannot scientifically validate this, my experience as a therapist indicates this phenomenon to me. A history of abuse, hurt, grief, etc., will build within a person and produce unwanted behaviors like depression, panic attacks, anxiety disorders, etc.

For example: have you ever had someone remind you of a significant person in your life and trigger an unwanted state change within you? This happened even though you knew they were not the individual that originally influenced your state. The stranger's reminding you of a significant other triggered the Gestalt of the memory of this significant other. This connection of memories gives Time-Lining its power. The memories result from the history of the person.

> *Usually the Gestalting or clustering of memories begins from what we call a Significant Emotional Experience of Pain (SEEP).*

Usually the Gestalting or clustering of memories comes from what we call a Significant Emotional Experience of Pain (SEEP). A Significant Emotional Experience of Pain (SEEP) refers to those times when we install learnings from one experience of high intensity. The model for Time-Lining consists of our memories Gestalting or clustering at the emotional level (see Figure 16:2). I (BB) believe that this happens neurologically through the activity of the neurotransmitters. Neurotransmitters refer to those chemical messengers that allow one nerve cell to communicate with another nerve cell. Any stimulus or anchor that fires off one memory will fire off the entire Gestalt.

Before I (BB) became aware of this model, I knew of its existence. In the pastorate I have had people dislike me because of a generalization. Some even left the church. In searching for a reason, I discovered that I reminded them of a father who abused them emotionally. My strong personality served as a trigger to fire off the entire negative Gestalt of their father's memories. One person said, "You even sound like my father!" A Gestalt always has a trigger (anchor). Whenever you see, hear or feel something that has similarity to the original trigger, the entire Gestalt will fire. Time-Lining, in reframing the content of the memory at a Meta-level, will result in a shifting of the submodality structure of the memory and the altering of the emotional part of the Gestalt. This will result in the removal of the trigger. The entire mental strategy alters in Time-Lining.

> *Time-Lining, in removing the emotional part of the Gestalt, will remove the trigger.*

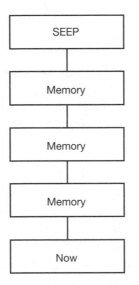

Other similar memories connected to the SEEP

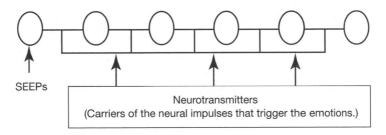

*Figure 16:2  Gestalts and Significant Emotional Experiences of Pain*

As you look at the line between the separate memories (See Figure 16:2), what does it contain? The line represents the neural impulses that trigger the emotions. You will remember that neurotransmitters are those chemical messengers that transmit information from one nerve cell to another nerve cell. The circles represent the memories (SEEPs). Our emotions result from the interactions of these memories with our body. You will recall the basic NLP model teaches us that our states result from the interaction of our internal representations, the word-meaning we give them and their inter-action with our body through the central nervous system. In Time-Lining we do not act on the linkage itself. But, by allowing the client to **let go** (reframe the memories) of the emotional content of the memory, the linkage of the memories metaphorically breaks as the neurotransmission changes. The memories remain but Time-Lining allows the participant to totally reframe the memory, thus changing their emotional response. By thus reframing the SEEPs, the individual metaphorically pulls out the string and the Gestalt will no longer fire as it once did.

You will remember that Through Time people arrange all their memories in front of them. Since all of their memories are in front of them, theoretically they will experience greater influence from their painful memories than will an In Time person. However, In Time people also Gestalt memories and they also experience their effects. Indeed, because In Time people have a tendency to associate into their past memories, they can "feel" their inten-sity more than Through Time people who tend to dissociate from memories.

Through Time people do Gestalt their memories more readily than do In Time people. When you ask a Through Time person to access a particular memory, they may have difficulty separating the Gestalt. Instead of seeing one memory, they may see several. When this happens, ask the client to imagine their memories as being in a photo album. Next, have them turn the pages back. This helps them access individual memories. (See "Trans-derivational Search" in Chapter Thirteen.)

## Developmental Periods

Though not formally a part of NLP, Time-Lining looks at the Significant Emotional Experience(s) of Pain (SEEP), and the Gestalt provides the areas of the change work. The location of the root cause of a negative state provides the key for a successful and complete therapy. Where does the client locate the root cause of the first SEEP of the problem? Once you locate the first SEEP, you can use Time-Lining to reframe the negative emotions from the entire Gestalt.

> *Once you locate the first SEEP, you can use Time-Lining to remove all the negative emotions from the entire Gestalt.*

Tad James, the primary developer of Time-Line Therapy™ drew from the work of sociologist Morris Massey in pointing out three major developmental stages through which all pass. Massey calls these three major periods the **Imprint Period** which occurs from birth to age seven. The **Modeling Period** begins at age eight and goes through age thirteen. And, the **Socialization Period** starts around age fourteen and goes through age twenty-one. Knowledge of these periods will assist you in locating and cleaning up the SEEP.

(**Note:** Crown House Publishing will soon publish John Burton's book, *States Of Equilibrium*, which presents a thorough treatment of developmental psychology. John relies heavily on the work of Jean Piaget but draws from several authors. I (BB) highly recommend this book as a thorough treatment of developmental psychology framed in the context of NLP and Meta-states.)

### Imprint Period

The child's mind acts like a sponge during the Imprint Period (birth to seven). The development of mental filters (a conscious mind) hasn't occurred at this young age. For this reason, the child will absorb the teachings and the behaviors of their parents and other significant adults. Because most of the learnings during this period locate within the unconscious, many of the memories will exist outside conscious awareness. The Meta-model in conjunction with Milton-model language patterns provide the tools for uncovering these repressed memories.

A child's concept of God/divinity develops during the imprint period. Guess whom they get this concept of God from? You guessed correctly, the father. If the father provides love and care to the child, the child will grow up with the belief that God also loves and cares for His children. If the father treats the children harshly and even abusively, the child will grow up believing God also treats His children harshly and abusively. Time-Lining offers a tool for re-imprinting these memories. Much of your work with Time-Lining and Significant Emotional Experiences will concern memories formed in the Imprint Period of the client's Time-Line.

> *Time-Lining offers a tool for re-imprinting these memories.*

### Modeling Period

During the Modeling Period (between eight and thirteen) the child both consciously and unconsciously begins to model the behaviors of people around them. Until age seven, the child does not distinguish between himself and their parents. However, around the age of eight, the child begins to notice the difference between himself and his parents. He also becomes aware of the other people around him. He begins to model the behavior of his heroes. Individual values begin to form at age eight. Massey teaches that our major values form during this period. According to Massey age ten has significance. What kind of significant events happened around age ten in your life to shape your values? Your world at age ten, Massey believes, shaped your values in life. When dealing with people who have problems with values, look for trouble during the Modeling Period.

## Socialization Period

The ages of fourteen to twenty-one mark the Socialization Period. During this stage the developing individual begins to interact with other persons. Relationships and social values form during this period. These relationships and social values usually last throughout life. Time-Lining provides the means to alter these values. If a client has difficulty in the social areas of his life, you may wish to look for the root cause first in this period. Again, such problems may go back to the Modeling or Imprint Periods as well.

## Beyond The Presenting Problem

Most clients do not give you the real problem when they first come in. Sue came to me distressed because the doctor was discontinuing her anti-depressant medication. Sue's husband had left her six years earlier. Since that time, Sue had grown dependent on medication. How could she live without the medicine? Her presenting problem concerned the time her husband left her. However, after questioning, the greater problem surfaced. Her mother died from cancer in Sue's early childhood. The memory of the death of her mother generalized (Gestalted) with the memory of the earlier divorce of her mother and father. The emotions surrounding the divorce of her husband merged with the emotions of her mother's death and the earlier divorce. Thus, the divorce with her husband presented only an example of a greater problem or SEEP. The greater problem consisted of the death of her mother and the earlier divorce of her mother and father. Sue's therapy required that I take her back to the root cause or the SEEP. The root cause lay way back when she learned that her mother and father planned to separate.

> For Time-Lining to have permanency, you must clear up the Greater Problem, the SEEP or the Root Cause.

The divorce from her husband presented just an example of Sue's real problem. The divorce provided one of the last beads on a long string of pearls of SEEPs. In questioning Sue, she related the greater problem, which concerned her discovery that her mother had terminal cancer. For Time-Lining to have permanency, you must clear up the Greater Problem, the SEEP or the Root Cause. Once you reframe the Greater Problem, other associated problems will go as well (see Figure 16:3). The client probably will not have awareness of their existence. Using Time-Lining it is possible to change the Gestalts of memories and the strategies associated with them.

The Greater Problem or the Root Cause operate as Meta-level structures that unconsciously control the client and produce the unwanted behavior. Healing requires accessing their neurology of the part and at the same time the client must access Meta-level resources that will heal/reframe the Greater Problem. Time-Lining provides a useful way to both uncover and elicit the strategy for the Greater Problem while at the same time the accessing of higher level resources that one can bring to bear on to the problem.

Our memories make a significant contribution to our personality. Time-Lining operates directly on the memories. The entire Gestalt and the strategies associated with it change with Time-Lining. Strategies form over time. It is possible to change entire strategies using Time-Lining. The reason for this is because Time-Lining works directly on the way we code the memories that create the strategies. Sue had quite a strategy for depression. Time-Lining blew the strategy completely out. Sue could not run the strategy any more. I knew the therapy had worked when Sue could no longer run the strategy for depression.

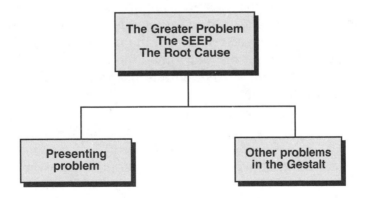

*Figure 16:3 The Greater Problem*

## Memory Management: Experiencing Your Time-Line

As you progress with your learnings, you gain more and more tools to assist you in Time-Lining. Now it is time to experience your Time-Line in a more practical sense.

Recall your personal Time-Line. I want you to *now* just dissociate from your body. Imagine yourself floating out of your body. Leave your body sitting or standing and float up above your body and the images on your Time-Line. Float way up high, see the whole continuum of the past, present and future. You can see the images on your Time-Line. Doesn't it feel good to get above all that? Yes, that describes simply the process of how people "get above it all." When you do this you go "Meta" to your Time-Line. You are dissociating when you "go above" your Time-Line.

Compare the relative brightness of the past and the future. If you have had a lot of pain in your past, your past may appear much darker than your future. If you see dark areas in your past, these may indicate some sort of abuse. Importantly, notice I said "may." If differences in the brightness between the past and the future appear, try brightening up your past close to the brightness of the future. Now, your future may be darker than your past. If true, try brightening up the future to even brighter than your past. Could you brighten either your past or your future Time-Line? If you could, did it change your perceptions? For some people it does, for others it doesn't. As we have discussed in the submodality section, the difference that makes the difference resides primarily in the Meta-level structures. However, for some people, especially the visually oriented, changing the brightness of their Time-Line can make some positive shifts. For this type of processor, "brightness" carries positive Meta-level meanings.

You still remained above your Time-Line? Good. Now, I want you to choose a memory from the past that has little importance to you. Please choose a minor memory. Save the heavy stuff for later. Float back over that memory and look down on it. You see yourself in the memory, correct? Good, OK, now take that memory out of your Time-Line and push it far away. Just keep pushing it farther and farther until it disappears. Make it darker as it goes away. Notice the blank area in your Time-Line where that memory was. Now, choose a new memory. Choose a pleasant memory. Take that memory and insert it into the blank space of the old memory.

OK, good. Remaining above your Time-Line, float out over your future. You do have a future Time-Line, don't you? The wisdom writer says, "Where there is no vision, the people perish."[31] This wise man knew that we all have the potential to dream big for the future. And, by dreaming big for the future, we become the future. What do you want for your future? What event do you wish to happen? In keeping with your ecology for your life, choose an image of yourself living and doing what you want to live and do. Make the image really compelling. You may need to increase the brightness or focus the colors. Experiment with the size of the image to make it powerfully compelling. For most people, making an image larger will increase the emotional component of the image.

Once you have the image, step inside of it. Wrap all the feelings of living and doing the person you desire for yourself around you. Once you experience the emotions of living as the person you desire to live, step out of the image. Seeing your self in the image, place the image in your future Time-Line. Choose a time in your future that you believe realistic for yourself to become that person. Good. Just stick it right in your future Time-Line. Good, remaining above your Time-Line over that future event, look back toward *now*. Notice how all the events between the present and that future event begin to align themselves in such a way for you to become that person. Now, float back over the present and drop into and associate with your body. As you look forward up your Time-Line, notice how all the events between then and now realign themselves in such a way that you cannot help but to become that person. Good. How does it feel to control your memories and your future dreams?

### Reframing Memories With The Fast Phobia Cure

> Using Time-Lining in conjunction with the Fast Phobia Cure provides a most effective tool in eliminating the visual component of SEEPs.

Using Time-Lining in conjunction with the Fast Phobia Cure provides a most effective tool in eliminating the visual component of SEEPs. Usually when you remove the visual component the accompanying kinesthetic disappears as well. When working with a client with a phobia, take them back on their Time-Line until they have arrived over the time of the installation of the phobia. **Do not have them associate into the moment of the phobia's installation**. Just leave them above their Time-Line and have them place an imaginary movie screen above their Time-Line. Run them through the Fast Phobia Cure. Do this after you have eliminated the negative emotions. That will make the procedure both more effective and much easier on the client.

I use this model often with victims of sexual abuse. Ask the client if they would like to have that picture(s) removed from their brain. If they say, "Yes," proceed with the Fast Phobia Cure on that particular memory. On rare occasions the Fast Phobia model will not effectively remove the visual image. In that case I use the Swish Pattern to completely remove the picture. Also, use the Swish Pattern to replace the deleted memory with a pleasant memory. The following section will explain this further.

### Replacing Memories With The Swish Pattern

In replacing memories on the Time-Line, do a Swish Pattern using the associated picture of the blank area on the Time-Line. Remember, following the Fast Phobia Cure, the client will have erased the visual component of the image of the memory. Ask them to form an associated picture of the blanked out area. Should some of the picture still remain, lead the client in forming an associated picture of whatever remains after the Fast Phobia Cure. Swish this associated picture with a dissociated picture of a pleasant memory that the client chooses to replace the old memory. The swish provides us with another powerful tool for replacing these old deleted memories. Remember, try swishing first with a large and small picture. If that doesn't work, swish using distance.

## Steps Into Time-Lining[32]

Use the following steps to assist you to begin the actual process of using Time-Lining. Following the steps listed will assist you in leading the client into the actual therapeutic process. From a study of Richard Bandler's therapies[33], Tad James developed the following procedure in leading the client into a therapeutic intervention.

### 1.  Establishing Rapport

Before any therapeutic intervention, always establish rapport with the client. Before moving into the actual interventions, test for rapport.

### 2.  Gathering Information

When a client comes in to you, they come at the effect of some cause. Your job involves moving them to cause. Using the Meta-model and other counseling skills you may know, gather as much information about the client as you think necessary. Remember, the Meta-model gets to the deep structure beneath the surface structure material. You make permanent changes at the deep structure. Spend at least thirty minutes to one hour gathering information before beginning therapy. Your goal concerns getting to the greater problem.

### 3.  Going From Effect To Cause

NLP and Time-Lining work primarily at the process level. When a client comes in and says, "I am depressed," you move them from effect to cause by asking, "How do you do that?" They will probably say, "What do you mean, 'How do I do that?'" You respond, "I want to know what you do inside your head for you to do the process of depressing yourself."

Depression illustrates a nominalization. Most of the problems that people bring to you are expressed as nominalizations. Can you put depression in a wheelbarrow? Will guilt, anxiety, fear and shame fit in a wheelbarrow? No, you move the client towards cause/choice when you turn their nominalized problem into a process.

The question, "How do you do that?" handles nominalizations. It will also handle any mind reads and cause and effect. When you ask the question, "How do you do that?" you tend to dissociate the client from their problem. Some clients may associate into their problem state, then they will dissociate (go Meta) in order to notice how they do the problem so they can describe to you how they do it. They must run the strategy of the problem if they actually do the problem. Do not have the client run the strategy of doing the problem if they have a phobia or heavy trauma. Otherwise, you want them to run the strategy of doing the problem. You can then calibrate (note their non-verbal behaviors, i.e. facial expressions, breathing, etc.) as they run their problem state. This will enable you to know when you complete the therapy. If they cannot run the strategy again, you are done.

### 4.   Teach Me How To Do That

After dissociating them from their problem with the question, "How do you do that?" you may wish to further dissociate them. Say to the client, "How do I do that?" They will probably respond again with, "What do you mean, 'How do I do that?'" Your response, "Just suppose that I work for a temporary agency and I need to fill in for you today. How would I do the process of depressing myself?" You want to learn their strategy of doing their problem. This question will force them to explain the processes going on inside their head to do the process of their problem. In explaining the problem, they will have to dissociate from the problem.

Recently a neighbor of mine called for help. Diane had serious health problems. If that wasn't enough, her mother attempted suicide a few weeks after coming to see me. Her mother almost succeeded. Diane spent most of the day in bed crying. In response to my question, "How do you do the process of crying?" Diane said, "I see myself over mother's casket." Diane made a picture (as do most people) of her problem. This example illustrates what you want. So I said to Diane, "So, I make a picture in my head of me standing over my mother's casket? Yes, that could make me cry."

> Bob: Diane, is the picture close or far off?
> Diane: Close.
> Bob: Could you send it far off and it still work?
> Diane: Yes.

Bob: Where is it located? Is it up high or low? Is it to your right or left?
Diane: It is low and down to my right.
Bob: Could you move it up to your left and it still works?

After struggling, Diane moved the image and said, "It still hurts but not nearly as bad."

### 5.   Scramble The Strategy

Now what happened? Diane's strategy for crying was to first see a picture of herself over the casket of her mother. Note: in order to see herself over the casket, Diane had to be dissociated. My first guess at the submodality driver for that picture was unsuccessful. Distance did not serve as a driver for Diane. However, when she moved the image from down right (kines-thetic) to up left (visual recall), her emotions changed.

This process scrambles the client's problem by interrupting the strategy. Such procedures interrupt the strategy. First, you need the client to give you the image and submodalities of the problem. Next, you test for drivers. You just experiment. And, if you wish, take the submodalities out to their limits. When you tell a client, "Send it far off and see if it still works," They will actually be trying this out as they are hearing the statement. Taking submodalities out to the limit comes from Bandler's model of the Compulsion Blow Out.[34]

If you should accidentally choose a submodality driver, you may lead them to destroy the strategy. In the above example, if distance served as a driver, they may send the picture off to the point where it disappears. The internal representation will disintegrate in their mind. In NLP we call this going over the threshold. If this should happen, they cannot run the strategy anymore. At times you may find that this series of questions may eliminate the problem. At best, it will scramble their strategy.

### 6.   Discover The Root Cause

The above process will often get to the root cause of the problem. Sometimes the process is only the first step, and you will need to ask some other questions in order to get to the root cause. When you complete step five, ask the client, "What is the root cause of this problem which, when you disconnect from it, will cause the problem to disappear? If you were to know, would it be before, during or after your birth?" Memorize this question. Should the client respond, "I don't know," say, "I appreciate that you think you don't know, you know, but just suppose you did... it would be... ?" If the client answers, "After my birth." You say, "Good, what year?"

If the client says, "Before." You say, "Good, was it in the womb or before?" If they say, "In the womb." You say, "Good, what month?"

I have had numerous clients go back into the womb for the root cause of their problem. Remember, the question of Time-Lining goes to the unconscious mind. When I first started doing Time-Lining, the wife of one of my minister friends came to see me. I (BB) asked her, "If you knew the root cause of your problem, which when you disconnect from it, will cause the problem to disappear, when would it have been, before, during or after your birth?" Sandra replied immediately, "Before birth." "Good, was it in the womb or before?" "In the womb." "Good, what month?" "It was the fourth month." Astonishment appeared all over her face, and mine. "I heard mother say, 'My God, the last thing I need is another child.'" My friend's wife was the fifth child. She grew up feeling unwanted. The root cause lay during her time in the womb.

Modern medical science gives ample evidence beyond doubt that the fetus responds to outside stimuli. Fathers speak to their children in the womb. They do this by talking to the fetus through the mother's abdomen. When fathers do this, the newborn child will respond to dad's voice and not to any other man. Studies indicate conclusively that the baby in the womb hears, feels and learns. These early experiences in the womb begin to shape attitudes and expectations about ourselves.[35]

In response to the question, "In the womb or before?" what options do we have if the client says, "Before?" Occasionally, you will receive this response. Time-Lining says that you respond, "Was it a past life or passed down to you genealogically?" Now, the Judeo/Christian community will obviously not believe in past lives. Also, some other religions have the same belief. And, in my area of North Carolina, I have received only two past life responses. During one of my NLP trainings I utilized Time-Line on a lady from Canada. She replied, "In a past life." What did I do? I matched her model of the world and proceeded. On many occasions clients mention the root cause of their problem as existing in the Time-Line of a parent or grandparent. Often they even go further back in the genealogies. What do you do in this case? You have them float up above their Time-Line and go all the way back to the root cause. Take them back no matter how many generations they must travel. This answer comes from their unconscious mind. Therefore, you must get all the way back to the root cause for for the change work to be permanent.

## Letting Go Of A Negative Emotion: Using Time-Lining

Negative emotions weigh like millstones around our necks. They rob us of energy that we could more productively use in any other pursuits. Using Time-Lining will help us solve the problems of negative emotions rapidly and effectively. The following procedures will work with any negative emotion including depression, guilt, shame, fear from the past, grief and sadness.

### Experiencing Your Time-Line: Letting Go Of Negative Emotions

The best way to learn Time-Lining as with any NLP technique involves experiencing it. You have experienced your Time-Line. And, you have experimented with memory replacement. Now, you will experience the letting go of a negative emotion. Before you begin the exercise, look carefully at the diagram in Figure 16:4. This diagram represents your Time-Line. The line going above your Time-Line illustrates your dissociating above your Time-Line. The numbers indicate four key positions involved in Time-Lining. **Position 1** lies above the Time-Line and represents your arrival just before you or the client get to the root cause or the SEEP. **Position 2** lies directly above the root cause. **Position 3** refers to the position above your Time-Line, fifteen minutes before the root cause. Note carefully the conceptual location of Position 3, for there is where you do the change work. As a conceptual place, in Position 3 we enter a place Meta (dissociated) to the problem. Also, we have positioned ourselves temporally before the problem ever occurred. And, we conceptually take all our present knowledge and resources (Meta-level structures) to that position enabling us to do some powerful change-work through reframing the problem by bringing those resources to bear on the problem. **Position 4** indicates your or the client's association into the event.

Make a mental picture in your mind of these four positions above your Time-Line. Now, select some experience that created a minor negative emotion in you. Someone could have hurt your feelings, or maybe you did something that caused you some minor guilt. Choose a minor negative emotion that you would like to let go. Get into your favorite place and position of relaxation. You may wish to have some relaxing music in the background. Take that memory and float up above your Time-Line. As you travel back on your Time-Line, you approach Position 1. From this position see the root cause of the event in front and below you.

From Position 1 go on to Position 2. At Position 2 you locate yourself directly above the root cause. Now, float down into the event (**Important:** Never associate yourself or anyone else into a trauma or phobia.). Associate into the event of the root cause totally. See what you saw, hear what you heard and feel what you felt at the creation of that emotion. Now disconnect from those emotions and float back up to Position 2. From Position 2, float back to Position 3, which lies fifteen minutes (further if you need to) before the root cause. From Position 3, turn and look towards the present. You will see the root cause of your negative emotion below and in front of you. Now, where is the negative emotion? And, any other negative emotion from that experience, have they disappeared, too?

Position 1: Position above the Time-Line, in the present
Position 2: Position directly above "The Root Cause"
Position 3: Fifteen minutes before "The Root Cause"
Position 4: Association into the event

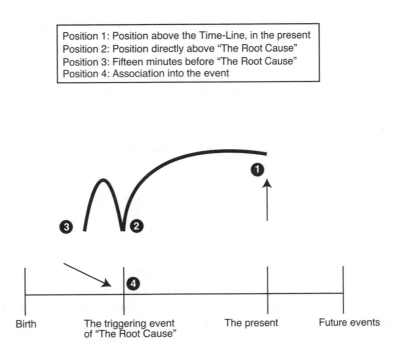

Birth  The triggering event of "The Root Cause"  The present  Future events

*Figure 16:4 Time-Lining Diagram*

If after looking toward the present you still experience negative feelings, remain in Position 3 and "give yourself permission" to let those negative emotions flow out of you. Remain there until all the emotions flow out. If you cannot let the emotions go completely, a part probably needs reframing. The section "When the Emotions Won't Let Go" will provide you with specific part's reframes for letting go of emotions from Position 4.

(1) **Follow steps 1 through 5 in Steps Into Time-Lining on page 372.**

(2) **Discover the Root Cause:** Ask the client, "If you knew the root cause of the negative emotion which when you disconnect from it will cause the negative emotion to disappear, when would that have been, before, during or after your birth?"

(3) **Once you get the root cause, have the client float up above their Time-Line. Once above their Time-Line, lead them back into the past towards the root cause of the negative emotion.** Say to the client, "Allow your unconscious mind to take you back to the root cause of the negative emotion. I want you to stop when you get close to it but not quite to it." Lead them to float back remaining above their Time-Line to Position 1 (see Figure 16:4). From this position they can see the event which presents the root cause of the negative emotion.

(4) **Have the client float back until they position themselves directly over the event at Position 2.** Once they have positioned themselves directly over the event, lead them to float down into the event and associate into their body. Associate them into the event. Say to the client, "Look through your own eyes, hear what you heard during that experience. And feel what you felt during that time." Ask them what emotions they feel and calibrate. Make a list of all emotions experienced by the client. In testing, use this list to make sure all the emotions go flat.

Why float people down into Position 4? Why have them associate into the experience? You will get better results if you have them experience these emotions just before they disconnect from them. One moment the client experiences all the pain and hurt from the root cause of the negative experience. The next moment those emotions disappear. This experience ratifies the change to the conscious mind. And, you want to ratify all changes to the conscious mind. Remember, do not associate someone into a traumatic experience, such as a phobia or a severe abusive episode. With Time-Lining, you don't have to. Just take them straight back to Position 3. For phobias use the Fast Phobia Model.

(5) **Float the client out of Position 4 and above their Time-Line. Ask the client to preserve what they have learned from the experience.** Say to the client, "You have learned something from this experience, haven't you?" When the client responds that they have learned something, say, "In that special place in your mind where you preserve such learnings, preserve what you have learned from this experience." Now I am presupposing that there is a special place in the mind to preserve such learnings. The mind will accept this description and create such a "special place."

This procedure works well as a reframe. Why preserve learnings? Even in the most severe trauma or abuse case, the client has learned something helpful. Suppose your client experienced a rape. Preserving the learnings would keep them on guard for future threatening situations.

You would not want them to have to go through rape again to learn the signs of another possible rape. The important thing is to always check with the client. Ask them if they have gained some knowledge they need to preserve. If they say, "Yes," then you say, "OK, in that special place in your mind where you preserve such learnings, I want you to preserve what you have learned from this experience." And, they will do it. Once they have preserved the learnings, you may now delete the memory with the Fast Phobia Cure if the client desires for you to do so.

(6) **Direct them to float back fifteen minutes before the event to Position 3 and look forward to the present.** Say to the client, "Remaining above your Time-Line, I want you to float back to about fifteen minutes before the event." Give them time to make the mental shift.

By observing their eyes and facial expressions, you can usually tell when they have reached Position 3. When you think they have arrived in Position 3, ask them, "Do you see the event below and in front of you?" When they say, "Yes," you reply, "Now where are all those emotions? Have all of those emotions that were there disappeared too?" On occasion give the client time to let the emotions go. With particularly heavy emotions, say to the client once they assume Position 3, "Now let those emotions flow right out of you." Pace them by repeating the phrase, "Let the emotions go." Repeat these words each time the client breathes out. As the client releases the emotions, you will literally watch a life change in front of you.

Recently I (BB) have added another language pattern that works well. As I observe the physiological changes in the client as the emotions leave, I will say, "And as you let those emotions go you will notice that the image below you and in front of you is changing, isn't it?" They will nod their head or say, "Yes." When they respond positively, say, "Great! That means it is working." And it does mean that it is working for these techniques work directly on the way the brain has coded that event. The submodalities will change as they reframe the problem and let the emotions go. Making this statement to the client, and their subsequent ratification, allows for further confirmation to the conscious mind that rapid change has now happened.

(7) **Test by floating the client back to Position 2. Lead them to associate into Position 4.** Ask the client, "Are you experiencing any of the negative emotions?" Make sure the emotions have flattened out. By that I mean that they no longer experience any of the previously felt negative emotions when associated into Position 4. If the client cannot

experience any negative emotions, you have almost completed the therapy. If any of the emotions remain, use the information in the section: "When the Emotions Won't Let Go."

(8) **Float the client out of Position 4 and above their Time-Line. Direct the client to come forward above their Time-Line.** Give the client the following directions: "I want you to come forward above your Time-Line but only as fast as you can allow all the other events between then and *now* with similar emotions to **LET GO**. Pay particular attention to these events. And, just before you get to them, should you experience any negative emotions from that experience, let me know and I will assist you in letting them go just as we have on the previous memories." As the client uncovers other painful memories, walk them through the procedure on each subsequent memory. With this section I depart from the way Tad James teaches it. He allows them to let them go on their own as they come forward. I have better results if I assist the client on each subsequent memory.

(9) **Future pace the client by associating the client into an imaginary time in the future. Ask them to choose a time that would have previously triggered the negative emotions.** Float the client above the time and out into the future. Ask them to choose an event that would have previously triggered the negative emotion. Float them down into that event fully associated. Say, "Now, try in vain to experience those negative emotions." If they cannot experience the negative emotions, you have completed the therapy. Should they respond negatively, continue to work with the emotion(s) they are now experiencing.

### When The Emotions Won't Let Go

Suppose the client cannot reframe all the negative emotions away when in Position 3, what then? Sometimes the client cannot let them all go. Or, when you test, you will discover that all the emotions haven't left. When a client cannot release the emotions, usually an objecting part needs reframing. The following reframes have proven most helpful. Memorize the language of each. Use them in order. If one doesn't work, go to the next one.

1. Say to the client, "I know there is a part of you that thinks you should have learned something from this event. And, I agree that it's important for you to preserve all the positive learnings in that special place you reserve for all such learnings. Then it would be **OK** to let the emotions **GO NOW**, wouldn't it?" We have found that this language pattern is useful in nearly all cases, and therefore we now include it as standard.

2.  If reframe number one doesn't work, say to the client, "The highest intent of the unconscious mind is to preserve the body. Now, I am sure that the part knows that your holding on to these negative emotions is harmful to the body. With that in mind, will that part give you permission to let the emotion **GO NOW?**"

3.  Should neither of these reframes work, discover the highest intent of the part. Continue stepping up or chunking up on the part. Keep asking, "What is the purpose/intent of the part?" Follow this line of questioning until you get its highest purpose/intent, which will give the client permission to let the emotion go. You may need to find some other part to perform the same function in a less harmful way. If you uncover conflicting parts, use the Visual Squash to integrate them.

### When The Emotion Hasn't Disappeared During Testing

You will encounter times when the emotion hasn't totally flattened in Position 4 during testing. If these techniques have not worked, it is likely that the problem has resulted from one or more of these three areas:

1.  **The client has not positioned themselves totally in Position 3.** Make sure the client dissociates from the memory above the Time-Line from Position 4. Then the client must not only position themselves above the memory, the client must also position themselves before the memory. Through trial and error we have learned that fifteen minutes before the memory works best. You will discover exceptions. When clients have lived for a long time associated into a negative memory, they will naturally re-associate into the memory. Watch your use of language and guide the client carefully to Position 3.

2.  **The client has not yet found the first event or root cause.** You will still get the release of a lot of negative emotions from SEEPs that do not go all the way back to the first event. At times a client will report that 90% or more of the emotion has disappeared. However, in NLP we don't accept 90%. We go for 100%. If just a small amount of emotion remains, the total Gestalt could regenerate. Continue working until all the negative emotions disappear. Many times your work will seem like peeling an onion. You will clean up one event only to discover another. Keep on keeping on until you get the first event and the emotion flattens out.

3.  **The client has a part that objects to letting the memory go.** See the section on "When the Emotions Won't Let Go."

**The Basic Principles Of Time-Line Therapy™** (Young, 1999):

- All problems exist in the "present"— although they refer to the "past." Usually the problem exists in a way that is confused, jumbled, unclear, and so on, at least to the conscious mind.

- What we need to do is to switch them to a different reality, a different model, in order to effect a change. By switching realities we get a different perspective on the "problem."

- We do that by introducing the metaphor of time as a line. This is a common metaphor in Western culture, the basis of our calendar system.

- As the brain has coded our experience, it is able to know which is going to be the most significant part of the story. It seems to be easier to do this separation process if we mark it out spatially.

- By asking the brain to find the key experience it will do this analogously—and move back along the line until it "locates" it. This is not about "truth"—there is no evidence that the event it chooses is something that happened for real. It does not matter. Quite often the brain will "make up" some experience to work on.

- Time-Line Therapy™ presupposes there is a root cause, and that the person will be able to identify it. In fact the brain will oblige the conscious questioning and come up with an answer which "makes sense."

*Alternative Procedure For Time-Lining (Young, 1999):*

- Have the person create an (imaginary) physical Time-Line on the floor.

- Have them walk back (backwards) along that line until they reach the critical place "in the past" for taking action.

- When the person is at that spot, have them dissociate from it, so that they can be aware of the event. They dissociate by stepping off the line.

- Then ask them to find a resource, either for themselves, or for the other person or people involved. In other words, they are going to a higher level of description—a Meta-position, in order to expand that particular model of the universe.

- They must be able to find a resource—either because they are moving to a Meta-reality or a universal reality—or in mundane terms, they have had a lot more life experience since then, and they know now what they did not know then.

- Have them apply the resource—put that "past" experience into a larger context. The situation has now changed anyway because of the Meta-awareness.

- Have them associate into that experience and come back up the Time-Line noticing how things have changed.

- And then you can future pace—extend the Time-Line into the future and have them explore it to see that things will be different in the future. "That's it."

---

For a more thorough study of Time-Lining consult the recently released *Time-Lining: Patterns For Adventuring In "Time"* (Bodenhamer and Hall, 1997, Crown House Publishing, Wales, UK).

---

## Thought Questions To Assist Your Learning:

1. How do you internally represent "Time?"
2. Describe the difference between Middle Eastern and Western "Time."
3. How does one use NLP to elicit a Time-Line? Describe the process.
4. How does an "In Time" person differ from a "Through Time" person?
5. Relate these kinds of "Time" processing (In Time, Through Time) to the Myers-Briggs Type Inventory.
6. What does "SEEP" mean and how does it relate to Time-Line processes?
7. What results did you get, or see others get, from some of the Time-Line processes?

# Endnotes

[1] Tad James, *The Basic NLP Training Collection* (Honolulu: Advanced Neuro Dynamics, 1990), pp. 16-17.

[2] Genie Z. Laborde, *Influencing With Integrity* (Palo Alto: Syntony Publishing, 1987), pp. 71-72.

[3] Tad James, *The Basic NLP Training Collection* (Honolulu: Advance Neuro Dynamics, 1990), p. 19. (Used with permission)

[4] Michael Hall, Ph.D. *Meta-states Journal. Meta-States Patterns in Business*, Vol. III, Number 6. (Grand Junction, CO: E. T. Publications, 1999), p. 2.

[5] Special thanks to Tommy Belk who assisted in the formulation and outlining of the presuppositions in the pattern given.

[6] Edited from Bernard F. Cleveland, Ph.D., *Master Teaching Techniques* (The Connecting Link Press, P. O. Box 716, Stone Mountain, Ga. 30086, (404) 979-8013), pp. 171-172.

[7] Ray L. Birdwhistell, *Kinetics and Context: Essays on Body-Motion Communication*. Allen Lane, 1971. (Originally published, Philadelphia: University of Pennsylvania Press, 1970).

[8] Steve and Connirae Andreas, *Heart of the Mind* (Moab: Real People Press, 1989), pp. 46-54.

[9] *Ibid.*, p. 51.

[10] Richard Bandler, *Using Your Brain For a Change* (Moab: Real People Press, 1985), pp. 43

[11] Harris, Randy Allen, *The Linguistics Wars* (NY: Oxford University Press, 1993).

[12] Read Richard Bandler and John Grinder's book *Reframing: Neuro-Linguistic Programming and the Transformation of Meaning* (Moab: Real People Press, 1982) for a more detailed study of reframing. Chapter IV deals with the "Advanced Six-Step Reframing Outline."

[13] Gratitude goes to Tad James for providing me with many of these examples. Members of one of his Accelerated Practitioner's Training generated them.

[14] Gordon, *Therapeutic Metaphors* (Cupertino: Meta Publications, 1978), p. 42.

[15] Robert Dilts, *Roots of Neuro-Linguistic Programming* (Cupertino: Meta Publications), p. 77.

[16] See David Gordon, *Ibid.*, p. 53.

[17] Matthew 5:39 (NASV).

[18] See Tad James, *The Basic NLP Training Collection Manual* (Honolulu: Advance Neuro Dynamics, 1990), p. 61. (Used with permission)

[19] Wyatt Woodsmall, *LifeLine Therapy* (Arlington: Advance Behavioral Modeling, 1989), p. 4.

[20] Proverbs 23:7.

[21] Edited from Burt Wasserman "'The Cure" for Headaches and Other Uncomfortable Feelings' in *Anchor Point* (Franktown: Cahill Mountain Press, Inc., April, 1993), pp. 4-7.

[22] Richard Bandler, *Using Your Brain For a Change*, pp.131-152.

[23] Robert Dilts, *Changing Belief Systems with NLP* (Cupertino: Meta Publications, 1990), pp. 11-13.

[24] Adopted from Connirae & Steve Andreas' video tape "Resolving Grief" (Boulder: NLP Comprehensive, 1987).

[25] This material edited and adapted from E. Gene Rooney, "Level IV" in *Neuro-Linguistic Programming: Skills for Communication and Change* (Reynoldsburg: L.E.A.D. Consultants, Inc., 1986), pp. 6-19.

[26] E. Gene Rooney, *Ibid.*, pp. 11-12.

[27]E. Gene Rooney, *Ibid.*, pp. 18-19.

[28]Proverbs 29:18 KJV.

[29]See Tad James and Wyatt Woodsmall, *Time-Lining and the Basis of Personality* (Cupertino: Meta Publications, 1988), pp. 17ff.

[30]Robert Dilts in his book *Changing Belief Systems with NLP* (Cupertino: Meta Publications, 1990) uses the concept of walking the Time-Line extensively. We direct the reader to this book for an excellent treatment of this concept in changing beliefs and re-imprinting.

[31]Proverbs 29:18 KJV

[32]Special thanks go to Tad James, Ph.D. for his inaugural work in Time-Line Therapy™. Advanced Neuro Dynamics, Honolulu, Hawaii.

[33]See Richard Bandler, *Magic In Action* (Cupertino: Meta Publications, 1984).

[34]For more information on the compulsion blowout see Steve and Connirae Andreas, Chapter V, "Eliminating Compulsions," in *Change Your Mind and Keep the Change* (Moab: Real People Press, 1987), pp.89-113.

[35]See Thomas Verny, M.D. *The Secret Life of the Unborn Child* (New York: Summit Books, 1981)

# Bibliography

Andreas, Steve and Connirae. (1987). *Change Your Mind and Keep The Change*. Moab, UT: Real People Press.

Andreas, Steve and Connirae. (1989). *Heart of the Mind.* Moab, UT: Real People Press.

Andreas, Steve and Connirae. (1987). *Resolving Grief.* Boulder, CO: NLP Comprehensive, VideoTape.

Atkinson, Marilyn. (1997). *"The Grammar of God."* Vancouver, BC: Unpublished Manuscript.

Bandler, Richard and Grinder, John. (1975). *The Structure of Magic, Volume I: A Book About Language and Therapy.* Palo Alto CA: Science & Behavior Books.

Bandler, Richard and Grinder, John. (1976). *The Structure of Magic, Volume II.* Palo Alto, CA: Science & Behavior Books.

Bandler, Richard and Grinder, John. (1979). *Frogs Into Princes: Neuro-Linguistic Programming.* UT: Real People Press.

Bandler, Richard and Grinder, John. (1982). *Reframing: Neuro-Linguistic Programming and the Transformation of Meaning.* Ut: Real People Press.

Bandler, Richard. (1985). *Magic in Action.* Moab, UT: Real People Press.

Bandler, Richard. (1985). *Using Your Brain for a Change: Neuro-Linguistic Programming.* UT: Real People Press.

Bandler, Richard and MacDonald, Will. (1988). *An Insider's Guide to Submodalities.* Cupertino, CA: Meta Publications.

Bateson, Gregory. (1979). *Mind and Nature: A Necessary Unity.* New York: Bantam.

Bateson, Gregory. (1972). *Steps to An Ecology of Mind.* New York: Ballatine.

Bateson, Gregory and Bateson, Mary Catherine. (1987). *Angels Fear: Toward an Epistemology of the Sacred.* NY: Macmillan Publishing Co.

Beck, A.T. (1976). *Cognitive Therapy and the Emotional Disorders*. NY: International University Press.

Berman, Sandford I. (Ed.). (1989). *Logic and General Semantics: Writings of Oliver L. Reiser and Others.* San Francisco: International Society for General Semantics.

Birdwhistell, Ray L. (1970). *Kinetics and Context: Essays on Body-Motion Communication.* Allen Lane, 1971. Originally published, Philadelphia, PA: University of Pennsylvania Press.

Bodenhamer, Bobby G. and Hall, L. Michael. (1997). *Time-lining: Patterns for Adventuring in "Time".* Wales, United Kingdom: Crown House Publishing.

Bois, J. Samuel. (1973). *The Art of Awareness: A Textbook on General Semantics and Epistemics.* Debuque, IO: Wm. C. Brown Co.

Bourland, David D. Jr. and Johnston, Paul Dennithorne. (1991). *To Be or Not: An E-prime Anthology.* San Francisco, CA: International Society for General Semantics.

Bourland, David. D. Jr., Johnston, Paul Dennithorne; and Klein, Jeremy. (1994). *More E-prime: To Be or Not II.* Concord, CA: International Society for General Semantics.

Chomsky, Noam. (1956). *Syntactic Structures.* The Hague: Mouton Publishers.

Chong, Dennis and Jennifer. (1991) *Don't Ask Why: A Book About the Structure of Blame, Bad Communication and Miscommunication.* Oakville, Ontario: C-Jade Publishing, Inc.

Cleveland, Bernard F. (1987) *Master Teacher Techniques.* Stone Mountain, GA: The Connecting Link Press.

DeLozier, Judith and Grinder, John. (1987) *Turtles All the Way Down: Prerequisites to Personal Genius.* Bonny Doon, CA: Grinder, DeLozier and Associates.

Dennett, Daniel C. (1991). *Consciousness Explained.* Boston: Little, Brown and Company.

Dilts, Robert. (1992-1997). *Visionary Leadership Skills.* Santa Cruz, CA: NLP University.

Dilts, Robert; Grinder, John; Bandler, Richard; and DeLozier, Judith. (1980). *Neuro-Linguistic Programming, Volume I: The Study of the Structure of Subjective Experience.* Cupertino. CA.: Meta Publications.

Dilts, Robert. (1983). *Applications of Neuro-Linguistic Programming.* Cupertino CA: Meta Publications.

Dilts, Robert B. (1983). *Roots of Neuro-Linguistic Programming.* Cupertino, CA: Meta Publications.

Dilts, Robert (1990). *Changing Belief Systems with NLP.* Cupertino, CA: Meta Publications.

Dilts, Robert B.; Dilts, Robert W.; and Epstein, Todd. (1991). *Tools for Dreamers: Strategies for Creativity and the Structure of Innovation.* Cupertino, CA: Meta Publications.

Donaldson, Rodney E. (Ed.) (1991). *A Sacred Unity: Further Steps to an Ecology of Mind.* NY: Cornelia & Michael Bessie Book, HarperCollins.

Ellis, A. (1979a). "Rational emotive therapy." In R. Corsini (Ed.). *Current Psychotherapies.* (2nd. ed.). Itasca, IL: F. E. Peacock, 185-229.

Fauconnier, Gilles. (1985). *Mental Spaces: Aspects of Meaning Construction in Natural Language.* MA: Cambridge University Press.

Freedman, Jill and Combs, Gene. (1990). *Symbol, Story, and Ceremony: Using Metaphor in Individual and Family Therapy.* NY: W.W. Norton & Co.

Goodwin, Paul A. (1988). *Foundation Theory: Report on the Efficacy of the Formal Education Process in Rural Alaska.* Honolulu, HI: Advanced Neuro Dynamics.

Gordon, David. (1978) *Therapeutic Metaphors.* Cupertino, CA: Meta Publications.

Hall, L. Michael. (1995). *Meta-states: A Domain of Logical Levels, Self-Reflexive Consciousness in Human States of Consciousness.* Grand Jct. CO: Empowerment Technologies.

Hall, L. Michael. (1996). *Dragon Slaying: Dragons to Princes.* Grand Jct. CO: Empowerment Technologies.

Hall, L. Michael. and Bodenhamer, Bob. (1997*). Figuring Out people: Design Engineering with Meta-Programs.* Wales, United Kingdom: Crown House Publishing.

Hall, L. Michael. and Bodenhamer, Bob. (1997). *Mind-lines: Lines for Changing Minds.* Grand Jct. CO: Empowerment Technologies.

Hall, L. Michael. (1997a). *Neuro-Linguistic Programming: Going Meta into Logical Levels.* Grand Junction, CO: ET Publications.

Hall, L. Michael. (1994). "The Precision Strategy." *Metamorphosis*, 1994c, May/June. Grand Jct. CO: ET Publications

Hall, L. Michael. (1998). *The Secrets of Magic: Communicational Excellence for the 21st Century.* Wales, United Kingdom: Crown House Publishing.

Hall, L. Michael. (1996). *The Spirit of NLP: The Process, Meaning, and Criteria for Mastering NLP.* Wales, United Kingdom: Crown House Publishing.

Hall, L. Michael and Bodenhamer, Bob. (1999). *The Structure of Excellence: Unmasking the Meta-levels of "Submodalities".* Grand Jct. CO: Empowerment Technologies.

Harris, Randy Allen. (1994). *The Linguistics Wars.* New York, NY: Oxford University Press.

Huxley, Aldous. (1954). *The Doors of Perception and Heaven and Hell.* NY: Harper & Row.

James, Tad. (1990). *The Basic NLP Training Collection.* Honolulu, HI: Advanced Neuro Dynamics.

James, Tad and Woodsmall, Wyatt. (1988). *Time-Line Therapy™ and the Basis of Personality.* Cupertino, CA: Meta Publications.

Johnson, C.E. (1994). "The 7%, 38%, 55% Myth." *Anchor Point*, July 1994, 32-36.

Korzybski, Alfred. (1941/1994). *Science and Sanity: An Introduction to Non-Aristotelian Systems and General Semantics,* (4th Ed & 5th Ed). Lakeville, CN: International Non-Aristotelian Library Publishing Co.

Kostere, Kim and Malatesta, Linda. (1990). *Maps, Models, and the Structure of Reality: NLP Technology in Psychotherapy.* Portland, OR: Metamorphous Press.

Laborde, Genie Z. (1987) *Influencing with Integrity.* Palo Alto, CA: Syntony Publishing.

Lakoff, George and Johnson, Mark. (1980). *Metaphors we Live by.* Chicage: The University of Chicago Press.

Langacker, Ronald. (1987). *Foundations of Cognitive Grammar, Vol. 1.* Stanford, CA: Stanford University Press.

Langacker, Ronald. (1991). *Concept, Image and Symbol: The Cognitive Basis of Grammar.* NY: Mouton de Gruyter.

Lefebvre, Vladimir A. (1971). *The Structure of Awareness: Toward a Symbolic Language of Human Reflexion.* Beverly Hills, CA: Sage.

Lefebvre, Vladimir A. (1972). "A Formal Method of Investigating Reflective Process." *General Systems: Yearbook of the Society for the Advancement of General Systems Theory,* 17. Ann Arbor, MI: The Society.

Lewis, Bryon A. and Pucelik, Frank. (1982). *Magic Demystified: A Pragmatic Guide to Communication and Change.* Portland: Metamorphous Press, Inc.

Mahoney, Michael J. (1991). *Human Change Processes: The Scientific Foundations of Psychotherapy.* NY: BasicBooks.

McDermott, Ian. (1997). *Unpublished Practitioner Handouts.* London: International Teaching Seminars.

Mehrabian, Albert. (1972). *Non-verbal Communication.* Aldine Atherton Inc.

Mehrabian, Albert. (1971). *Silent Messages.* Wadsworth Publishing Co. Inc.

Miller, George. (1956). "The Magical Number Seven, Plus or Minus Two: Some Limits on Our Capacity to Process Information." *Psychological Review: 63*:81-97.

Miller, George A; Galanter, Eugene; and Pribram, Karl H. (1960). *Plans and the Structure of Behavior.* NY: Holt, Rinehart and Winston Co.

O'Connor, Joseph and Seymour, John. (1990). *Introducing Neuro-Linguistic Programming: A New Psychology of Personal Excellence.* Great Britain: Mandala.

Osherson, Daniel N. and Smith, Edward E. (Eds.). (1992). *Thinking: An Invitation to Cognitive Science, Vol. 3.* Cambridge, MA: The MIT Press.

Overdurf, John and Silverthorn, Julie. (1996). "Beyond Words: Languaging Change Through the Quantum Field." Audio-tapes. PA: Neuro-Energetics.

Pzalzgraf, Rene. (1991). *"Miltonesque Meta-model, Part 3." Rapporter #40: February and March*

Pentony, Patrick. (1981). *Models of Influence in Psychotherapy.* NY: The Free Press.

Rooney, Gene. (1986). *Neuro-Linguistic Programming: Skills for Communication and Change.* Reynoldsburg, OH: L.E.A.D. Consultants, Inc.

Rossi, Ernest L. and Cheek, David B. (1988). *Mindbody Therapy: Methods of Ideodynamic Healing in Hypnosis.* NY: W.W. Norton & Co.

Russell, Bertrand. (1960). *Our Knowledge of the External World.* NY: Mentor Book Edition, New American Library.

Seamands, David. (1988). *Healing for Damaged Emotions.* Wheaton, Illinois: Victor Books.

Schmidt, Gerry and Ewing, Lara. (1991). "NLP in Business." NLP Training Workshop Audio-Tapes, Sept. 13-16, 1991. Boulder, CO: NLP Comprehensive.

Siegle, Robert. (1986). *The Politics of Reflexivity: Narrative and the Constitutive Poetics of Culture.* Baltimore: John Hopkins University.

Steier, Frederick (Ed.). (1991). *Research and Reflexivity.* Newburg Park, CA: Sage Publications.

Tolman, Edward C. (1948). "Cognitive Maps in Rats and Men," *Psychological Review, 55,* pages 189-208.

Verny, MD, Thomas. (1981). *The Secret Life of the Unborn Child.* New York, NY: Summit Books.

Wasserman, Burt. "'The Cure' for Headaches and Other Uncomfortable Feelings" in *Anchor point.* (1993). Franktown: Cahill Mountain Press, Inc.

Watzlawick, Paul; Beavin, Janet H.; and Jackson, Don D. (1967). *Pragmatics of Human Communications: A Study of Interactional Patterns, Pathologies, and Paradoxes.* NY: W.W. Norton.

Weinberg, Harry L. (1959/1993). *Levels of Knowing and Existence: Studies in General Semantics.* Englewood, NJ: Institute of General Semantics.

White, Michael and Epston, David. (1990). *Narrative Means to Therapeutic Ends.* New York: Norton.

Whitehead, A. N., and Russell, B. (1910). *Principia Mathematica.* Cambridge: Cambridge U. Press.

Woodsmall, Wyatt. (1996). "What is Wrong With Logical Levels," IANLP Conference, Austin, Texas, April 26, 1996.

Woodsmall, Wyatt. (1989). *Lifeline Therapy* (1989). Arlington, VA: Advance Behavioral Modeling.

Young, Peter. (1997). "Let's Hear It for Nominalisations." *Rapport # 38,* pp. 35-38.

Young, Peter. (1999). *Personal Communication.* United Kingdom.

Zagler, Zig. (1984). *See You At The Top.* Gretna: Pelican Publishing Company.

Zagler, Zig. (1984a). *Secrets of Closing the Sale.* Old Tappan: Fleming H. Revell Company.

Zink, Nelson. (1993). "Going Meta: Logical Levels, the Structure of Dissociation." *Anchor Point.* July, 1993, pp. 12-15.

Zink, Nelson. (1994). "Levels of Learning." *Anchor Point.* Oct. 1994, pp. 9-11.

# Glossary Of Terms

*Accessing Cues*: How we use our physiology and neurology by breathing, posture, gesture, and eye movements to access certain states and ways of thinking. These are observable by others.

*As-If Frame*: To "pretend." To presuppose some situation is the case and then act upon it as if it is true. This encourages creative problem-solving by mentally going beyond apparent obstacles to desired solutions.

*Analogue*: An analogue submodality varies continuously from light to dark; while a digital submodality operates as either off or on, i.e. we see a picture in either an associated or dissociated way.

*Analogue Marking*: Using voice tone, facial expressions, gestures, or a touch to emphasize certain words non-verbally as you are talking to someone. The marked out words give an additional message.

*Anchoring*: The process by which any stimulus or representation (external or internal) gets connected to, and so triggers, a response. Anchors occur naturally and in all representational systems. They can be used intentionally, as in analogue marking or with numerous change techniques, such as Collapse Anchors. The NLP concept of anchoring derives from the Pavlovian stimulus-response reaction, classical conditioning. In Pavlov's study the tuning fork became the stimulus (anchor) that cued the dog to salivate.

*Association*: Association contrasts with dissociation. In dissociation, you see yourself "over there." Generally, dissociation removes emotion from the experience. When we are associated we experience all the information directly and therefore emotionally.

*Auditory*: The sense of hearing, one of the basic representational systems.

*Behavior*: Any activity that we engage in, from gross motor activity to thinking.

*Beliefs*: The generalizations we have made about causality, meaning, self, others, behaviors, identity, etc. Our beliefs are what we take as being "true" at any moment. Beliefs guide us in perceiving and interpreting reality. Beliefs relate closely to values. NLP has several belief change patterns.

*Calibration*: Becoming tuned-in to another's state and internal sensory processing operations by reading previously observed noticed non-verbal signals.

*Chunking*: Changing perception by going up or down levels and/or logical levels. Chunking up refers to going up a level (inducing up, induction). It leads to higher abstractions. Chunking down refers to going down a level (deducing, deduction). It leads to more specific examples or cases.

| | |
|---|---|
| *Complex Equivalence:* | A linguistic distortion pattern where you make meaning of someone else's behavior from the observable clues, without having direct corroborating evidence from the other person. |
| *Congruence:* | A state wherein one's internal representation works in an aligned way. What a person says corresponds with what they do. Both their non-verbal signals and their verbal statements match. A state of unity, fitness, internal harmony, not conflict. |
| *Conscious:* | Present moment awareness. Awareness of seven +/- two chunks of information. |
| *Content:* | The specifics and details of an event, answers *what?* And *why?* Contrasts with process or structure. |
| *Context:* | The setting, frame or process in which events occur and provide meaning for content. |
| *Cues:* | Information that provides clues to another's subjective structures, i.e. eye accessing cues, predicates, breathing, body posture, gestures, voice tone and tonality, etc. |
| *Deletion:* | The missing portion of an experience either linguistically or representationally. |
| *Digital:* | Varying between two states, a polarity. For example, a light switch is either on or off. Auditory digital refers to thinking, processing, and communicating using words, rather than in the five senses. |
| *Dissociation:* | Not "in" an experience, but seeing or hearing it from outside as from a spectator's point of view, in contrast to association. |
| *Distortion:* | The process by which we represent the external reality in terms of our neurology. The modeling process by which we inaccurately represent something in our neurology or linguistics, can occur to create limitations or resources. Distortion occurs when we use language to describe, generalize, and theorize about our experience. |
| *Downtime:* | Not in sensory awareness, but "down" inside one's own mind, seeing, hearing, and feeling thoughts, memories, awarenesses; a light trance state with attention focused inward. |
| *Ecology:* | Concern for the overall relationships within the self, and between the self and the larger environment or system. Internal ecology: the overall relationship between a person and their thoughts, strategies, behaviors, capabilities, values and beliefs. The dynamic balance of elements in a system. |
| *Elicitation:* | Evoking a state by word, behavior, gesture or any stimuli. Gathering information by direct observation of non-verbal signals or by asking meta-model questions. |

| | |
|---|---|
| *Empowerment:* | Process of adding vitality, energy, and new powerful resources to a person; vitality at the neurological level, change of habits. |
| *Eye Accessing Cues:* | Movements of the eyes in certain directions indicating visual, auditory or kinesthetic thinking (processing). |
| *Epistemology:* | The theory of knowledge, how we know what we know. |
| *First Position:* | Perceiving the world from your own point of view, associated, one of the three perceptual positions. |
| *Frame:* | Context, environment, meta-level, a way of perceiving something (as in Outcome Frame, "As If" Frame, Backtrack Frame, etc.). |
| *Future Pace:* | Process of mentally practicing (rehearsing) an event before it happens. One of the key processes for ensuring the permanency of an outcome, a frequent and key ingredient in most NLP interventions. |
| *Generalization:* | Process by which one specific experience comes to represent a whole class of experiences, one of the three modeling processes in NLP. |
| *Gestalt:* | A collection of memories connected neurologically, based on similar emotions. |
| *Hard Wired:* | Neurologically based factor, the neural connectors primarily formed during gestation, similar to the hard wiring of a computer. |
| *Incongruence:* | A state of being "at odds" with oneself, having "parts" in conflict with each other. Evidenced by having reservations, being not totally committed to an outcome, expressing incongruent messages where there is a lack of alignment or matching between verbal and non-verbal parts of the communication. |
| *Installation:* | Process for putting a new mental strategy (way of doing things) inside mind-body so it operates automatically, often achieved through anchoring, leverage, metaphors, parables, reframing, future pacing, etc. |
| *Internal Representations:* | Meaningful patterns of information we create and store in our minds, combinations of sights, sounds, sensations, smells and tastes. (IR) |
| *In Time:* | Having a time line that passes through your body: where the past is behind you and the future in front, and 'now' is inside your body. |
| *Kinesthetic:* | Sensations, feelings, tactile sensations on surface of skin, proprioceptive sensations inside the body; includes vestibular system or sense of balance. |

**Leading:**    Changing your own behaviors after obtaining rapport so another follows. Being able to lead is a test for having good rapport.

**Logical Level:**    A higher level, a level *about* a lower level, a meta-level that informs and modulates the lower level.

**Loops:**    A circle, cycle, story, metaphor or representation that goes back to its own beginning, so that it loops back (feeds back) onto itself. An open loop: a story left unfinished. A closed loop: finishing a story. In strategies: loop refers to getting hung up in a set of procedures that have no way out, the strategy fails to exit.

**Map of Reality:**    Model of the world, a unique representation of the world built in each person's brain by abstracting from experiences, comprised of a neurological and a linguistic map, one's internal representations (see Model of the World).

**Matching:**    Adopting characteristics of another person's outputs (behavior, words, etc.) to enhance rapport.

**Meta:**    Above, beyond, about, at a higher level, a logical level higher.

**Meta-levels:**    Refer to those abstract levels of consciousness we experience internally.

**Meta-model:**    A model with a number of linguistic distinctions that identifies language patterns that obscure meaning in a communication through distortion, deletion and generalization. It includes specific challenges or questions by which the "ill-formed" language is reconnected to sensory experience and the deep structure. These meta-model challenges bring a person out of trance. Developed in 1975 by Richard Bandler and John Grinder.

**Meta-programs:**    The mental/perceptual programs for sorting and paying attention to stimuli, perceptual filters that govern attention, sometimes "neuro-sorts," or meta-processes.

**Meta-states:**    A state about a state, bringing a state of mind-body (fear, anger, joy, learning) to bear upon another state from a higher logical level, generates a gestalt state—a meta-state, developed by Michael Hall.

**Mismatching:**    Offering different patterns of behavior to another, breaking rapport for the purpose of redirecting, interrupting, or terminating a meeting or conversation.

**Modal Operators:**    Linguistic distinctions in the meta-model that indicate the "mode" by which a person "operates": the mode of necessity, possibility, desire, obligation, etc. The predicates (can, can't, possible, impossible, have to, must, etc.) that we utilize for motivation.

| | |
|---|---|
| *Model:* | A description of how something works, a generalized, deleted or distorted copy of the original; a paradigm. |
| *Modeling:* | The process of observing and replicating the successful actions and behaviors of others; the process of discerning the sequence of IR and behaviors that enable someone to accomplish a task. |
| *Model of the World:* | A map of reality, a unique representation of the world which we generalize for our experiences. The total of one person's operating principles. |
| *Multiple Description:* | The process of describing the same thing from different perceptual positions. |
| *Neuro-Linguistic Programming:* | The study of excellence. A model of how people structure their experience; the structures of subjective experience; how the person programs their thinking-emoting and behaving in their neurology, mediated by the language and coding they use to process, store and retrieve information. |
| *Neuro-Semantics®:* | A model of meaning or evaluation utilizing the meta-states model for articulating and working with higher levels of states and the Neuro-Linguistic Programming model for detailing human processing and experiencing; a model that presents a fuller and richer model offering a way of thinking about and working with the way our nervous system (neurology) and linguistics create meaning (semantics). |
| *Nominalization:* | A linguistic distinction in the meta-model, a hypnotic pattern of trance language, a process or verb turned into an (abstract) noun, a process frozen in time. |
| *Outcome:* | A specific, sensory-based desired result. A well-formed outcome that meets the well-formedness criteria. |
| *Pacing:* | Gaining and maintaining rapport with another by joining their model of the world, by matching their language, beliefs, values, current experience, etc.; crucial to rapport building. |
| *Parts:* | A metaphor for describing responsibility for our behavior to various aspects of our psyche. These may be seen as sub-personalities that have functions that take on a "life of their own"; when they have different intentions we may experience intra-personal conflict and a sense of incongruity. |
| *Perceptual Filters:* | Unique ideas, experiences, beliefs, values, meta-programs, decisions, memories and language that shape and influence our model of the world. |
| *Perceptual Position:* | Our point of view; one of three mental positions: first position —associated in self; second position—from another person's perspective; third position—from a position outside the people involved. |

| | |
|---|---|
| *Physiological:* | The physical part of the person. |
| *Predicates:* | What we assert or predicate about a subject, sensory-based words indicating a particular RS (visual predicates, auditory, kinesthetic, unspecified). |
| *Preferred System:* | The RS that an individual typically uses most in thinking and organizing experience. |
| *Presuppositions:* | Ideas or assumptions that we take for granted for a communication to make sense. |
| *Primary levels:* | Refer to our experience of the outside world primarily through our senses. |
| *Primary states:* | Describe those states of consciousness from our primary level experiences of the outside world. |
| *Rapport:* | A sense of connection with another, a feeling of mutuality, a sense of trust; created by pacing, mirroring and matching; a state of empathy or second position. |
| *Reframing:* | Changing the context or frame of reference of an experience so that it has a different meaning. |
| *Representation:* | An idea, thought, presentation of sensory-based or evaluative-based information. |
| *Representational System (RS):* | How we mentally code information using the sensory systems: Visual, Auditory, Kinesthetic, Olfactory, and Gustatory. |
| *Requisite Variety:* | Flexibility in thinking, emoting, speaking, behaving; the person with the most flexibility of behavior controls the action; the Law of Requisite Variety. |
| *Resources:* | Any means we can bring to bear to achieve an outcome: physiology, states, thoughts, strategies, experiences, people, events or possessions. |
| *Resourceful State:* | The total neurological and physical experience when a person feels resourceful. |
| *Satir Categories:* | The five body postures and language styles indicating specific ways of communicating: leveler, blamer, placater, computer and distracter, described by Virginia Satir. |
| *Second Position:* | Point of view; having an awareness of the other person's sense of reality. |
| *Sensory Acuity:* | Awareness of the outside world, of the senses, making finer distinctions about the sensory information we get from the world. |
| *Sensory-Based Description:* | Information directly observable and verifiable by the senses, see-hear-feel language that we can test empirically, in contrast to evaluative descriptions. |

| | |
|---|---|
| *State:* | Holistic phenomenon of mind-body-emotions, mood, emotional condition; the sum total of all neurological and physical processes within an individual at any moment in time. |
| *Strategy:* | A sequencing of thinking-behaving to obtain an outcome or create an experience; the structure of subjectivity ordered in a linear model of the TOTE. |
| *Submodality:* | The distinctions we make within each rep system, the qualities of our internal representations. |
| *Synesthesia:* | A "feeling together" of sensory experience in two or more modalities, an automatic connection of one rep system with another. For example, a V-K synesthesia may involve perceiving words or sounds as colored. |
| *Third Position:* | Perceiving the world from the viewpoint of an observer; you see both yourself and other people. |
| *Time-line:* | A metaphor for how we store our sights, sounds and sensations of memories and imagination; a way of coding and processing the construct "time." |
| *Through Time:* | Having a time line where past, present and future are in front of you. For example, time is represented spatially as with a year planner. |
| *Unconscious:* | Everything that is not in conscious awareness in the present moment. |
| *Universal Quantifiers:* | A generalization from a sample to the whole population— "allness" (every, all, never, none, etc). A statement that allows for no exceptions. |
| *Unspecified Nouns:* | Nouns that do not specify to whom or to what they refer. |
| *Unspecified Verbs:* | Verbs that do not describe the specifics of the action, how they are being performed; the adverb has been deleted. |
| *Uptime:* | State where attention and senses are directed outward to the immediate environment, all sensory channels open and alert. |
| *Value:* | What is important to you in a particular context. Your values (criteria) are what motivate you in life. All motivation strategies have a kinesthetic component. |
| *Visual:* | Seeing, imagining, the rep system of sight. |
| *Visualization:* | The process of seeing images in your mind. |
| *Well-Formedness Condition:* | The criteria that enable us to specify an outcome in ways that make it achievable and verifiable. A well-formed outcome is a powerful tool for negotiating win/win solutions. |

# The User's Manual For The Brain PowerPoint Overheads

## Bob G. Bodenhamer DMin & L. Michael Hall PhD

An outstanding set of PowerPoint overheads to accompany the most comprehensive guide to date covering the NLP Practitioner course, *The User's Manual For The Brain.* The whole course is summarised by over 200 pages of slides making this an essential resource for NLP Practitioner trainers who wish to use *The User's Manual For The Brain* as the basis for their trainings. The overheads are designed by two of the most important theorists working in the field of NLP today.

**CD ISBN: 9781899836512**

# The User's Manual for the Brain, Vol. II: Mastering Systemic NLP

## L. Michael Hall PhD &
## Bob G. Bodenhamer DMin

This much anticipated volume continues in the tradition of Volume 1 as the most comprehensive manual published to date covering the NLP Practitioner course. The authors introduce the latest advances in the field and invite you to reach beyond Practitioner level to Master level where you will distill the very essence of NLP. It includes exciting new work on Meta-programs; Meta-states, and Submodalities. This book is packed with case studies, seminar demonstrations, discussions and trance scripts.

*As a sequel to Volume 1,* User's Manual for the Brain, Volume II *is a Master's level Curriculum for NLP practitioners. It takes a systemic approach to integrating NLP skills, presuppositions, models, processes, and applications with the four meta-domains, Meta-States, Meta-Modalities, Meta-Programs, and the Meta-Model, to arrive at the gestalt that is NLP. Moreover, the course content is conveyed in such a way as to install the attitudes of mastery and the "power of wizardry" that combines passion, motivation, and dedication. Readers will get a fresh new look at the presuppositions of NLP for shaping the prerequisite attitudes of NLP mastery.*—Judith E. Pearson, Ph.D.

**Hardback    476 Pages    ISBN: 978189983688**

# Secrets of Personal Mastery
## L. Michael Hall PhD

What conceptual states do you have and 'never leave home without'? What *attitudes* do you seem to take everywhere you go? Do you tend to think optimistically? Do you tend to see the dark side of things?

When we have recourse to such *high level states of mind*, we access a 'place' or 'attitude' that has more influence and more power than just an everyday frame of mind. These states-upon-states, or Meta-states, *govern* our experience.

So what if you had the ability to alter those Meta-states, and the executive powers that lie at the higher levels of your mind?

*Secrets of Personal Mastery* enables you to *access your executive levels* and *take charge of your mental-emotional programming*. Treating *mind* as an emergent process of our entire mind-body-emotion system, this book teaches you that it is not so much *what* you are thinking that controls your destiny and experiences, but *how* you're thinking – *your frames of reference determine your experience of life*.

To achieve your personal mastery, this book guides you through various Thought Experiments that work upon your 'executive' mind powers. As you partake in these processes you will enter into the higher management of your own mind at all its levels, and that will prepare you for the ultimate development of excellence – accessing your personal genius. Exploring the structures that now organise and govern the very basis of your life, *Secrets of Personal Mastery* takes you through a course 're-structuring' that addresses:

▲ the mind and emotion            ▲ the excellence of expertise

▲ the tragedy of complacency      ▲ identity and existence

▲ madness and genius              ▲ language and semantics

▲ procedures and magic            ▲ the mind-muscle connection

▲ personal and interpersonal development.

**Paperback  224 pages  ISBN: 9781899836567**

# Hypnotic Language

## John Burton &
## Bob G. Bodenhamer DMin

We each shape our own reality. Perceptions and cognitive processes unique to each of us determine our individual perspective on the world, and we present to ourselves what we are programmed to see. But what if we could change our perceptions and cognitive processes – and consequently our reality?

One way of achieving this is by harnessing the power of hypnotic language. This remarkable book examines the structures of the hypnotic sentence, and the very cognitive dimensions that allow hypnotic language to be effective in changing our minds. Defining the three facets that allow the mind to be susceptible to hypnotic language patterns, *Hypnotic Language* puts these insights into practice in case examples that demonstrate the application and effect of hypnotic language. Teaching us how to create the most effective hypnotic scripts, it provides new language patterns that address beliefs, time orientation, perception, spiritual matters and states of mind, and devises new hypnotic language applications that emphasise the importance of *Gestalt principles* and *cognitive factors*.

An invaluable resource for hypnotherapists, psychologists, NLP practitioners and counsellors, *Hypnotic Language* promotes a new and deeper understanding of hypnotic language, clearly defining the divide between the conscious and unconscious mind – and those language paths that link the two. Providing a wealth of scripts for hypnotic trance, it presents innovative and original ways to induce cognitive change that enable you to access your unconscious mind – and the infinite resources it holds.

Hardback  320 pages  ISBN: 9781899836352